Constitutional Knowledge and Its Impact on Citizenship Exercise in a Networked Society

Ana Melro
University of Aveiro, Portugal

Lídia Oliveira
University of Aveiro, Portugal

A volume in the Advances in Electronic Government, Digital Divide, and Regional Development (AEGDDRD) Book Series

IGI Global
DISSEMINATOR OF KNOWLEDGE

Published in the United States of America by
IGI Global
Information Science Reference (an imprint of IGI Global)
701 E. Chocolate Avenue
Hershey PA, USA 17033
Tel: 717-533-8845
Fax: 717-533-8661
E-mail: cust@igi-global.com
Web site: http://www.igi-global.com

Library of Congress Cataloging-in-Publication Data

Names: Melro, Ana Luisa Rego, 1981- editor. | Oliveira, Lidia, 1968- editor.
Title: Constitutional knowledge and its impact on citizenship exercise in a networked society / Ana Melro and Lidia Oliveira, editors.
Description: Hershey, PA : Information Science Reference, [2019] | Includes bibliographical references.
Identifiers: LCCN 2018052159| ISBN 9781522583509 (h/c) | ISBN 9781522583516 (eISBN)
Subjects: LCSH: Political participation--Technological innovations. | Electronic government information. | Information society--Political aspects.
Classification: LCC JF799.5 .C67 2019 | DDC 323/.042--dc23 LC record available at https://lccn.loc.gov/2018052159

This book is published in the IGI Global book series Advances in Electronic Government, Digital Divide, and Regional Development (AEGDDRD) (ISSN: 2326-9103; eISSN: 2326-9111)

British Cataloguing in Publication Data
A Cataloguing in Publication record for this book is available from the British Library.

All work contributed to this book is new, previously-unpublished material.
The views expressed in this book are those of the authors, but not necessarily of the publisher.

For electronic access to this publication, please contact: eresources@igi-global.com.

Advances in Electronic Government, Digital Divide, and Regional Development (AEGDDRD) Book Series

ISSN:2326-9103
EISSN:2326-9111

Editor-in-Chief: Zaigham Mahmood, University of Derby, UK & North West University, South Africa

MISSION

The successful use of digital technologies (including social media and mobile technologies) to provide public services and foster economic development has become an objective for governments around the world. The development towards electronic government (or e-government) not only affects the efficiency and effectiveness of public services, but also has the potential to transform the nature of government interactions with its citizens. Current research and practice on the adoption of electronic/digital government and the implementation in organizations around the world aims to emphasize the extensiveness of this growing field.

The Advances in Electronic Government, Digital Divide & Regional Development (AEGDDRD) book series aims to publish authored, edited and case books encompassing the current and innovative research and practice discussing all aspects of electronic government development, implementation and adoption as well the effective use of the emerging technologies (including social media and mobile technologies) for a more effective electronic governance (or e-governance).

COVERAGE

- ICT within Government and Public Sectors
- Public Information Management, Regional Planning, Rural Development
- Current Research and Emerging Trends in E-Government Development
- Frameworks and Methodologies for E-Government Development
- Issues and Challenges in E-Government Adoption
- Case Studies and Practical Approaches to E-Government and E-Governance
- Emerging Technologies within the Public Sector
- E-Government in Developing Countries and Technology Adoption
- Online Government, E-Government, M-Government
- E-Citizenship, Inclusive Government, Connected Government

IGI Global is currently accepting manuscripts for publication within this series. To submit a proposal for a volume in this series, please contact our Acquisition Editors at Acquisitions@igi-global.com or visit: http://www.igi-global.com/publish/.

The Advances in Electronic Government, Digital Divide, and Regional Development (AEGDDRD) Book Series (ISSN 2326-9103) is published by IGI Global, 701 E. Chocolate Avenue, Hershey, PA 17033-1240, USA, www.igi-global.com. This series is composed of titles available for purchase individually; each title is edited to be contextually exclusive from any other title within the series. For pricing and ordering information please visit http://www.igi-global.com/book-series/advances-electronic-government-digital-divide/37153. Postmaster: Send all address changes to above address.

Titles in this Series

For a list of additional titles in this series, please visit:
https://www.igi-global.com/book-series/advances-electronic-government-digital-divide/37153

Private Sector Innovations and Technological Growth in the MENA Region
Maryam Ebrahimi (Azad University, Iran)
Information Science Reference • ©2019 • 217pp • H/C (ISBN: 9781522570868) • US $195.00

Multi-Level Governance in Developing Economies
Tugba Ucma Uysal (Mugla Sitki Kocman University, Turkey) and Ceray Aldemir (Mugla Sitki Kocman University, Turkey)
Information Science Reference • ©2019 • 303pp • H/C (ISBN: 9781522555476) • US $195.00

Security Frameworks in Contemporary Electronic Government
Ryma Abassi (Carthage University, Tunisia) and Aida Ben Chehida Douss (Carthage University, Tunisia)
Information Science Reference • ©2019 • 306pp • H/C (ISBN: 9781522559849) • US $195.00

Optimizing Regional Development Through Transformative Urbanization
Umar G. Benna (Benna Associates, Nigeria)
Information Science Reference • ©2019 • 348pp • H/C (ISBN: 9781522554486) • US $215.00

Strategic Management and Innovative Applications of E-Government
Andreea Molnar (Lancaster University, UK)
Information Science Reference • ©2019 • 308pp • H/C (ISBN: 9781522562047) • US $180.00

Economic and Geopolitical Perspectives of the Commonwealth of Independent States ...
Oxana Karnaukhova (Southern Federal University, Russia) Alexandra Udovikina (Independent Researcher, Russia) and Bryan Christiansen (PryMarke LLC, USA)
Information Science Reference • ©2018 • 323pp • H/C (ISBN: 9781522532644) • US $200.00

Innovative Perspectives on Public Administration in the Digital Age
Aroon P. Manoharan (University of Massachusetts – Boston, USA) and James McQuiston (Kent State University, USA)
Information Science Reference • ©2018 • 332pp • H/C (ISBN: 9781522559665) • US $195.00

For an entire list of titles in this series, please visit:
https://www.igi-global.com/book-series/advances-electronic-government-digital-divide/37153

IGI Global
DISSEMINATOR OF KNOWLEDGE

701 East Chocolate Avenue, Hershey, PA 17033, USA
Tel: 717-533-8845 x100 • Fax: 717-533-8661
E-Mail: cust@igi-global.com • www.igi-global.com

Editorial Advisory Board

List of Reviewers

Table of Contents

Detailed Table of Contents

The protection of fundamental rights is one of the essential elements of European identity. Thus, knowledge of the law is crucial for the realization and guarantee of fundamental rights: knowing the law must be the first of the fundamental rights that assist us. Despite the abundance of declarative texts, the lack of identification and visibility and the lack of knowledge about the gracious and contentious ways, continue to be barriers to the full affirmation of those rights. The authors present a review on the legal structure of this novel space in which we move: a common space without borders, a space of democracy, an area of freedom, security, and multiculturality. Elencare which rights to citizens and how to access them intends to give shape to a future portal of enlightenment. The approach will be tripartised by the portuguese constitutional system, the European Convention on Human Rights and the European Union.

This chapter is developed along three conceptual axes: citizenship; knowledge society: transparency; and trust and participation. It begins by explaining the concept of citizenship and its historical roots, the Greek polis and the Roman civitas; the revival of cities in the Late Middle Ages and their consolidation in the Modern Age. It analyzes the citizenship construct with the affirmation of each inhabitant as a citizen involved in improving the several plans of the quality of urban life. The second axis evaluates the characteristics of knowledge societies as promoting factors to a citizenship based on socio-political indicators that build trust between the citizen. The third axis deals with transparency and trust as active disseminators of timely and relevant information to the public and its impact on corruption, as a barrier against a broad citizenship. At the methodological level, the study combines bibliographic research with a field research by questionnaire.

This chapter addresses the right of access to information, reinforced as a fundamental rule for citizens in the Brazilian constitutional norm of 1988, now regulated, more closely, from the enactment of the law on access to information in 2011. It represents an important legislative instrument of reinforcement of the principle of publicity, as well as the main infraconstitutional standard guaranteeing access to information. The requirement of a clear and transparent accountability environment by the public manager is a republican assumption of massive participation by society. This is because the right of access to information of a public nature provides a better control

This chapter seeks to assess the trends in rights-based development (RBD) and citizenship in Zimbabwe based on constitutional knowledge to proffer options on how the public can become constitutionally knowledgeable towards developing the nation. The chapter is informed by constitutional knowledge gathered through qualitative data from document analysis and literature on this discourse. The chapter first discusses the provisions of RBD and citizenship in Zimbabwe in light of the constitution. It assesses the trends in RBD and citizenship in Zimbabwe past, present, and the future to analyze the trends in the changes in the development of the nation, based on constitutional knowledge. Lastly, it proffers policy options on ways to nurture constitutionally knowledgeable citizenry.

Traditionally, public administration has always preferred to work behind closed doors. However, the concept of participatory democracy, which developed especially after the 1950s, encouraged citizens to participate more in the decision-making mechanisms of the state. Turkey experiences many problems in exercising the right to information, which was enacted in 2003, arising from the administration's attitudes and behaviors and also from the legislation. Foremost among these are the fact that citizens have not been made sufficiently aware of this right and that the administration is reluctant to share information. An analysis of the data and statistics in Turkey shows a rising trend in the exercise of this right by citizens between 2004-2015. However, considering the size of Turkey's population, the rate can still be deemed low. Post-2015 figures show a radical decline in citizens' exercising of the right to information. This situation may be explained by the painful process that Turkey experienced from 2015 onwards and the state of emergency implementations that followed.

Corruption is a human phenomenon that covers the whole world. It is a fact that public corruption gains more prominence than private corruption, because the state has the duty of accountability in a transparent way to taxpayers. As a result of this, the authors focus on the analysis of public corruption, which involves agents and public resources of the state. Therefore, this study has the main objective to verify if there is a relationship between IPC corruption (corruption perception index) and HDI (human development index), which posits the hypothesis that the greater the corruption, the lower the HDI indexes. In addition to the CPI and HDI variables, they also analyze the GDP of the countries in a secondary way. The global data analyzed indicate a high correlation between greater corruption and a lower index of human development, which may suggest problems of accountability.

The central idea of this chapter is to discuss the notion of privacy arising from the use and exchange of messages through the use of mobile phones and whether police officers in charge of patrolling and public security may have access to the messages contained therein without proper judicial authorization. The authors focused on the position of the Brazilian Superior Court of Justice (STJ) on the subject, based on the decision rendered in the Appeal in Habeas Corpus (RHC) n. 51.531/RO. At this trial, protection was given to the new forms of communication and data contained in mobile phones under the constitutional terms of protection of privacy and non-unlawful obtaining of evidence, so that it will be necessary to issue a court order to get any informational elements found in messaging applications installed on a smartphone.

Dealing with the subject of the fundamental rights of people involved in medically assisted reproduction, this chapter focuses on the issues surrounding the LGBTI+ population (lesbians, gays, bisexuals, transsexuals, intersexuals, and new genders that are being recognized). Within this group, the importance of biological children, even amongst those who cannot naturally reproduce, is also highlighted. Firstly, the author points out the laws that determine the child's protection, then compares them to real-life examples of actual situations of homophobia including physical and psychological abuse, understanding that children are also subject to the same abuse, not only due to sexual orientation discrimination and gender identity but also from having to grow up in a so-called unusual family structure. The author looks for an answer that will help strengthen the child's fundamental rights both before and after birth.

This chapter deals with the dignity of the human person and moral harassment, bringing some specific considerations about Brazilian reality. The scientific objective is to demonstrate the concrete existence of an impact on the principle of human dignity when harassment occurs in the environmental work. It is a theme that is in the discussion guide mainly from the beginning of this century, although abuse and humiliation have always been practiced in labor relations, with the same current scope, which is a tool to achieve generally derogatory ends of the human condition and intensified by the action of globalization in the contemporary world. Besides impact directly on the person, moral harassment in the work environment results in consequences for society, for company (organization), and the state.

The municipality is the basic territorial organization for almost all the Member States of the European Union and has approximately the same attributions in all these. Even so, the territorial structure of municipalities differs in each of the Member States, and it is possible to group them into two large groups: those that have implemented reforms with a consequent reduction in the number of these entities and those with a high number of municipalities. Although Spain is a neighbor of Portugal and Portugal gets some influences from France, in fact the territorial organization of municipalities corresponds to very different realities. Through this research you can see that Portugal did reform its municipalities while France and Spain failed to do so. However, they all recognize that there is a need to reform the territorial structure of municipalities.

Foreword

Without constitutional knowledge or fundamental rights knowledge, it is very hard (or even impossible) to protect and promote the citizenship exercise in a networked society. And it must to be given importance not only to the theory constitutional and fundamental rights issues but also to the constitutional and fundamental rights law in force. And if it is very important the theory, we must never forget the practice of the constitutional and fundamental rights law. What our societies put in practice?

This book will show very interesting and different constitutional and fundamental rights knowledge and its impact on citizenship exercise in a networked society point of views. It will cross the “new world”. For example, in USA, where it seems to exist a specific lack in freedom of speech of a uniform standard which leads to dangerously inconsistent punishments and poses the ultimate threat to constitutional knowledge and citizenship exercise, a real chilling of speech, school districts could and should erect a virtual schoolhouse gate by implementing a standard.

Then in Europe the book provides a comprehensive picture of the importance of citizenship education curricula and the use of information technologies (ICT) in Portuguese schools. In other chapter it will be seen very clear that Portugal did reform its municipalities while France and Spain failed to do so. And how this important subject is connected with the constitutional and fundamental rights knowledge and its impact on citizenship exercise in a networked society.

It’s time to go again to the other side of the Atlantic. In Brazil, the fifth biggest country in the world, sixth in population, there are very strong and objective clues that reflect that the absence of a citizenship education and constitutional education affects the rising rate of dissemination of fake news in Brazil. Brazil has a very important Information Access Law that seeks to improve the full constitutional citizenship instrument. Indeed, the requirement of a clear and transparent accountability environment by the public manager is an assumption of massive participation by society. And not only from a republic point of view: see Norway, Sweden, Denmark, Spain, Belgium, between others.

On other hand bullying and harassment in work context put in danger and cause damage to the human dignity environment. The real and productive work is always done it with human dignity environment. It is very important to analyse from a scientific structural point of view the citizenship, the knowledge society, the transparency, the trust and participation.

All these variables are connected with the rationality against corruption. Less corruption, more economic justice. Less corruption, more social justice, more political justice, more cultural justice. More accountability. Developed mentality. It is very clear that social networks have a big influence in the exercise of citizenship. The book shows what happens in, for example, Portugal. The interest of this work is that the results suggest that it is possible to promote the exercise of citizenship through social networks (for example in Portugal). The problem is that social networks are like a double-edged sword. We can find a very close connection between corruption and human development index and unfortunately Brazil is a "good example" to check that: "The global data analyzed indicate a high correlation between greater corruption and a lower index of human development which may suggest problems of accountability".

This book tries to prove that knowing the law must be the first of the fundamental rights that assist people. And this will be done through not only from the Portuguese constitutional point of view, but also from the European Convention on Human Rights and the European Union itself. Of course it must be considered the protection of the communication and digital security of mobile phones as a fundamental right to privacy. There is no other way and the Brazilian Superior Court of Justice sentences confirm that with precision.

In the field of taxation in international trade, a chapter brings to the discussion the importance of transparency has becoming proportional to the growing complexity of the terms in which cross-border trade in goods takes place. Thus the requirements and effects of transparency are reflected in a digital context of dematerialization. And also here the dematerialization could not be synonymous of less human rights and duties. So, it's important to pay attention to this because the theory itself will not save them.

Time to go to Africa. The correspondent chapter "seeks to assess the trends in rights-based development (RBD) and citizenship in Zimbabwe based on constitutional knowledge to proffer options on how the public can become constitutionally knowledgeable towards developing the nation". Id est, we will not have human development if people don't know their own fundamental rights and duties.

Last but not least, we have some "problems relating to the right to information in Turkey". As we can read: "An analysis of the data and statistics in Turkey shows a rising trend in the exercise of this right by citizens between 2004-2015. However, considering the size of Turkey's population, the rate can still be deemed low. Post-2015 figures show a radical decline in citizens' exercising of the right to information. This situation may be explained by the painful process that Turkey experienced from 2015 onwards and the state of emergency implementations that followed".

Above all the book as a message of hope because it gives more than one world geographical point of view. And gives some possible solutions to some constitutional and human rights and duties. It shows obstacles but also shows chances to improve human quality of life. This book brings lots of enthusiasm and courage. Because to have a better human rights and duties world one cannot stay sitting on the sofa. Bravo to the Organizers, to the Authors and to the Publisher, because this book is again a good step in the right direction.

Gonçalo S. de Melo Bandeira
Polytechnic Institute of Cávado and Ave, Portugal

Gonçalo S. de Melo Bandeira *was born in Porto, Portugal, and received the LLD-Juridical-Criminal Sciences, Faculty of Law, University of Coimbra (2009); Master in Public Law from the Faculty of Law of the Portuguese Catholic University (2003); and Degree in Law from the Faculty of Law of the University of Coimbra. He is an Adjunct Professor of Public Law by the (State) School of Management of the Polytechnic Institute of Cávado and Ave (IPCA) – Superior Public Education of Portugal, European Union and a Researcher at the JusGov-University of Minho. He collaborates with several Portuguese and foreign universities. Between 2009 and 2013, he was a Guest Professor at the Portucalense University Infante D. Henrique, Porto and a Researcher at the Max-Planck-Institut für ausländisches und Internationales Strafrecht, Freiburg im Breisgau, Baden-Wüttemberg, Deutschland-Germany, 2005, 2006, and 2011. He has been a Professor and Researcher-Guest at several Brazilian Public, Private, and Cooperative Higher Education Institutions. He has several publications in Portugal and abroad. His works are mainly on fundamental rights, economic, social and financial criminal law, including cybercrime. He collaborates with the written press.*

Preface

The functions of official national and international institutions may contribute to the communication and dissemination of the Fundamental Laws and, consequently, to an effective exercise of the sovereignty of the people, one characterized by being informed and clarified. The relation of this book is that of knowledgeable citizens are, just so, sovereign citizens.

However, access to information is not always synonymous with literacy. That is, free access to all the legislation, all the documentation and explanation of it, but if there is no competence for its reading and even interest in the demand, this has an empty result.

Thus, the communication and dissemination of the Constitutions are important factors for the exercise of sovereignty by the people, but they cannot be considered the only ones. Such communication should be carried out through the relevant mechanisms, but also through the media (television, radio, Internet, among others).

But prior to this communication, strategies for the literacy of the Constitutions (and other legislation) should be devised, since only then does access to information translate into true knowledge of it. This literacy is included in the precepts advocated in the Charter on Education for Democratic Citizenship and Human Rights Education, that is, the idea of an Education for Democratic Citizenship is only understood with the comprehension of what are the Constitutions, which include Fundamental Rights and Human Rights.

Moreover, Luísa Neto had already defended a similar position when, in citing Malala Yousafzai, stated that "the deepening of knowledge is inseparable from the development of (transverse and specific) competences that generate knowledge", and there is therefore "a clear interpenetration between the process of transmitting scientific knowledge and the basic dimension of deepening the democratic culture" (Neto, 2016).

Communication and dissemination will take place through education, with the aim of developing true popular sovereignty and, consequently, a democratic culture. Nonetheless, it is argued, like the author did, that it is not through the definition of a closed and imperceptible programmatic content that this education for citizenship and the informed exercise of popular sovereignty will be done, but rather through permanent dialogue between government, educational institutions, research and development centers, etc. And also between private organizations and citizens, whether private associations, companies, which resort to their civil responsibility and contribute to the exercise of that sovereignty.

Communication is therefore closely related to education, since it is not sufficient to have access to the means, resources and mechanisms if it is not schooled for its use, if it does not detain the necessary literacy for a critical usage.

It is believed that these communication, education and dissemination contribute to the formation of constitutional norms throughout its duration, since they fulfill their constitutional role. By fulfilling this constitutional role, it is thus ensured that constitutional norms accompany societal evolution and adapt to new demands.

THE CHALLENGES

With the importance of the national Constitutions to the exercise of a full citizenship, knowledge of these laws has been urgent for some years now. This widespread knowledge would allow for the exercise of a more enlightened national citizenship. What knowledge do the citizens of the Constitutions of their countries have? What importance does this knowledge have for the effective development of national citizenship? What role is expected to be played by national and worldwide institutions? In the Network Society what are the best strategy to make the Constitution known? Which citizens participate through the Internet know the Constitution? Citizens use their knowledge of the Constitution to substantiate their participation?

Citizenship exercise is a broader concept which include the concepts of Constitutional awareness, Treaties on Human Rights and participation awareness, digital access to the institutions and documents and many others. The goal was to analyze how this awareness occurs in the different countries and how the citizenship participation is made (if existing). It was of greater importance to analyze the role of digital tools in the dissemination of the Constitutional documents as well as in enhancing citizen participation. The publication aims to reflect on the several formats, goals, actors and tools Constitutional awareness takes into account, including its effectiveness on Information Society. This publication will contribute to the knowledge on the concept of Citizenship exercise.

SEARCHING FOR A SOLUTION

Generally, it is incumbent upon the official internal bodies, including the Constitutional Court, when it exists, to review (in)constitutionality of legislation, norms, court decisions, international agreements, decisions on electoral acts, organization of political parties, referendums, and other functions.

But who should assume a role of communicator and disseminator of the Constitutions? Is it the competence of the Constitutional Court to contribute to the development of an informed citizenship and, consequently, to the exercise of the sovereignty of the people? This role of the Constitutional Court is questioned considering that it is the maximum body of guarantor of the constitutionality, which means that it is the guarantor of the sovereignty of the people present in the Constitution (among other aspects).

The national official bodies do not only have the powers to supervise, determine (in)constitutionality and the judgment of appeals, they go even further when they are present in discussions on specific issues, when they assume the role of contributing to critical reflection. And this is precisely what is intended for the exercise of sovereignty of the people, to do it critically, for citizens to inform themselves, clarify, seek to know more, seek education for the Constitution, for rights and duties and for the participation of economic and political organization.

But, in order to guarantee that the sovereignty of the people is exercised through the knowledge of the Fundamental Law, it is also suggested that the document of the Constitutions be elaborated and made available digitally and in print, with annotations that allow its comprehension distributed by schools, by the training entities, by all bodies responsible for the education of citizens and by other public entities.

It is not considered that it is only the role of internal institutions to ensure the communication and dissemination of the Constitution, but it is considered that these have a fundamental role, and they are the guarantee of their effective application.

ORGANIZATION OF THE BOOK

The book is organized into 14 chapters. A brief description of each of the chapters follows:

Chapter 1 discusses the protection of fundamental rights as one of the essential elements of European identity. It claims that knowing the law must be the first of the fundamental rights that assist us. The authors present a review on the legal structure of this novel space in which we move: a common space without borders, a space of democracy, an area of freedom, security and multiculturality.

Chapter 2 analyses the concept of citizenship and its historical roots, the Greek polis and the Roman civitas; the revival of cities in the Late Middle Ages and their consolidation in the Modern Age. It analyzes the citizenship construct with the affirmation of each inhabitant as a citizen involved in improving the several plans of the quality of urban life. It also evaluates the characteristics of knowledge societies as promoting factors to a citizenship based on socio-political indicators that build trust between the citizen. And, finally, deals with transparency and trust as active disseminators of timely and relevant information to the public and its impact on corruption, as a barrier against a broad citizenship.

Chapter 3 addresses the right of access to information, reinforced as a fundamental rule for citizens in the Brazilian constitutional norm of 1988, now regulated, more closely, from the enactment of the law on access to information in 2011. It represents an important legislative instrument of reinforcement of the principle of publicity, as well as the main infraconstitutional standard guaranteeing access to information. The requirement of a clear and transparent accountability environment by the public manager is a Republican assumption of massive participation by society.

Chapter 4 starts focusing on the first amendment to the United States Constitution which protects the freedom of speech. While the Supreme Court held in 1969 that students "do not shed their constitutional rights at the schoolhouse gate," since then the Court has limited students' freedom of speech, stopping short of considering the boundaries of off-campus, online speech. Lower court holdings vary, meaning that a student engaging in certain online speech may not be punished at all in one state but would face harsh criminal punishments in another. The lack of a uniform standard leads to dangerously inconsistent punishments and poses the ultimate threat to constitutional knowledge and citizenship exercise: chilling of speech.

Chapter 5 focuses on the peoples' access and presence in social networks, and how essential it is to follow this form of access and sharing information, especially when it comes to publicizing the rights and duties of citizens. In this sense, the present study focused on the analysis of the profile of Portuguese citizens that uses social networks to support the different themes that make up the concept of citizenship.

Chapter 6 seeks to assess the trends in rights-based development (RBD) and citizenship in Zimbabwe based on constitutional knowledge to proffer options on how the public can become constitutionally knowledgeable towards developing the nation. The chapter is informed by constitutional knowledge gathered through qualitative data from document analysis and literature on this discourse. The chapter first discusses the provisions of RBD and citizenship in Zimbabwe in light of the constitution. It assesses the trends in RBD and citizenship in Zimbabwe, past present and the future, to analyze the trends in the changes in the development of the nation, based on constitutional knowledge. Lastly, it proffers policy options on ways to nurture constitutionally knowledgeable citizenry.

Chapter 7 analyses how Turkey experiences many problems in exercising the right to information, which was enacted in 2003, arising from the administration's attitudes and behaviors and also from the legislation. Foremost among these are the fact that citizens have not been made sufficiently aware of this right and that the administration is reluctant to share information.

Chapter 8 presents a study based on the understanding that the citizens' lack of awareness of the rights inherent to the very guarantee of human dignity, as well as of the whole historical process that gave rise to the guarantee of such rights, is one of the reflexes that the absence of a citizenship education and for citizenship provoke, even affecting the high rate of dissemination of false news in Brazil. There is a recurrent need to deal with this type of problem, especially aggravated by the presidential race of 2018, where there is an increase in the reproduction of news whose reliability of the source is not verified, although they are evidently false, exaggerated and sensationalist. While analyzing this problem, the study seeks to examine the harm of this practice to the exercise of citizenship.

Chapter 9 discusses transparency as a quality that transcends many areas of law and which is based on a fundamental principle that transcends the entire legal system and whose scope extends to all public and private actions to which legal relevance can be recognized. In the specific field of taxation in international trade, the importance of transparency has become proportional to the growing complexity of the terms in which cross-border trade in goods takes place. Indeed, the more complex the exchanges are, the greater the level of control over them, and the greater the degree of transparency required, both as regards the form of control and the specific terms in which transactions are performed.

Chapter 10 analyses corruption as a human phenomenon that covers the whole world. It is a fact that public corruption gains more prominence than private corruption, because the state has the duty of accountability in a transparent way to taxpayers. As a result of this, we focus in the present work on the analysis of public corruption, which involves agents and public resources of the State. Therefore, this study has the main objective to verify if there is a relationship between IPC corruption (Corruption Perception Index) and HDI (Human Development Index), which posits the hypothesis that the greater the corruption, the lower the HDI parents, it is also intended to analyze in the case of Brazil in the global scenario.

Chapter 11 discusses the notion of privacy arising from the use and exchange of messages through the use of mobile phones and whether police officers in charge of patrolling and public security may have access to the messages contained therein without proper judicial authorization. The authors focused on the position of the Brazilian Superior Court of Justice (STJ) on the subject, based on the decision rendered in the Appeal in Habeas Corpus (RHC) n. 51.531/RO.

Chapter 12 focuses on the issues surrounding the LGBTI + population (lesbians, gays, bisexuals, transsexuals, intersexuals and new genders that are being recognized). Within this group it is also highlighted the importance of biological children, even amongst those who cannot naturally reproduce. Firstly, we will point out the laws that determine the child's protection. We then compare them to real life examples of actual situations of homophobia. Including physical and psychological abuse. Understanding that children are also subject to the same abuse, not only due to sexual orientation discrimination and gender identity but also from having to grow up in a so called unusual family structure.

Chapter 13 deals with the dignity of the human person and moral harassment, bringing some specific considerations about Brazilian reality. The scientific objective is to demonstrate the concrete existence of an impact on the principle of human dignity when harassment occurs in the environment work. It is a theme that is in the discussion guide mainly from the beginning of this century, although abuse and humiliation have always been practiced in labor relations, with the same current scope, which is a tool to achieve generally derogatory ends of the human condition and intensified by the action of globalization in the contemporary world.

Chapter 14 discusses the municipality as the basic territorial organization for almost the Member States of the European Union and has approximately the same attributions in all these. Even so, the territorial structure of municipalities differs in each of the Member States, and it is possible to group them into two large groups: those that have implemented reforms with a consequent reduction in the number of these entities, and those with a high number of municipalities. Although Spain and France are very close to Portugal, in fact the territorial organization of municipalities corresponds to very different realities.

Ana Melro
University of Aveiro, Portugal

Lídia Oliveira
University of Aveiro, Portugal

REFERENCES

Council of Europe. (2010). *Education for Democratic Citizenship and Human Rights Education (EDC/HRE)*. Retrieved from https://www.coe.int/web/edc/charter-on-education-for-democratic-citizenship-and-human-rights-education

Neto, L. (2016). A educação para a democracia: um propósito de solidariedade social e intergeracional. In *Educação e(m) Democracia*. Porto: Editorial UP.

Acknowledgment

The editors would like to acknowledge the help of all the people involved in this project and, more specifically, to the authors and reviewers that took part in the review process. Without their support, this book would not have become a reality.

First, the editors would like to thank each one of the authors for their contributions. Our sincere gratitude goes to the chapter's authors who contributed their time and expertise to this book.

Second, the editors wish to acknowledge the valuable contributions of the reviewers regarding the improvement of quality, coherence, and content presentation of chapters. Most of the authors also served as referees; we highly appreciate their double task.

Ana Melro
University of Aveiro, Portugal

Lídia Oliveira
University of Aveiro, Portugal

Introduction

The Swiss philosopher Jean-Jacques Rousseau discussed the concept of sovereignty of the people, in 1762 in his book *The Social Contract* (or, in the original, *Du Contrat Social or Principes du Droit Politique*). For Rousseau, the origin of popular sovereignty resides in the social pact established among all people. The social contract is then "a form of association that defends and protects with all common force the person and property of each associate and by which each one, uniting himself to all, obeys, however, but himself and remain as free as before" (Rousseau, 1999, p. 23). It is understood, therefore, that this social contract confers on the people sovereignty, because it is through it that "each of us puts in common thy person and all the power on the supreme direction of the general will; and we collectively receive each member as an indivisible part of the whole" (Rousseau, 1999, p. 24).

The sovereignty of the general will is, according to the philosopher, inalienable and indivisible. Unalienable because "since sovereignty is nothing other than the exercise of the general will, it can never be alienated, and that sovereign power, which is a collective person, can only be represented by itself" (Rousseau, 1999, p. 32). Indivisible "because either the will is general, or it is not - or is it of the whole people, or is it only part of it. In the first case, this declared will is an act of sovereignty and constitutes the law. In the second, it is nothing more than a private act, or it is an act of magistracy - at most, a decree." (Rousseau, 1999, p. 33).

Also Sieyès, in 1789, in his work *Qu'est-ce que le tiers état?*, reflected on the concept of sovereignty when attributed to the people or the general will, nevertheless, differs from Rousseau since it considers that the popular sovereignty derives of the existence of a Nation, considering, above all, the historical motives that contributed to this existence.

In addition, in the studies of Emmanuel-Joseph Sieyès, the people are sovereign because it has a Constitution, although it exists before this one. As the author points out,

> *The nation exists above all, it is the origin of everything. Its will is always legal, it is the law itself. . . . In each part the constitution is not the work of the constituted power, but of the constituent power. . . . This is like this and in no other way that the constitutional laws are fundamental. The first ones, those who establish the legislature, are founded by the national will before any constitution; they form the first degree. The second ones must be established in the same way by a special representative will. Thus all the parts of the government answer to themselves and depend in last case on the nation. (Sieyès, 2002, p. 53)*

From the analysis of Sieyes and the importance that the author attributes to the Constitution, we move on to the meaning of the sovereignty of the people present in the written Constitutions. The texts, as we know them today, are an achievement of the Liberal Revolutions and, not infrequently, the result of successive revisions. If some revisions were more punctual in terms of changes, others went deeper. Nevertheless, the sovereignty of the people has never been called into question, but rather has been intensified with the formal reception of international instruments, such as the Universal Declaration of Human Rights.

In general, the Constitutions are texts that guide the conduct of citizens, which aggregate the set of rights and duties of these citizens, whether individual or collective, whether or not they are members of civil society, without exercising public office (not counting on democratic participation, which presupposes that it is everyone's duty, even if their absence is not sanctioned); either to carry out this public exercise.

If the Fundamental Laws are this document, then it is understood that it would not make sense that the people were not sovereign, since it exists only because there is a people, because there is a group of citizens who have been granted citizenship, which is reviewed in the principles there defined and for which and through which the Nation and the State guarantee their existence and carry out their functions, evolving as the people (society) present new requirements. Sovereignty is present here, in the constant and frequent consultation that the Constitutional, Representative and Right State should do to the people, either directly or indirectly, in order to continue to perform their functions and fulfill their purposes.

But if the people are sovereign, certain conditions have to be guaranteed for this sovereignty to be fully exercised, conditions that depend on the bodies responsible for allowing access to information about the Constitutions, but also on the role of the citizens themselves in seeking to be informed about the text and what implies what is written there. Freedom implies responsibility and it can take many forms, one of which is the search for information, the obtaining of knowledge.

Nowadays, there is a plurality of means to access content (data-information-knowledge), whether through television, radio, or even more, the Internet (perceived as content), which can be accessed through platforms, such as television, computer, mobile phone and tablet (perceived as tools). This is generally the case, but it is important to highlight access to information on the Fundamental Laws.

There are various mechanisms through which citizens can access the Constitutions and their meaning. The first of these is the very document which, as a rule, is available online on various pages of the dependence of the State or the Constitutional Court, when it exists.

In addition, the media are responsible for disseminating the Constitutions in a variety of ways, either through news that mention it directly or indirectly; with a negative or positive connotation; using legal language or more accessible one; referring to the people and their sovereignty, to the role of the Constitutional Court or to specific articles stemming from certain discussions.

It is hoped that there are various means by which the (sovereign) people can access the Constitutions and explanatory texts of it or the news about when the Constitution is involved and why. But who is responsible for reporting on the Constitution and in what format? Who should have as competence the communication and dissemination of the Fundamental Law (and consequent education for the Constitution, for citizenship and democracy)?

This section ends with the role of the people in building their own sovereignty, through the search for information, knowledge and constant updating on the Constitution, the rights and duties embodied therein, economic organization and the organization of political power.

It is the citizens' responsibility to seek information on the Fundamental Law of their Country; on the matters under discussion in which they imply, directly or indirectly, in the Constitution; on the electoral programs of political parties. It is also within its competence to update knowledge on the matters contained in the Constitution (in particular, constitutional revisions) and other international documents that were formally received by the Constitution. Citizens must also seek to clarify existing doubts regarding the Constitution through the means at their disposal. It is also a civic duty of citizens, especially those most enlightened in this matter, to inform others whenever this is necessary and even informally.

Internal and international official institutions and people must work together for knowledge about the Constitutions to be guaranteed, so that, consequently, the sovereignty of the latter is also guaranteed and exercised.

Hopefully this book will contribute to the broadening of knowledge in diverse areas, such as Constitution, Network Society, and Human Rights, and will be an effective contribution to the interdisciplinary development of the scientific areas that are present here.

REFERENCES

Rousseau, J.-J. (1999). *O Contrato Social*. Mem Martins: Publicações Europa-América.

Sieyès, E.-J. (2002). *Qu'est-ce que le tiers état?* Paris: Éditions du Boucher.

Section 1
Constitutional Knowledge

This section highlights the importance of constitutional knowledge and of other important official documents in fundamental rights to the full exercise of citizenship.

Chapter 1
The New Paths of Fundamental Rights in the 21st Century:
Globalization and Knowledge in a Digital Age as a Proposal

Fátima Monteiro Pacheco
Instituto Superior de Contabilidade e Administração do Porto (ISCAP), Portugal

Dora Resende Alves
Universidade Portucalense Infante D. Henrique, Portugal

ABSTRACT

The protection of fundamental rights is one of the essential elements of European identity. Thus, knowledge of the law is crucial for the realization and guarantee of fundamental rights: knowing the law must be the first of the fundamental rights that assist us. Despite the abundance of declarative texts, the lack of identification and visibility and the lack of knowledge about the gracious and contentious ways, continue to be barriers to the full affirmation of those rights. The authors present a review on the legal structure of this novel space in which we move: a common space without borders, a space of democracy, an area of freedom, security, and multiculturality. Elencare which rights to citizens and how to access them intends to give shape to a future portal of enlightenment. The approach will be tripartised by the portuguese constitutional system, the European Convention on Human Rights and the European Union.

DOI: 10.4018/978-1-5225-8350-9.ch001

INTRODUCTION AND PROPOSAL: A NEW FORMAT FOR THE DECLARATIONS OF RIGHTS

The authors wish to emphasize here that the fundamental rights, in reality of the Portuguese legal system, by virtue of the principle of assimilation of foreigners and stateless persons, are intended to protect portuguese citizens resident in the national territory and resident abroad, although they contemplate a special treatment for european citizens. The principle of universalism attributed to all individuals, just because they are, rights and duties. This principle is enshrined in article 12 Constitution of the Portuguese Republic (CPR) of 1976, which states that fundamental rights are 'rights of all'. It is intended a brief approach to the universalist perspective of fundamental rights, defending the existence of a tendency to universalize respect for human dignity as the basis of all human rights (Martins, 2010, pp. 526-537).

Furthermore, the functioning of a democratic and pluralist society requires the guaranteeing momentum of the law, and therefore international law and European Union law have come to broaden the block of fundamentality and strengthen the protective capacity of the legal system. Thus, where national jurisdictions do not fully protect, it is essential to know if, where, and how the citizen can obtain protection. For this reason, there's a believe that judicial integration and the emergence of the European judicial area implies that the populations are aware of the content of the European Convention on Human Rights (ECHR) and of the Charter of Fundamental Rights of the European Union (CFREU) and understand the functioning of its supervisory mechanisms.

To point out, the communicational age we live in also means that justice can respond to the new challenges of technological evolution. Starting from this reality, what moved the authors to the elaboration of this work - necessarily brief - was the desire to provide the community with information about the current constitutional system and about the systems of regional protection of fundamental rights that citizens can enjoy through the use digital tools and access to platforms for dissemination and clarification. It is already an uncontroversial fact that technology and information technology enable solutions in a digital environment that enable the sharing of information and the dissemination of knowledge in order to allow access to the law by all those who are part of this planning.

It is in this context that the work intends to bring the proposal studied to a new "era of Rights", by means of the creation of a digital platform with informative content, accompanied by several links directed to the Constitution of the Portuguese Republic; for the ECHR and European Union (EU) and CFREU institutional treaties, accompanied by small clarifications on the content and functions of each diploma. Here stands a believe that the construction of a portal of fundamental rights would be an element of true democracy in the service of equality of citizens. If such a portal were to be realized, it would be a further step towards enabling the invocation of such rights by private individuals, as well as a further step in the institutionalization of human rights protection systems: the digitization phase.

For the moment, and because it is an ambition that can not be achieved here, a brief summary of the legal structure of this novel space in which we are moving is presented: a common space without borders, a space of democracy, a space of freedom, security and multiculturalism, which - necessarily - also goes through the fundamental rights of individuals. It is the desideratum that moves this work and which intends to give shape to a future portal of enlightenment, under the terms referred to above.

Such an approach will necessarily be tripartite: a first point will be devoted to the portuguese constitutional system; a second point will refer to the subsidiary regional system established by ECHR; finally, a third point will be devoted to the protection system experienced by the European Union. Let us then see, in a necessarily abbreviated form, each of the mentioned moments, reiterating the importance of its digital application.

BACKGROUND

It is already an unwavering fact that the protection of fundamental rights is one of the essential elements of European identity. Thus, knowledge of the law is crucial for the realization and guarantee of fundamental rights: knowing the law must be the first of the fundamental rights that assist us. However, despite the abundance of the declarative texts of rights that surround us, the lack of identification and visibility of the same and the lack of knowledge about the graceful and contentious routes that the republic provides, continue to be barriers to the full affirmation of those rights as rights of all.

In fact, European states live under a plurality of rights: in the same territorial space coexist several legal orders and various mechanisms of judicial protection, whose relationship is not established by hierarchical criterion, but by means of a reciprocal coordination method. Each of the existing orders – internal, Union, and regional international – constitutes a distinct legal system. The Treaties constitute an autonomous legal order founded on its primacy; The Constitutions form a distinctive arrangement that relates to that of the Union; and the regional international order, founded on the subsidiarity of its intervention, acts if and when domestic law does not ensure equivalent protection.

CONSTITUTIONAL SYSTEM IN LEGAL ORDERS

The National Constitutional System: Systematization, Characterization, and Categorization of Rights and Forms of Guardianship

This first moment will be devoted to the portuguese constitutional system. It will refer to the systematization of the constitutional text, the characterization of the Portuguese organizational and constitutional model, the various categories of fundamental rights envisaged, as well as a reference to its general and specific legal regime. It will also be stated its form of guardianship.

Systematization and Characterization

The portuguese catalog of fundamental rights is very complete, but the number and content of the norms on fundamental rights has been added and changed in each of the seven constitutional revisions that it has known. Portugal is a sovereign Republic, based on the dignity of the human person (article 1, all of Portuguese Constitution), which is why the protection of fundamental rights is particularly evident.

The constitutional text begins by stating the Fundamental Principles (articles 1 to 11) which make explicit portuguese constitutional identity and which, because of their essentiality, constitute material limits of revision. Then, in the first part, it presents the Fundamental Rights and Duties (articles 12 to 79) which include the general principles (Title I - articles 12 to 23), the "rights, freedoms and guarantees" (Title II - articles 24 to 57) which are the rights of personal, civil and political nature and 'economic, social and cultural rights and obligations' (Title III - articles 58 to 79), which generally do not have that nature, benefit, part of them, from the specific legal regime attributed to rights, liberties and guarantee (article 17). It should be pointed out that other fundamental rights which enjoy the same specific legal regime are dispersed both in the constitutional text and at the infra-constitutional level (articles 21, 22, 103 (3), 124 (1) and 72 and 483 of the Portuguese Civil Code of 1966) (Alves, 2015, May).

In its second part the constitutional text clarifies the Economic Organization (articles 80 to 107), and in the third the Organization of Political Power (articles 108 to 276).

Finally, in a fourth part, it deals with the Guarantee and Revision of the Constitution (articles 277 to 289) and ends with the Final and Transitory Provisions (articles 290 to 296).

It is, therefore, a constitution of a democratic rule of law and a state of fundamental rights, of an promissory nature and open to "social inclusiveness" and to inter-constitutionality, committed to the realization and promotion of material equality.

Categorization of Fundamental Rights

Fundamental rights are foreseen in the first part (or dispersed), preceding political and socio-economic organization, stating and recognizing a vast and quite complex catalog of rights and duties based on the dignity of the human person. These rights reflect the subjective and fundamental legal position of individuals in the face of the state and embrace a material, plural, open and universalist perspective (article 16) of fundamental rights. They are, therefore, rights that aim to protect and guarantee the essential values of the human. On the other hand, they are linked to the economic constitution and to the principle of economic and social democracy, which lends to our fundamental law a very expressive dimension of sociability. The consecration of these rights at the constitutional level translates their supremacy into the state legal system.

It should be noted that fundamental rights may be foreseen outside the catalog but included in the constitutional text (articles 20, 21, 22, 61 and 62); outside of Part I, but also included therein (articles 103 (3) and 124 (1)); or may be present in ordinary internal laws (as in articles 72 and 483 of the Portuguese Civil Code); as well as in texts of international law and European Union law.

It also follows from article 16 of the CRP that the scope and meaning of fundamental rights may be broader than that arising from its constitutional consecration, stating that there may be laws and other applicable rules of international law that contain fundamental rights, where should include the prediction of rights provided for in CFREU. It is therefore an open or non-typical clause that reflects the non-exhaustive list of fundamental rights in Portuguese fundamental law.

The rights listed in Title II ('rights, freedoms and guarantees') are rights of individual freedom, of a personal nature, which aim to ensure the non-intervention of the public authorities, which is why they have a subjective dimension (first generation rights and status negativus). It is a set of rights inherent to man (right to life, personal integrity), as well as some rights claiming benefits from the State (article 36 (6). The rights of political participation (freedoms) - also mentioned here - are attributed to citizens and imply their guarantee by those powers, which is why they reveal an objective dimension (second generation rights and *status activus*). Also included in this Title are rights to benefits that require the State to perform positively with a view to their realization, which is why they have an active dimension (third generation rights and *status positivus*) and are not universal. And, finally, solidarity rights that are based on a differentiation between individuals according to their needs (fourth generation rights) (Alves, & Moreira, 2018, July). "Guarantees" means the right of each person to demand the protection of their rights, recognition of the existence of appropriate procedural means to safeguard it and the establishment of certain important institutional guarantees (articles 27 (2), 54 5, 56, 2 (2) and 64 (2)), which ensure that they are enforceable.

The triology indicated in Title II benefits from the same specific legal regime of protection and its content is determined at constitutional level. As Vieira de Andrade (2001, p.184) mentions, this system of rights, freedoms and guarantees includes benefits that imply a state behavior of 'bounded implementation of the Constitution'. The law regulates the feasible constitutional norms and concretizes those not feasible, by means of legislative measures that, although they give freedom of formation to the legislator, do not understand the power of appreciation of the necessity of the legiferation. As example of directly applicable rights are: freedom of assembly and demonstration or *habeas corpus*, right to initiative and private property, right to work (in its negative aspect), right to protection of health; and illustrating a right that lacks implementation measures, there are to be seen: the right to just and equal conditions of work or the right to vote (Canotilho, 2003, pp. 396-480).

Being of a different structure in the face of 'economic, social and cultural rights', they are presented as a category of norms of a prescriptive nature, of determinable or determinable content at the constitutional level, directly applicable, enjoying a reservation of law, binding public entities and private, and may only be restricted in the cases provided for in the Constitution or directly based thereon (article 18) (to see Miranda, 2014, p. 406; Canotilho & Moreira, 2007, p. 310; Miranda & Medeiros, 2010, p. 310; Canotilho, 2003, p. 437).

The precepts that fill them have a higher normative than other categories of fundamental rights, and their regime apply to constitutional precepts of a similar nature (article 18, paragraph 1, *ex vi* article 17). It is clear from their mandatory nature that such rights enjoy "reserve of the Constitution" and reserve of parliamentary legislative competence (article 165 b). By virtue of their constitutional determinability they can be enforceable by themselves or not feasible. The former are immediately effective by direct constitutional means, not requiring the interposition of the legislator, against the law, if it establishes inconsistent restrictions with the constitutional text. They are independent of mplementing mediation by the public authorities, granting their holders subjective powers to demand behavior, usually abstention or compulsory benefits (article 25, 1). The second (not feasible), whose effective exercise by the holder, depends on subsequent regulation, are also constituted by preceptive norms, although its normativity is based on its determinable content at constitutional level. They depend on concrete legislative action, by astringing the legislator to adopt positive measures to comply with, conformed or implement the constitutional tasks (article 49), under penalty of unconstitutionality by omission (article 283), compensation for damages caused by the fault, and resistance of individuals to commands that offend them.

Already listed in Title III ('economic, social and cultural rights and duties'), by reduction, designated as 'social rights' (Alves & Silva, 2015), are not homogeneous. They have to do with the economic status of individuals, or with fundamental living conditions and are part of a social conception of the State, that is, aim to guarantee fundamental living conditions and assign rights to certain specific social categories. Many of them presuppose the incumbency of the State towards their realization (articles 58, 59, 63, 64, 65, 66, 73, 74), but some have a *status negativus* (articles 61 (1) and 62) and are addressed to the society itself (articles 67, 68, 69). Some are universal (articles 58, 61 (2), 63, 78, 79), others relate only to certain social categories (articles 59 (1), 60 68, 69, 72, 77) or institutions which lack specific protection (articles 67 and 76 (2)) (Canotilho & Moreira, 2007, p. 294). As Jorg Pölakiewicz, the Portuguese constitutional text has the "most detailed catalog of all Western Europe" (1994, 347) (Botelho, 2017, p. 157).

These rights have a differentiated regime of rights, freedoms and guarantees, although they have a minimum, nuclear or principal content, which can be determined constitutionally, even though, in most cases, they require a concrete or conforming interposition of the ordinary legislator (in the case of the social security system, of the national health service, or universal basic education, compulsory and free), being rights under "reservation of law". The rules that enshrine them are, therefore, specific rules that are embodied in the power to grant their holders the right to receive benefits or activities concretized by the State, by means of ordinary legislation.

In the words of Vieira de Andrade, they are "norms of legislation, and do not confer on their owners true powers to demand, because they aim, first, to indicate or impose constitutionally on the State measures for greater satisfaction or concrete realization of protected assets" (2001), differing from programmatic norms. In this regard, they are also mandatory rules binding the public authorities on the duty to produce legislation in order to achieve, them are also prohibited by *non facere*.

Thus, the social norm is an imposition of legislative action, it is true, but the tasks of the legislature are not always determined at the constitutional level: they are not feasible, they lack normative concreteness, and their conformation by the courts is forbidden. In fact, if they are not directly applicable, legislative intervention is necessary, with the legislator (primary recipient) having the breadth of content. The intervention of the law therefore has an expansive meaning and it is up to the legislator to define the measure of the right to ensure, thus fulfilling the constitutional enunciation. In this way, social law is objectified in legislation, within a framework of taxation for the legislator, which is bound by a constitutional 'action' mandate.

Afonso Vaz, stating that the Constitution should not be intended for what it has reserved for social policy, even though it imposes on the public authority the obligation to ensure to all "a minimum indispensable for a dignified existence" and that - in this context - the social rights would be " constitutional precepts which enunciate the right as fundamental but do not precede the constitutional measure of law, before the State is responsible for promoting or scheduling the realization of the right, that is to confer, expansively, the Legal protection measure of right" (1998, pp. 435-451).

This is, therefore, of somewhat limited effectiveness. It is worth noting that, due to its lower determinability, such norms do not assign real subjective rights to individuals. They attribute, however, a "subjective legal position" (pretension) embodied in "rights to benefits by legal claims", individualisable. Indeed, many of them present an intense determination of their *minimum* content, capable of sustaining an unconstitutionality by omission (article 283) because lack of the necessary measure to make the norm feasible; as well as, constitute a factor of normative interpretation, or, in Vieira de Andrade's words, a 'legal standard of judicial control of norms' (2001), able to lead to a more favorable solution to the fundamental right. However, even if they do not allow individuals to be direct recipients of the constitutional provision that envisages them, depending on a limited legislative action by the "reserve of the possible" - the principle of the protection of trust implies the strict foundation of any legislative act that so as to safeguard the prohibition of social retrogression and the fundamental obligation to ensure to all the minimum necessary for a dignified existence.

Affirming Cristina Queirós (2002, p. 151) that the general normative binding of social rights guaranteed by standards of constitutional level, which are not merely "appeals to the legislator" but as a "parameter of judicial control" when the evaluation of the constitutionality of restrictive or discordant legal or regulatory measures, suffraging that their non-compliance may give rise to "unconstitutionality by omission", and stating that such rights imply the consecration of the principle of social backlash.

Guardianship Momentum

The effectiveness of fundamental rights depends on the possibility of judicial and non-judicial control. Accordingly, the Constitution establishes the possibility for the courts (article 20, paragraph 1) to control, on a diffuse basis, the constitutionality of the legal norms (article 204), and should not apply those that prove contrary to the Constitution and to the principles contained therein, which include fundamental rights. In fact, the Constitutional Court can appeal against decisions of courts that refuse to apply any rule based on its unconstitutionality or that apply a rule whose unconstitutionality was raised during the proceedings (article 280 (1) (a) and (b) and (5) (6)), which means that internal control of respect for fundamental rights rests primarily with the Constitutional Court.

On this point it should be clarified that, in Portuguese law, there are several types of unconstitutionality, namely: by action or omission, total or partial; material, formal or organic; original or supervenient; antecedent or consequent. The guarantee mechanisms of the Constitution are constitutional (positive) surveillance and constitutional review. Supervision may be preventive of unconstitutionality by action; successive abstract of unconstitutionality by action (in "main way" or "path of action"); successive unconstitutionality by action; and inspection of unconstitutionality by omission (only of legislative measures). On the other hand, the supervisory bodies are the Constitutional Court and the other courts. While the Constitutional Court has the exclusive right of preventive, successive, abstract, supervisory review of unconstitutionality by omission, as well as the judgment of the appeals of other courts in constitutional matters, the ordinary courts decide on the constitutional issues raised in the cases they judge, and their decisions are recurrable to the Constitutional Court. The modalities of supervision can thus be classified according to the subject (of any acts or standards); as to the nature of the bodies involved (political or jurisdictional); (diffused or concentrated); as to the time or moment of control (preventive or successive); (abstract or concrete); interest (objective or subjective); and finally, as to the process (principal or incidental) and by action or omission. The effects of supervision, on the other hand, depend on the type of unconstitutionality, and judgments (articles 204 and 280) refer to concrete, diffuse or concentrated supervision - importing the disregard of the norm to the concrete case; the pronouncements (articles 278 and 279) refer to abstract preventive oversight - importing the veto of decrees and prohibition of ratification of treaties; those of declaration (articles 281 and 282) to the successive abstract inspection, importing general obligatory force; Finally, verification (article 283) refers to the inspection by omission, importing appreciation and knowledge to the competent bodies.

Back to the main subject, the 'rights, freedoms and guarantees' can see their exercise suspended in 'state of siege' and 'state of emergency' (articles 19, 134 (d) and 138), situations that only happen to exceptional, transitory and anomalous title. Such exceptionality justifies subjecting such statements to the verification of tight assumptions, requirements and limits, with some rights being absolutely intangible, as in the case of articles 24, 25, 26 (1), 29 (1) (2) (3) (4). If this is not the case, citizens have the right to resist (article 21), as well as, incidentally or through the judge of the case, they may request that the constitutionality of such measures be reviewed by the Constitutional Court, as already was reported.

In addition, citizens, in case (also) of violation of such rights, also have the right to petition the organs of sovereignty and the Ombudsman (articles 52 (1), 23 and 281 (2)), requesting them to initiate procedures for the abstract supervision of the norms that would harm them, thus filling the lack of an autonomous right of action before the Constitutional Court. In the same sense, the legislator requires a special speed in all cases that have to do with such rights (article 20, paragraph 5, for example, subpoena for the protection of rights, freedoms and guarantees).

In the name of constitutional integrity and identity, this category of rights constitute material limits of revision (article 288 (d)), and reservation of law in a formal sense (article 165, paragraph 1 (b)). On the other hand, all administrative activity of the State must respect the intangibility of its essential content, which means that the republic defends the constitutional order and the subjective positions in which these rights are translated, in an institutionalized and organic way, being unconstitutional the rules that infringe such impositions.

Finally, it is worth mentioning the extra-contractual civil liability regime of the State (Law 67/2007 of December 31) and other public entities that gives concretization to the article 22 of portuguese Constitution. The established regime seeks to protect citizens in respect of actions or omissions in the State which may harm fundamental rights. Such possibility constitutes an irreplaceable instrument of defense against the violation of these rights (of domestic and international origin), constituting such virtuality a guarantee that assists to all the individuals. In this respect, the states were left to be demanded only by other states, so that they could be also by individuals. As well, they have since been granted the status of subjects of international law and the concomitant right of access to international jurisdictional bodies.

Violation of 'economic and social rights', not benefiting from the special protection granted to rights under Title II (articles 17 and 18), may give rise to unconstitutionality by omission (article 283), which will always depend - on the one hand - on the degree of constitutional determination of the rule in question and, therefore, on the existence of an mandatory imperative minimum content - on the other - of the communication of such omission to the Constitutional Court by the (restricted) entities that may request it, due to the lack of active procedural legitimacy of citizens for this purpose. In fact, as has already been mentioned, since these rights are subject to a law, it is up to the legislator to define the measure and content of the right to be provided and to be carried out by the State, thus transferring the realization of the fundamental right of responsibility of the constituent legislator to that of the legislator ordinary. That is why the protection of such rights is clearly politicized.

The concepts of "essential content" or "minimum content" are not equivalent to whom the social rights do not have a "minimum content" due to the lack of a constitutional measure which provides for the content of the provision, and the legislation itself fulfills with the determination of "originating entitlement to benefits" or "subjective pretension to benefits" (Vaz, Carvalho & Botelho, 1998, pp. 345-346). It is stated that the content of the precepts of social rights and the corresponding claims is determined by the Constitution, 'only in a minimum', depending more on options of the ordinary legislator's own options, with 'autonomous conformation power', and therefore subject to a more 'attenuated' control by the courts, although some of its precepts constitute concrete constitutional impositions (Andrade, 2001, p. 378). And warning that the guarantee of the "essential content" of social rights, as a rule, does not correspond to the constitutional core of the right, rather to its "legal content", highlighting the difference between essential content declared irreversible by the constitutional legislator and nucleus of legislative, reversible (Queiroz, 2006, p.120).

The constitutional protection of this category of fundamental rights is therefore lower than that offered to 'rights, freedoms and guarantees', even though offended citizens may trigger the mechanism of popular action (article 52 (3)). for the defense of constitutionally protected social assets and enjoy the operation of the Administrative Procedure Act (article 267), regarding administrative acts that affect the essential content of these rights.

The Regional System of the European Convention on Human Rights: Tutored Rights and the Institutional System

The recognition of fundamental rights at the constitutional level can not fail to consider the internationalization of their protection through the international instruments that have been recognized at European level (Alves, & Moreira, 2018, July). Referring in particular to the ECHR (1953) and to the court it has set up: the European Court of Human Rights, to which Portugal acceded in 1976 (Botelho, 2010).

ECHR is an instrument of international law that is part of domestic law (approved and published in Portuguese official journal, Series I, 236/78, Law 65/78 of 13 October), which, pursuant to (2) of article 8 of Portuguese Constitucion, is directly applicable in this legal system. By virtue of its supra-legal position it must be applied even if it contradicts the ordinary laws. Due to its immense importance, it has become possible (since 2007) to carry out an extraordinary review of internal judgments which have become final (article 449 (1)(g) of the Portuguese Criminal Procedure Code and article 771 (f) of the Portuguese Civil Procedure Code) whenever they are in contradiction with the case law of the European Court and there has been an multitude of legislative changes and judicial practices.

That court, which has a mandatory and permanent jurisdiction, has jurisdiction to examine all matters relating to the interpretation and application of the ECHR (article 32 of the ECHR). In addition, it can appreciate the decisions of the portuguese Constitutional Court, which is why its dynamic and evolving jurisprudence has been incorporated into the densification and expansion of fundamental rights protected by the republic. Nonetheless, the fact that the Convention (article 35 (1)) provides for the right to an individual right of action against any natural or legal person implies that its applicability is only possible when the internal system not provide equivalent protection (Article 53)

The Convention has direct effect (invocability in court) in the domestic legal order and prevalence over portuguese ordinary laws, pursuant to articles 8 (2) and 277 (2), and article 70 of Law 28/82 of 15 November (Organic Law of the Portuguese Constitutional Court). About the rule of exhaustion of internal media to be seen Fausto de Quadros (1990, pp.124-126).

It should also be noted that, in order to avoid the plurality of international proceedings on the same cases, the European Court will not know complaints lodged in other international instances.

Tutelated Rights and Institutional System for the Guarantee and Enforcement of Judgments

The Convention, whose objective is to ensure the protection of human rights, did not create new rights, but rather recognized those in respect of which all States parties agreed on their fundamentality and unavailability. It is thus a catalog which sets out a 'common lowest common denominator' for national rights and which recognizes a tight range of rights. As it is: the right to life; prohibition of torture and inhuman or degrading punishment; the right to liberty, security; fair trial, respect for private and family life; freedom of thought, conscience and religion; of expression; of assembly and association; right to marriage; effective recourse and equality.

Such rights, essentially civil and political in nature, have been successively supplemented by additional Protocols, which must be ensured to all persons dependent on the "jurisdiction" of the States parties. This means that a State may be held liable for breach of the Convention even if an individual is outside its territory as soon as it is under its authority or effective control. In addition, only States parties, when acting in a legislative, administrative or judicial capacity, may be sued in the European Court. These Protocols include the right to property, education and free elections; prohibition of imprisonment for debts, freedom of movement; prohibition of the death penalty; procedural guarantees in case of expulsion of foreigners; double degree of jurisdiction in criminal matters; indemnification for judicial error; *non bis in idem*; equality of spouses and the general prohibition of discrimination, to name a few.

The Convention has institutionalized a guarantee system whose application falls primarily on the States (courts) - the European Court should only intervene when the Member States fail to do so - and it enables them to choose the most appropriate measures to implement it ("margin of discretion"). In this way, the national court has become the natural judge of the Convention - even if individuals are allowed - once domestic resources have been exhausted or exhausted direct access to the European Court (articles 34 and 35 ECHR). Whenever this happens, the victims (specific and personal interest in acting) have only six months, from the knowledge of the final internal decision, to bring the action, under penalty of non-admissibility. It should be noted that the concept of victim has been interpreted in an evolutionary way and refers to direct, potential or indirect victims, provided that they are alive and that they justify this quality throughout the proceedings. In the course of the operation of the complaint, it is also important to point out that States should provide the European Court with all the means of assistance necessary for its effective examination, as well as assist in relevant fact-finding missions. On the other hand, the manifest lack of grounds or the absence of material injury leads to the inadmissibility of individual petitions.

If the applicant's right is not satisfied by means of an amicable settlement (article 38), the court judges decides on the merits of the case, certifying the existence of a breach of convention. The European Court therefore has declarative competence, since it rules on the existence or otherwise of breach of the Convention (article 41); since it provides a reasonable remedy to the victim if the domestic law of the offending State does not allow, if not imperfectly, to obviate the consequences of such infringement (article 41). The functioning of the system at issue, therefore, obliges a State which breaches the Convention to redress the consequences of the unlawful act; to perform the obligation breached; to cease the unlawful act; and to repair the damage caused.

The decisions of this tribunal are binding on States (articles 44 and 46 ECHR) and, in the end, the Committee of Ministers of the Council of Europe has the function of monitoring the effective implementation of its judgments.

The system allows to harmonize, at minimum level, the national legal systems of Human Rights. However, the judgments of the European Court in practice constitute a kind of precedent for all European courts. In this way, it is up to the judges to ensure that the rights guaranteed in the Convention are respected within their legal order.

The European Union System: The Evolution of the Protection System and of the Institutional System

It is already common place that the Court of Justice of the European Union (ECJ) - signed in its mission of guaranteeing compliance with the law for the interpretation and application of treaties - has proved to impose the consequences of primacy, leaving in the shadows the defense of fundamental rights (Martins, 2007, 122). In fact, although the original treaties included a number of relevant provisions on the subject, those provisions had a functionalist dimension in that they were linked to the objective of creating the common market. In the absence of a catalog of fundamental rights, it was the device of of the judicial body of the then European Community to explore the way for the construction of a genuine system of protection. This fact shows that this system emerged as an internal system of an autonomous "multilevel" Union and, differently, the ECHR system, as seen, was specifically established to be an international system of protection, external to States, dismissal of state functions and own normative production. Also on the social rights side (Alves, 2018).

In a second stage, the Court would integrate fundamental rights by way of the general principles of law, incorporating the common constitutional traditions, as some case-law: judgment of 12/11/69, *Stauder*, Rec. 1969, p. 419, and judgment of 17/12/70, Internationale Handelsgesellschaft, 11/70, Rec. 1970, p. 1125, judgment of 13/07/1989, Wachauf, 5/88, Col. 1989, p. 269, judgment of 24/3/1994, Bostock, C-2/92, Col. 1994, p. I-955, among others.

And in a third phase, the rights provided for in international instruments (not only the ECHR), building a block of fundamentality, the respect of which would ensure, within the framework and objectives of the treaties,, as to see on case-law: judgment of 14/5/74, Nold, 4/73, Rec. 1974, p. 491; judgment of 15/5/86, Johnston, 222/84, Col. 1986, p. 1651; judgment of 13/12/79, Hauer, 44/79, Rec. 1979, p. 2727; judgment of 28/10/75, Rutili, 36/75, Rec. 1975, p. 1219, Judgment of 10/09/1987, Demirel, 12/86, Col. 1987, 3719, judgment of 15/05/1986, Johnston, 222/84, 1951, among others. Indeed, it was in 1969, in the judgment in Stauder v. city of Ulm (of 12/11/1969, 29/69, [1969] ECR 419), that the Court abandoned its restrictive position by stating in Paragraph 7 that 'the contested provision does not disclose any factor capable of calling into question the individual fundamental rights contained in the general principles of Community law, which the Court ensures compliance with'. On the other hand, in 1974, in the judgment Nold, (4/5/73, p. 491), it stated that international instruments could provide "indications" to be considered in the context of the protection of fundamental rights. Therefore, such traditions and rights of conventional origin, while not being sources of Community law, would have been communitarianised by contributing to a broader conception of fundamental rights in the Union.

By virtue of this construction, the Union was bound by fundamental rights (Duarte, 2006), even if its concrete content was uncertain, since it depended on a revelation of case-law. In other words, it was for the Court to decide, on a case-by-case basis, whether or not a fundamental right would form an integral part of Union law. In addition, although the legal basis for its protection remained non-existent, the Court was thus able to ease conflicts with the courts constitutional provisions that refused to diminish the protection of individuals by virtue of their States' membership of the Communities. Thanks to such methodology, the European Court has identified a body of rights which it was responsible for ensuring and that successive revisions of the Treaties would be constitutionalised.

The elaboration of a formal list of fundamental rights was to respond to the inadequacies of the praetorian system of protection, contributing to its certainty, by making the TFEU enter a fourth phase of evolution. For this reason, the Cologne European Council in 1999 approved the creation of an *ad hoc* body whose purpose was to present a draft Charter of Fundamental Rights of the European Union (Martins, 2017, p. 249). Once the consensus of the Member States was established, the Charter would be accepted solemnly at the Nice European Council and proclaimed by the Presidents of the European, Parliament, Council and Commission. The intention was therefore to constitutionalize an autonomous catalog of fundamental rights, limited to the reaffirmation of the rights already revealed by the Court. Indeed, paragraph 5 of the Preamble states that the Charter "reaffirms" rights whose origin derives from the constitutional traditions and common international obligations of its Member States, the ECHR, the Social Charters approved by the EU and the Council of the European Union. Europe, as well as the case law of the TFEU and the European Court (Duarte, 2006).

Subsequently, under the Treaty of Lisbon, pursuant to article 6 (1) TEU, Charter was treated as the legal value of the Treaties and, consequently, it acquired judiciality and could be invoked in the courts of the EU and nationals, under the terms of its article 51 (1) fist part. In this context, article 6 TEU presents the system of protection of fundamental rights of the Union: its first paragraph recognizes the value of Charter, the second authorizes the adhesion to the ECHR (Pacheco, 2017c), and the third confirms the vocation for the opening of the system, by traditional route of general principles of law - so that a European pluralism in the protection of fundamental rights will continue to reside in the Union's judicial system (Pacheco, 2011).

With regard to situations where there is a breach of convention through EU primary law, it must be pointed that because the Union is not yet part of the ECHR, member states will have to maintain their responsibility. In fact, according to the case-law of the European Court, the transfer of competence of states to international organizations does not relieve them of any responsibility. If such violation results from the implementation of secondary law, the European Court does not refuse to exercise such supervision, especially in cases where state protection "is manifestly deficient". That fact, however, ends up invested by the member states in a kind of control power of indirect conventionality. Therefore, because such a practice could jeopardize the primacy of the DUE, it is legitimate to consider the advantages or disadvantages of EU accession to the ECHR. To escape the main theme of the present work, this paper does not present any doctrinal positions on the problem, even though we indicate the work of Pacheco (2017c), a work that equates and develops the most significant doctrinal positions.

The Rights Protected by the Charter

The systematisation of Charter does not follow the classic dichotomy of fundamental rights (Pacheco, 2016). Starting with a Preamble, it contains seven titles: Dignity, Freedom, Equality, Solidarity, Citizenship, Justice and Final Provisions. It is a vast catalog: in the wake of a universalist conception, advocated by the Universal Declaration on Human Rights, it brings together, in the same document, very heterogeneous and innovative rights, systematized under the prism of indivisibility, interdependence and uniqueness of rights. In this way, it marks the awareness of the equal importance of the civil, political and social dimension of the fundamental rights that assist individuals, extending the *acquis* of fundamental rights in the EU.

Although its terminology refers to "rights, principles, and objectives" Charter does not indicate the differentiation between these concepts, making equitable if all the norms have the same legal force. Its precepts are based on the essential values of human dignity, fundamental freedoms, equality among persons, solidarity, citizenship and justice, and the categorization of each in the said triology is not governed by criteria of a hierarchical nature. Thus, the integration of its precepts into the categories indicated will have to be determined by the interpretation of its legal nature, making it impossible to check whether the content of each precept establishes a subjective right, if such content is not available to the legislator, if each of them will have direct applicability and immediacy, or will require further implementation by national laws and practices.

In Title I, Charter begins by reaffirming the inviolability of the dignity of the human being (article 1, all af the Charter as flollows), in which all other rights are anchored,, including the rights to life (article 2), to physical integrity (article 3), prohibition of torture and inhuman or degrading treatment or punishment (article 4) and prohibition of slavery and forced labor (article 5).

Title II provides for classical freedoms: the right to liberty and security (article 6), respect for private and family life (article 7), the right to marry and to establish a family (article 9), freedom of thought (article 10), freedom of expression and information (article 11), freedom of assembly and association (article 12) and freedom of the arts and sciences (article 13); social rights (Pacheco, 2017b), such as professional freedom and the right to work (article 15), the right to education (article 14); economic rights, such as freedom of enterprise (article 16) and property rights (article 17); third generation rights, such as the protection of personal data (article 8); the rights of aliens: the right of asylum (article 18) protection in case of removal, expulsion or extradition (article 19).

The principle of equality before the law is also recognised in Title III (articles 20, 23) and the prohibition of discrimination on grounds of nationality (article 21 (2)) and in relation to other suspect categories - sex, ethnic origin, religion or belief, disability, age and sexual orientation - retaking the Treaty of the European Community, articles 12 and 13, and 14 ECHR lists, while adding the motivations based on genetic characteristics. Rights are also recognized for certain categories of persons in need of special treatment - children (article 24), elderly persons (article 25) and disabled persons (article 26). The inclusion of respect for cultural, religious and linguistic diversity (article 22) in this title is also justified by the importance of the principle of non-discrimination.

In a universe of 50 legal norms there are 12 precepts qualified as solidarity rights, which are part of Title IV of the Charter. Its negotiation started from a " minimum common denominator" to all States, allowing a potential irradiation effect across the entire legal system of the Union. The right to information and consultation of workers within the undertaking is enshrined (article 27), right of collective negotiate and action (article 28), right of access to employment services (article 29), protection in the event of unfair dismissal (article 30), fair and just working conditions (article 31), the prohibition of child labor and the protection of young people at work (article 32), protection of family and professional life (article 33), the right to social security and social assistance (article 34). Not all should be framed as social rights, encompassing third generation rights, such as: environmental protection and consumer protection (articles 37 and 38), health protection and access to services of general economic interest (articles 35 and 36). Moreover, not all social rights (Schutter, 2000, p.33) are recognized in the form of individual subjective rights, which can be immediately invoked by individuals. Many have been poured out in the form of principles (Balaguer Callejón, 2005, pp. 109-122) (the norms on environmental or consumer protection), in need of implementing measures by the Member States. As refered, in contrast to the rights, which must be respected, the principles must be observed and their implementation promoted, and can not be invoked before they are implemented in concrete policies. The principles thus lay down an obligation on the part of the Union to recognize a specific value, to be enforceable against the authorities which must observe them and to promote them through its normative development, in the strict exercise of its powers, although they can not be invoked individually on the same terms as can be. As Olivier De Shutter states: «*Certains des droits de la Charte ne figurent dans le droit de l`Union qu`en tant que príncipes généraux du droit, invocables donc uniquement dans le champ d`application du droit de l`Union, et nom pas de manière indépendante, mais seulement en combinaison avec une norme de droit primaire (constitutionnel) ou dérivé (législatif) qui fait figurer telle situation comme relevant, ratione materiae, du droit européen*» (2000, p. 96).

On the other hand, not all social norms are found in this title (Alves, 2018). There are social rights in the titles of freedom, such as freedom of association, access to professional and continuing training and freedom of undertaking; as well as in the title of equality, as in the case of equality between men and women, in the field of work and remuneration. In addition, social rights with expression, such as the right of the representatives of the workers to the protection of the enterprise, were outside the Charter. The presence of these rights is fundamental to the exercise of freedoms, essentially as regards the conditions for free movement, without which it would not be possible to have a common code of European values and a European social policy. The inclusion of social rights - as rights, principles or objectives - has contributed to overcoming a Union that is essentially market driven and guarantees economic freedoms, and social values can now be better promoted.

Title V deals with citizenship and retakes the norms already in force, doubling its formulation. The statute covers the right to elect and be elected to the European Parliament and municipal elections (articles 39 and 40), the right to good administration (article 41), right of access to documents (article 42), the right to petition the Ombudsman and the Parliament (articles 43 and 44), freedom of movement and residence (article 45) and diplomatic and consular protection (article 46). These rights reflect the symbolic and political burden they carry: they are attributed to individuals as members of a political community and are granted to nationals of the Member States. However, the rights reserved exclusively to citizens, are those of electoral participation, of diplomatic and consular protection. As a result, most of these rights can benefit citizens of third countries. In this sense, freedom of movement and permanence now appears as a possibility for third-country nationals legally resident (article 45 (2)) (Pacheco, 2017c).

Finally, Title VI enshrines the right to effective judicial action and fair trial (article 47), the presumption of innocence and the rights of defence of the defendant (article 48), the principles of legality and proportionality of offenses and penalties (article 49) and the right not to be judged or punished more than once for the same offense (article 50) already contained in the ECHR or its protocols.

Title VII includes the general provisions concerning the scope (articles 51 and 52) and the interpretation (articles 52 (3) to (7) and 53) of the rights and principles, the level of protection and the prohibition of abuse of rights (article 54). This title is intended to establish the scope - personal and material - of the Charter, the meaning and scope of the rights assigned, the level of protection that these rights confer on their holders and the implications that their possible abusive use may give rise to. It should be noted that although the provisions of the Charter can not extend the competences of the Union as defined in the Treaties under article 51 (1), the institutions and bodies of the Union are bound to respect it, as are the Member States when they apply Union law.

The Charter's final provisions implicitly imply a general principle of openness to the ECHR system and the common constitutional traditions of the Member States.

Accordingly, in accordance with article 52 (3), where the rights contained in the Charter coincide with those of the ECHR, their meaning and scope must be identical. However, should the EU law confer greater protection, it must be provided to its holders. In turn, (4) article 52 of the Charter reproduces the same reasoning regarding constitutional traditions, saying nothing about the possibility of applying the highest level of protection conferred by the EU law. Article 53 is a non-regression clause which seeks to preserve the minimum level of protection conferred by the various legal orders in the field of fundamental rights - that of the Union, those of the Member States and international law.

The Court of Justice of the European Union's Protection of Rights

Under Article 19 (1) of the TEU, the Court of Justice of the European Union ensures compliance with the law in the interpretation and application of the Treaties. The Court intervenes in several titles, exercising the function of ordinary, international, administrative and constitutional jurisdiction. It is therefore for the Court of Justice of the European Union to review the constitutionality of secondary legislation and to ensure the protection of fundamental rights in relation to EU law and state measures implementing or enforcing it.

Relations between the national courts and the Court of Justice have developed within the framework of the cooperation which the mechanism of the questions referred for a preliminary ruling (article 267 TFEU) is the best vehicle. However, it is worth noting that all judges (from all levels) are attached to the application of the DUE, ensuring the full effect of this legal system, which was an illustration of the Europeanisation of national courts.

By virtue of the aforementioned procedure for judicial cooperation, the national courts which have referred the question referred for a preliminary ruling by the Court of Justice, applying (or not) the Union rule to the *sub-judice* case, thus guaranteeing uniformity of that system in all Member States.

In view of the characteristics of the system, it will be for States to ensure effective judicial protection of the rights conferred on individuals by Union law and non-contractual liability for their infringement (Pacheco, 2017a). For that reason, the conditions laid down for the compensation of damage by the legislation of a State can not be less favorable than those relating to similar claims of an internal nature (principle of equivalence), nor can they be organized in such a way as to render virtually impossible or excessively difficult to achieve reparation (principle of minimum effectiveness), aiming at both principles to ensure judicial protection that does not jeopardize equality between European citizens (Proença, 2017).

The successive penetration of the European Union law on the exercise of the judicial function has obliged the Member States to reform national legal rules and to redefine the functioning of their judicial area, making it possible for individuals to rely on European Union law - or derivatives that impose clear, precise and unconditional obligations or which recognize rights - in the 'EU decentralized courts', that is, national courts. It is therefore incumbent on the Member States to designate the competent judicial bodies and to regulate the remedies which ensure the safeguarding of the rights which are part of the European legal order. This means that internal judges are bound by the non-application of national laws affecting fundamental rights guaranteed by the EU, irrespective of the instance in which they are involved, where such standards are in the field of application of the Union law, and without having to wait for its legal elimination.

SOLUTIONS AND RECOMMENDATIONS

It has become clear that the plurality of jurisdictions can provide individuals with greater access to justice, which is no longer confined to national courts. Thus, polycentric fundamentalism - resulting from the plurality of declaratory texts of rights and the various mechanisms of judicial protection - can contribute to the emergence of a common European order in the field of fundamental rights. In this framework, by seeing their fundamental rights violated, individuals can benefit from all cooperation mechanisms, in particular through the creation of interconnected judicial networks, an increasingly inter-institutional dialogue, an increasingly active dissemination of such texts and jurisdictional mechanisms, as well as databases with access to the public. All this maximizes the protection of fundamental rights.

FUTURE RESEARCH DIRECTIONS

The communicational era requires that justice also benefit from technological developments. In this context, citizens should be given access to the law through the use of digital tools and platforms for dissemination and clarification. The state of the art in technology and computer science already allows the dissemination of solutions, in a digital environment, that allows access to the world of the law. It was with this conviction that the authors presented the proposal for the construction of a new "era of rights", through the creation of a digital platform with information content, accompanied by links to the portuguese Constitucion; for the ECHR and for the EU (CFREU), accompanied by small clarifications on the content and functions of each diploma. The authors believe that the construction of such a portal of fundamental rights would be an element of true democracy in the service of equality of citizens, which would increase their invocation in court, giving a further stage to the movement of institutionalization of systems of protection of rights of man: the phase of the digitization.

CONCLUSION

After the continent was rebuilt from a fratricidal war and survived barbarism, the European project was the "candidate of hope" towards a future of peace. The Europe that was made based on freedom and respect for difference, in search of a new soul. This new soul was the idea that Europe was building itself. Prisoner of the market and aiming for fundamental rights, Europe was the paladin of a community of rights that survived the liquidity of the times.

However, what are the proclamations of rights if people do not know them and / or can not do them? The answer seems linear: to disclose and protect. And for tutelage it is necessary to institute "remedies" for those who need them. The Authors attempted this desideratum: first they presented the fundamental rights that Portugal enshrines and guardianship; then the international texts that best enshrine them and how they can be organized and should be given to knowledge.

This research received no specific grant from any funding agency in the public, commercial, or not-for-profit sectors.

REFERENCES

Alves, D. R. (2015, May). *Os direitos sociais na Constituição portuguesa. Conexão com o direito da União Europeia*. Paper presented at the meeting of Conferência Ibérica - "O Controlo Constitucional dos Direitos Sociais em ciclos de Crise Económica", Universidade Portucalense, Porto, Portugal.

Alves, D. R. (2018). Os direitos sociais na constituição portuguesa: sua conexão com o direito da União Europeia. In *Temas Constitucionais – o direito constitucional no Brasil e na Península Ibérica* (pp. 11–33). São Luís, Brasil: SVT Editora.

Alves, D. R., & Moreira, F. C. (2018, July). *A Convenção Europeia dos Direitos do Homem e os seus laços com os direitos de segunda geração*. Paper presented at the meeting of IV Congresso Internacional Dimensões dos Direitos Humanos: "Direitos Humanos de 2ª Geração", na Universidade Portucalense, Porto, Portugal.

Alves, D. R., & Silva, M. M. M. (2015). *O Estado Social e os Direitos Sociais - Um Novo Paradigma? In Cadernos de Dereito Actual, 3* (pp. 351–361). Santiago de Compostela: Espanha.

Balaguer Callejón, F. (2005). *La configuración normativa de princípios e derechos constitucionales en la Constitución Europea*. RDCE.

Botelho, C. S. (2010). *A Tutela Directa dos Direitos Fundamentais*. Coimbra: Almedina.

Botelho, C. S. (2017). *Os direitos sociais em tempos de crise*. Coimbra: Almedina.

Canotilho, J. J. G. (2003). Direito Constitucional e Teoria da Constituição (7.ª ed.). Coimbra: Almedina.

Canotilho, J. J. G., & Moreira, V. (2007). *CRP Constituição da República Portuguesa Anotada (4.ª edição)*. Coimbra: Coimbra Editora.

de Andrade, V. (2001). Os Direitos Fundamentais na Constituição Portuguesa de 1976 (2.ª ed.). Coimbra: Almedina.

Duarte, M. L. (2006). *União Europeia e Direitos Fundamentais - no espaço da internormatividade*. Lisboa: aafdl.

Duarte, M. L. (2011). *União Europeia - Estática e dinâmica da ordem jurídica eurocomunitária*. Coimbra: Almedina.

Martins, A. M. G. (2007). A Proteção dos Direitos Fundamentais em Portugal e a Constituição Europeia. *REE, 1*(2).

Martins, A. M. G. (2010). *A igualdade e a não discriminação dos nacionais de Estados terceiros legalmente residentes na União Europeia – da origem na integração económica ao fundamento na dignidade humana*. Coimbra: Almedina.

Martins, A. M. G. (2017). *Manual de Direito da União Europeia*. Coimbra: Almedina.

Miranda, J. (2014). *Manual de Direito Constitucional*. Coimbra: Coimbra Editora.

Miranda, J. & Medeiros, R. (2010). *Constituição da República Anotada* (2nd ed.). Coimbra: Coimbra Editora.

Pacheco, F. (2011). *O Sistema de Protecção dos Direitos Fundamentais na União Europeia – Entre a Autonomia e o Compromisso. In Julgar* (pp. 11–28). Coimbra: Coimbra Editora.

Pacheco, F. (2016). *Tempo, vínculos e direitos: quando circular e permanecer não tende a ser o estatuto fundamental dos nacionais dos Estados-Membros, UNIO*. EU Law Journal.

Pacheco, F. (2017a). *Crise e viabilidade dos sistemas de segurança social: as facetas da cidadania europeia na jurisprudência recente do TJUE. Revista do Direito de Língua Portuguesa, REDILP Ano IV (9). Faculdade de Direito da Universidade Nova de Lisboa*. Quid Iuris.

Pacheco, F. (2017b). *Algumas reflexões sobre o conteúdo dos direitos sociais na União Europeia. In Os novos horizontes do constitucionalismo global*. Braga: APPCDM - Artes Gráficas de Braga.

Pacheco, F. (2017c). Cidadania Europeia: da livre circulação de pessoas ao gozo do essencial dos direitos conferidos pelo estatuto fundamental dos nacionais dos Estados-membros. In *Viagens Intemporais pelo Saber: Mapas, Redes e Histórias*. Porto: ISCAP, Centro de estudos interculturais – CEI.

Pacheco, F. (2017c). *Em nome da autonomia do Direito da União: algumas considerações sobre um parecer polémico. Debater a Europa, 16*. Aveiro: Imprensa da Universidade de Coimbra.

Polakiewicz, J. (1994). *Soziale Grundrechte und Staatszielbestimmungen in den Verfassungsordnungen Italiens, Portugals und Spaniens*. Zeitschrift für ausländisches öffentliches Recht und Völkerrecht.

Proença, C. C. (2017). *Tutela Jurisdicional Efetiva no Direito da União Europeia*. Lisboa: Petrony.

Quadros, F. (1990). O princípio da exaustão dos meios internos na Convenção Europeia dos Direitos do Homem e a ordem jurídica portuguesa. *Revista da Ordem dos Advogados*, *50*(1), 124-126.

Queiroz, C. (2006). *O Princípio da não reversibilidade dos Direitos Fundamentais – princípios dogmáticos e prática jurisprudencial*. Coimbra: Coimbra Editora.

Queiroz, C. (2006). *Direitos Fundamentais – Teoria Geral*. Coimbra: Coimbra Editora.

Schutter, O. (2000). La contribution de la Charte des droits fondamentaux de l'Union européenne à la garantie des droits sociaux dans l'ordre juridique communautaire. *Revue Universelle des Droits de l'Homme*, *12*(1-2), 33–47.

Vaz, M. A. (1998). *O enquadramento jurídico-constitucional dos «direitos económicos, sociais e culturais» in Juris et de Jure – nos 20 anos da Faculdade de Direito da UCP*. Porto: Universidade Católica Portuguesa.

Vaz, M. A., Carvalho, R., & Botelho, C. S. (1998). *Direito Constitucional*. Coimbra: Coimbra Editora.

KEY TERMS AND DEFINITIONS

Constitution: Maximum document of a political community, with two basic functions: the need to order, limit, and legitimize political power (social pact); and to recognize, constitutionalize and guarantee the rights and freedoms of individuals (declaration of rights). Through constitutions the political community defines its common goals, creates its institutions, establishes the limits to the exercise of powers and reveals its system of values. The current functions of the Constitution are the construction of the political and legal unity of a State. In this sense, the constitution is intrinsic to the ontic figure of sovereign state. The Constitutions legitimize themselves in a substantive and formal plane: conditioning the power to the pursuit of the ends and to the respect of principles (among them the one of the guarantees of the fundamental rights) and, linking its exercise to the observance of democratic rules.

ECHR (European Convention on Human Rights): A treaty of international law that links the Portuguese State to the international legal order, which enshrines the rights and freedoms that embody the political and cultural values of Western democracies. The Convention has institutionalized a system of protection that is intended to be applied internally, so at the first moment of application are the domestic courts, which are bound to enforce it and to compensate victims if it has been violated. Only if this mechanism fails will individuals be able to access its court: the European Court of Human Rights. Underlying the intervention of the European Court is the principle of subsidiarity in view of the exhaustion of internal fundamental rights protection mechanisms. The rule of exhaustion and the right to an effective remedy are complementary: States must comply with the provisions of the Convention and, if violated, must provide victims with the effective means of redressing the damages suffered.

EU: An international entity set up and created by the EU Treaty in 1992 which led to a "new phase in the process of European integration initiated with the institution of the European Communities", which aimed at deepening economic integration and creating the conditions for future political integration of Europe. Signed at Maastricht, the new treaty was based on the European Communities (supplemented by the policies and forms of cooperation then instituted). The EEC, established in 1957 by the TR, was renamed EC. This, in turn, coexisted with the ECSC (1951) and the EAEC (1957). The three treaties formed the Communities and the EU, although autonomous, was not intended to replace them. As it is a single act of International Law, the TEU was composed of three parts with distinct intentions: it instituted the European Union; regulated the Common Foreign and Security Policy (CFSP); and the provisions relating to justice and home affairs (CJAI). On the other hand, it introduced changes to the institutional treaties by inserting diplomatic clauses in the title dedicated to the final provisions. The EU was structured in three distinct pillars (Communities, CFSP, and CJAI), with two logics of operation, corresponding to integrationist (community pillar) and cooperative (intergovernmental pillars) methods.

European Law: Law of International Organizations with a European geographical scope, with special emphasis on the Council of Europe, in particular with regard to the application of the ECHR. The EU law should be included in "European law" in its broadest sense, ie the legal systems produced and coexisting on the European continent. It is not unusual for the small and large European designation as regards fundamental rights. The first one refers to EU Europe and the second to Europe of the Council of Europe, both with specific sources, shared values, and common spaces of action.

Fundamental Rights: A set of rights recognized and guaranteed by higher norms of the legal systems or coming from other sources, which contain values transcendent to the own material constituent power, considered worthy of protection by a certain normative system. They consecrate subjective and basic positions of consecrated and established individuals at the constitutional, formal and material levels, designating the effective rights of the people before a concrete political organization. The term fundamental rights applies to internal orders. Respect for the fundamental rights is one of the most identifiable signs of a given legal order.

Human Rights: Are a set of legal rules that recognize to individuals in general fundamental rights and freedoms inherent to all "humanity" that, by their nature, must be secured before the States. These rights are characterized by their qualities of universality, abstraction, essentiality, inalienability and priority over positive law. The human rights international law was developed after World War II and includes different rules regarding the sources from which they originate and the universal or regional scope in which they apply. It is a special and autonomous branch of international law, of customary and conventional origin, linked to the progressive affirmation of the individual's international subjectivity.

Principles: Unlike the rules, the principles do not constitute subjective rights directly demandable or immediately materialized. These are constitutional and programmatic rules that establish and finalize the purposes and tasks to be achieved, the application of which depends on the adoption of measures of implementation or execution by the legislative bodies. By requiring regulatory or administrative intervention to become effective, the principles can serve as a judicial basis and give rise to new Union powers. These are therefore impositive legal standards of 'optimization' that need to be densified. Possessing indeterminate content, they lack concrete mediations. In the event of a conflict, they are 'object of weighting and harmonization between', allowing balancing of the antagonistic interests, which is not the case with legal rules.

Treaty of Lisbon: It is a treaty of continuity, although it introduces a very important body of amendments to previous treaties. Entering into force on 1 December 2009, it opens a 'new stage in the process of creating an ever closer union among the peoples of Europe'. By maintaining the international nature of the constituent treaties and allowing for the coexistence of different legal regimes, this treaty amended the TEU and the TEC, extinguishing the European Community. The reform of the Treaties has given rise to two new international texts, with the same legal value, on the basis of which the new EU Statute is framed. The Union is founded on the Treaty on European Union (TEU) and on the Treaty on the Functioning of the European Union (TFEU), replacing and succeeding the European Community. The Treaty establishing the European Atomic Energy Community, which was established in 1957, is not part of the original law, but has not changed since that time.

Chapter 2
Knowledge Society:
Participation, Transparency, and Trust as Factors of Citizenship

Artur Parreira
Universidade Santa Úrsula, Brazil

Rui Duarte Moura
Universidade Lusófona de Humanidades e Tecnologias de Lisboa, Portugal

Ana Lorga da Silva
https://orcid.org/0000-0001-7514-8278
Universidade Lusófona de Humanidades e Tecnologias de Lisboa, Portugal

ABSTRACT

This chapter is developed along three conceptual axes: citizenship; knowledge society: transparency; and trust and participation. It begins by explaining the concept of citizenship and its historical roots, the Greek polis and the Roman civitas; the revival of cities in the Late Middle Ages and their consolidation in the Modern Age. It analyzes the citizenship construct with the affirmation of each inhabitant as a citizen involved in improving the several plans of the quality of urban life. The second axis evaluates the characteristics of knowledge societies as promoting factors to a citizenship based on socio-political indicators that build trust between the citizen. The third axis deals with transparency and trust as active disseminators of timely and relevant information to the public and its impact on corruption, as a barrier against a broad citizenship. At the methodological level, the study combines bibliographic research with a field research by questionnaire.

DOI: 10.4018/978-1-5225-8350-9.ch002

INTRODUCTION

The chapter addresses the concept of citizenship and its relation to other concepts currently under focus, namely human sustainability in its five major dimensions (environmental, economic, social, cultural and political), the knowledge society and its impact on individual behavior and the participation and intervention of citizens in political processes at various levels.

The concept of citizenship has been an important focus of reflection: this reflection begins in the Greek polis, especially with the worship of justice and the connection between the individual and community destiny, expressed by the philosopher Solon, which is the basis of the construction of the concept. Solon first established, objectively, the causal link between violation of law and disruption of social life (Jaeger, 2001). In Rome, where the situation was not very different from what was lived in Greece, the concept was more formal: Rome was a slave society, based on the 'gens' (patrician families), which held citizenship and political rights. The plebs, made up of non-noble and foreign Romans, did not fit any kind of juridically defined right; only in the third century BC, after long political conflicts, were created institutions proper to the plebeian population, such as the Tribunate and the Assembly of the Plebe (Cardoso, 1985). The period following the fall of the Roman Empire (V century) in the High Middle Ages saw the vertical fall of the meaning of citizenship inherited from Antiquity: the constant barbarian invasions made Europe a territory in which institutions and customs were confronted. worlds barbarian and roman. A peculiar type of social organization (nobility, clergy and serfs) arose, with a central concern: fidelity to the masters, as a guarantee of security.

The picture just began to change with the formation of national states, centralized, favoring the development of cities and, consequently, the classic notion of citizenship, linked to the granting of political rights associated with urban life. Thus, began a new relationship between politics, economy and society, nourished by the dynamism of the emerging mercantile capitalism and, later, by the religious reforms of the fifteenth century. These acquisitions were consolidated by the Enlightenment philosophers and materialized in the French Revolution and the American Constitution and today embody the multidimensional construct of citizenship: civil and political rights; rights and measures of a more social nature, linked to the world of work, education, health and housing (mainly carried out in the nineteenth and twentieth centuries); finally, the most universal idea of rights linked to the very sense of humanity, defended mainly in the last third of the twentieth century and, today, as objectives of sustainable development (ODS-ONU, 2015).

Knowledge Society

Another theme focused on the chapter is the journey towards a knowledge society, which will have an undoubted impact on the construction of citizenship, which will materialize in different behavioral contexts (Barker, 1968), but certainly no different from today's societies.

Knowledge societies are not a new thing: all human societies have focused on the acquisition of knowledge and derived technologies, to dominate their support context and guarantee their sustainability (Nhacuongue and Ferneda, 2012). What is new in knowledge societies is the systematic search for information and the evaluation of the impact of all decisions on the quality of life of society. This society systematically uses study and learning to increase the information component and proportionally reduce the material and energy components in the technologies it uses (Coutinho and Lisboa, 2011).

To use the technology properly, it is essential that users acquire competence. In this perspective, the educational level of the population is an important indicator of the capacity of society to use knowledge and demonstrate competence. The Organization for Economic Co-operation and Development report (OCDE, 2014) showed levels of schooling in member countries that could serve as a basis for a minimum indicative standard for entry into a knowledge-based society: 82% of the population in those countries with 25-34 years of age completed at least upper secondary education; 39% completed higher education. And he proposed the goal of 85% for high school by 2016 and 45% for higher education by 2018.

The postulate that underlies this hypothesis considers that the collective use of knowledge is a function of the existing level of education, since the level of education of citizens conditions the choice of decision makers and, consequently, the informational quality of socio-political decisions (Castells, 2003).

The third axis of the reflections followed in this chapter addresses characteristics of the knowledge society that can be determinant factors for citizenship to be valued as a basic condition of living: sociopolitical participation, transparency, trust and smoothness of processes (anticorruption).

Paths that open access to meaningful information are explored, thus avoiding that transparency is confused with the simple disclosure of information, but is also relevant, accurate and reliable for the recipient (Forssbæck and Oxelheim, 2014). Transparency is rooted in the principle of impartiality with respect to divergent or opposing interests, allowing an objectivity to generate a sense of trust in the publics in presence (Nunes de Almeida, 2014).

'Trust', in turn, means a sense of self-confidence, as well as a firm belief in the reliability, honesty, effectiveness, or loyalty of someone (Dictionary of the Portuguese Language, 2013).

We distinguish two levels of trust based on Ketzer (2016): a basic level that configures social relations with the world, institutions and unknowns, which can be called trustworthiness (for Mistzal, 1996); and a deep level in which trust is explicit and situated at the level of moral relations, presupposing good will of the parties and involving the institution of promises.

Reliability is the level of trust that matters in citizenship; when it is broken, the person becomes socially resentful and the loss of this reliability compromises social relations. Ultimately, any breach of trust (Ketzer, 2016) can occur with the formal system based on laws, regulations, and institutional practices.

Transparency is even more important since it is a factor of confidence in the smoothness of political decisions and anti-corruption standards, a very strong aspiration of the population (Parreira, Silva and Moura, 2018), eager to enjoy a firm belief in reliability, honesty, efficacy and loyalty of institutions and public agents. The lack of transparency and guarantee of impartiality is, on the contrary, associated with pronounced levels of corruption, leading in general to the loss of confidence and the sharp reduction of citizen participation (Parreira, Silva and Moura, 2018).

These themes are firstly explored theoretically, in the corpus of the chapter; and then through an empirical study presented, whose results are taken by the authors' proposals for their proposals and conclusions.

THE CONSTITUTION OF CITIZENSHIP

The concept of citizenship has historically been an important focus of reflection on the configuration of the ways of living in European society and the like. This reflection began in the Greek polis, crossed the Roman empire and then the Middle Ages and the Renaissance, as mentioned in the introduction. However, it was revived and recast by the illuminists of the seventeenth century, who decisively influenced their incorporation into the social and political life of the industrial societies that were emerging and affirming themselves, when they were adopted politically by the French Revolution and the Anglo-Saxon world, incorporation into the United States Declaration of Independence. Philosophers like Locke and Rousseau conceived the ideas of a liberal democracy, relying on reason and opposing divine law (Locke, 1689). Locke's ideas directly influenced the wording of the American Constitution of 1776.

The French Constitution of 1791 enshrined rights such as equality, liberty, security, property, free expression of thought, due process of law, ample defense and political rights; it exerted, therefore, great influence on the constitutions of other countries, such as Mexicana (1917), Soviet (1918), German of the Weimar Republic (1919), which ended with the seizure of power by Hitler (Tolfo, 2013).

The idea of the rights and guarantees of the French revolution was taken up by the United Nations Organization, which left negotiations after the Second World War.

These rights are generally considered to be first generation: they are civil and political rights, impose on the State the duty to respect the sphere of freedom of the individual; represent a means of defending individual freedoms against the excessive demands of public authorities.

Second generation rights emphasize the principle of equality between citizens. They mark the passage from the liberal state (of an individualist character) to the social state (of a more solidary and inclusive nature): they materialize with the implementation of public policies and services, supported by social benefits, assumed by the constitutions (Mexican, 1917; Soviet, 1918; German of Weimar, 1919). These constitutional texts protect work, education and health rights, attributing to the State the satisfaction of these community needs.

Later, the third-generation rights were explicitly described: solidarity rights, characterized by collective or diffuse ownership, such as consumer law and environmental law, collective concerns that were previously not evident, such as environmental protection, care of the various forms of historical and environmental heritage, cultural diversity, peace (Scholz, 2017).

Human rights are universal, natural and historical, directly linked to human nature and beyond legal boundaries and state sovereignty (Benevides, 2009); its most striking example is the Universal Declaration of Human Rights (1948), established by the United Nations (UN), art. 1, from the French Constitution of 1791, declaring that "all human beings are born free and equal in dignity and rights, confirming the constitutional protection of human rights among democratic countries."

This perspective of universality has as counterpart the universality of the duties of citizenship. A citizen must act for the benefit of society, and the latter must provide basic rights to life, such as housing, food, education, health, leisure, work, security, environment. The idea of citizenship is thus eminently political; its rooting in universal values is mediated by local political values and decisions. In any case, there is currently a set of principles, values and practices that the authors consensually associate with the construct of citizenship:

- Being subject, not object.
- Being a citizen, not a consumer.
- To be master of a personal destiny, not mere factor of production or human capital.
- Being a person who exists for himself, is aware of himself as an 'I' in a world where he integrates but is different from himself.
- Being a person who is aware of the relationship with another selves-in-the-world.

This conception fosters attitudes and behaviors that define, at the level of practices, the concept of citizenship:

- Respect for you, for the other and for nature.
- Personal affirmation through positive attitudes towards self and others: self-esteem, initiative to improve things, orientation to the common good.
- Concept of city and love of the city, perceived as a people with vital meaning, community of citizens equal in their relationship; on the physical plane, a sense of security and aesthetics; in the community lifestyle, adoption of conscientious attitudes, care for the environment, not wastefulness, involvement in socio-political life.
- Notion of essential equality of citizens, compatible with ancillary differences (respect and valorisation, initiatives against inequality and marginalization).
- Acceptance of the construction of norms of relationship in common life shared and sustained by all, based on the concept of fundamental rights and duties, subject to collective debate to reassess their positivity and equity.

THE TRAITS OF A KNOWLEDGE SOCIETY

The advances of current societies towards future societies may follow multiple paths. One of the ways of this development is to build societies based on the use of information technologies and guided by scientific knowledge in the decisions they make about their own organization: they will be societies whose functioning will have as fundamental support the information transformed into knowledge based, in principle, on the level of the sciences that are the central nucleus of their culture and of their way of seeing reality (Masson and Mainardes, 2011).

In the study presented, the characteristics of this society are understood as the integrative context conducive to the consolidation of the other behavioral patterns studied: trust, transparency and a strong reduction of practices of corruption.

Information and Knowledge

The information allows to obtain a map of reality; knowledge is information transformed into an instrument to deal with each reality. While information is in consciousness and serves only as the attribution of meanings, knowledge includes mediate or immediately the relation of the subject to reality and its action on it. For the current level of knowledge, the reality, the existing one, comes in three categories:

- Matter: what has mass and, in case of gravity, weight.
- Energy: a force that produces work, i.e., results, behavior, movement.
- Information: meaning of an existing for a subject.

Without awareness of a subject there is no meaning and without meaning there is no existence, because there is no information describing the possible existing (Saldanha, 2013). Applying these concepts to society, one can affirm with Amaral (2006) that:

(...) the concept of 'knowledge societies' is preferable to that of the 'Information Society' since it better expresses the complexity and dynamism of the changes that are taking place ... the knowledge in question is not only important for growth but also to strengthen and develop all sectors of society. Amaral (2006, p.9, cited in Dziekaniak and Rover, 2011, p.2)

The level of knowledge of a society can be defined based on the distinction between data, information and knowledge made by Davenport and Prusak (Table 1).

Data are stimuli to which the subject can assign meaning and transform into information; information is in the subject's consciousness, allowing him to situate himself in a context, his world; the knowledge, finally, is the operationalized information, made instrument to deal with the reality.

From Table 1, a continuum of knowledge can be drawn (Table 2). In this continuum, the zero level means null processing of information, own of a closed system, that processes only matter / energy. The knowledge above level 5 is not yet given in our experience and is not therefore included in the continuous.

This continuum will be used as a framework of criteria to evaluate to what extent the results of the empirical research carried out in our study configure appropriate characteristics to define a knowledge society. From this perspective, it is proposed as a first postulate that a society, to be definable as a knowledge society, must be

Table 1. Continuum data to knowledge

Data	Information	Knowledge
Distinct facts have no meaning in themselves, they are events, phenomena or stimuli, matter to construct information.	Data to which the individual gave meaning, relevance and purpose (Drucker, 1988); shape the view of the individual over the real; impact their behaviour.	Structure of meanings for evaluation and incorporation of new experiences and information; information to be applied and guide action.

Source: Adapted from Davenport and Prusak (2000).

Table 2. Levels in the knowledge continuum

Level 0	Null information processing: closed system (object) that processes only matter / energy, in a field where meanings are assigned by an external (subject) processor.
Level 1	Information about the existence of an object, where the level of knowledge is limited to the identification of the type of object; does not allow its effective manipulation, it only assigns meaning to the object and thus guides the subject in the real field.
Level 2	Information that is partial knowledge of the object: it allows to manage it, for it includes the knowledge of tools for this, especially those that assure the operability of the management; but it does so in a very imperfect way, because it ignores many of the conditions of the object and its connections with the context. Risk of perverse effects in this management, due to this lack of knowledge.
Level 3	Information that is relatively extensive knowledge of the object: it allows to handle it very effectively, because it already has knowledge of many connections to the context, partially contextualizing the operations on the object. Generally dangerous perverse effects associated with extensive interventions with unawareness of important impacts on the context.
Level 4	Very extensive information about the object: it can explain it globally and, in the details, it allows to handle the object in an extensive and secure way, situate it in the context of support and attend to its essential connections to other contexts. Concern over effective control of potentially harmful effects.
Level 5	Almost complete knowledge of the object explains the object in the global and its various facets and movements; allows to construct the object from its inexistence, based on accessible resources, situate it in the context of support and manage its connections to the global context. Effective prevention of many potentially harmful effects.
Level >5	Knowledge of all intra-interobject connections, ability to create existing from the knowledge itself (level of conceivable knowledge, but not measurable distance from level 5, because it is outside current human experience).

Source: The authors (2018).

located at least at level 4 of the continuum in all the fundamental sectors of its functioning. This requires, among other things, that the application of knowledge to intervention over the real based on operational knowledge of the means that enable it. These means are what is called technology, which is a concrete and therefore specific way of applying knowledge.

Technologies depend on the instruments of intervention and are therefore limited expressions of the knowledge they apply. In turn, the improvement of technologies leads to the amplification and precision of the knowledge they embody (Ferreira and Axt, 1999), an informational circle that concretizes Morin's (1990) idea of recursion.

Historically, the substitution of one technology for another gives rise to what may be called technological revolutions, which are characterized by the emergence of new technologies, like the concept of scientific revolution of Kuhn (1962), in which new scientific paradigms arise.

In the eighteenth century technologies based on the intensive use of matter (animals, human arm, etc.) were replaced by 'new technologies' of intensive use of energy (steam engine), triggering the industrial revolution; currently, intensive energy technologies have been replaced by technologies for the extensive use of information, with natural changes in the production paradigm (Parreira, 2018). A knowledge society systematically uses study and learning to increase the information component and proportionally reduce the material and energy components in the technologies it uses (Coutinho and Lisboa, 2011).

Knowledge as Competence

To use the technology properly it is essential to acquire the competence by the users. The development of these skills is the basis for the effective use of technology and knowledge. There are multiple definitions of competence, but all converge to the definition that is most compatible with reflection now underway: competence is the effective management of knowledge of the real and the instruments that allow to apply this knowledge on concrete conditions of a defined context.

A human system is competent when:

- Can create or acquire knowledge about the real.
- Organizes, stores and creates effective ways of accessing this knowledge.
- It has a way of distributing and getting this knowledge to the actors who will apply it.
- Has a way of effectively applying this knowledge, using the appropriate technologies in its present (Gomes, 2002).

Knowledge societies practice the systematic search for information and seek to ensure that all decisions with an impact on the quality of life of society are based on the competencies required by the decision (Rato, 2010).

UNESCO published a synthesis paper in this area (Seddoch, quoted in Bernheim and Chauí, 2008, p.36):

- Create a higher education accessible to all, based on merit.
- Reconfirm the fundamental missions of the national higher education systems (to educate, train, conduct research, contribute to the sustainable development of society as a whole).
- Strengthen the critical and prospective role of higher education.
- Promote the academic freedom and autonomy of higher education institutions, while maintaining their responsibility towards society.

A Knowledge Society Has Diverse Means of Production and Distribution of Knowledge

The production of knowledge is, therefore, a nuclear activity in knowledge societies. It focuses on all areas with implications in the individual and collective quality of life of societies. Knowledge is produced in diverse centers, starting with universities and research centers, but also in companies and schools at all levels. If we recognize that the knowledge society is a learning society (Hargreaves, 2003), then basic and average schools themselves are committed to innovative learning experiences. The motors of this revolution are the appreciation of teachers, special attention to students with high skills or difficulties, the valorization of the arts, the diversity of forms of learning, highlighting the means of diffusion of knowledge as powerful as those based on the internet, where individual subjects can assume the role of producers of socially usable knowledge.

SOCIOPOLITIC TRANSPARENCY, CONFIDENCE, AND PARTICIPATION

The third axis of this chapter opposes corruption and transparency and relates transparency and trust as generators of socio-political participation and full citizenship.

Corruption as Anti-Citizenship

The term 'corruption' means deterioration, decomposition, putrefaction; deterioration of a substance by rotting or rust. Banerjee, Hanna and Mullainathan (2012) define corruption as an incident, in which a bureaucrat (or an elected agent) violates a rule to earn some amount of money or equivalent. The United Nations Anti-Corruption Policy Guide (2003, quoted in Hancock and Bradley, 2014, p.9) notes that "definitions of corruption vary from country to country according to cultural, legal or other factors and with the understanding that in each country one has the nature of the problem ". Transparency International defines corruption as "the abuse of power entrusted to private gain"; and the World Bank defines as corrupt practice "the offer, delivery, receipt or solicitation, direct or indirect, of any value to unduly influence the actions of another party." (Hancock and Bradley, 2014, p.9).

According to Klitgaard (1994), corruption mainly involves three variables: the opportunity to experience the illegal act, the possibility of corrupt action being discovered, and the likelihood of the perpetrator being punished; and proposes three levels of analysis of the phenomenon.

The first level is the individual, where corrupt behavior is causally linked to the motivations of the actors: motivation is at the root of all intentional behavior - and corruption is intentional behavior.

The second level is the organizational level, where many corruption behaviors occur. They are clearly influenced by the organization's culture and climate, which act as a facilitator or even as a direct cause.

The third level is the sociopolitical one, whose complexity is great, since it integrates several levels and sectors, including the previous ones. Several causal factors or facilitating conditions are pointed out, namely:

- A culture of pursuit of advantage, with low appreciation of the ethical stance and the idea of common good.
- A network of connectors, which drive corruption behaviors.
- Actors in leadership positions motivated by patterns of corruption.

In the point 'The picture of a knowledge society' results of studies carried out by the authors on the subject are presented, to obtain a clarifying and sufficiently precise definition (Table 1).

It is the relational behaviors (shown in black in Table 1) that construct the essence of what is defined as corruption: a way of deciding and acting in violation of ethics, supported by the construction of a network of decision makers that define the standards of action accepted by network. These behaviors are all above the 88th percentile of the scale - the highest position of which had a numerical value of 9.25, corresponding to. It is extremely appropriate to designate this behavior as corruption (Parreira and Silva, 2016). One can therefore adopt them as a precise definition of the construct as it sheds light on the reason for the impact of corruption and can open a way of accessing the roots of the problem.

The Impact of Corruption

Brei points to the functionalist position that corruption results "can be a stimulus to the development process, not irreparable damage to society, and acceptable at a given historical moment" (Brei, 1996, p. 105). However, this possible positive contribution is submerged by a series of clearly perverse effects. The UK Anticorruption Plan (Hancock and Bradley, 2014) states that if left unchecked, corruption harms the community and the integrity of public and private institutions; allows criminals to bypass border controls and facilitate illegal trafficking in goods; creates unnecessary costs and undermines the ability to promote sustainable growth (Brei, 1996; Hancock and Bradley, 2014). According to Pellegrino and Gerlaugh (2004, p. 438) corroborated by Rock and Bonnett (2004), "the increase of a standard deviation in the corruption index is associated with a reduction of investments of 2.46 percentage points, which reduces growth economic growth at 0.34% per year. "These data show that corruption has a destructive impact on the economic, social and political dimensions of sustainability.

Transparency and Socio-Political Participation as Barriers to Corruption and Citizenship Factors

The expression 'transparency' refers to the quality of what is transparent, namely a body that is allowed to pass through the light and allows to distinguish, through its thickness, the objects that are behind.

In an administrative sense, the concept of transparency configures concrete relationships between individuals and groups, which are perceived by observers (Chevalier, 1988). Transparency can be analyzed from several perspectives, such as active disclosure (Oliver, 2004). disclosure of policy choices (Fox, 2007) and increasing the flow of information to the public in a timely, comprehensive, relevant, high-quality and reliable manner in relation to public performance (Ferranti, Jacinto, Ody and Ramshaw, 2009). In compliance with transparent administrative procedures, the State and Public Administration, as well as private entities, should be obliged to disclose information before, during and after the decisions and ensure that anyone can access the procedures and processes related to them (Silva, 2010).

Transparency is a concept that must be applied in accordance with the context of reference (Merloni, 2008), but whose common denominator is to avoid shadowing the law. Your study can not be isolated from other principles such as advertising, motivation, impartiality, efficiency and legality. Particularly as regards the link between the concept of transparency and the concept of impartiality, it should be emphasized that the transparency of the decision-making procedure is an important guarantee of impartiality.

In this sense, the decision-making process seems to be inseparable from impartiality, and the efficiency principle becomes fundamental considering the need to improve the performance of public institutions and agents (Gonçalves, 2013).

Within the framework of a knowledge society in which citizenship and socio-political participation are fundamental conditions for living, it is called for access to information that has meaning and meaning and demonstrates the capacity to use it, avoiding that transparency is confused with simple and is only observable, but also relevant to the recipient, as well as accurate and reliable (Forssbæck and Oxelheim, 2014).

Figure 1. Concept of transparency; degrees and characteristics
Source: Adapted from Capelli et al. (2014)

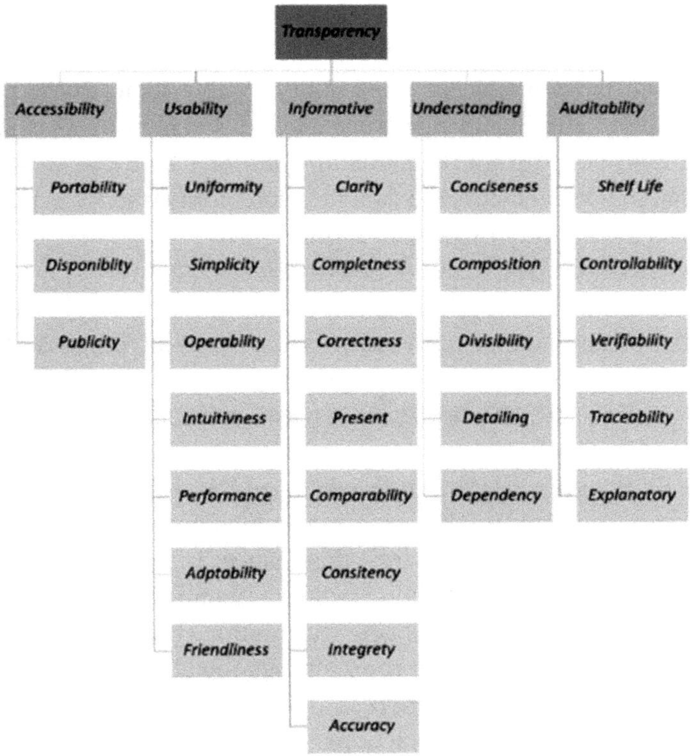

Around this subject there have been efforts to establish mechanisms that allow reliable information to be made available to society. In this sense, Capelli et al. (2014) proposed to construct the concept of transparency applied to the administrative context based on twenty-eight characteristics associated with five degrees of transparency:

In short, transparency requires that information be accessible, that it can be used, that it demonstrates quality, that it is understandable and that it is valid. The authors consider that all the mentioned characteristics must be present in the administrative transparency. However, it should be mentioned that transparency is a state that can vary according to the characteristics of the concept and needs of a social nature, since the characteristics of transparency are qualities and can have different perceptions according to the reference contexts (Merloni, 2008).

It should be noted, however, that although several interpretations can be admitted, there is a common denominator to all of them, which is based on the crucial objective of preventing gloomy activities by maintaining full transparency with regard to the processes and behavior of public and private entities. Regarding the public thing, it cannot be admitted that a democratic State of law hides matters of public relevance to the interested parties in general and to the subjects directly affected (Mello, 2013).

This perspective calls for an intimate relationship between the principle of transparency and the principle of impartiality to contribute to the existence of objectivity, exemption and equidistance in relation to divergent or opposing interests, configuring a sense of trust for the public in question (Almeida, 2014). That is, it can be said that transparency has the dual function of impartiality in public matters and trust in this impartiality (Ribeiro, 1996).

The term 'trust' means a sense of self-confidence, as well as a firm belief in someone's reliability, honesty, effectiveness, or loyalty (Dictionary of the Portuguese Language, 2013). In the administrative sense it is an act of relying on the truthfulness of certain facts in the light of previous experiences.

According to Ketzer (2016) two levels of trust can be distinguished: a basic level that configures social relations with the world, institutions and unknowns, which is called reliability, and a deep level in which trust is explicit and situates moral relations, assuming good will of the parties and involving the institution of promises.

Reliability, which is the level of trust that matters in the domain of citizenship and the knowledge society, does not produce resentment at the level of social relations when it is broken, but by losing trust in the world one becomes socially resentful. The loss of this reliability compromises social relations and, ultimately, can break any relationship of trust (Ketzer, 2016) with the formal system based on laws, regulations and institutional practices.

Transparency is more important since it is generally a factor of anti-corruption and citizen participation, which corresponds to a very strong aspiration of the population (Parreira, Silva and Moura, 2018), who are eager to enjoy a firm belief in reliability, honesty, efficacy and loyalty of the institutions and public agents, mainly.

The lack of transparency and fairness is generally associated with differentiated levels of corruption and generates the loss not only of reliability but also of confidence in the surrounding world.

Previously, the three levels of analysis of the phenomenon of corruption (Klitgaard, 1994) were mentioned: the individual, the organizational and the sociopolitical. At this last level, corruption assumes very complex institutional bases based on the 'culture of advantage' with devaluation of the ethical stance and the idea of common good, in networks of connectors that stimulate corrupt behavior and in actors motivated by patterns of corruption.

In this case, the lack of transparency has very serious consequences in terms of the loss of trustworthiness in the surrounding world and the remoteness of citizens about their socio-political participation, preventing the consolidation of citizen practices and the deepening of the knowledge society.

THE EMPIRICAL RESEARCH

Starting from the ideas exposed above, a field research was carried out, subdivided into two parts:

- In the first part, the picture of a knowledge society, as represented by the sample subjects;
- The second part of the study focused on transparency as the main anticorruption factor and citizen participation as the engine of smarter decisions.

As a whole the research aimed to clarify the extent to which the characteristics attributed by the subjects of the sample to the knowledge society are the context conducive to the consolidation of the other concepts studied: transparency, trust and rejection of corrupt practices.

The study continues previous studies (Parreira et al., 2015, Parreira, Lorga da Silva and Rego, 2016) carried out within the scope of the CPES (Centro de Pesquisa e Estudos Sociais).

Research Instruments

To characterize a knowledge society, a questionnaire survey was conducted in which respondents were asked to express their idea of what a future knowledge society would be. In the data collection, a questionnaire was used consisting of three sections:

- The first section is the basis of the first part of the study and consists of 13 items, similar to those suggested by Kumpikaitė (2007), quoted above. This part of the questionnaire allows to characterize the representation that the respondents make of a knowledge society, indicating to what extent they consider each characteristic as belonging to that society (point a); and then also assess the position of their current society in that characteristic (point (b)). Table 2 presents these data.
- The second section evaluates the perception of the constructs corruption and transparency by the subjects interviewed, in order to confirm if they have a clear and consistent notion of the two concepts, having 12 items dedicated to the characterization of corruption and nine items dedicated to the characterization of transparency.
- The third section, consisting of six items, focuses on citizen participation and trust.

Data collection took place between June and September 2017.

The Sample

The survey sample comprised 138 respondents, students and teachers from three universities in Brazil (Rio Janeiro) and Portugal. The students are mainly working students, as can be seen in the sample.

This is a convenience sample, explained by the scarcity of resources that could be directed to this work.

The researchers were concerned, however, with obtaining a sample of a representative size, despite the limitations of available means; and also took care that the subjects included had a reasonable knowledge of the problematic in focus. Despite being a sample of university students, the included students are working students, having, therefore, experience of non-university work contexts.

First Part: The Picture of a Knowledge Society

The study that portrays a knowledge society is an exploratory field research, which gave continuity to another study presented at a Congress in Buenos Aires.

The study had two main objectives:

- Obtain a relatively detailed characterization of the representation of a knowledge society by university students and professors.
- Assess how far away from the knowledge society respondents place the society in which they are inserted.
- Evaluate in which way the characteristics of the knowledge society are perceived as factors of trust, active participation for full citizenship, and barriers against corruption.

Table 3. Sample characteristics

N=138									
Age	%	Gender	%	Degree	%	Work	%	Country	%
<21	15,9%	F	59,4%	PhD	26,1%	Professor	44,2%	PT	66,7%
[21,31[	37,0%	M	40,6%	Master	31,8%	Student	23,3%	BR	33,3%
[31,41[	19,6%			Licence	39,2%	Technician	10,9%		
[41,51[	9,4%			Middle Level	2,9%	Administrative	21,6%		
≥51	18,1%								
Total	100%		100%		100%		100%		100%

Source: The authors (2018).

Guiding Hypotheses:

H1: Future Knowledge societies are represented as significantly different from present ones, in all their main characteristics.
H2: The characteristics of the knowledge society regarding the free and open circulation of information on all operations and activities are perceived as strong barriers against corruption.
H3: Leaders open to divergent thinking are the decisive factor for citizen participation.
H4: The participation of informed citizens increases the transparency of political decisions.
H5: Transparency of decisions is perceived as the strongest barrier against corruption.

Table 4 presents the characteristics of this type of society and its distance from the current ones, in the participants' perception.

The picture of the future knowledge society drawn by the respondents differs substantially from that of the current society to which they belong. The characteristics it will present will have an obvious impact on the type of citizen and the citizenship standards they will promote. This impact on citizenship patterns may, in fact, be different from one society to another within a common range: the traits of these societies may have different configurations, both quantitatively (extension of each trait) and qualitative (trait profiles many different). Despite the likely differences, it is expected that all of them promote similar patterns of behavior and an idea of citizenship convergent with what can be inferred from this research. Thus, the realization of knowledge societies with these traits will lead to significantly different indicators of current societies, confirming Hypothesis 1 (Table 4).

The differences between the two societal profiles are all statistically significant ($p = 0.05$ or $p = 0.005$) and very pronounced in the most relevant traits for the issue of citizenship (traits 10, 11, 12 and 13). Some of these traits will be highlighted in the second empirical study, which will help to better understand the impact of this type of society on citizenship behaviors and to define these behaviors with greater precision.

The distances in the traces 'extensive connectivity between people' (1,92) and 'ethical behavior and responsibility' (2,07) are insignificant, suggesting that respondents consider the differences between the two types of society as regards connectivity between people and the valorization of ethical and responsible attitudes; but when we go to the practical level the distances are much greater: in the unacceptability of corruption (6,66); in the requirement of transparency of acts and decisions (6,16); in rejecting inequality (5,60); in the observance of a society situated at least at level 4 of the knowledge continuum, in all essential sectors of functioning (4,95).

Table 4. Traits of a knowledge society

Traits of society		Average	sd	Difference observed
1. A society that will be characterized by the extensive connectivity between people, through various existing virtual networks.	Knowledge society	8,83	1,372	**1,92**
	Actual society	6,91	2,085	
2. A society in which the majority of citizens will value ethical behavior and social responsibility.	Knowledge society	7,78	2,372	**2,07**
	Actual society	5,71	1,346	
3. A company which bets on the free movement of information.	Knowledge society	8,45	1,778	**2,75**
	Actual society	5,70	1,547	
4. A society with very easy access to knowledge through the instruments of access to information.	Knowledge society	8,33	1,699	**3,20**
	Actual society	5,13	1,347	
5. A society that accepts the diversity of people and conditions that exist and seeks its systematic use.	Knowledge society	8,02	2,203	**3,67**
	Actual society	4,35	1,778	
6. A learning society in which people are motivated to acquire solid knowledge and to guide their behavior.	Knowledge society	8,29	1,682	**3,94**
	Actual society	4,35	1,346	
7. A society committed to sustainable decisions and practices in all its areas of operation.	Knowledge society	7,93	2,131	**4,25**
	Actual society	3,68	1,548	
8. A society in which the leaders will be motivated to leave no important factor out of their decisions, making an effort to integrate everyone.	Knowledge society	7,34	2,334	**4,38**
	Actual society	2,96	2,516	
9. A society that will avoid waste, including human waste.	Knowledge society	7,71	2,688	**4,56**
	Actual society	3,15		
10. A society situated at least at level 4 of the knowledge continuum, in all essential operating sectors (see table describing levels of knowledge).	Knowledge society	8,01	2,114	**4,95**
	Actual society	3,16	1,689	
11. A society in which inequality will be less than it is today and class separation will be less rigid.	Knowledge society	7,89	2,362	**5,60**
	Actual society	2,29	1,547	
12. A society in which the transparency of acts and decisions will be the habitual practice of rulers and social and economic.	Knowledge society	7,98	2,619	**6,16**
	Actual society	1,82	1,841	
13. A society whose behavior patterns will be incompatible with corrupt practices.	Knowledge society	8,47	2,099	**6,66**
	Actual society	1,81	1,548	

Source: The authors (2018).

Second Part: Transparency as a Factor of Anti-Corruption and Socio-Political Participation

The study on transparency as an anticorruption and participation factor is an exploratory field research that continued another study on barriers to corruption in the knowledge society presented in 2016 at the Laemos international conference, in Viña del Mar. In this study, corruption and wasteful behaviors in the field of threats to one or more dimensions of human sustainability are integrated, exploring the link between those behaviors and the concept of transparency and trustworthiness, as well as the role attributed to socio-political participation as factor of development and consolidation of those characteristics.

Tables 5 and 6 show the perception of the respondents about the 'corruption' construct and the 'transparency' construct, respectively, as well as the value they attribute to each dimension of the constructs; table 6 shows the most striking indicators of citizens' socio-political participation.

Table 5. Dimensions of the corruption construct

Dimensions of the corruption construct	N	Average
Steal someone with gun threat	138	3,578
Theft or theft of an object	138	3,842
Use company products without authorization and without declaring	138	5,910
Giving someone false information to take advantage of a business	138	6,860
Fake data to be admitted to an institution	138	7,256
Usar a sua posição para guardar para si parte do pagamento de um cliente à sua empresa, às escondidas do cliente	138	**8,272**
Use privileged knowledge coming from your social position, to gain profits in a business, impossible to obtain without this knowledge	138	**8,361**
Being in a contest and influencing someone from the institution to be placed ahead of other competitors	138	**8,538**
Use your position to get a payout from a contestant with a promise to favor you	138	**9,158**
Receive money from a vendor, with the promise that he will win the deal	138	**9,377**
Use your social position to secretly influence a business and make a profit out of it	138	**9,409**
Secretly propose payment to an employee of a potential client, to gain an advantage over the other competitors	138	**9,429**

Source: The authors (2018).

The relational behaviors (shown in black in Table 5) that constitute the essence of what is defined as corruption: a way of deciding and acting in violation of ethics and supported by the construction of a network of decision makers that define the standards of action accepted by network. These behaviors are all above the 88th percentile of the scale used - whose highest position had the numerical value of 9.25, corresponding to 'It is extremely appropriate to designate this behavior as corruption' (Parreira and Silva, 2016). One can therefore adopt them as a fairly precise definition of the construct.

The data in Table 6, regarding transparency, reveal that the concept is very present in the reality lived by the respondents: all indicators of institutional transparency have values that are equal to or above "very applicable" (7.62 of the scale used), indicating that the concept is clearly understood globally and in each of its dimensions.

Tables 5 and 6 confirm that the respondents know quite well the essential concepts focused in this research. Comparing those results with the results in the table 7 (which shows the results regarding the factors that impact on citizens' participation in politics, namely, decisions that affect their life in the shortest or longest term), the close relationship between them becomes evident.

Respondents consider that higher levels of schooling do not have a very positive effect on citizens 'participation in politics (4,51) or on politicians' acceptance of greater citizen participation (4,25), which a position around the mean.

The factors to which respondents attributed the most positive impact on citizens political participation refer to increased citizen participation through greater transparency of institutions and their leaders (7.75) and, in return, greater transparency in government decisions due to the participation of informed citizens (7,17), which

Table 6. Dimensions of the corruption construct

Dimensions of the construct Transparency	N	Average	sd
Total information on the execution of the project, control and correction of deviations	138	7,3989	2,25671
Know who takes the economic decisions in the institution	138	7,7789	1,65768
Declaration of financial values in games in competitions	138	7,8006	1,66115
Publication of all competitor bids	138	7,8226	1,76675
Publication of the outcome of the evaluation of the proposals	138	7,8482	1,72786
Complete information on how to handle complaints	138	7,8535	1,75247
Total opening of the tendering procedure	138	8,1245	1,43488
Complete information about the final results of the project	138	8,2370	1,60181
Publication of the accounts of public institutions	138	8,4233	1,51408

Source: The authors (2018).

means that both are enhanced through greater transparency and participation. The values in these criteria are above 7.09 (scale position corresponding to the 75th percentile).

It should be noted that respondents realized that penalizing acts of corruption is a less effective barrier to avoiding them than learning attitudes of transparency, loyalty to others and responsibility for their actions. The importance of these attitudes is confirmed - using the modeling method of structural equations - by the positive and slight relation (0,217), which shows that the school is perceived as a source of some irreplaceable preventive learning of acts of corruption (including attitudes of frankness, loyalty and responsibility for their actions) and the data show that being consciously aware of these attitudes has undoubtedly an impact on the transparency of the acts and decisions of the leaders.

Insofar as the transparency of leaders leads to the construction of a society guided by ethics and social responsibility (Table 7), the results support the hypothesis of the study on the role of transparency of leaders and institutions in the context of the decisions taken (H5).

Regarding the free and open circulation of information characteristic of the knowledge society as a barrier to corruption, facilitated access to knowledge is crucial as a guide to social and political intervention. There is a positive and slight relationship in terms of transparency in decisions, confirming H2 (Table 8).

On the other hand, there is also a positive and slight relation regarding the attention of the managers to all the factors that involve the decisions (Table 9).

These findings lead us to the issue of involving informed citizens to increase the transparency of policy decisions (H4), confirming that this is a fundamental condition for increasing transparency and improving the quality of government decisions; this requires, in turn, the active participation of citizens. Effectively, Table 10 shows a positive and moderate relationship between the active participation of citizens, the production of better-quality policies, and increased transparency of decisions.

Table 7. Society is guided by ethics and social responsibility

Constant	7,089 (,552)
The transparency of leaders and institutions is a decisive condition	,158** (,067)
N	138
R^2	,039

*** p<0,01; ** p<0,05; * p<0,1 *(Standard errors in parentheses)*
Source: The authors (2018)

Table 8. Bet on the transparency of decisions

Constant	6,288 (,714)
Easy Access to Knowledge	,259*** (,0053)
N	138
R^2	0,025

*** p<0,01; ** p<0,05; * p<0,1 *(Standard errors in parentheses)*
Source: The authors (2018)

Table 9. Managers attentive to all decision factors

Constant	6,458 (,692)
Easy Access to Knowledge	,195** (,086)
N	138
R^2	0,07

*** p<0,01; ** p<0,05; * p<0,1 *(Standard errors in parentheses)*
Source: The authors (2018)

Table 10. Increased transparency of government decisions

Constant	4,178 (,732)
The active participation of citizens leads to better quality political decisions	,504*** (,091)
N	138
R^2	,357

*** p<0,01; ** p<0,05; * p<0,1 *(Standard errors in parentheses)*
Source: The authors (2018)

Respondents are more appreciative of leaders being open to face-to-face debate and criticism than simply to participate, supporting hypothesis H3: leaders open to discuss divergent information and ready to encourage brainstorming are a relevant condition for participation active participation of citizens; in turn, increases the transparency and quality of the decisions, with a positive and strong relationship in the regression model (Table 11).

Table 11. Active citizen participation and better-quality policy decisions

Constant	0,756 (,592)
Officials open to discuss information that is divergent and ready to encourage the confrontation of ideas	,788** (,069)
N	138
R^2	,426

*** p<0,01; ** p<0,05; * p<0,1 *(Standard errors in parentheses)*
Source: The authors (2018)

Undoubtedly, the intervention of well-informed citizens increases the transparency of leaders and institutions, which in turn is decisive as a barrier to corrupt behavior, as H5 states.

CONCLUSION

At first, the results of the empirical research allowed to obtain a detailed characterization of the representation of a knowledge society and to evaluate the distance that this society is in relation to the current society. Respondents pointed out very significant differences between the features of the knowledge society and current society, namely patterns of citizenship, unacceptability of corruption, demands for transparency of acts and decisions, rejection of inequality and observance of a high society level.

The verified results confirmed the hypotheses according to which: the present societies walk in one way or another to become societies of knowledge (H1); a knowledge society must be at least at the level 4 of the knowledge continuum in all the fundamental sectors of its functioning (H2).

Secondly, research focused on transparency, exploring the relationship between corruption behavior and the concepts of transparency and trustworthiness, as well as the role attributed to sociopolitical participation.

The results obtained on the 'corruption' construct show that it is 'relational behaviors' that define what is defined by corruption, especially the way of deciding and acting in violation of ethics, supported by a network of decision makers who define the norms of action.

In the 'transparency' construct, there were two types of findings from the perspective of the respondents: higher education does not significantly impact a greater participation of citizens in political life or a greater acceptance of citizen participation by politicians; but greater transparency of institutions and their leaders induce greater sociopolitical participation of citizens, and greater citizen participation leads to increased transparency in government decisions.

To the extent that greater transparency of leaders leads to a society guided by ethics and social responsibility, it is confirmed H6: Transparency of decisions is perceived as a strong barrier against corruption.

There is also confirmation of H3 that free and open information circulation in the knowledge-based society is a barrier to corruption, since facilitating access to knowledge is crucial for the transparency of decisions and encourages greater attention of the leaders to all factors that involve decision making.

On the other hand, a positive and moderate relationship is identified between the active participation of citizens, the production of better-quality policies and the increase of transparency of decisions, confirming H5 according to which the participation of informed citizens increases the transparency of the decisions.

Finally, insofar as the active participation of citizens increases the transparency and quality of decisions through greater openness of the leaders to the frontal debate and critical reflection, Hypothesis 4 confirms that it is open leaders to the divergent thinking the factor decisive for citizen participation.

It can thus be affirmed that in the knowledge societies the government and the various public and private agents in positions of political and technical leadership will adopt measures that minimize material, financial and human waste, developing transparent practices in the political, economic and social dimensions, pondering all the key factors for good decision-making and seeking to build inclusive societies.

In this way, the concept of citizenship promoted in knowledge societies will include the fundamental rights that are now commonly accepted, both first and second generation and third generation:

- The right to a personal affirmation as an autonomous person, free to express, question and defend their own ideas.
- The right to own property of various types and sizes.
- The right to be treated as equal before the institutions and with equity by the authorities.
- Right to equitable access to essential goods offered in societies, such as health, education, housing, security, and paid work.
- The right to active participation in the social, cultural and political life of society and its institutions.

Holder of such rights, the citizen will be socially motivated to:

- To assume behaviors of respect and solidarity with their fellow citizens, knowing how to accept differences and not to question the equality of all as people.

- Obtain information, acquire knowledge and strive to integrate this knowledge into their individual and collective action.
- Fulfill your part in building the quality of life, avoiding waste and contributing to healthier and harmonious environments.
- Act in favor of social inclusion and the reduction of socioeconomic and cultural inequalities.
- Comply with ethical standards in all economic and social relations.
- Intervene socially, culturally and politically for a better and broader citizenship.

REFERENCES

Almeida, J. N. (2014). *Transparência e proporcionalidade no Financiamento dos Serviços de Interesse Económico Geral*. Porto: Vida Económica.

Banerjee, A., Hanna, R., & Mullainathan, S. (2012). *Corruption*. Working Paper 12-08, Massachusetts Institute of Technology. Disponível em http://econwww.mit.edu/files/6607

Barker, R. G. (1968). *Ecological psychology*. Stanford, CA: Stanford University Press.

Bei, Z. A. (1996). A corrupção: Causas, consequências e soluções para o problema. *RAP*, *30*(3), 103–115.

Bernheim, T. C., & Chauí, M. (2008). *Desafios da universidade na sociedade do conhecimento: cinco anos depois da conferência mundial sobre educação superior*. Brasília: UNESCO.

Capelli, C. (2009). *Uma Abordagem para Transparência em Processos Organizacionais Utilizando Aspectos* (Unpublished doctoral dissertation). Pontifícia Universidade Católica do Rio de Janeiro.

Capelli, C., Engiel, P., Leite, J., Nunes, V., Tanaka, A., Santos, G., & Benjamim, K. (2014). *A Evolução do Modelo de Maturidade em Transparência Organizacional*. Rio de Janeiro: Universidade Federal do Estado do Rio de Janeiro. Disponível em https://www.researchgate.net/publication/303912288_A_Evolucao_do_Modelo_de_Maturidade_em_Transparencia_Organizacional/download

Cardoso, C. F. (1985). *A Cidade Estado Antiga*. São Paulo: Ática.

Castells, M. (2003). A Era da Informação: Economia. In *O Poder da Identidade*. Lisboa: Fundação Calouste Gulbenkian.

Chevalier, J. (1988). *Lê mithe de la transparence Administrative*. Paris: Centre Universitaire de Recherces Administratives et Politiques de Picardie, Informacion et Transparence Administrative, PUF.

Coutinho, C., & Lisboa, E. (2011). Sociedade da Informação e da Aprendizagem: Desafios para a Educação no Séc. XXI. *Review of Education*, *18*(1), 5–22.

Davenport, T., & Prusak, L. (2000). *Working Knowledge: How Organizations Manage What They Know*. Boston: Harvard Business School Press.

Dicionário da Língua Portuguesa. (2013). Porto: Porto Editora.

Dziekaniak, G., & Rover, A. (2011). Sociedade do conhecimento: características, demandas e requisitos. *DataGramaZero – Revista de Informação*, *12*(5). Disponível em http://www.egov.ufsc.br/portal/conteudo/artigo-sociedade-do-conhecimento-caracter%C3%ADsticas-demandas-e-requisitos

Ferranti, D., Jacinto, J., Ody, A. J., & Ramshaw, G. (2009). *How to improve Governance: A New Framework for Analysis and Action*. Washington, DC: Brookings Institution Press.

Ferreira, J., & Axt, M. (1999). Conhecimento, tecnologia e sociedade: Em busca de referências interpretativas da ação. *Interface*, *3*(5), 95–109. doi:10.1590/S1414-32831999000200009

Forssbæck, J., & Oxelheim, L. (2014). The Multi-Faceted Concept of Transparency. *IFN Working Paper, nº 1013*. Estocolmo: Research Institute of Industrial Economics.

Fox, J. (2007). Government Transparency and Policymaking. *Public Choice*, *131*(1-2), 23–44. doi:10.100711127-006-9103-3

Glennerster, R., & Shin, Y. (2008). Does Transparency Pay? *IMF Staff Papers*, *55*(1), 183–209. doi:10.1057/palgrave.imfsp.9450028

Gomes, E. (2002). Gestão do conhecimento: definição conceitual, múltiplos usos e interpretações. In *Jornada de Prospecção Tecnológica e Gestão do Conhecimento: contextos de Sociedade da Informação, gestão do conhecimento e Prospecção tecnológica - uma tentativa de visão sistêmica, 1*. Brasília: Disponível. Retrieved from http://www.cgee.org.br/arquivos/pro0202.pdf

Gonçalves, L. (2013). *Direitos sociais: cidadania, política e justiça*. Rio de Janeiro: Sinergia.

Hancock, M., & Bradley, K. (2014). *UK Anticorruption Plan*. Disponível em www.gov.uk

Hargreaves, A. (2003). *O Ensino na Sociedade do Conhecimento: a educação na era da insegurança*. Porto: Porto Editora.

Jaeger, W. (2001). *Paideia: A formação do homem grego*. Rio de Janeiro: Martins Fontes.

Ketzer, P. (2016). A irredutibilidade do conceito de confiança na epistemologia do testemunho. *Conjectura: Filosofia e Educação, 21*(3), 496–513. doi:10.18226/21784612.v21.n3.03

Klitgaard, R. (1994). *A corrupção sob controle*. Rio de Janeiro: Jorge Zaha.

Kuhn, T. S. (1970). *The Structure of Scientific Revolutions. Enlarged* (2nd ed.). Chicago: University of Chicago Press.

Masson, G., & Mainardes, J. (2011) A Ideologia da Sociedade do Conhecimento e suas Implicações para a Educação. *Currículo sem Fronteiras, 11*(2), 70-85. Retrieved from http://www.curriculosemfronteiras.org/vol11iss2articles/masson-mainardes.pdf

Mazzali, R., & Ercolin, C. A. (2018). *Governança corporativa*. Rio de Janeiro: Editora Fundação Getúlio Vargas.

Mello, C. A. B. (2013). *Curso de Direito Administrativo. 30ª edição*. Malheiros Editores.

Merloni, F. (2008). *La Transparenza Amministrativa*. Milano: Giuffrè.

Misztal, B. (1996). *Trust in modern societies*. Cambridge, UK: Polity Press.

Morin, E. (1990). *Introduction à la pensée complexe*. Paris: ESF.

Nhacuongue, J. A., & Ferneda, E. (2012). A construção do conhecimento na atualidade: um olhar sobre o impacto da tecnologia. *DataGramaZero – Revista de Informação, 13*(7). Disponível em https://repositorio.unesp.br/handle/11449/114787

OCDE. (2014). *Perspectivas das políticas de Educação em Portugal*. Lisboa: OCDE – Organização para a Cooperação e o Desenvolvimento Económico.

Oliver, R. (2004). *What is Transparency?* New York: The McGraw-Hill Companies In.

Parreira, A. (2017). Inovação, Novas Tecnologias e Complexidade. In Utopia, Anarquia e Sociedade. Coimbra: Almedina.

Parreira, A., & Silva, A. L. (2016). The use of numerical value of adverbs of quantity and frequency in the measurement of behavior patterns: transforming ordinal scales into interval scales. *Revista Ensaio – Avaliação e Políticas Públicas em Educação, 90*.

Parreira, A., Silva, A. L., & Moura, R. (2018). Transparência e Cidadania Organizacional: anticorrupção e sustentabilidade. In Emprego, Desenvolvimento e Coesão Social: Que Perspetivas para a Regulação Económica e Social? Lisboa: Associação Portuguesa de Profissionais em Sociologia Industrial, das Organizações e do Trabalho.

Pellegrino, L., & Gerlaugh, R. (2004). Corruption's Effect on Growth and its Transmission Channels. *Kyklos*, *57*(3), 429–457. doi:10.1111/j.0023-5962.2004.00261.x

Pítsica, G. (2012). Cidadania, transparência, proteção do erário e os Tribunais de Contas. *Revista Controle*, *10*(2), 98–110.

Rato, H. (2010). Crise e Democracia: Resolução da Crise e Aprofundamento da Democracia. In Investigação e Prática em Economia. Parede: Principia.

Ribeiro, M. (1996). *O Princípio da Imparcialidade da Administração Pública*. Coimbra: Almedina.

Rock, M. T., & Bonnett, H. (2004). The Comparative Politics of Corruption: Accounting for the East Asian Paradox in Empirical Studies of Corruption, Growth and Investment. *World Development*, *32*(6), 999–1009. doi:10.1016/j.worlddev.2003.12.002

Rubinstein, F. (2011). *Notas sobre a Transparência fiscal no direito financeiro*. São Paulo: Ed. RT.

Saldanha, G. S. (2013). Transgramáticas: Filosofia da Ciência da Informação, linguagem e realidade simbólica. *Tendências da Pesquisa Brasileira em Ciência da Informação*, *6*, 1–30.

Scholz, J. M. (2017). As apropriações dos direitos humanos no Brasil: O caso da Declaração Universal dos Direitos Humanos (1948) *Passagens. Revista Internacional de História Política e Cultura Jurídica*, *9*(2), 214–243. doi:10.15175/1984-2503-20179204

Silva, S. T. (2010). *Direito Administrativo Europeu*. Coimbra: Editora Coimbra. doi:10.14195/978-989-26-0183-0

Chapter 3
The Information Access Law as a Full Constitutional Citizenship Instrument

Marcilio Barenco Correa de Mello
Ministério Público de Contas do Estado de Minas Gerais, Brazil

ABSTRACT

This chapter addresses the right of access to information, reinforced as a fundamental rule for citizens in the Brazilian constitutional norm of 1988, now regulated, more closely, from the enactment of the law on access to information in 2011. It represents an important legislative instrument of reinforcement of the principle of publicity, as well as the main infraconstitutional standard guaranteeing access to information. The requirement of a clear and transparent accountability environment by the public manager is a republican assumption of massive participation by society. This is because the right of access to information of a public nature provides a better control of public expenditures, while allowing, on the other hand, promotion of social control of a diffuse nature. It should be pointed out that, with greater knowledge of their own rights, the citizen goes through a faster inclusion process, either in the subjectivation of a minimal role of rights that he does not know, or in the clarification of his duties as a participant in the process of state maintenance.

DOI: 10.4018/978-1-5225-8350-9.ch003

INTRODUCTION

The advent in 2011 of the Law of Access to Information in Brazil, represented significant advance public policy of government transparency, providing the legislating awakening of reaffirmation of constitutional citizenship, whether the regulation of freedom of information as a constitutional fundamental right, whether as a form greater efficiency to the principle of publicity, to allow access to any citizen to information previously reserved for gestational decision spheres of public administrations federal, state, county and municipal.

But much has to speak. Democracy while based on the "power of the people, by the people and for the people" challenges the encouragement of public transparency in order to re-found the popular legitimacy as a perennial form of citizenship. The access to information law gained new ally the principle of publicity (Art. 37, CR / 88), with guidelines imposed on public bodies to publicize their data in apertus locus, which contains at least provide clear accounts, concise, intelligent and intelligible.

Another band, after almost seven years of the right legislative innovation study released by the Union of the Comptroller General (CGU) subordinate to the federal executive branch, in disclosure of the 3rd Assessment Scale of Brazil Transparent Index - Open Data. Brazil (n.d.) it found that 69.8% of the 2,238 municipalities surveyed - a total of 5,570 - were graded below 5 (regular). Only 209 municipalities surveyed - corresponding 9% of the total - had a satisfactory note (between grades 9 and 10), including 14 municipalities headquarters of Capital Units of the Federation (out of 27).

The figures draw the gap between the standard cogent Act prescribed by law and pragmatism of its fulfillment. Much is revealed, above all, the failure of internal and external control bodies, allowing insurmountable obstacle to access of information to citizens in the ambience of "local government", now jettisoning them full active political participation, now jettisoning them of salutary social control - here diffuse character - dependent passive public transparency[1] as relevant in times of substitutes deviation scandals of public money and corrupting practices.

But not only. Failure to comply with the Access to Information Act (LAI) administration by public officials - active public transparency[2] - revela that participatory presence of the population is in its infancy, not only demands and CLAIMS public data open goals but as a true policy of good governance and approach an essentially dialogic public administration. The greater the transparency, the greater the concern of constitutional citizenship, a virtuous two-way street. Depriving the citizens of basic information on economics, finance, government, politics, people, family, society, science, technology, communication, budget, health, education, security, among others, provides up increasingly vilification to "right to the future" of future generations yet unborn.

Collaboration and active participation of society in acts of management and control require revisiting the institute of dialogical public administration, especially from the perspective of classical doctrine of Peter Häberle (1997) in the erection of an "open society the interpreters of the Constitution" where the classical view (restricted to judges and courts) of posthumous contours of constitutional hermeneutics welcomes innovative contributions of the people who has legitimacy to coin the norm, perhaps interpret it, serving as a guidance level for the legislator / judging.

The information transmutes is ancillary element to the essential to the full exercise of constitutional citizenship, without which amputate up "senses" indispensable to the creation of a protective network of society, whether in support of their rights, is in favor of the exchequer which is constituted by efforts of the citizens themselves.

In this vein, public managers need to elect the active and passive public transparency as issues of "agenda", not only uplifts them to themselves the title of good managers, but mainly for inclusion of citizenship as the basis of participation popular active.

Such foundations are due to obligations treatise that Brazil is a signatory own and forced to comply. If we consider that the foundation of the Inter-American System of Human Rights - the Pact of San José, Costa Rica - signed in 1969 by the Federative Republic of Brazil, which entered into force in mid-1978 already aquilatava prescription of free peering, receive and disseminating information and ideas of any kind (Pact of San José, n.d.). We see that apparent "youth" of the right of access to information under Brazilian law is more "late" than current.

Based on the spread of the right to information in centuries past in several countries (eg two hundred years in Sweden), we have an atmosphere arising from democratic ideals globalized, expressing the public interest in fostering to today's social control and the call popular active participation by the republican foundation of citizenship, core element fastened in a Democratic State of Law, serving double bias: higher calling popular active participation through "access to information" and greater transparency (active and passive) as effective mechanism to combat corruption and embezzlement of public funds.

If we consider the breadth and possibilities stemming from the Access to Information Act n. 12,527 / 2011, we are facing the inauguration of a progressive system of checks and balances, enhancer not only of social control, but knowledge of other rights constitutionally set in allocation of society, away from the "secret" as a trademark of totalitarian states, with segregation of all stripes.

Here we highlight larger ballast and speed in obtaining information as the apex of the right to information, since founded long in Brazilian constitutional norm, whether through effective communication, which is the oportunização made possible by information and communication technology (ICT), which imposed a duty of disclosure of data through electronic official sites, notably the so-called "Transparency Portals".

It boosts up increasingly, government strategy of promoting the coordinated actions of plural forums of popular participation (public hearings), accountability, providing for sanctions for breach of the LIA, stipulating tight deadlines to provide information subject to liability.

However, the gratuitous advance in providing information, shaft coupled to tight requirements. Let me explain. The first is the payment of fees required for the reproduction of documents in the exercise of public transparency passive, sometimes only means of material evidence of illicit commission.

The second is the essential qualification of the applicant, that prima facie, cause fear and embarrassment, especially when directed to that bad manager who will be monitored and subjected to possible civil, administrative and criminal liability for the commission of illegal acts, ímprobos and malbaratamento money public.

After all, we can not but point out the factors that represent circumstantial advances in fighting corruption, all the more diffuse and open manner, allowing greater engagement for the awakening of full constitutional citizenship.

In fact, the citizen empowerment in access to information and public transparency, will have the power to bring it closer to the governments, giving them the opportunity to better understand their rights, while to foster the creation of a new culture of "citizenship" participatory network, the supervision and development of public policies essential to life in society organized the law of Democratic States.

THE RIGHT TO PUBLIC INFORMATION ADMINISTRATION

Access to administrative public information, even before being a duty imposed on the public manager, constitutes a civil right historically incorporated into the slow progress of the generations of constitutional rights. Herein lies its essence though constitutionally recognized human right, and therefore, a fundamental right, keeping correspondence to the principle of publicity and transparency.

In all fairness, freedom of expression as enshrined since the French Revolution (1789), brought attention to the right of access to administrative public information, in our times being common goal of democracies, far beyond the ideologies of the right to "freely express" and "manifest freely" (Constitution of Brazil, 1988).

In this sense, the historical evolution of this right to information lies beyond the classical generation of constitutional rights (1st generation - public liberties, 2nd generation - equality and 3rd generation - fraternity)[3], to identify him in Paulo Bonavides (1988) as a constitutional right to 4th generation, requirements established by political globalization related to democracy, information and pluralism. It is stated here that the globalization of fundamental rights equivalent to universalize them in institutional harvest where residing in legal normativity, introduces the 4th generation rights in the institutionalization phase of the Social State, comprising the implementation of the open society of the future in maximum dimension of universality, the apex of the relations of pluralistic coexistence.

Augusto Martínez, the right of access to public information is unfolding landmark ideas driven by neoconstitutionalism imposing a new constitutional state model based on the centrality of the human person (Martinez, 2015).

Highlight the conceptual transition from the dogma of administrative law linked to the public interest and pure administrative discretion (beyond the law), for, constitutionalising them, converge it to the ideals of human dignity, driven by fundamental rights and democracy, set new constitutional airs (legality block) for the actors of public administration (managers).

Now the government is presented in a decentralized manner in the search for greater efficiency to the recipients of their services (citizens), the observance of the constitutional principle of publicity comes from a constitutional dimension imminently rules (Constitution of Brazil, 1988).[4]

Such facts are logical consequence and imbrincada from the evolution of generations of constitutional rights, boosting the state - then absentee - for your new level of social justice agency propellant affirmative action. So much so that the right of access to information has been recognized in the Universal Declaration of Human Rights (1948), covering not only the very right itself, but above all the duty of the State.

Here we also cover the prism principle of freedom of information, added to the right of citizens to be informed, lifting them definitively to the basic human need to condition (fundamental). Then we have the aggregation of the ideals of public freedoms of expression and opinion, the right to stay informed by the State, arising therefore legal framework of the duty of transparency of the state entity (Barros, 2008).

In this scenario, the right of access to information can be hoisted to the achievement level of the requirements inherent in the principle of human dignity, accompanied at the heart of the evolution of fundamental rights and the principle of human dignity, with very spirit of public liberty and citizenship of the social fabric. Loped administrative public harvest, cotejamos such right of access to administrative information on the fundamental rights of the citizen role, among others (Constitution of Brazil, 1988).

Therefore, before being standard formally constitutional in Brazilian law, we reproduce his status materially constitutional law, greater expression of citizen participation in the spheres of decision of Public Administration, and as tight as only security elements of state and society, and more recently, the rights to privacy (Constitution of Brazil, 1988)[5].

So it was erected citizen participation in Public Administration to be revealed in the preparation of objective standards related to the Government, whose orbit legislating mainly reaches the infra legislator.

We have for attention which highlights Ramiro Sales (2014) as to the immediate applicability of fundamental rights outlined in the Brazilian constitutional rule, all by virtue of Article 5, paragraph 1, of the Constitution of 1988, namely: direct application in a particular case, compliance by infra-constitutional norms, interpretation of paradigm acts or legal norms of loved and state powers, parameter to judicial review and, finally, the imposition of the duty of concreteness by the state government.

However, it should be emphasized that the constitutional right of access to administrative public information has brought voluntary restraint exercise, although classified by the classical doctrine as effective rule contained[6] by providing in Article 5, paragraph XXXIII, in verbis:

Art. 5 [...]

XXXIII - everyone is entitled to receive from government agencies information of private interest, or of collective or general interest, which shall be provided within the law, subject to liability, except for those whose secrecy is essential to the security of society and the state. (Emphasis added)

Regulating the time prefixed on the request for access, the Federal Law n. 12,527 / 2011 established in its article. 10 c / art. 11, § 1, the assumptions and deadlines for exercising the right to ascend the administrative information, regulating art. 5, item XXXIII of the Constitution of the Republic of 1988, but let's see:

Art. 10. Any interested party may submit request for access to information to agencies and entities referred to in art. 1 hereof, for any legitimate means and the request contains information identifying the applicant and the specification of the requested information.

[...]

Art. 11. The public body or authority must authorize or grant immediate access to the information available.

Paragraph 1 is not possible to grant immediate access, as provided in the caput, the agency or entity receiving the request shall, within a period not exceeding twenty (20) days:

I - communicate the date, place and method to perform the query, perform playback or obtain the certificate;

II - state the reasons in fact or in law the refusal of all or part of the intended access; or,

III - report that does not have the information, indicate if your knowledge, the body or entity which controls it, or even refer the application to that agency or entity, cientificando him of the shipment of your order information.

Paragraph 2. The period specified in paragraph 1 may be extended by ten (10) days, with the express reasons, which will be made aware of the applicant. (My italics)

In addition, the Federal Law n. 12.527/2011, as well as identifying the applicant need delimiting the prefixed terms, demanded the possibility of charging to own expenses documentary playing the organ or consulted public entity, despite the search services and providing information are free, in verbis:

Art. 12. The search service and providing the information is free, except in the case of reproduction of documents by the agency or public entity consulted, in which case you'll be charged only the amount necessary for reimbursement of the cost of services and materials used.

Single paragraph. Will be free to reimburse the costs provided for in the caput everyone whose economic situation does not allow it to do so without prejudice to support themselves or family, declared under the Act [...].

So even though there was no forecast infra standard of access times to administrative information, it was defensible the right of access administrative information for their own material densification of existing constitutional provision, now made possible by fully collated procedure regulatory infra standard: Access to Information Act.

For right by the very fundamental constitutional commandment about the desired public information will be those recorded publicist essentially excluded to relating to state security, society and the right to personality, these facts expression of constitutional rule originated.

ThereforeWe are faced with the necessity of realization of a fundamental right constitutionalised, whose density material allows its fulfillment immediately, despite the advent of the Federal Law n. 12.527/11, which regulates the access procedure to administrative public information on degree of infra normative abstraction.

For effectiveness and realization of the right of access to administrative information, there to implement the subjective dimension of this right, recognized in Canotilho (2011) as one that spells out those rights in its own characteristics Collating of subjective rights to citizens, ie the transfer of the right to private sphere of the individual with effect in legal relations undertaken to authorize from plan your claim.

For Sales (2014) the evolutionary study of the right of access to information and features involving such a right, it is essential to understand the right subjectivized citizens, as well as its revindication, loved bound by duty to inform and finally, the protective forms of the full exercise and acquired defense features (negative for non-infringement) and delivery (by affirmative fulfillment of duty).

They reside here four status where the individual can position in the State, in the classical theory of Jellinek (2018), that is subject to duties or obligations (taxable) in its sphere of protected individual equity (negative rights or abstention), and subject to positive rights (positive rights or civitas) with the existence of political rights (active citizenship).

In this area, the access to information law brings a facet of the full exercise of citizenship, while the individual becomes subject to obligations, but above all, recipient rights (positive or negative), whose inclusion in a social rule of law will take place completely, allowing even the participation in social diffuse control, whose public transparency assumption is mainspring for full exercise of subjectified rights (access to administrative information).

Therefore, that subjectivity of the right of access to information depends even before the objective dimension of the right itself, constituted as seen lines ago in content for human and fundamental rights, treated as estruturan principlestes of constitutional norms, substantially constitutional essence in the foundations of the state and society.

For *Alexy (2017),* the structural principles of the state play a central role of the legal system, radiating up the vertically integrated legal relations between the State versus citizen, and flatter between third parties (individuals), consecrating themselves in the objective order of principles that guide every legal system, resulting in three consequences the systemic constitutional construction: a) limiting of infra law; b) legal system of open character, with sopesamento values in each case, there is no single solution to the case; and, c) duration of the open legal system in the face of moral.

This time, irradiation of fundamental rights as positive law, is to spread the idea of justice among the branches of law, fact also applies understanding the right of access to administrative information, while fundamental principle of constitutional law. Access to information should be guided by the purposes and constitutional functions, meaning the implementation of the idea of dialogic public administration (democratic), strong popular emancipation instrument (full constitutional citizenship).

The issue of below legal means of access to information, in concretization the fundamental right carries with it a set of subprinciples to be scrutinied.

1. ROL ACCESS RIGHTS TO PUBLIC INFORMATION ADMINISTRATIVE SUBPRINCIPLES

The appreciation of the set of constitutional provisions and information access law has given rise to a range of subprinciples the right to public information, notably: Maximum Advertising or Secrecy minimum, disclosure, Modernity, Promotion of Open Government, Participation, Motivation No need, procedure Adequate Quality Information and gratuity (Sales, 2014).

This list of subprinciples exploits the concreteness of fundamental constitutional rule, leaving imbrincados each other to perform the major principle of right of access to administrative information, while forming a minimal scope of the company's participation requirements in state decisions, while their fellow citizens they are recipients of state public goods and services, subject to individual and collective rights.

The rules work in the legal system of parameterized way, graduating meanings and values; since the principles are presented as true optimization warrantsgeneral and abstract nature, with effect at different levels and functions (Alexy, 2017). The higher the principled, generally more difficult it will be the realization of the rights. On the other band, the principles also serve as vectors of standards and interpretations incompatible with the core to be preserved. Therefore, the right of access to administrative information stems from higher principles, namely the principle of access to information, principle of transparency, principle of publicity, democratic principle and the rule of law.

In order to safeguard him while the necessary fundamental principle autonomy created a range of subprinciples that act due delegated by sobreprincípios consolidated constitutionally. No wonder, Article 3 of the Federal Law n. 12.527/2011, brought forming elements that range, namely:

Art. 3. The procedures laid down in this Act are intended to ensure the fundamental right of access to information and must be executed in accordance with the basic principles of public administration and to the following guidelines:

I - compliance with advertising as a general rule and secrecy as an exception;

II - dissemination of information of public interest, regardless of requests;

III - use of means of communication made possible by information technology;

IV - promoting the development of the transparency in public administration culture;

V - development of social control of public administration.

These guidelines express the nature subprinciple, induction of systemic and legal instruments set involving the right of access to administrative information.

So we have the subprinciple of Maximum Advertising reinforces the primacy of sobreprincípio Advertising constitutionally post[7] in full nature (Constitution of Brazil, 1988). This is because the trailer subprinciple of Maximum Advertising, we have the subprinciple of Secrecy Minimum, which makes room for restrictive lien information of interest to the state and society, as well as relating to the privacy of the individual, in fact.

In truth, the Rule Maximum Advertising opens spectrum light to public transparency much more useful and almost full, make the Secrecy Minimum something small, exceptional and opaque. There will be cases where the preservation of secrecy is essential to legal security reserves, without, however, encompass the chances maximized public policies (and their spending) in essential services provided by the state, allowing its inspections diffusely by the citizen. Here lies the touchstone of social control.

From this premise, defended the idea that the maximum disclosure should reach the information, the ones who should provide it, and addressed to individuals (passive or active), by means of appropriate administrative structures (Sales, 2014).

Without neglecting the Minimum secrecy, the Federal Law n. 12.527/2011 conceptualized in his art. 4, items III and IV, the information written exception to the rule, as delimiting whole subjected to temporarily publicist restrictions based on essential security of the state and society, and that may cause damage to the constitutionally protected right to privacy (Constitution of Brazil, 1988).[8]

Already with regard to subprinciple Disclosure is inscribed in performance function of the right of access to public information by entering in the communication obligation context, involving the concepts of active and passive public transparency and proactive duties of public administrations, concerning the activities carried out, sector or general public policies, organization, services, asset management, procurement, contracts, government programs, projects, provision of public spending accounts, tax expenditures and own revenues, among others.

Such disclosure should take place within easy access, via electronic site (Portals Transparency), with express indication of Citizen Assistance Service (SAC or Ombudsman), with powers to receive requests and provide information of procedural movements.

In addition to form a educational-preventive environment and social orientation, subprinciple of Disclosure performs the purpose of public interest, enabling social participation in the reorganization of a dialogic public administration, to promote the debate to build bridges that lead to maximum effectiveness Republican goals.

Regarding the subprinciple of Modernity, it reinforces the idea of a Public Administration oped to meet the principle of efficiency, with the use of resources made possible by information technology, involving not only data processing systems, *software* or hardware, but above all human aspects, administrative and organizational (workflows, people and information). We are thinking far beyond the possession of dependable and efficient information (modern management), including rapid and hyaline access (public transparency) to the recipients of the Access to Information Act (citizen).

In this context, we must identify the Internet as important mechanism for democratization of administrative information, which objectivity, transparency passive and easy intelligibility, become essential components.

Pitch of subprinciple the Promotion of Open Government, to promote the cultural development of transparency in public administration, we recorded the secretiveness of the paradigm shift of the acts of government, rooted by potestade overcome the antiquated acts of empire, within the context democratization of information while fundamental right.

The withholding of public information limits the civic activity of citizens, reducing the necessary supervision to *res publica*, Leaving under suspicion public officials, injuring death the educational, informative and social orientation character provided for in the Constitution of the Republic of 1988.[9]

Moreover, ware to subprinciple participation, which also has the aspect of democratization of public administration, we have here the greatest expression of the promotion to full citizenship, whether as a subject of obligations, but above all, the citizen as subject of rights, a contemporary trend of individual or collective presence in the political and governmental decisions.

Simplification of the ideas, decentralization, participatory encouragement, cooperation and peaceful coexistence are landmarks of the democratization of public administration. Of course, arise will be possibilities greater social control with administrative participatory methodology, fostering negotiation and conciliatory possibilities with better education of the public interest and acceptance of acts emanating from the authority on outdated unilateralism and power.

Odete Medauar brings the various forms of participation in society, whether in the broad sense, with popular participation in acts of management, but also in the choice of their representatives of the executive and legislature by direct vote, secret, universal and periodic, or, through political parties. Already in the strict sense, adds the idea of popular participation by citizens or civil servants, that the functional linkages integrate and influence its institutions as well as through trade unions or particular activities (Medauar, 2003).

Thus, social participation becomes wider precedent to provide social control, dependent on access to administrative public information, without which such function is mitigated by the absence of the object to be scrutinized and monitored. That is why the information should be provided finalisticamente whenever possibleIn future decision-making acts, consultations and public hearings for greater implementation of administrative democratization.

An act of citizen's quality of participation is dependent on the formation of integrative cultural environment, taking for granted the right to access to public information, leaving as well, as a pillar of democratic rule of law.

We also have the subprinciple of Motivation No need, with the aim to deconstruct the creation of unnecessary requirements that impede access by fronting limiters and restrictive requirements for exercising the right securitized by simply identifying the applicant and specifying the required information.

As seen lines ago, the identification of the applicant is obstacle to the free exercise of the right of access to information, while exposing the person who seeks support surveillance of public events, sometimes riddled administrative illicit acts with criminal consequences, exercising the right to citizenship in his own name, but in typical collective function in procedural replacement. If we have the Maximum Advertising as subprinciple ínsito the implanted system, requiring the exercise of passive transparency regardless of provocation, the exercise of active transparency (with request for information), dispenses with pre-qualification and nomination of the applicant being diametrically opposed legal commands.

The specification information requestada It has merely indicative nature, not to allow the specific obstacle is access except those assumptions Secrecy Min.

Again, the subprinciple Procedure Suitable takes place in facilitating access through objective procedure, expeditious, transparent, clear, modern, guidance and open to challenge.

We also have the subprinciple Quality of information characterized by the availability, authenticity, integrity, and Firstness today (Global Regulation, 2011).

Finally, we have the subprinciple of Gratuity covering the search service and provision of data, except those intended for reproduction of documents, the costs of which should not stick exclusively to the amount necessary to compensate the cost of reprographic services.

You are here limitation to assess illegal activity mechanism under the Public Administration and proof material, sometimes lies in production documentary evidence, costly obstacle to the applicant acting in his own name in order to protect collective rights.

Of course, with all principological framework now espoused, created an environment more secure legal relations and fundamental right to protection of the citizen, where overcoming the regulatory gap of state duty, no longer is impediment to the exercise of full rights of access to information, the exercise of constitutional citizenship assumption.

But Right now assured emerged new duties. Public transparency brought with it the duty of social control more effective by its diffuse and open nature, enabling the participation of society and its members as my public spending tax and participants in shaping public policy.

TRANSPARENCY TO PUBLIC SOCIAL CONTROL

As a right of holders to participate in public affairs, every citizen holds portion of state sovereign power in the definition of public policies, either in the formation of decision-making spheres, is in control of the realization of finalistic state objectives.

The people plays not only a quantitative benchmark for the vote, but rather a communicative unpersonalized mass legitimate government democratic process, being endowed with so political rights (Silva, 2012).

The core of the new constitutional citizenship is based precisely on citizen participation in administrative decisions and political control and public management. The filing complaints with government agencies is effective instrument of control of legality of acts and accountability of bad managers, much more now with the exploitation of the right of access to administrative public information.

The popular inclusion in the administrative democracy model meets the objectives of equality between citizens, while members of the human race, chamber turning to the universality of fundamental constitutional rights.

Be protagonist of the political power game is no longer a privilege of the few, but results from the exercise of ordinary rights affections to any citizen whose access to information and control culture should be internalized early on in society, in order to leverage the performance of full citizenship.

The diffusion of knowledge and administrative public information, efficient tools and spaces of social control by the citizens, they become indispensable to the administrative democratization process with the permanent reaffirmation of legitimacy of social control.

To Vanice Valle (2011) the construction of spaces for dialogue and a dialogic public administration, move through the good governance exercise conditions - whose legal status is still open - but that is embedded democratic ideals represent state way of relating to participatory social systems and decision-making processes that affect all recipients; cooperating to achieve the common objectives through respect and cooperation, will be easier assimilation of the effects of acts of administrative management in which also participated in the production.

Thus, transparency as a right of assumption access to administrative public information becomes attribute of good democratic governance, breaking paradigms of state-owned reserve given information it produced itself.

In this context, we have the birthplace of the control function, whose democratic participation induces social form of exercise, especially for the effective diffuse character (open) your exercise. Let me explain: where there is a citizen exercising the right to participate in public policy development and management, there will be a citizen exercising social control of its efficiency and effectiveness.

As we see, the social control becomes part of the essence of democratic and dialogical system of public administration. In this drive, we have the awakening of citizenship. The active and conscious participation with the right assessment, opinion and formation of public policy decisions volvidas society, has its summit in pluirma integration actors in shaping the public interest to be pursued by the state.

However, this interaction depends largely on the degree of transparency offered by one, in particular by mechanisms of information technology and its availability for the World Wide Web: Internet.

The available public information gained contour fundamental right with a positive impact on the prospects for social rights, where better communication and dissemination raises the recognition instilled immediately in the policies of destination: the citizen.

Of course, the social control here post, performs the legitimacy of society or social groups to actively participate in decisions and the development of standards stimulating behaviors increasingly virtuous in the seat of formation of collective decisions. This is the great plateau to be reached for the full constitutional citizenship as a formative element of democracy, through the exercise of civil, political and social rights.

Such improvement of democratic participation allows the creation of collegiate instance decisions while away from unilateral decisions not openly discussed with the recipients, all for the benefit of their own community.

In this sense, the information became powerful instrument inclusive of the population right exercise and social control mechanism of public administration, representing today's culture to be fostered in democratic regimes and Law States.

Access to information is valid ambience assumption of rational decisions, whether in training of management acts, either in shaping the supervision of acts already performed. Provide them with democratic character, assumes that oportunize the actors to equal participation in decisions affecting them, and, in our times, full development of assumption of society.

Public transparency is prerequisite for good governance and administration, while promotes the culture of constitutional citizenship to members of society.

CONCLUSION

The right of access to administrative information has become an important instrument available to the citizen, giving him the political powers in shaping the decision-making process within the state administrative relations. The aspiration of a better quality of life in the open information society, it is human right positivado as a fundamental right of the citizen.

While the information is used for the recognition of individual and collective rights that Law democratic states give their citizens, provides an active participation in the idealization of public policies that will serve as the motto for implementation of goods and services essential to their own community.

Hand other, besides the formation of cultural ideals of a participatory society in state decisions, we have to contemplate the broad accessibility to administrative public information, the space to hold a duty of citizenship, namely the monitoring of the use of public resources as a foundation republican.

The supervisory powers granted to citizens by the Access to Information Act (Law no. 12.527/2011), forced the state entities to broaden the dissemination of government actions and management, allowing them to give notice of their actions and revealing to information as a public good belonging to all society.

The evaluation and monitoring of public administration by the data open to society, require more zealous, ethical and responsible attitudes by the public manager who knowing of the existence of submission to an open control by society, makes its shrouded political and administrative decisions of greater caution with public affairs.

Finally, the right of access to information is great cultural challenge of Brazilian society. There is need to create an active participation of political consciousness of citizens "tax" in favor of the fight against corruption and bureaucracy. Notwithstanding, the major breakthrough in popular participatory efficiency through access to public information, lies in the consolidation of full citizenship in constitutional democracy seat, through the full exercise of their civil, political and social.

REFERENCES

Alexy. (2007). Teoria dos Direitos Fundamentais (2nd ed.). São Paulo: Malheiros.

Alvarenga. (2011). *Aristides Junqueira. Reflexões sobre improbidade administrativa no direito brasileiro.* São Paulo: Editora Malheiros.

Anastasia. (n.d.). *Exposição de Motivos do Projeto de Lei do Senado nº 349/2015.* Disponível em: https://legis.senado.leg.br/sdleg-getter/documento?dm=4407647&disposition=inline

Barros. (2008). *O Estado (in) transparente: limites do direito à informação socioambiental no Brasil (Doutoramento em Desenvolvimento Sustentável, Política e Gestão Ambiental)*. Brasília: Universidade de Brasília.

Barros. (2008). *O Estado (in)transparente: limites do direito à informação socioambiental no Brasil* (PhD thesis). University of Brasilia, Brasilia.

Bonavides. (2018). *Curso de Direito Constitucional* (33rd ed.). São Paulo: Malheiros.

Bonavides, P. (1988). Curso de Direito Constitucional (33ª ed.). São Paulo: Malheiros.

Brazil. (n.d.). *The Comptroller General*. Available in https://relatorios.cgu.gov.br/Visualizador.aspx?id_relatorio=20

Canotilho, J. J. (2011). *Direito Constitucional e Teoria da Constituição* (7th ed.). Coimbra: Almedina.

Carvalho, F. (2018). *Manual de Direito Administrativo* (32nd ed.). São Paulo: Editora Atlas.

Constitution of Brazil. (1988). Retrieved from http://english.tse.jus.br/arquivos/federal-constitution

Cunha, J. (2018). Curso de Direito Constitucional (13ª ed.). Salvador: Editora Juspodivm.

Di Pietro, . (2018). *Direito administrativo* (31st ed.). Rio de Janeiro: Editora Forense.

Fagundes. (2010). O controle dos atos administrativos pelo Poder Judiciário (8ª ed.). Rio de Janeiro: Editora Forense.

Filho. (2018). Curso de direito administrativo (13ª ed.). São Paulo: Editora Revista dos Tribunais.

Freitas. (2018). *O artigo 22 da LINDB e os novos contornos do Direito Administrativo sancionador.* Disponível em: https://www.conjur.com.br/2018-jul-25/opiniao-artigo-22-lindb-direito-administrativo-sancionador

Global Regulation. (2011). *Ex vi arts. 4 and 7, item IV of the Federal Law n. 12,527 / 2011*. Retrieved from https://www.global-regulation.com/translation/brazil/2895611/law-no.-12%252c527-of-november-18%252c-2011.html

Häberle. (1997). *Hermenêutica Constitucional: a sociedade aberta dos intérpretes da Constituição – contribuição para interpretação pluralista e procedimental da Constituição. Tradução de Gilmar Ferreira Mendes*. Porto Alegre: Fabris.

Jacoby Fernandes, J. U. (2018). *Lei nº 13.655/2018 e o resgate da segurança jurídica para os gestores públicos e órgãos de controle.* Disponível em: https://www.jmleventos.com.br/pagina.php?area=coluna-juridica&acao=download&dp_id=181

Jellinek, Mendes, & Branco. (2018). Curso de Direito Constitucional (13th ed.). São Paulo: Saraiva.

Martínez. (2015). Derecho al acceso a la información pública em el Uruguay. In *Acesso à Informação Pública*. Belo Horizonte: Fórum.

Martínez. (2015). Derecho al acceso a la información public in el Uruguay. In *Access to Public Information* (p. 220). Belo Horizonte: Forum.

Mattos. (2010). *O limite de improbidade administrativa: comentários à Lei nº 8.429/92* (5th ed.). Rio de Janeiro: Editora Forense.

Medauar. (2003). *O direito administrativo em evolução.* São Paulo: Revista dos Tribunais.

Ministério Público Federal. (2018). *Nota Técnica Conjunta nº 1/2018.* Disponível em: http://www.mpf.mp.br/atuacao-tematica/ccr5/notas-tecnicas/docs/Nota%20Tecnica%201_2018.pdf

Motta. (2018). *Alterações na LINDB valem para todos, não só para o controle, 2018.* Disponível em: https://www.conjur.com.br/2018-jun-14/interesse-publico-alteracoes-lindb-valem-todos-nao-controle

Neto & Freitas. (2018a). *A função normativa da administração pública e a Lei 13.655/2018.* Disponível em: https://www.conjur.com.br/2018-jun-14/opiniao-funcao-normativa-administracao-publica-lindb

Neto & Freitas. (2018b). *O artigo 22 da LINDB e os novos contornos do Direito Administrativo sancionador.* Disponível em: https://www.conjur.com.br/2018-jul-25/opiniao-artigo-22-lindb-direito-administrativo-sancionador

Neto. (2018). *Resposta aos comentários tecidos pela Consultoria Jurídica do TCU ao PL nº 7.448/2017.* Disponível em: https://www.conjur.com.br/dl/parecer-juristas-rebatem-criticas.pdf

Oliveira. (2012). Ativismo judicial, pragmatismo e capacidades institucionais: as novas tendências do controle judicial dos atos administrativos. *Revista Brasileira de Direito Público, 10*(39), 9-36.

Pact of San José, Costa Rica. (n.d.). *Article 13 - Freedom of thought and expression*. Retrieved from https://www.oas.org/dil/access_to_information_American_Convention_on_Human_Rights.pdf

Pereira. (Ed.). (2015). *Segurança jurídica e qualidade das decisões públicas: desafios de uma sociedade democrática, Brasília. 2015*. Disponível em: https://antonioaugustoanastasia.com.br/wp-content/uploads/2015/09/segurancajuridica.pdf

Sales. (2014). *O Direito de Acesso à Informação Pública Administrativa*. Rio de Janeiro: Lumen Juris.

Silva. (2012). Transparência e Controle social: Controle externo, controle social e cidadania. In *Revista do Tribunal de Contas do Estado de Minas Gerais, Ano 1, n. 1, Edição Especial*. Belo Horizonte: Tribunal de Contas do Estado de Minas Gerais.

Valle. (n.d.). *Direito fundamental à boa administração e governança*. Belo Horizonte: Fórum.

ENDNOTES

1. Provision of public information in response to specific claims by individuals or legal entities.
2. Public Disclosure of data opened by the public administration itself.
3. Dimensions of constitutional rights.
4. Article 37 of the Constitution of the Federative Republic of Brazil 1988.
5. Article 5, paragraph X of the Constitution of the Federative Republic of Brazil 1988.
6. Are those in which the constituent legislator regulated seconds interest in the matter, leaving scope for restrictive action by racing infra legislator or government, under which the law may establish or the general concepts contained therein, in casu within being established.
7. Art. 37 of the Constitution of the Federative Republic of Brazil 1988.
8. Art. 5, section X of the Constitution of the Federative Republic of Brazil 1988.
9. Art. 37, paragraph 1, of the Constitution of the Federative Republic of Brazil 1988.

Chapter 4
Erecting a Virtual Schoolhouse Gate

Maryam Ahranjani
University of New Mexico, USA

ABSTRACT

The very first amendment to the United States Constitution protects the freedom of speech. While the Supreme Court held in 1969 that students "do not shed their constitutional rights at the schoolhouse gate," since then the Court has limited students' freedom of speech, stopping short of considering the boundaries of off-campus, online speech. Lower court holdings vary, meaning that a student engaging in certain online speech may not be punished at all in one state but would face harsh criminal punishments in another. The lack of a uniform standard leads to dangerously inconsistent punishments and poses the ultimate threat to constitutional knowledge and citizenship exercise: chilling of speech. Recent interest in technology-related cases and the presence of a new justice may reverse the Court's prior unwillingness to address this issue. In the meantime, this chapter argues that school districts should erect a virtual schoolhouse gate by implementing a uniform standard.

INTRODUCTION

Congress shall make no law … abridging the freedom of speech. - Amendment I

This chapter address the extent to which the First Amendment to the U.S. Constitution extends protections to public K-12 students' speech online.

DOI: 10.4018/978-1-5225-8350-9.ch004

The Framers of the United States Constitution – the oldest and shortest written constitution in the world – felt so strongly about the importance of free speech that they included it in the very first amendment to the main document. In fact, a number of the Framers wanted to include free speech and other individual rights in the main document and only agreed to sign once it was promised to them that there would be immediate additions (Emerson 1977). In 1791, just four years after ratification of the U.S. Constitution, the Bill of Rights – the first ten amendments – were adopted.

As the final arbiter of the Constitution and its amendments, the U.S. Supreme Court's role in ensuring protection of civil rights cannot be overstated. While the other two branches of government – the legislative and executive – can have an influence on rights, the Supreme Court has an independent and critical role in reviewing the work of the other branches (Rotunda & Nowak 2017). In the past eighty or so years, the U.S. Supreme Court has repeatedly interpreted the provision to include the rights of public school students to freely speak, and decline to speak, in the school context.

In 1969, the Court declared that students – and teachers – do not "shed their constitutional rights at the schoolhouse gate." In *Tinker v. Des Moines Independent School District* (1969), the Court recognized the important role that public schools play in preparing youth for citizenship. They declared that student speech on campus may not be censored unless the school officials show a reasonable apprehension that the student speech will lead to material disruption or collide with the rights of others. In *Tinker*, Justice Fortas famously wrote, "It can hardly be argued that either students or teachers shed their constitutional rights to freedom of speech or expression at the schoolhouse gate."

In the almost fifty years since *Tinker* was decided, the Supreme Court has decided exactly three cases concerning the extent of students' freedom of speech. Those cases include *Bethel v. Fraser* (1986), *Hazelwood v. Kuhlmeier* (1988), and *Morse v. Frederick* (2007). The reluctance to consider more cases and create more useful guidelines highlights the Court's deference to school officials. Further, the Court's refusal to grant certiorari in *Bell v. Itawamba County* (2015), indicates another concern of the justices – how to handle the impact of technology on rights.

This chapter argues that the schoolhouse gate now extends to off-campus, online speech. The advent and widespread use of the internet by young people has exponentially increased the opportunities for students to speak such that there is now a virtual schoolhouse gate. The Supreme Court simply has not caught up. In fact, according to Connor Mitchell and Carolyn Schurr Levin of the Student Press Law Center (2017), the leading non-profit in this space, the Court has declined a number of opportunities to review the extent to which students' freedom of speech both in K-12 and higher education extends to online speech. Lower courts have explored this question and have reached different conclusions and drawn different lines.

The implications of this question are considerable. Over 90% of American children are enrolled in public schools, and almost all students have an online presence. According to the National Center for Education Statistics, the vast majority of Americans use the internet (2018). According to the Pew Research Center, 92% of teens report going online at least daily, and a quarter of teens report being online almost constantly (Lenhart 2015). If the vast majority of young people rely on online communication, their very ability to organize, express themselves, and shape their and our futures depends on the boundaries we set.

BACKGROUND

The Structure of Government

The United States Constitution divides federal government into three branches, and the states mostly mirror this structure in their respective state governments (Rotunda & Nowak 2017). The legislative branch consists of the bicameral Congress, made up of the U.S. House of Representatives (whose members are apportioned according to population) and the U.S. Senate (two members per state). Congress passes laws. The executive branch, comprised of the elected President and his cabinet members who are heads of various agencies, enforces the laws passed by Congress. Finally, the judicial branch – composed of federal district courts, federal courts of appeals or circuit courts, and the Supreme Court – reviews laws to ensure compliance with the Constitution.

The three branches check and balance one another's power by reviewing one another's actions, thereby stabilizing government and virtually eliminating concerns of unchecked power (Rotunda & Nowak 2017). For example, the current President of the United States, Donald Trump, has attempted to undo years of civil rights advances by changing policies of the Department of Justice and issuing executive orders. Upon review of his actions, courts have struck down or limited the reach of his actions, including the so-called Muslim ban, and the efforts to cut funding of cities that call themselves sanctuaries from federal immigration enforcement (Winkler 2017).

Role of the Supreme Court

The nine-member Supreme Court is the highest federal court, and it is the final decision-maker regarding the Constitution. The Constitution usually only applies to state (government) action (Rotunda and Nowak 2017). There are some exceptions, but private action generally does not invoke constitutional rights such as freedom of speech. When the Supreme Court decides a case, their decision generally precludes further litigation on the same issue because of the doctrine of stare decisis. Pursuant to stare decisis, once the Court has decided a matter, the matter is already settled and cannot be re-litigated.

Another important point about the Court's reach is the idea that the Court only decides whether a law violates or does not violate the Constitution (Rotunda & Nowak 2017). That is, it provides a floor of rights. Congress and state legislatures, as well as state constitutions, may provide more expansive rights if they choose.

However, the Court does sometimes overturn itself, and it has done so in the First Amendment context. An often-cited example is the Court's change of heart regarding the flag salute. In the 1940 case of *Minersville School District v. Gobitis*, the Court considered whether the expulsion of Lillian and William Gobitis from their Pennsylvania public schools for refusing to salute the flag as part of a daily school exercise violated their First Amendment rights. The Gobitis children were Jehovah's witnesses and believed that the Bible forbade saluting graven images like the flag. The Court upheld their expulsion.

Just three years later, the Court reversed itself in a case called *West Virginia v. Barnette* (1943). During the height of World War II, the West Virginia Board of Education voted to require teachers and students to salute the flag in school. When the children of Jehovah's Witnesses refused to perform the salute, they were sent home, threatened with transfer to reform school for criminally delinquent children, and their parents faced prosecution for causing juvenile delinquency. In *Barnette*, the Court recognized the importance of the state's goal of promoting national unity, but it held that coercing patriotism contradicts the First Amendment. Writing for the majority, Justice Jackson famously said, "If there is any fixed star in our constitutional constellation, it is that no official, high or petty, can prescribe what shall be orthodox in politics, nationalism, religion, or other matters of opinion or force citizens to confess by word or act their faith therein."

Notwithstanding occasional reversals, the Court's adherence to its own precedents has provided stability and predictability in terms of the public's awareness of the protections and limitations of constitutional rights. The nine Justices of the Supreme Court are well-respected jurists who are nominated by the sitting President of the United States when a vacancy arises and confirmed by the members of the U.S. Senate after enduring a hearing process in front of the Senate Judiciary Committee. The justices occupy a vaulted, respected position in the legal profession, and they enjoy life tenure, which frees them from political and other pressures.

Important Values Underlying the First Amendment

Internationally renowned American constitutional law scholar Erwin Chemerinsky outlines the four theories as to why the Supreme Court regards the freedom of speech as a fundamental right (2017). Supreme Court justices refer to these values in their opinions, both as support for their conclusions and to acknowledge and explain deviations from one or more underlying values.

The first theory is self-governance, which articulates the crucial role free speech plays in a democracy. Most scholars agree that political speech is at the core of what is protected by the First Amendment. The second theory is discovering truth. The idea here is that free speech is essential to discover the truth. Of course the internet and social media have tested the limits of this value because any person is able to speak to millions of others in an instant. Justice Oliver Wendell Holmes felt that the marketplace of ideas would promote a clash of ideas and ultimately produce truth (Chemerinsky 2017). Critics worry that not everyone has access to the marketplace of ideas and that it's wrong to assume that truth will triumph over falsehood. Response: government determination of truth and censorship of falsehoods is worse.

The third theory supporting free speech as a fundamental right is advancing autonomy. Based in human rights values, advancing autonomy recognizes that speech is an essential aspect of personhood and autonomy. Some critics of this theory note that other aspects of autonomy are not granted fundamental right status and one's free speech may infringe on another's autonomy or self-fulfillment. Lines must be and have been drawn to recognize when there are clashes of rights, but there is no question that hurt feelings at the very least and violence may result from allowing wide latitude for speech under this theory. The white nationalist protesters in Charlottesville, Virginia tested the boundaries (Katz 2017). And more recently the Pittsburgh synagogue shooter who voiced his hatred for Jews repeatedly online before killing eleven adults in their house of worship exemplifies the dangers at the outer limits (Chavez, Grinberg, and McLaughlin 2018).

Finally, recognizing free speech as a fundamental right promotes tolerance. In other words, if everyone feels free to speak, then we all have to recognize one another's point of view, even if we disagree. Critics of this theory question whether tolerance should be regarded as a basic value. While tolerance is not an enumerated constitutional right, there is no question that the Framers, escaping religious and speech intolerance in England, were very much motivated by tolerance as a fundamental value.

Dean Chemerinsky points out that the theories are not mutually exclusive and none is without problems. However, they do exist, the justices do refer to them, and there is no question that they have influenced First Amendment jurisprudence in the absence of detailed constitutional language. With regard to speech, all the First Amendment says is, "Congress shall make no law … abridging the freedom of speech." As lofty as the language is, it provides very little actual guidance with regard to critical questions such as whether all speech has the same value, whether some restrictions make sense, and, if so, where to draw the lines.

The Supreme Court and Students' First Amendment Rights

The Court only hears between 60 and 80 cases each year, representing less than 1% of all appellate petitions filed ("About the Court" 2018). It has granted certiorari – or agreed to hear – dozens of cases regarding the scope of various First Amendment free speech protections. With regard to the relatively narrow area of public school students and their free speech rights, four major cases set the scene for the question of online speech protections. Those cases are *Tinker v. Des Moines Independent School District* (1969), *Bethel School District v. Fraser* (1986), *Hazelwood v. Kuhlmeier* (1988), and *Morse v. Frederick* (2007).

In *Tinker*, as explained earlier, the Court first expressed a broad support for the idea that schoolchildren and teachers enjoy constitutional freedoms inside and outside of public schools (1969). The Court overturned the censorship of the students' black armbands in protest of the Vietnam War because their speech did not "materially and substantially interfere with the requirements of appropriate discipline in the operation of the school." The affirmed the idea first offered in *Barnette* that expressive conduct, particularly when it is political in nature, is akin to pure speech that may only be violated under limited circumstances. Justice Fortas wrote:

In our system, state-operated schools may not be enclaves of totalitarianism. School officials do not possess absolute authority over their students. Students in school as well as out of school are "persons" under our Constitution. They are possessed of fundamental rights which the State must respect, just as they themselves must respect their obligations to the State. In our system, students may not be regarded as closed-circuit recipients of only that which the State chooses to communicate… Students are entitled to freedom of expression of their views.

Under the facts in that case, since the students' wearing of the armbands did not disrupt school and did not "collide with the rights of others," the school could not punish the speech. In *Tinker*, the Court said that unless there was an actual disruption or school authorities could reasonably "forecast substantial disruption of or material interference with school activities," censorship violated the students' First Amendment rights.

The *Tinker* standard of actual or reasonably forecasted material and substantial disruption has not been overturned in fifty years. However, in *Bethel, Hazelwood*, and *Morse*, the Court drew more lines around student speech. In *Bethel*, it ruled that schools could prohibit speech they considered "vulgar, lewd, or plainly offensive" because such speech contradicted the fundamental values of public school education. Justice Brennan's concurring opinion introduced the idea that schools do not have the authority to punish off-campus speech, although in subsequent years some lower courts instead have held that off-campus speech that school officials deem inappropriate may be punished.

In *Hazelwood*, a school prohibited student journalists from publishing a school newspaper issue including controversial topics. When the case was appealed to the Supreme Court, a majority held that the First Amendment allows school officials to censor content in school-sponsored publications that bear the imprimatur of the school as long as the school's actions are "reasonably related to legitimate pedagogical concerns." The Court deferred to school officials' judgment in determining when speech might be considered a product of the school itself by parents and members of the public.

For almost twenty years, the Court did not consider another student speech case. However, in 2007 it agreed to hear a case about whether schools could punish students for speech perceived by school officials as promoting illegal drug use at an off-campus, school-sponsored activity (*Morse v. Frederick)*. The case arose when a principal allowed students to participate in the Olympic torch relay coming through Juneau, Alaska. The event occurred during school hours but across the street from the school. Joseph Frederick was a sassy student who later admitted that he purposely used non-sensical language when he unfurled a banner that read "Bong Hits 4 Jesus" during the televised torch rally. Principal Deborah Morse tore up the banner and suspended the student for promoting illegal drug use, which was against school policy.

The Court upheld the punishment, pointing out that the speech in *Morse* was distinct from the speech in *Tinker, Fraser*, and *Kuhlmeier*. The main effect of the *Morse* decision was to expand schools' authority to regulate speech that occurs off-campus but at a school-sponsored event. If the First Amendment is a big piece of cheese, these cases – and the Court's silence – have created big holes such that students' First Amendment rights now look like a block of Swiss cheese.

But what of speech that occurs off-campus and *not* at a school-sponsored event? Online speech has grown exponentially in frequency, and yet, the Court has yet to determine the boundaries of regulating it. In early 2016, the Supreme Court declined to grant certiorari to the case of *Bell v. Itawamba County School Board* (2015). In that case, the Fifth Circuit upheld disciplinary action imposed on Taylor Bell, a high school senior who recorded a rap song containing threatening language off-campus and posted it to his own Facebook page and later to YouTube. Bell posted the song off-campus on his personal computer. The Fifth Circuit considered whether off-campus speech directed at school officials and reasonably understood by them to be threatening, harassing and intimidating speech that could create a substantial disruption violated the Tinker standard.

The court reasoned that school officials acted within their authority since the recording described violent acts to be carried out against two named sports coaches employed by the school, the student intended the recording to reach the school community and the school reasonably forecasted a substantial disruption at school. Bell appealed the decision to the U.S. Supreme Court, and just a few days after Justice Antonin Scalia passed away unexpectedly, the Court denied cert.

The Supreme Court's refusal to grant certiorari means the various standards imposed by lower circuit courts will continue to cause confusion at best and trample on students' rights and their futures at worst. Observers note a number of potential reasons that the Supreme Court has elected to stay out of this question. In general, the Court generally recognizes that school officials are in the best position to make decisions regarding school functioning. Second, the consequences of a ruling both in favor of and limiting free speech are high. Bullying and cyberbullying are very real threats to student safety, and speech that might be tolerated when spoken seems more harmful when written and posted online. On the other hand, a ruling limiting free speech would be difficult to implement, and lower courts have struggled to draw meaningful lines. Finally, the Court generally is not known for being technology-savvy, and it generally lags behind the other branches of government in terms of understanding and interpreting regulations of technology.

ARGUMENT

The lack of a national standard for off-campus, online speech fails to give notice, offers school officials unfettered discretion which leads to inconsistent discipline, and may chill students' speech. In considering a solution, a balance must be struck between the schools' important and legitimate safety and pedagogical concerns and the societal values associated with free exercise of speech in an era where most speech occurs online and through social media.

In *Goss v. Lopez* (1975), the U.S. Supreme Court held that school suspensions for less than ten days only require "rudimentary precautions" whereas shorter suspensions require minimal procedural (notice and hearing) protections. Aware of the additional measures that must be taken once a student is expelled for ten or more days, school officials often suspend students for less than ten days, but many students receive multiple suspensions throughout a school year that add up to more than ten days missed, but receive no corresponding procedural due process protections or educational services that often attach only to longer suspensions (Ross, 2016).

Different Approaches Across the Country

Federal appellate courts are split on when and how schools may regulate online, off-campus speech. In an exhaustive analysis of holdings related to online, off-campus speech, Ferry identified several different approaches (Ferry, 2018). She found that while the majority of federal appellate courts apply *Tinker*'s material and substantial disruption standard, their approach to applying the exceptions from *Fraser, Kuhlmeier*, and *Morse* vary. She found that the Second, Seventh, and Eighth Circuits apply the foreseeability threshold to the *Tinker* test. The Third Circuit also applies foreseeability but focuses on the student's intent, thereby narrowing the possibility for censorship. The Fourth Circuit also applies *Tinker* but focuses on a "sufficient nexus" between the speech and harm. Rather than focusing on the speaker's intent, the Eleventh Circuit adopted a pro-school test that applies both *Tinker* and the "true threat" test. The Fifth Circuit employs a flexible, fact-specific inquiry that seems to favor school officials.

Of all the federal appellate courts, the Ninth Circuit has adopted the most student-friendly approach by refusing to apply Tinker unless there is an identifiable threat of school violence. Ferry concludes that the First, Sixth, Tenth, and D.C. Circuits have not yet addressed off-campus online speech.

Since the "true threat" doctrine supports school officials' concerns and is part of the author's recommended approach, it is worth explaining further. The Supreme Court first articulated the true threat doctrine in a per curiam (or slam dunk) opinion in case called *Watts v. United States* in 1969. In *Watts*, a speaker made threatening speech about the president, but the Court held that the speech was protected as political speech. While the Court made it clear that speech that is considered a true threat is unprotected, it has never clearly defined what constitutes a true threat. However, where speech purposely or knowingly communicates an intention to inflict unlawful harm on another person or persons, it is likely to be considered a true threat not worthy of protection. One challenge with the true threat test is whether the threat is assessed from the perspective of the speaker or the target of the speech and courts have used both perspectives.

Balancing School Officials' Concerns With Students' First Amendment Rights

Arguments for School Officials

The Supreme Court has repeatedly recognized two important arguments in favor of school officials: 1) they need flexibility as they are the ones on the ground making decisions based on the needs of their particular students and schools, and 2) they have a duty to maintain safety and order.

The Supreme Court has extended special deference to government actors in "special needs" environments such as public schools. In the public school context, the Court has repeatedly held in *New Jersey v. T.L.O.* (1985), *Bethel v. Fraser* (1986), *Vernonia School District v. Acton* (1995), *Board of Pottawatomie County v. Earls* (2002) and other cases that since school officials are acting in loco parentis ("in the place of parents"), they have a special duty to maintain safety and order. In too many public schools, teachers and staff feel overworked and underpaid, and the burnout rate is high. Courts give deference to school officials out of respect for the unique challenges they face and a realization that local decision-making necessarily happens swiftly. As a nod to these needs, judges feel that they are not in the best position to second-guess school teachers and staff.

Arguments in Favor of Students' Individual Rights

On the other hand, some justices – including Justices Abe Fortas, Thurgood Marshall (the first African American Supreme Court Justice) and William Brennan – have recognized the vital importance of schools as training grounds for citizenship, and in order to be engaged citizens, students must learn and exercise their rights and responsibilities. Since schools are the one public institution that touches most students, it is the one institution that is uniquely situated to promote all the values underlying speech as a fundamental right. In recent years, civic education programs and courses have been cut in favor of "core" courses that prepare students for standardized testing. Without these designated opportunities to learn about active citizen engagement, most public school students will only learn about their free speech rights if they are allowed to exercise them.

Building on the constitutional values, advocates and scholars point out very serious challenges with the harshness of current censorship practices. Noted constitutional and education law scholar Professor Catherine J. Ross makes a powerful argument that many minor infractions resulting in school exclusion involve violations of school speech codes (2016). Professor Ross points out that students are often disciplined for out-of-school speech in disproportionately harsh ways, and disciplinary referrals are an important predictor of involvement in the juvenile justice system. The school-to-prison pipeline has been well-documented in the literature and includes not just the disturbing overall problem of school discipline leading to criminal convictions and recidivism, but also disparities in discipline across race, gender, disability, and class lines. Low-income black and brown boys are far more likely to be disciplined for the same behavior as higher-income white boys and girls. The New York Civil Liberties Union reports that the use of "profane language" is one of the top ten reasons students are suspended (Ross, 2016). In America today, students are arrested rather than sent home when they protest in ways that evoke disapproval from schools.

According to Professor Ross, schools respond disproportionately to speech for which adults could never be punished, and for which young people could not be punished outside of school, with potentially life-changing consequences. Ross points out that even if a student has the resources to pursue a civil suit and is lucky enough to prevail, unless the student obtains an injunction, the penalty will be applied before resolution of the lawsuit (Ross, 2016).

She provides the example of Adam Porter's case. Before the Fifth Circuit Court of Appeals found his drawing of a violent attack on his school was protected speech, Adam had already been arrested, kept in jail for four days, threatened with expulsion, sent to an alternative school with at-risk youth, and dropped out of school. Even though the court ruled that his First Amendment rights were violated, "no one could turn back the clock and restore his route to a high school diploma" (Ross, 2016).

Building on robust scholarship documenting the existence and dangers of the school-to-prison pipeline, in a 2017 law review article the author coined the term "prisonization" to describe the practice of students being treated like little prisoners by being subjected to zero tolerance policies, metal detectors, armed police officers in schools, cameras, drug-sniffing dogs, and other law enforcement techniques (Ahranjani, 2017). Today, with millions of students attending prisonized schools, the dangers of censorship extend far beyond mere censorship of articles as in *Hazelwood* or suspension from school as in *Tinker* and *Bethel.*

The Supreme Court and Technology

While all these factors and perhaps others explain why the Court would want to stay out of the question of students' free speech online, the Court's recent foray into technology in a different constitutional context provide hope that it may move past its fear of technology. In the past decade, the Court has considered three cases regarding whether the Fourth Amendment's warrant requirement extends to GPS tracking and cell phones. These cases indicate a sea change in terms of at least a majority of the Court's willingness to extend constitutional protections to current technologies.

In 2012, in *United States v. Jones*, the Court ruled that police need a search warrant to use a GPS tracking device to monitor a person's life, particularly if there was no urgent public safety rationale. In *Riley v. California* (2014), the Court unanimously ruled that if officers seize a smartphone at the time of an arrest, they need a warrant before viewing its contents. Finally, in deciding the 2018 case of *Carpenter v. United States*, the Court considered whether police need a search warrant to obtain cellphone location information that is routinely collected and stored by wireless providers. It concluded that the government did indeed violate the Fourth Amendment when it did not obtain a search warrant to access historical records containing the physical locations of cell phones.

Since the appointment of conservative Brett Kavanaugh to the Supreme Court in October, 2018 to replace the more moderate Anthony Kennedy, it remains to be seen how the Supreme Court will rule on cases considering cases at the intersection of civil rights and technology. The Heritage Foundation, a conservative think tank, points out that while he served on the D.C. Circuit, Justice Kavanaugh did not hear many technology cases, but he certainly proved himself to be an originalist and a textualist who firmly believed in the limited role of judges to decide the law rather than what it should be (Snead, 2018). As an originalist and a textualist, he likely will resist the urge to *create* law.

Carpenter v. United States (2018) was a 5-4 decision in which Chief Justice Roberts, a conservative appointed by then-President George W. Bush, sided with the liberal Justices Kagan, Sotomayor, Ginsburg and Breyer in the relatively narrow holding in terms of scope. Justice Kavanaugh replaced his mentor Justice Kennedy, who voted with the dissent. However, even if Kavanaugh adopts his predecessor's stance, the outcome in the case would have been the same.

If, in fact, the Court could overcome its reluctance to get involved in public school affairs and its fear of technology, the implications are tremendous. By way of example, consider students' recent exercise of their first amendment right to speak to protest the second amendment's right to bear arms. In the wake of the shooting resulting in 17 deaths in a Parkland, Florida public high school, students at Marjory Stoneman Douglas High and across the country mobilized to ask for adults to make schools safer (Gray 2018). Students mobilized online and organized thousands of walk-outs all over the country and the world at 10 a.m. on March 14, 2018. They also organized a national march in Washington, DC on March 24, 2018, just five weeks after the shooting rampage, and smaller marches were held in countless other cities.

Without online communications, these tremendous efforts never would have occurred. While some schools affirmatively support walkout efforts as political expression and civic activism, others warned students they would be punished for walking out. Without national standards protecting student speech, students learn different lessons about the importance of civic engagement. Without the Supreme

Court or Congressional action to extend free speech rights to online communications, the very future of democracy is at stake when some voices are discouraged and punished.

SOLUTIONS AND RECOMMENDATIONS

The American system of democracy is at once fragile and strong. Our Constitution has withstood the test of time, yet civil rights that took decades to establish have been eroding at an alarming pace at the direction of the Trump administration.

Scholars have proposed that in the absence of Supreme Court precedent, school districts should simply adopt policies that reflect best practices (Ferry, 2018; Shaver, 2017). In carefully considering the various circuit court approaches, Ferry thoughtfully proposes a model standard for school districts to adopt, which the author has changed slightly. Ferry's proposed standard would first consider whether the speech in question occurred off- or on-campus. If it occurred on-campus, the *Tinker* standard would apply. If it occurred off-campus, there must be an initial assessment of whether the online speech caused a material and substantial disruption, a true threat, or neither. The author adds that the true threat could be assessed either from the perspective of the speaker or the recipient.

Pursuant to longstanding doctrine, true threats could be punished immediately. Where the online speech creates a material and substantial disruption to school functioning, it could be punished if the speaker intentionally caused the disruption, and courts should look at content and form of the speech in determining intent. If the online speech creates no disruption and does not constitute a true threat, it should not be punished.

This test incorporates all the elements considered by lower courts, recognizes schools' important interests, and ultimately heavily weights students' First Amendment rights in a way that is consistent with the theories underlying free speech as a fundamental right. Children have been at the forefront of many social movements, from the civil rights movement to the anti-Vietnam War movement to gun violence to climate change. Cultivating their voices has been and will be critical to the continuing growth of our democracy. Allowing them the space to exercise free speech in the medium that currently presents itself gives them the opportunity to pressure-test democratic values.

FUTURE RESEARCH DIRECTIONS

A valid critique of this case by international readers is that an expansive vision of free speech is a uniquely American concept. In fact, when the Pew Research Center polled 38 countries in 2015, it found that Americans are more tolerant of not only free speech than citizens in the other countries polled, but also more supportive of free press and the right to internet usage without government censorship (Gray, 2016). Interestingly, Latin America was the region second most likely to support these three freedoms, with Europe in third place, Asia in fourth, Africa in fifth, and the Middle East in last place. In terms of a country-by-country analysis, after the U.S., the countries whose populations are most supportive of free expression are Poland, Spain and Mexico. It follows that generally countries with strong support of free expression also support student speech, including online speech.

One critique of Americans' support for free expression is, of course, that speech can be incredibly harmful. For example, comparative constitutional law scholar Mila Versteeg now based at the University of Virginia in Charlottesville has pointed out that the 2017 rally in Charlottesville in which heavily armed white nationalists invaded a progressive university town to protest, and the protests led to violence and death, would not have happened in Europe (2017).

Professor Versteeg points out that while the European Court of Human Rights protects free speech, it also recognizes that it must be balanced against other societal interests and is not absolute. She argues that the European approach is more neutral and refuses to rely on the values articulated in the earlier section on values underlying the First Amendment because the burden to discern when the speech is harmful and to respond to harmful speech then falls on fallible and busy individual human beings rather than the government to police.

However, the increased and increasing access to the internet as a forum for speech makes it even more difficult for government to draw and enforce lines. It seems likely that other countries may move closer to the American approach to free speech given the internet's omnipresence in the lives of all people across borders. In fact, to some extent, the internet erases borders and limitations for its users. Young people in the internet era can and do share information instantaneously.

A recent Knight Foundation survey of over 10,000 American high school students and over 550 high school teachers indicated that American high school students value First Amendment freedoms even more than adults (Policinski, 2017). For example, 91 percent of youth respondents said that it was important to be able to "express unpopular opinions" (Polcinski, 2017). For better or worse, American youths' expansive views likely will influence youth in other countries.

Therefore, the author argues that what the U.S. Supreme Court does and does not decide with regard to students' online free speech rights is relevant to Latin American and European observers in the near term and less relevant in Asia, Africa, and the Middle East, where citizens and governments are not as supportive of strong speech rights. Further study is necessary. Very little has been written comparing different countries' treatment of rights to free speech for children. The author hopes to engage in such study to explore the extent to which Americans' expansive view of free speech applies to and influences other countries.

CONCLUSION

In terms of today's youth and online speech, adults have a responsibility to nurture this speech but also think about whether and what lines may be drawn to protect them from hate, bullying, and other negative speech while recognizing the importance of cultivating students' voices. While the United States is peerless with regard to its expansive speech protection by law, it is worth watching our jurisprudential development since at least two regions – Latin America and Europe – are not far behind. Monitoring U.S. court decisions may provide an insightful perspective of what issues arise in a country with expansive protections and may inform other countries' development of laws relating to student online speech.

REFERENCES

About the Court. (2018). *The Justices' Caseload*. Retrieved from: https://www.supremecourt.gov/about/justicecaseload.aspx

Ahranjani, M. (2017). The Prisonization of America's Public Schools. *Hofstra L. Rev., 45*(1097).

Bell v. Itawamba County School Board, 799 F. 3d 379 (2015).

Bethel v. Fraser, 478 U.S. 675 (1986).

Board of Education of Pottawatomie County v. Earls, 536 U.S. 822 (2002).

Carpenter v. United States 585 U.S. __ (2018).

Chavez, N., Grinberg, E., & McLaughlin, E. C. (2018, October 31). *Pittsburgh synagogue gunman said he wanted all Jews to die, criminal complaint says*. Retrieved from https://www.cnn.com/2018/10/28/us/pittsburgh-synagogue-shooting/index.html

Chemerinsky, E. (2017). *Constitutional Law*. Alphen aan den Rijn, The Netherlands: Wolters Kluwer Law & Business.

Emerson, T.I. (1977). Colonial Intentions and Current Realities of the First Amendment. *U. Pa. L. Rev., 125*(737).

Ferry, K. A. (2018). Reviewing the Impact of the Supreme Court's interpretation of "Social Media" as Applied to Off-Campus Student Speech. *Loy. U. L.J.*, 49(*717*), 771.

Goss v. Lopez, 419 U.S. 565, 581 (1975).

Gray, A. (2016, November). Freedom of speech: which country has the most? *World Economic Forum*. Retrieved from https://www.weforum.org/agenda/2016/11/freedom-of-speech-country-comparison/

Gray, S. (2018, March). Thousands of Students Walked Out of School Today in Nationwide Protests. Here's Why. *Time Magazine*. Retrieved from http://time.com/5195960/national-school-walkout-march-14/

Hazelwood v. Kuhlmeier, 484 U.S. 260 (1988).

Katz, A. (2017, August). Unrest in Virginia: Clashes over a Show of White Nationalism in Charlottesville Turn Deadly. *Time Magazine*. Retrieved from http://time.com/charlottesville-white-nationalist-rally-clashes/

Lenhart, A. (2015). *Teens, Social Media and Technology Overview*. Retrieved from http://www.pewinternet.org/2015/04/09/teens-social-media-technology-2015/

Levin, C. S. (2016). *Legal analysis: how far can schools go in limiting student speech online*. Retrieved from http://www.splc.org/article/2016/06/legal-analysis-student-speech

Minersville School District v. Gobitis, 310 U.S. 586 (1940).

Mitchell, C. (2017). *Supreme Court Declines to Hear Free Speech Case*. Retrieved from http://www.splc.org/blog/splc/2017/04/keefe-certiorari-denied

Morse v. Frederick, 551 U.S. 393 (2007).

National Center for Education Statistics. (2018). *Fast Facts: Computer and Internet Use*. Retrieved from: https://nces.ed.gov/fastfacts/display.asp?id=46

New Jersey v. T.L.O. 469 U.S. 325 (1985).

Polcinski, G. (2017, February). *Good News for the First Amendment*. Retrieved from: https://knightfoundation.org/articles/good-news-for-the-future-of-the-first-amendment

Riley v. United States, 573 U.S. __ (2014).

Ross, C. J. (2016). Bitch, Go Directly to Jail: Student Speech and Entry Into the School-to-Prison Pipeline. *Temp. L. Rev.*, 88(*717*), 724.

Rotunda, R. D., & Nowak, J. E. (2017). *Treatise on Constitutional Law – Substance & Procedure*. Thomson West.

Shaver, E.A. (2017). Denying Certiorari in Bell v. Itawamba County School Board: A Missed Opportunity to Clarify Students' First Amendment Rights in the Digital Age. *Brook. L. Rev., 82*.

Snead, J. (2018). *Judge Kavanaugh and Technology Issues.* Retrieved from: https://www.heritage.org/courts/report/judge-kavanaugh-and-technology-issues

Tinker v. Des Moines Independent School District, 393 U.S. 503 (1969).

U.S. v. Jones, 565 U.S. 400 (2012).

Vernonia School District v. Acton, 515 U.S. 646 (1995).

Versteeg, M. (2017 August). What Europe Can Teach America About Free Speech. *The Atlantic.* Retrieved from: https://www.theatlantic.com/politics/archive/2017/08/what-europe-can-teach-america-about-free-speech/537186/

Watts v. United States, 394 U.S. 705 (1969).

West Virginia v. Barnette, 319 U.S. 624 (1943).

Winkler, M.B. (2017). Executive Order "Protecting the Nation from Foreign Terrorist Entry into the United States": Violating First Amendment Rights or Altering Constitutional Provisions Granting Foreign Policy Powers to the President. *W. Mich. U. T.M. Cooley L. Rev., 34*(79).

Chapter 5
Impact of Social Networks in the Exercise of Citizenship in Portugal

Cátia Rosário
Universidade Lusófona de Humanidades e Tecnologias de Lisboa, Portugal

Ana Lorga da Silva
https://orcid.org/0000-0001-7514-8278
Universidade Lusófona de Humanidades e Tecnologias de Lisboa, Portugal

ABSTRACT

In a society where access and presence in social networks is common to most of the population, it is essential to follow this form of access and sharing information, especially when it comes to publicizing the rights and duties of citizens. In this sense, the chapter focused on the analysis of the profile of Portuguese citizens that uses social networks to support the different themes that make up the concept of citizenship. Likewise, the results obtained allow to state that although most respondents do not use social networks to follow and/or support institutions, movements, or organizations associated with the exercise of citizenship, there is room for such. That is, the results suggest that it is possible to promote the exercise of citizenship through social networks in Portugal.

DOI: 10.4018/978-1-5225-8350-9.ch005

INTRODUCTION

Technological progress and globalization have brought several changes in the paradigms of society, namely in terms of access and sharing of information and knowledge.

The definition of information society proposed in the Green Book for the Information Society in Portugal (1997) is still current, considering that this concept refers to “a mode of social and economic development in which the acquisition, storage, processing, distribution and dissemination of information conducive to knowledge creation and to the needs of citizens and businesses, play a central role in the economic activity, wealth creation, citizens’ quality of life and cultural practices.”

In this way and as mentioned by Coutinho and Lisbôa (2011) the idea underlying the concept of Information Society is of a society inserted in a process of constant change. This change is based on the rapid advances of science and technology. Considering information as the raw material of knowledge and communication, several authors appear that have been considering that the essential is the knowledge resulted by access to information and not information itself. Similarly, UNESCO in 2005 suggested at the World Summit on the Information Society that the term would be changed to the Knowledge Society and in its World Report “Towards Knowledge Societies” considered that the term should be applied to societies which benefit their diversity and ability to encourage knowledge sharing.

Given the distinction and relationship between the Information and Knowledge Society, it should be noted that it would not have been possible to achieve the current level of ease of access and information sharing without Information and Communication Technologies (ICT).

The massification of ICT contributes to greater ease and increase, not only in access to information, but also in the interaction between individuals and between individuals and institutions.

Virtual social networks are currently an effective way of communicating and sharing information, accessible to a large proportion of the population.

Mosseberg, Wu and Crawford (2013) state that “Further, social networks foster collaboration, joint learning, and the speedy exchange of information between users. Thus, social networks have the potential to provide a new platform for communication between citizens and government officials, or for deliberation and discussion among citizens.” (Mossberg, Wu and Crawford, 2013, p.352)

Given the expansion of the use of social networks, it is possible to state that the framework of civic participation in actual society has been changed, since there are no geographic barriers to the information and performance of individuals. That is, social networks enhance the exercise of citizenship, given that, according to several studies, Internet users are more often more social, have more friends and contacts and are socially and politically more active than non-users (Castells and Cardoso, 2005).

The term citizenship, mentioned above, refers to a whole set of civil, political and social rights and duties. This is a multidimensional concept and as highlighted by Alvaro, (2011) there are plenty of authors who propose different approaches and dimensions for this concept. Martim and Mogarro (2010, p. 192) propose eight themes in the constitution to the concept of citizenship:

- State and nation: laws, principles, institutions and Constitutional Body in democratic regimes;
- Religion and religions as a manifestation of culture and spirituality;
- Relationship of the human being with nature, environment and socio-economic organization;
- Diversity of races, ethnicities and cultures: multiculturality and social inclusion;
- Family structure and role and gender roles at work and in the family;
- Health and quality of life (including aspects such as sport, food, safety, hygiene and sexuality);
- Civility, social coexistence and regulation of interpersonal relationships;
- Media and new information and communication technologies and how to use them effectively, safely, and ethically.

Considering that social networks are, as mentioned, a means accessible to the sharing of information, and can thus enhance the exercise of citizenship, it is considered relevant to analyse if this occurs in Portugal. It is also sought to verify the predisposition of users of social networks to use them to become more active citizens. For this purpose, a questionnaire was made available through the Google Forms tool. This questionnaire deals with various themes of the concept of citizenship mentioned above, as well as the profile of the users of social networks.

The questionnaire has been available during the period from September 1 of 2018 to September 28 of 2018, with the objective to obtain as many responses as possible, which were analysed using descriptive statistics.

The general objective of this study is to identify the extent to which citizens who use social networks do so to know their rights and duties as citizens.

Since the concept of citizenship is quite abundant, several dimensions have been used referring to the various themes in which citizenship can be exercised.

The specific objectives were:

- Identify the profile of social network users;

- Identify the profile of users of social networks that use them in the exercise of citizenship and in which themes are socially more active;
- Identify the profile of users who are available to use social networks to be socially more active and which subjects are available to do so.

Based on the above, it is intended that the present exploratory study provide relevant information on the previously described objectives, enabling the formulation of suggestions on how social networks are being and can be used for the exercise of citizenship in Portugal.

THE NEW PARADIGM OF CITIZENSHIP IN THE INFORMATION AND KNOWLEDGE SOCIETY

Over the last decades, there have been several economic, social and environmental changes resulting from aspects such as globalization and access to more information and more quickly. In this sense, Neto, Júnior and Valentim (2013) emphasize that it is practically impossible to face the current world without considering the importance of knowledge and information in society.

Talking about knowledge and access to knowledge cannot be done without considering the information, since it is only through information that knowledge is constructed.

Coutinho and Lisbôa (2011) mention that one of the first authors to refer to the concept of Information Society (SI) was Fritz Machlup, in 1962, in his book "The Production and Distribution of Knowledge in the United States". But the development of this concept may in fact be attributed to Peter Drucker, who in 1966 referred to a post-industrial society in which the power of economics was based on a new good that is information.

For Neto *et al* (2013), the term "information society" originated in the 1970s, based on discussions about the post-industrial society and what would be its defining characteristics. That is, there was an awareness and recognition of the importance of information, not only in political and economic terms, but also in social, cultural and educational terms.

For Oliveira and Bazi (2008)

the Information Society is striding towards a Knowledge Society, assuming different contours in that, because of this explosion of information made available, the individual is led to develop an awareness critical to what is being presented, to analyse the relevance of this to their needs, to take proactive positions in the search and use of information and to establish relationships between information processed, to produce knowledge. (Oliveira and Bazi, 2008, p.124)

According to these authors, the term Information Society comes from the "boom" of information technology and telecommunications, which allowed the creation of the so-called cyberculture, neologism defined by Levy, in 1999, as the mode of thought and values that developed through the growth of cyberspace, defined through communication from the global interconnection of computers, encompassing not only the material infrastructure of digital communication, but also the oceanic information universe it houses, as well as the human beings who navigate and nourish this universe.

That is, the Information Society was created in this essentially postmodern computational scenario, in which the individual perceived a certain anguish in the impact generated by the speed with which the technology evolved and made the information available. This evolution occurred mainly through the media, such as television and the Internet and in this sense, Information and Knowledge Technologies were and are fundamental in the creation and dissemination of knowledge.

Sarkar (2012) considers that

Information and Communication (ICT's) are referred to as the varied collection of technological gear and resources which are made use of to communicate. They are also made use of to generate, distribute, collect and administer information. ICT is a force that has changed many aspects of the way we live. Information and Communication Technologies consist of the hardware, software, networks, and media for collecting, storage, processing, transmission and presentation of information (voice, data, txt, images), as well as related services. (Sarkar, 2012, p.31)

UNESCO defines ICT as

Diverse set of technological tools and resources used to transmit, store, create, share or exchange information. These technological tools and resources include computers, the Internet (websites, blogs and emails), live broadcasting technologies (radio, television and webcasting), recorded broadcasting technologies (podcasting, audio and video players and storage devices) and telephony (fixed or mobile, satellite, visio/video-conferencing, etc.). (UNESCO, 2018)

There are several phases of ICT evolution that can be identified and can be followed in several books, journals, and of course online, for instance at The ICT Lounge site, shortly described here, ITC evolution comprises, the creation of electromagnetic calculator during World War II, computers, personal computers (desktops and laptops), microprocessors, internet, Bluetooth, and the wireless links.

The internet allowed to break the geographical barriers at several levels, it also contributes to accelerate the development of social networking, as the wireless development arising the mobile phones, those accompanying the evolution of ITC nowadays contains almost "the life" from large number of people all over the world as they are the main instrument to communicate, not only by voice and "conventional" SMS, but also by photos, music, e-mail and several applications where social networks are included, ones can say that "people have the world in the hands".

The past decade has witnessed the emergence of participatory Web and social media, bringing people together in many creative ways. Millions of users are playing, tagging, working, and socializing online, demonstrating new forms of collaboration, communication, and intelligence that were hardly imaginable just a short time ago. Social media also helps reshape business models, sway opinions and emotions, and opens up numerous possibilities to study human interaction and collective behavior in an unparalleled scale. (Tang and Liu, 2010, p.22)

The widespread use of ICT is observed in all aspects of life, in business, finance and financial services, marketing, education, social network, and so many aspects of daily life that is difficult to enumerate all of them.

According to Liu and Ying (2010)

Social network sites are those web-based services that allow individual to construct a public or semi-public profile within a bounded system, articulate the list of other users with whom they share a connection, and view and traverse their list of connections and those made by others within the system. (Liu and Ying, 2010, p. 749)

According to Aggarwal (2011) "social networks have become very popular in recent years because of the increasing proliferation and affordability of internet enabled devices such as personal computers, mobile devices and other more recent hardware innovations such as internet tablets."

In general, a social network is defined as a network of interactions or relationships, where the nodes consist of actors, and the edges consist of the relationships or interactions between these actors. A generalization of the idea of social networks is that of information networks, in which the nodes could comprise either actors or entities, and the edges denote the relationships between them. (Aggarwal, 2011, p.2)

ICT and Social networking brought us a lot of benefits, it's easy to communicate informally and professionally, the change and acquisition of knowledge is much easier than even a decade later, despite this there are "dangers" that must be prevent. The incorrect divulgation of knowledge it's a reality, people should know how to select information, should be "taught", but also the divulgation of erroneous or misleading information controlled, there are already some mechanisms to control the wild dissemination of information some websites control the information, and social networks, partially control the contents. Other concern is the use of ICT by children, without parental control, in this case there is not much to do, apart from an attempt to re-educate the population.

Social networking allows people to stablish connection with ones one previously don´t know, individually or with organized groups that shares the same interests at all levels, sport, nature, culture, politics, etc., once again, one may be aware about who is in the "other side".

Nowadays all personal information and work can be available online on clouds as OneDrive, Google Drive. iCloud, among others, part of that information is there voluntary, it means that people know how to use the clouds and wants to have everything available anywhere since internet is available, despite that several persons doesn't realise that using internet and agreeing with privacy policies are allowing the access of their data. As known information in clouds, leads to the danger of inappropriate use of the stored data by thirds as already happened and divulgated, by the social communication.

As is well known, among the most used social networks in Portugal are Facebook, Instagram, Twitter, LinkedIn and still Myspace, also they are channels where the subject citizenship is present in several forms, for those reasons it is briefly described how these social networks appeared and their evolution over time.

Myspace a social media network was born on 2003, MySpace users must be 14 or older as mentioned in Reoder, 2018. It was the largest social networking site in the world, from 2005 to 2009, had a significant influence on pop culture and music and created a gaming platform, the use of Myspace has decreased since 2015.

Facebook is as described in Oremus, 2014 and Mulen, 2016, is a social networking service was born on February 2004, 4, in a Harvard dormitory room by Mark Zuckeberg, along with fellow Harvard College students and roommates Eduardo Saverin, Andrew McCollum, Dustin Moskovitz and Chris Hughes. Firstly, they launched thefacebook.com, a website where college students could post information about themselves, trade messages, and become virtual "friends" with one another. When Facebook appeared, there were already social networks one of them was Friendster founded in 2002. Initially the idea was Facebook to be non-profit, but it started to be profit in 2009. Open to all the public with 13 years old or more, it's the social networking service that grew and expanded more at all levels: social, commercial, cultural using private (created by the users) and non-private groups all over the world.

Instagram is a photo and video-sharing social networking service owned by Facebook, Inc., it was launched in 2010, as Facebook only people with 13 years old or more can possess an account on it; Instagram's platform also allows to change private messages between the linked users.

Twitter founded in 2006 is an American online news and social networking service "a social media marketing" as written by Nations, 2017. On Twitter the users post and interact with messages known as "tweets". Tweets were originally restricted to 140 characters, but on November 7, 2017, this limit was doubled for all languages except Japanese, Korean, and Chinese according to Wikipedia, it also can be used from 13 years old.

LinkedIn is a social network for professionals, but it can be used form 13 years old:

Whether you're a marketing executive at a major company, a business owner who runs a small local shop or even a first year college student looking to explore future career options, LinkedIn is for anybody and everybody who's interested in taking their professional life more seriously by looking for new opportunities to grow their careers and to connect with other professionals. (Nations, 2018).

LinkedIn also has ways to send messages to the ones are linked.

The evolution of the knowledge society and the growing impact of ICT on citizens 'lives influence the way citizens' rights and duties are known and exercised. That is, one of the areas strongly affected by the use of ICT, namely by social networks, is the exercise of citizenship. In this sense, it becomes relevant to define this concept, which is so broad and to some extent abstract, it becomes difficult to define and classify.

According to article 4 of the Constitution of the Portuguese Republic, the concept of "Portuguese citizenship" concerns Portuguese citizens, who are all those who are considered as such by law or by international convention. It is thus verified that the Constitution does not define the concept of "citizenship", but this can be considered the "right to have rights and duties". That is, this is what makes citizens of Portugal and is what allows to have the rights, but also the duties, which are enshrined in the law.

The United Nations Educational, Scientific and Cultural Organization published its Global Citizenship Education: topics and learning objectives report in 2015, which states that

the concept of citizenship has evolved over time. it extended to all - for example, only men or those who possessed properties could be citizens. In the last century, a more comprehensive understanding of citizenship was gradually introduced under the influence of the development of civil, political and social rights. Today, the notions of national citizenship vary from country to country, thus reflecting differences of political and historical context, among other factors. (UNESCO, 2015, p.14)

According to Martins and Mogarro (2010)

The concept of citizenship is generally understood as the set of rights and duties of the individual who belongs to a community, who is now called a citizen. democratic societies, the authors also emphasize the civic, cultural and political participation (in the form of volunteering, associative), as inherent dimensions to the concept of citizenship and to the need to promote a culture of individual and social responsibility. This dimension has led some authors to emphasize the importance of education in citizenship rather than citizenship and differentiate between passive citizenship (right to vote, access to education, duty to pay taxes and comply with laws) of active citizenship, understood simultaneously as a right and duty to participate in the social and political life of the community. (Martins and Mogarro, 2010, p.187)

Álvaro (2011) highlights the relationship between information and knowledge technologies with the exercise of citizenship as long as we have witnessed the emergence of a networked society, characterized by a new notion of time and space and by a growing interactivity between people using technology.

Hingels, A, Saltelli, A., Manca, A.R., Mascherini, M. and Hoskins, B. (2009), Martins and Mogarro (2010) and Álvaro (2011) say that through the internet, time, space, information, communication and human relations have changed profoundly, leading to the abolition of borders and the creation of spaces and virtual communities open to a new sociability, new conception of citizenship.

It is understood in this way that we are faced with a broad and comprehensive concept, formed by several themes.

According to Castles (2000) the rights conferred on citizens can be grouped into five dimensions:

- Civil, which includes rights such as religious freedom, race, gender, among others.
- Politics, which includes the right to vote and political freedom.
- Social, related to labour rights, education, among others.
- Cultural, which includes the rights of preservation of language and culture from different origins.
- Gender, which refers to equal rights.

Martins and Mogarro (2010), propose eight dimensions that meet the five dimensions proposed by Castles (2000). Of the eight dimensions, seven of them refer to the five dimensions in a disaggregated way and the last one corresponds to the media and ICT.:

- State and nation - Laws, principles, institutions and organs of sovereignty, in democratic regimes. Portugal as a nation-state and as part of wider spaces: its relationship with the rest of the Iberian territory, integration in the European Union and its place in relation to other European countries, membership in the world of Lusophony and the privileged dialogue with the countries Portuguese speakers; democracy as a political regime; the organs of sovereignty; institutions of reference; some rights and duties of the citizen in democratic regimes.
- Religion and religions as manifestation of culture and spirituality. In this topic it is suggested: a secular education but including references to the existence of multiple religions; the promotion of tolerance for different religious manifestations or their absence or denial; the differentiation between religion and spirituality, religion and fanaticism; the different rituals; celebrations and places of worship of religions as cultural manifestations of peoples.
- Relationship of the human being with nature, environment and socioeconomic organization. Here the importance should be on recycling waste; sustainable development; renewable energies; the conservation of animal and plant species; the relations between the city and the countryside; the interior and the coast; the north and the south; with reference to work contexts and professions associated with industry, agriculture and services in the world today; and debates on specific environmental dilemmas.
- Diversity of races, ethnicities and cultures - multiculturality and social inclusion. In this theme, the cultural traditions of different peoples should be known and valued.
- Family structure and role and gender roles at work and in the family. A diversified conception of the concept of family should be adopted, with references to the different types of families (traditional, nuclear, reconstructed, single-parent, or otherwise), and equal valuation of all types, emphasizing the protective role the family plays for its members (especially for children) and the importance of affective ties between its members.
- Health and quality of life (including aspects such as sports, food, safety, hygiene and sexuality). In this case, the focus is on the promotion of healthy lifestyle habits (sports, healthy eating, and rejection of legal or illegal drugs that alter behaviour and / or perception); approach to sexuality issues, not

only from the medical point of view, but also from the affective-relational point of view; associated with health is the issue of quality of life.

- Civility, social coexistence and regulation of interpersonal relations. Cooperation and collaboration, tolerance, autonomy, critical thinking, responsibility for choices, equity, and the promotion of participation in school and community life, as well as non-violent conflicts, using peaceful means, such as the negotiation, mediation and dialogue processes.
- Media and new information and communication technologies, and how to use them effectively, safely, and ethically. In this theme, it is recommended to use a balanced and ethical medium and information technology, rather than merely promoting its use in quantity, with problematization of aspects, illusions, advantages and disadvantages of communication in the virtual domain, preventing cyberbullying.

POTENTIAL OF SOCIAL NETWORKS FOR MORE ACTIVE CITIZENSHIP

The number of social platform options is quite extensive, as mentioned earlier. As each platform can be targeted to different types of audiences and purposes. Nevertheless, in all the different social platforms, it is possible to create and follow institutions, groups or organizations that are dedicated to the defence and support to the exercise of citizenship. However, based on the different themes that make up the concept of citizenship, people can choose to follow and support different aspects of this concept.

It is indisputable that in Portugal, nowadays, access to the internet and the presence in social networks is a common practice for a large part of the population. This easy access allows to access and share information almost instantaneously. In this way, social networks can be used to promote the participation of people in the exercise of citizenship. Not only to raise awareness of the rights and responsibilities as citizens, but also as a means of empowering more active participation in society.

In this work it is aimed to identify how the Portuguese who use social networks use them to know and exercise their right to citizenship. For this purpose, a questionnaire was elaborated in which eight dimensions of the citizenship citation were considered, in order to identify which are the most popular in social networks.

This exploratory study was carried out based on the questionnaire available on the Google Forms platform.

It has been online since September 1 of 2018 until September 28 of 2018, the questions are in Portuguese (the questionnaire link is https://goo.gl/forms/3GYUthfAcars5g413) since the goal was a sample of Portuguese individuals.

The link was sent to 400 e-mails and approximately 50% of them (203) have answered.

Analysis of the Questionnaire

The obtained results were treated using the software IBM SPSS Statistics version 21 and since this is an exploratory study, the answers obtained were treated using descriptive statistics, presented in this section.

It is firstly presented the general characterization of respondents who answered the questionnaire presented.

Following is the characterization of the respondents who said to use social networks.

Finally, the analysis is made to the type of content associated to the exercise of citizenship that the respondents follow or are willing to follow.

Among respondents 61.8% are female and 38% are male.

Most respondents have Portuguese nationality 92.16% as can be seen in figure 1 below.

Figure 1. Nationality of respondents
Source: The authors (2018)

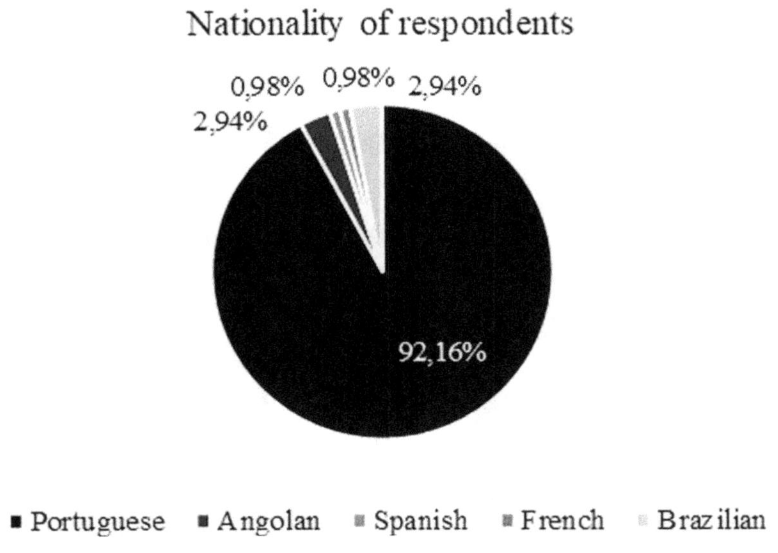

The average of the age of respondents is 40.44 years old, with a coefficient of variation of 23.3%, so the age of respondents presents a moderate dispersion, as can be seen in figure 2 presented next.

The respondents were asked about the region where they live and should choose one of the following hypotheses: metropolitan area of Lisbon, centre, north, Alentejo, Algarve, Region Autonomous Region of the Azores and Autonomous Region of Madeira.

There are no respondents from Alentejo, Algarve, Autonomous Region of the Azores and Autonomous Region of Madeira and the respondents are distributed by 66.6% of the metropolitan area of Lisbon, 28.4% of the centre, and 2.9% of the north.

Respondents were also asked to provide information on their level of education. In this case, 5.9% have the 3rd cycle (high school), 31.4% have completed high school, 42.2% have a degree, 16.7% have a master's degree and 3.9% have a PhD.

Profile of Social Network Users

Of the 203 respondents in this study, the vast majority claimed to use social networks - 97.1% answered yes and only 2.9% answered no.

Among those using social networks, it was intended to know for how many years they have used them. In this case 1% used it for less than 1 year, 2.9% used it 1 year ago or less than 5 years ago, and 82.4% 5 years, so the majority uses social networks at more than 5 years.

Figure 2. Age of respondents
Source: The authors (2018)

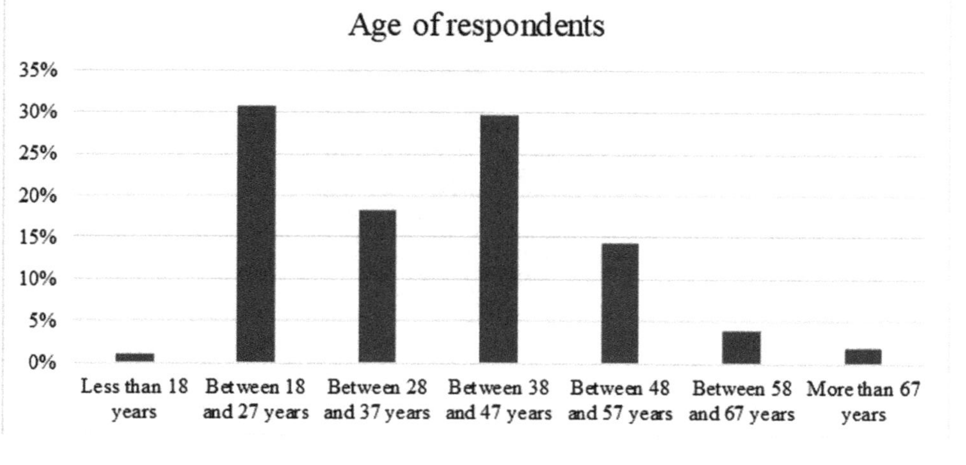

From those who use social networks, it was asked if they use Myspace, Facebook, Instagram, Twitter, LinkedIn, Netlog or others. As shown in figure 3, next, most respondents responded to Facebook and / or Instagram.

Respondents who claimed to use social networks were then asked to respond to the question "Does the social networks they use follow any movement associated with the concept / exercise of citizenship?". Regarding to this question, the majority of respondents answered "no" (57.8%) and 39.2% answered "yes".

Profile of Users of Social Networks That Use Them in the Exercise of Citizenship and in Which Themes Are Socially More Active

Respondents who answered that did not follow any institution or movement associated with the exercise of citizenship, were asked to justify why aren't doing so. To this end, the respondents were asked to answer the following hypotheses:

- No interest,
- Never considered the possibility of following one of these movements;
- Has not aware of the existence of any movement.

In this case, the majority (about 47.5%) said they did not follow because they have no knowledge of any institution / movement. 36.1% stated that they never considered this hypothesis and 16.4% did not do so by choice, that is, it was not of interest.

Figure 3. Social networks where respondents are present
Source: The authors (2018)

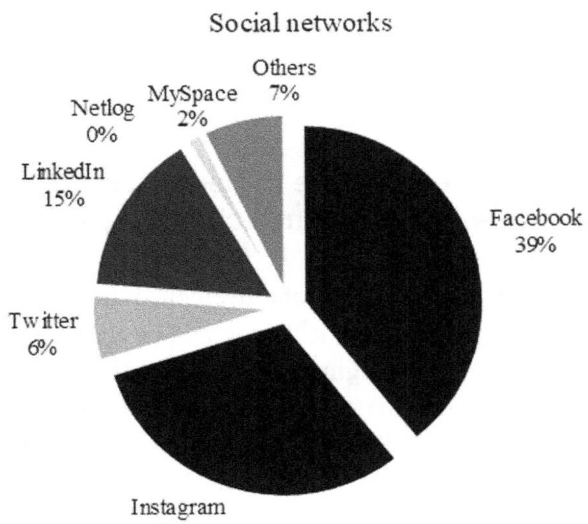

Of respondents who claim to follow some type of institution or movement associated with citizenship, they were asked to indicate what or which themes they follow, defending freedom and equality of choice:

- State and Nation (laws, principles and organs of sovereignty, promoting democracy and equality)
- Religion (as freedom of religious choice)
- Relationship of the human being with nature, environment and socio-economic organization;
- Diversity of races, ethnicities and cultures (movements against xenophobia and racism)
- Family structure and role and gender roles at work and in the family (parental, gender and work equality)
- Health and quality of life (promotion of healthy living habits, including aspects such as sport, food, safety, hygiene and sexuality)
- Civility, social coexistence and regulation of interpersonal relations (cooperation and collaboration, tolerance, autonomy, critical thinking, responsibility for choices, equity and even promoting participation in school and community life
- Medium and new information and communication technologies (effective, safe and ethical use)

The results obtained are shown next in Table 1.

As can be seen in the table 1 presented, the majority of people who said to follow some type of movement or institution associated to the exercise of citizenship, follow the themes Health and quality of life, State and Nation and Diversity of races, ethnicities and cultures. The less common theme is religion.

As shown in table 2, in most cases, respondents stated that they only follow 1, 2, 3 or 4 of the 8 themes presented.

Profile of Users Who Are Available to Use Social Networks to Be Socially More Active and Which Subjects Are Available to Do So

Respondents who did not follow any type of movement or institution associated with the exercise of citizenship were asked if they would be willing to do so. 78.7% of the respondents were available to begin to follow any of these types of movements / institutions. In this sense, the question was raised as to which or which themes they preferred to follow. The results obtained are presented in table 3, where it can be observed that Health and quality of life is the most popular subject, followed

Table 1. Represents the distribution of percentage of individuals that follows at least the mentioned category

Movements or institutions associated with the exercise of citizenship	Percentage
State and Nation	16.1%
Religion	3.2%
Relationship of the human being with nature, environment and socio-economic	7.0%
Diversity of races, ethnicities and cultures	13.6%
Family structure and role and gender roles at work and in the family	10.7%
Health and quality of life	26.3%
Civility, social coexistence and regulation of interpersonal relations	10.4%
Medium and new information and communication technologies	12.7%
TOTAL	100%

Source: The authors (2018)

Table 2. Represents the distribution of percentage of the individuals that follow 1 to 7 categories

Number of options	Percentage
1	20%
2	20%
3	27.5%
4	20%
5	5%
6	5%
7	2.0%
8	0,5%
Total	100%

Source: The authors (2018)

by Family structure and role and gender roles at work and in the family, State and Nation and Medium and new information and communication technologies.

As in the case of respondents who follow social movements, in this case, respondents who do not follow social movements but who are willing to do so reveal, as it is possible to see in table 4, that they are available to follow up to 5 themes, revealing once again that not all the dimensions that make up the concept of citizenship appear to be attractive enough for respondents.

Table 3. Represents the percentage of individuals that are open to follow at least the mentioned category

Movements or institutions associated with the exercise of citizenship	Percentage
State and Nation	13.7%
Religion	7.2%
Relationship of the human being with nature, environment and socio-economic	5.0%
Diversity of races, ethnicities and cultures	12.4%
Family structure and role and gender roles at work and in the family	15.7%
Health and quality of life	22.2%
Civility, social coexistence and regulation of interpersonal relations	10.7%
Medium and new information and communication technologies	13.1%
TOTAL	100%

Source: The authors (2018)

Table 4. Represents the distribution of percentage of the individuals that are open follow 1 to 7 categories

Number of options	Percentage
1	21.7%
2	15.2%
3	15.2%%
4	21.7%
5	15.2%
6	4.3%
7	5.0%
8	1.5%
Total	100%

Source: The authors (2018)

SOLUTIONS AND RECOMMENDATIONS

The concept of citizenship due to its various components is not clear for much of the Portuguese population, as one of the motivations of the authors to carry out this study is well known, as may be suggested by the results obtained by the same study, since there is a high percentage of people who do not follow movements associated with citizenship - 57.8% - that when asked if they are willing to follow, among these 39.2% expresses willingness to do so.

It is thought that individually concepts such as State and Nation, Religion, Relationship of Human being with nature, environment and socioeconomic organization, Diversity of races, ethnicities and cultures (movements against xenophobia and racism), Family structure and role and gender roles at work and in the family (parental, gender and work equality), Health and quality of life (promotion of healthy living habits, including aspects such as sport, food, safety, hygiene and sexuality), Civility, social coexistence and regulation of interpersonal relations (cooperation and collaboration, tolerance, autonomy, critical thinking, responsibility for choices, equity and even promoting participation in school and community life, Medium and new information and communication technologies (effective, safe and ethical use), are citizens, but they do not associate them with the concept of citizenship.

It is suggested that a rigorous analysis be made of the means that disseminate the various items that make up this concept, encouraging adequate entities and gaps to do so in a more efficient way and contextualize them as components of citizenship.

The citizenship theme presents several dangers due to its nature, several of its components lead and can lead to fanaticism especially in fields such as politics, religion, family, races, ethnicities as is common knowledge, however through social networks these manifestations can be stopped and even avoided, due to the development of algorithms associated with social networks. On the other hand, hackers also improve their invasion techniques. There will always be this duality, but not only regarding citizenship.

FUTURE RESEARCH DIRECTIONS

Social Networks change each day, and means of communication by voice, text and image such as WhatsApp, Viber, among others can also be considered as Social Networks not in the most conventional sense of social network concept. The same arrives for instance with YouTube, a video sharing service, people communicate share personal information, with the ones they are more "protected", because they choose or at least they have the opportunity to choose more or less thoughtfully the ones they intend and with really connect.

WhatsApp can be considered as social network transmitting concepts of citizenship, in the sense that users in addition to sending personal messages, are also passing on chain contact information for contact; from this information, depending on the groups and connections, much of it transmits information with citizenship contents in a conscious or unconscious way.

The authors intend to enlarge the work by doing a deeper research about the most used ways of communication and how they are used as social network, in the context of citizenship. YouTube it's a clearer way of dissemination of citizenship concepts by the videos that people see, the channel and network in general is organized in the way that once one visualize one of this subjects it suggests new videos related with it.

The results of the presented study suggest that most of the respondents who answered that do not follow social networks associated with citizenship, are motivated to follow it. But some citizens end up following the themes associated with citizenship, without having this notion, since they are not fully aware of the concept of citizenship. In this sense, YouTube could be used to analyzing this situation by the type of music videos visualized (which will induce users to follow others with affinities), or by the themes themselves, which are not exclusively musical and many of them are associated with the various items that constitute the concept of citizenship. The study can be performed not by questionnaire as performed in this study, but directly by algorithms of analysis of channel utilization in the Portuguese reality.

It is also possible to follow a line of research aimed at the perspective of entities, movements or organizations that clarify or support the exercise of citizenship.

In this sense, it would be important to identify the themes of citizens' rights and duties that are more present in social networks, distinguishing and "accounting" if they are in an official / institutional way or not.

Likewise, the profiles of the social networks used for this disclosure should be identified and subsequently analyzed to what extent these networks are able to adequately pass the information intended and correctly for the citizens.

As mentioned earlier, social networks present some dangers and can be used less correctly. In this sense, it can be analyzed how social networks are being used with the opposite effect to what is intended to defend citizens' rights and duties. That is, social networks can be used as a way of promoting discrimination and inequality. Thus, it will be important to study the extent to which this type of initiative reaches the users of social networks and then compare these two strands - Social networks in the promotion of citizenship vs Social networks against citizenship.

CONCLUSION

It is indisputable that in Portugal nowadays, access to the internet and presence in social networks is a common practice for a large part of the population. This easy to access and share information almost instantly. In this way, social networks can be used to promote the participation of people in the exercise of citizenship. Not only to raise awareness of the rights and responsibilities of citizens, but also as a means of enabling them to participate more actively in society.

The main objective of the exploratory study was to study the profile of the user of social networks that uses them as a way of informing themselves and participating in movements or institutions associated with the exercise of citizenship. Likewise, it was intended to analyse the extent to which respondents who do not follow any movement / institution are available to do so.

Our sample is mostly composed of female gender elements, with a mean age of approximately 40 years and living mostly in the Lisbon region and the central region of the country, being representative because it corresponds to regions with higher population density. Most respondents completed high school or college, using almost all social networks.

The results show that most respondents have a presence on social networks, being Facebook and Instagram the most popular networks. However, most people do not use them to follow or support any type of movement, cause or organization associated with the exercise of citizenship.

Of the individuals who accompany movements associated with citizenship, it was observed that the most followed themes are Health and quality of life, State and Nation and Diversity of races, ethnicities and cultures and the less common theme is Religion.

As for respondents who do not use social networks for the exercise of citizenship, most do not do it out of ignorance or because they never thought about doing so. In this sense, when interviewed about whether they would be willing to do it and if yes in which themes, once again it is verified that there is a greater predisposition for the themes associated with Health and quality of life is the most popular subject, followed by Family structure and role and gender roles at work and in the family, State and Nation and Medium and new information and communication technologies. The less popular themes were Religion and Relationship of the human being with nature, environment and socio-economic.

With this study, in addition to what has already been described, it turns out that in the case of users who use social networks with relative ease, they do not seem to be fully informed about the concept of citizenship. In this sense, agencies and institutions should promote the awareness of the concept of citizenship and the various themes that make up the concept. That is, the various dimensions of citizenship should be appropriately disseminated, with information of easy access, where people can be clarified and expressed freely and with respect, thus promoting their right to exercise citizenship. In this way, education for citizenship should be promoted, in the most diverse instances, from schools, to other institutions. This is because, when users use social networks, they should already be informed about their rights and duties so that they are not misled and then they can be more active citizens.

REFERENCES

Aggarwal, C. C. (2011). *An Introduction to Social Network Data Analytics*. Boston, MA: Springer. doi:10.1007/978-1-4419-8462-3

Álvaro, A. (2011). *Cidadania Digital: O Papel das TIC no Exercício da Cidadania dos Adultos* (Masters dissertation). Escola Superior de Educação de Coimbra, Coimbra, Portugal.

Castells, M., & Cardoso, G. (2005). *A Sociedade em Rede: Do Conhecimento à Acção Política*. Imprensa Nacional – Casa da Moeda.

Castles, S. (2000). Underclass or Exclusion: Social Citizenship for Ethnic Minorities. In Citizenship, Community and Democracy. London: Macmillan Press. doi:10.1007/978-1-137-09068-3_2

Coutinho, C., & Lisbôa, E. (2011). Sociedade da Informação, do Conhecimento e da Aprendizagem: Desafios para Educação no Século XXI. *Review of Education, 18*(1), 5–22.

Diário da República Eletrónico. (n.d.). *Constituição da República Portuguesa: Princípios Fundamentais*. Retrieved from https://dre.pt/web/guest/legislacao-consolidada/-/lc/337/201811301945/127959/diploma/indice

Hingels, A., Saltelli, A., Manca, A. R., Mascherini, M., & Hoskins, B. (2009). *Growing Cohesive Societies: The Characterization of Active Citizenship*. The 3rd OECD World Forum on "Statistics, Knowledge and Policy, Busan, Korea.

Iniciativa Nacional para a Sociedade da Informação. (1997). *Livro Verde para a Sociedade da Informação em Portugal*. Missão para a sociedade da Informação, Lisboa.

Liu, Y., & Ying, X. (2010). Review of Social Network Sites: Definition, Experience and Applications. In *Proceedings of The Conference on Web Based Business Management* (pp.749-752). Scientific Research.

Mansell, R., & Tremblay, G. (2015). *Renovando a visão das Sociedades do Conhecimento*. São Paulo, CETIC.br.

Martins, M., & Mogarro, M. (2010). A Educação para a Cidadania no Século XXI. *Revista Iberoamericana de Educación, 53*, 185–202.

Mossberger, K., Wu, Y., & Crawford, J. (2013). Connecting citizens and local governments? Social media and interactivity in major U.S. cities. *Government Information Quarterly, 30*(4), 351–358. doi:10.1016/j.giq.2013.05.016

Mulin, J. (2016). *This Is How Facebook Has Changed Over the Past 12 Years.* Retrieved from https://www.eonline.com/uk/news/736977/this-is-how-facebook-has-changed-over-the-past-12-years

Nations, D. (2017). *What Is Twitter, and Why Is it So Popular?* Retrieved from https://www.lifewire.com/what-is-twitter-3486519

Nations, D. (2018). *What Is LinkedIn and Why Should You Be on It?* Retrieved from https://www.lifewire.com/what-is-linkedin-3486382

Neto, J., Valentim, M., & Júnior, O. (2013, May). *Information Society, The Knowledge or Communication? Issues of information's appropriation.* Paper presented at the V Seminário em Ciência da Informação, Londrina.

Oliveira, A., & Bazi, R. (2008). Sociedade da Informação, transformação e inclusão social: A questão da produção de conteúdos. *Revista digital de Biblioteconomia e Ciência da Informação*, *5*(2), 115-131.

Oremus, W. (2014). *Facebook Was Born 10 Years Ago. Here's What It Looked Like.* Retrieved from http://www.slate.com/blogs/future_tense/2014/02/03/facebook_10th_anniversary_social_network_turns_10_looks_back_at_its_history.html?via=gdpr-consent

Reoder, L. (2018). *What is Myspace?* Retrieved from: https://www.lifewire.com/what-is-myspace-2654923

Sarkar, S. (2012). The Role of Information and Communication Technology (ICT) in Higher Education for the 21st Century. *The Science Probe*, *1*(1), 30–40.

Tang, L., & Liu, H. (2010). *Community Detection and Mining in Social Media Synthesis*. Morgan & Claypool.

UNESCO. (2018). *Information and communication technologies (ICT) Glossary.* Retrieved from http://uis.unesco.org/node/335129

Chapter 6
Constitutional Knowledge, Rights-Based Development, and Citizenship in Zimbabwe:
Past, Present, and Future

Innocent Chirisa
University of Zimbabwe, Zimbabwe

Emma Maphosa
University of Zimbabwe, Zimbabwe

Abraham Rajab Matamanda
https://orcid.org/0000-0001-5260-5560
University of Free State, South Africa

Wendy Wadzanayi Mandaza-Tsoriyo
Great Zimbabwe University, Zimbabwe

Kudzai Chatiza
University of Zimbabwe, Zimbabwe

ABSTRACT

This chapter seeks to assess the trends in rights-based development (RBD) and citizenship in Zimbabwe based on constitutional knowledge to proffer options on how the public can become constitutionally knowledgeable towards developing the nation. The chapter is informed by constitutional knowledge gathered through qualitative data from document analysis and literature on this discourse. The chapter first discusses the provisions of RBD and citizenship in Zimbabwe in light of the constitution. It assesses the trends in RBD and citizenship in Zimbabwe past, present, and the future to analyze the trends in the changes in the development of the nation, based on constitutional knowledge. Lastly, it proffers policy options on ways to nurture constitutionally knowledgeable citizenry.

DOI: 10.4018/978-1-5225-8350-9.ch006

INTRODUCTION

The current socio-economic and political landscape in Zimbabwe has brought a different meaning to the role of the constitution to the citizens. As such, there seems to be changes in the level of participation and knowledge of the constitution from the past, and the present. The level of knowledge tends to increase with time. The aim of this chapter is to assess the trends in rights-based development (RBD) and citizenship in Zimbabwe based on constitutional knowledge to proffer options on how the public can become constitutionally knowledgeable towards developing the nation. For the politicians, the constitution is a political document meant to sustain those in power and not fully representing the public. Unlike in the past, the public is now aware of some of the provisions stated in the constitution, especially on issues of gender which has been mainstreamed by most organizations in the country. Albeit this increasing awareness and knowledge of the constitution, there remains some ambiguity among the citizenry with regards knowledge on rights based development. This is contrary to the fact that the state should make some efforts to publicize the constitution since it seems little is being done in terms of full participation and interpretation of the constitution. It remains known to the policy-makers (the state or the government) and those who are studying along those lines yet the rest of the public remains ignorant. The constitution, as the 'mother law' in the land, has to adhere to the closures and the preamble of the act. Constitutional knowledge and rights based development is based on participation. Rights based development (RBD) is a process of development primarily aimed at human development and is informed by principles of rights, equality, social justice, participation and human dignity . Of late, the public has been given room to participate during the drafting of these policies, but it appears as if the powers are limited since some issues are not considered in policy-making.

The chapter is structured as follows: introduction to the study, the research methodology and theoretical framework which outlines the various schools of thought informing the study. The theoretical framework is followed by a review of literature on the global and regional experiences in constitutionalism. This part is preceded by a section which presents the results on constitutional development and rights based development in Zimbabwe. The results are followed by a discussion of the results and comparison with literature. The last section provides a conclusion of the study with some policy recommendations.

METHODOLOGY

The research follows a qualitative research approach. This approach provides a better understanding of the constitution-making and trends in rights based development. This study employs a case study of Zimbabwe. Secondary data sources such as textbooks, government reports, journals were the main sources of data. The data was analyzed based on themes emerging from the data- thematic analysis.

THEORETICAL PERSPECTIVES

Constitutional theory and elite theory of constitutional making process are discussed in this section. Constitutionalism by definition is the limitation of political power to ensure the enjoyment of rights and liberties guided by the rule of law (Lang and Wiener, 2017). The basic proposition of this theory is that groups and individuals within networks and institutions are driven and act primarily on the basis of mediating between conflicting material interests rather than on the guide of public interest. The diversity of interest is reflected in competition and conflict over access to economic resources, political freedoms and social justice (An-Nai'm, 2006). Consequently, leaving the groups with conflicting interests on their own, can result in societal disorder and conflicts (Sciulli, 1992). As a result, this theory argues that voluntary intervention among the different society groups should occur for a non-autocratic direction of social change (Sciulli, 1992). Thus a society jointly crafts laws as a mechanism for mediating the differences and conflict in access to social justice, political power and economic resources without the intervention of an external power which is the government/ state (An-Nai'm, 2006). Under the theory of fact a group ignores rights and interests of any other group external to it (Rosenfeld, 1994). In addition, the Madison theory also explains the relationship between the constitution and politicians (Griffin and Griffin, 1998). Madison claims that problems in the constitution emanates from a clash of personal interests of legislators against public interest responsibilities (Griffin and Griffin, 1996). The major challenge in the injustice of state laws is that of faction where few interest driven groups make decisions which inform national laws. Faction is the basis of divergences of interests within a society. This difference in interests groups in society is a reality that cannot be eliminated but at best can be managed using control mechanisms. Governments possess limited power to refuse to succumb to the influence of these influential interest groups. In a bid to militate against the competing interests, and to allow for a fair representation of almost all interest groups, Madison proposes that the constitution should be made through a majoritan rule process (Martin and Benjamin, 2014).

Rights Based Development (RBD) is an alternative development paradigm that became famous in the 1990s and is based on the United Nations Human Development Charter. Other origins of the paradigm were associated with the development crises among donor aid project in developing countries (Nelson and Ellen, 2008). This crisis was characterized by higher disparities in society, increasing poverty, lack of recognition of the role of development agencies in development and lack of accountability of the donor agencies. This led to the adoption of human based development (Cornwall and Nyamu-Musembi, 2004). The RBD approach differs from the conventional development models that emphasis economic development and market liberalization (Uvin, 2004). This approach to development has been more famous with international aid and donor agencies where it has been used to evaluate the success of projects mainly through emphasis on social changes and human welfare betterment (Nelson and Ellen, 2008). However, governments of the developing world have gradually embraced this development philosophy.

There are different typologies of human RBD (OCED, 2013). The common denominator is that that RBD aims at development that furthers the achievement of the basic human rights through building the capacity of duty holders as well as the citizens' claim the protection of their rights (Gready and Ensor, 2005). It is pertinent to note that the degree of accountability assumed by the government in fulfillment of human rights derives from the philosophy and ideologies of the state and the nature of power relations between the state and the civil society (Uvin, 2004). The achievement of human development is a shared responsibility between the different actors such as the state and the civil society (Andrew, 2007). This explains the promotion of a collaborative approach to development which places constitutional knowledge at the heart of RBD. The structures behind the violation of human rights and freedom and the social-economic arrangements (institutions) perpetuating deprivation tend to be exposed (Chambers, 2006). As a result the approach also focuses in eliminating exploitative institutional arrangements as a way of empowering citizens to take part in their own- development towards the attainment of human betterment (Nelson and Ellen, 2008). This shows the linking of the development paradigm to the law and constitutional arrangements.

In a bid to attain economic or physical development, human rights and human development forms the foundational step (Uvin, 2004). The development paradigm is increasingly being directed towards human development and empowerment as a strategy for poverty alleviation (Hickey and Mitlin, 2009; United Nations, 2016). It is also pertinent to note the absence of a universal rights-based approach to development (Cornwall and Nyamu-Musembi, 2004). The common principles guiding the RBD approach include participatory development, capacity building, empowerment, social equality and inclusivity, good governance (accountability, transparency and devolution) and the rule of law (Gready and Ensor, 2005; Nelson and Ellen, 2008).

LITERATURE REVIEW

No single definition exists to define a constitution. In its simplest terms, it is described as an important document used to inform the formulation of all public policies (Beeman et al. 2012). A constitution is also as a form of the supreme law of any country (Griffin, 1996). It can also be defined as an assemblage of laws, institutions and customs based on the problem of reason which seeks to attain a certain public good (public interest) (Madhuku, 2010). The constitution can also be defined as blue print in which the values of the state are enshrined (Katz, 2012). Therefore, it forms the system by which a society is ruled since it contains a framework for all the institutions and any other laws. The constitution has its origins in religious morals and value systems (An-Nai'm, 2006; Compton, 2014).

In the United States, stages in the constitution-making process include proposal of a bill, consultation and amendment by individual states and finally adoption of a constitution (Haws, 2009). The constitution-making process is usually called for by a special convention. Following the provisions of this convention, a draft is prepared and is subsequently challenged and altered through public consultation. The process give citizens ownership of the constitution-making process (Griffin, 1996). It is made through public debate by all interested stakeholders including the opponents and supporters of the constitution (Edling, 2003). It is drafted based on the need to provide checks and balances to the state assemblies which threatened the rights of the poor in America. Public debate is a procedure in the formulation or amendment of the Constitution for legitimacy reasons. The debates are also necessary to bring about a shared interpretation of the constitution. The need for a shared interpretation of the constitution is based on the government belief of ruling by agreement.

The process of consultation and the outcome is largely shaped by the structuring of power relations within society. The constitutional tradition is that of limitations on the constitutional powers vested in the president and the government. As a federal, there is a separation of powers between the law and the government in USA to ensure that the constitution is driven by the needs of the society (An -Naim, 2006). Despite the provision to limit elite capture in constitution-making in United States, the rich and elite groups (business associations) have a greater influence on constitution-making as compared to minority (Martin and Benjamin, 2014). The first constitution was made in 1787. Once formed the constitution is not cast in stone but is subjected to constant review to ensure it remains relevant under changes in the socio-economic and political environments (Edling, 2003). Rather than constitution-making being a decision of the state, in the United States, constitutional change is driven by the civil society (Griffin and Griffin, 1996). Social, economic, technological and political change makes demands for change of power arrangements and responsibilities of not only the government but other stakeholders as well. The bill of rights and property rights are important components of the United States constitution. Concerning property rights, the state takes due consideration to the protection of private property since the inception of United States' first constitution. The right to property is as important as the right to life (Paul and Dickman, 1989). This is because the economy of the United States is largely based on real estate property equity.

Another important example of constitution-making is China. The shift from a socialist to a liberalized economy had an important impact in shaping China's constitution. Under the socialist economy, the focus of the constitution was on increasing the government's power to control citizens rather than increasing the power of citizens (Chen, 1999). The first constitution to be made in China reflected interest of the ruling government which controlled the constitution-making process. Thus during the socialism era, constitution-making in China suffered from elite capture by the warlords. Other than interests of warlords, ideologies of the president and the president's conception of a real China also shaped objectives of constitution law under socialism. Constitutional law by the Chinese government became concrete in 1982. After this period, there was a major shift from socialism orientation towards economic liberalization. The shift is credited with the economic transformation of China. Changes in the political economy were also accompanied by changes in China's administrative framework and power relations. The grassroots and civil society assumed more powers and influence in law formulation. The role of civil associations in constitution-making was strengthened (Fai et al. 2015). As far as constitution-making process is concerned religious value systems also feed into constitutional law (Qing, 2013). This improved participation of the public in law formulation and improved ownership of the constitution by the public.

For the regional experience, South Africa shares most characteristics in Zimbabwe particularly with regards to the fact that the constitution has a British origin. However colonial law was adjusted at the end of the apartheid era. Under the post-apartheid South African constitution, the president enjoys ceremonial rather than executive powers. The 2004 constitution of South Africa excludes the right to development. However, it recognizes the right of citizens to economic, social, cultural, political and environmental rights. Among these rights include the right to food, education, health, clean environment and social justice. Whilst the government assumes accountability for ensuring citizens' rights are met, a separate and autonomous commission-South African Human Rights Commission is responsible for monitoring implementation of rights (Tlakula, 2004). As far as constitution-making is concerned, the constitution is reviewed by the judiciary before it is gazetted (Ndulo, 2010). After the constitution of rights is formulated it is the responsibility of the Human Rights Commission in liaison with the courts and the judiciary to oversee and monitor the implementation the constitution particularly the parts that relate to human rights and liberties (Tlakula, 2004). The provision of information to the public is one of the important initiatives taken to make the state more transparent and accountable to citizens. This positively contribute towards reducing misuse of the nation's sources and corruption among government officials.

The active role of citizens and civil society in implementation of the constitution is an important aspect for fostering the provisions of the constitution (Phama and Madi, 2016). The civil society is responsible for research and advocacy to raise awareness of citizens' rights. This is an important move towards communicating the constitutional provisions to the society. Other institutions employ litigation (taking the government to court over allegations of negligence) to force the government to respond to the rights of citizens. Community organizations also collaborate in implementation of rights such as health and environment conservation for the benefit of the society (Phama and Madi, 2016). Aggressive petitions by the civil society have yielded positive results of the rise in spending on health, education and housing by the government. Petitions also led to review of policies that increase accessibility of human rights (Andreassen and Crawford, 2013). This led to an improvement in the government's concern towards human development and consequently improvements on RBD in South Africa.

The current Constitution of 2010 in Kenya was a radical change from the former constitutions (Lumumba *et al.* 2014). In terms of the contents, more emphasis was placed on the rights of citizens (Ghai, 2014). Furthermore, the constitution limits the powers exercised by the state to reduce manipulating of state powers for private interest (Murunga *et al.* 2014). The constitution also seek to reduce exploitation of minority citizens under the ethnicity system. In addition the Constitution is also motivated to remove colonial injustice where colonial constitution served the interest of the ruling class through unfair land appropriation laws. The reform of constitutional order in Kenya is initiated by the civil society. The civil society organizes itself (political mobilization) and lobby for the amendment of the constitution (Murunga *et al.* 2014). Besides the civil society, the government is a critical stakeholder in amendment of the constitution since the government can call for amendment of sections of the constitution that hampers execution of government responsibilities (*ibid.*). Other than the government, the courts are also key actors in the formulation of the constitution. Once formed, the constitution is subject to renewal and constant adjustment to promote effective human development. For example the reason why the current 2010 was amended was to get rid of the excess limitations imposed on human rights (Ambani and Mbondenyi, 2015).

Kenya's constitution of 2010 has three overarching objectives which are nation building, state restructuring and equal access to social and economic resources. Nation building focuses on inclusive development, equal rights and social justice whilst nation restructuring places a particular emphasis on restructuring the administrative framework to ensure good governance that is accountable, transparent, participatory and decentralized. The rights and responsibility of citizens under the 2010 constitution come under many different forms and include the right to human dignity, the right to life (though this right is exercised subject to limitations), the right to information where every citizen has the right to access information on any matters of interest. Furthermore Kenya's 2010 constitution entitles citizens to political rights where citizens have the right to vote, the right to participate in any elections and compete for office and the right to petition and demonstrations when they feel aggrieved (Mbondenyi and Ambani, 2014).

The constitution also provides economic rights such as the right to property and the right to a clean environment. The right to property includes the right to both movable and immovable property. It is the responsibility of the state to protect the claims of the citizens to property and where citizens' private property is appropriated, full compensation should be provided (Mbondenyi and Ambani, 2012). However, this right doesn't apply for informally acquired properties for example unregistered residential property. Thus claims of land and property ownership by the minority groups like squatters remain vulnerable. Other than the economic right, the constitution also gives equal weight to the issue of environmental rights. This is critical given the high volumes of dumping and the impact this is likely to have on the environment and human health. Therefore to protect public health, the public is entitled to a clean and healthy environment through the environmental right. However these rights like any other rights in the nation are exercised subject to limitations. The duty to ensure the provision of all rights ultimately rests with the government though the public has a role to cooperate with the government towards the realization of this right (Mbondenyi and Ambani, 2014). Other than the government and the public, the Human Rights Commission, the courts and the judiciary also monitor implementation and address any issues regarding the interpretation and implementation of these rights (Mbondenyi and Ambani, 2012). In addition, implementation of these provisions is determined by social- economic and political factors such as political will and commitment, interests of elites, economic changes (Ghai, 2014).

RESULTS: FOCUS ON ZIMBABWE

This section provides an overview of the constitutional developments in Zimbabwe which include the human rights which inform RBD. The section also analyse trends in rights based development, based on the constitutional provisions and challenges in implementation of these for effective human development.

The constitution making process in Zimbabwe is initiated by the central government. The government proposes a draft constitution which is later debated with the public through consultative meetings. After this the draft bill is amended to take into account the views emerging from consultations. Despite consultation the government through the executive and the president has the final decision as to adoption and suspension of a constitution in Zimbabwe. Constitutional law is the prime law of Zimbabwe as it supersedes and guides the formulation of all subsidiary legislation on economic, social and political development (Ndlovu, 2015; Matamanda *et al.* 2018).

The first constitution to be implemented in Zimbabwe following independence was the 1979 constitution. The constitution was based on the provisions of the Lancaster House Constitution which maintained interests of the white minority and a few ruling elites (Hatchard *et al.* 2004; Magaya, 2015). Public participation was ignored under this constitution. Furthermore, the 1979 Constitution vested little powers within the president (Sibanda, 1991). This led to a revision of the constitution creating the 2000 Referendum, which was meant to domesticate some of the provisions of the 1979 Constitution and address inequality (Magaya, 2015). The rights spectrum was broadened from political rights to include social rights (Zimbabwe Government, 2000). The right to participation was also included. To foster participation, the constitution advocated for devolution of powers to undertake development planning at lower levels. Other than the right to participation, law on property was adjusted to facilitate state ownership and compulsory acquisition of land and property limiting the right to compensation (Moyo, 2016). This made expropriation of land easier under land reform. The other adjustment was the increase in executive powers of the president where the president is immune from any checks by the judiciary or the civil society. The 2000 referendum was further revised in 2013 to create the operative 2013 constitution. Constitutional reform up to 2013 was intended to streamline practice with global developments on human rights and participatory development by the United Nations and Africa Union human rights provisions (Dzinetsa, 2012; Chirisa *et al.* 2013). Furthermore, constitutional reform was also meant to enhance the capacity of government and the society to address new challenges arising in the social, economic and political aspects (Raftopoulos and Mlambo, 2009).

Despite the reform, the 2013 Constitution retained most aspects of the 2000 Constitution. Major aspects such as the administrative frameworks and citizens' rights have remained almost the same. The 2013 constitutional provisions on rights based development are captured under human rights in chapter 4 of the Constitution of Zimbabwe Amendment (No. 20) of 2013. These include right to participation, inclusion and equality, right to housing, right to property, right to water, right to health and sanitation and the right to the environment (Government of Zimbabwe, 2013). These rights form the basis for assessing rights based development in Zimbabwe.

Property rights are a key aspect of RBD addressed by the constitution of Zimbabwe. Property ownership (land, real estate property) is important assets for poverty alleviation (Chambers, 1997). Furthermore secured property rights are economic assets that can be traded on the property market increasing capital formulation by citizens (Desoto, 2000). The right to property is provided under section 71 which provides the right for every citizens to own, lease or dispose property. Homeownership is one of the aspects of property ownership important in development planning in Zimbabwe. Homes despite being economic assets are also important for shelter under section 28 of the 2013 Constitution and the state is obliged to take all possible action to ensure citizens have access to adequate shelter (Government of Zimbabwe, 2013). In line with the provisions, the government has taken attempts to provide land to developers at subsidized costs, providing loans and directly engage in housing construction since independence in a bid to improve housing access (Moyo, 2014). This partially improved access to housing. However the privatization of housing to has further worsened access to housing. Under privatisation, the responsibility of the central government is to guard the interests of citizens to prevent manipulation and profiteers in the housing market. Despite this, engagement of housing cooperatives worsened access to housing for the poor. Other than poor housing infrastructure, poor housing quality and housing provided in most housing cooperatives lack formal tenure (Moyo, 2014). Politicisation of access to land is another challenge where land is allocated on a partisan basis. This promotes inequality in access to land and housing hence the persistence of housing challenges and informal housing in Zimbabwe (Government of Zimbabwe, 2015).

Besides the state assuming responsibility for housing provision, the state also owns of all land in the country (Government of Zimbabwe, 2013). Withdrawal of private property rights to farmers after fast track land reform negatively affected farmers' potential to use land as collateral security (Richardson,). Likewise in peri- urban areas most homeownership programs introduced in the post 2010 fast track program lack private property rights since the concern has been centered on shelter in the quantitative dimension (Kamete, 2006). The absence of private tenure undermine the capacity of these beneficiaries to use their land and houses as capital assets. Hence a constraint on the right to property.

One distinct area of strength of the 1979 constitution was the strong protection to private property rights which was altered in subsequent constitutions (Linington, 2001). Compensation law was changed to allow land expropriation for 'public interest' by the state without adequate compensation (Vollan, 2013). This law promoted the interests of ruling party elites on private property. This is because compensation is determined by a government valuation board only on the basis of improvements made on land, rather than having markets guiding the pricing of the land. This has further alienated the land rights of citizens as well as limit the role of markets in the land market and made the government an active actor in land acquisition and transfer (Moyo, 2016). In addition, courts and the judiciary have limited authority to question the fairness of the compensation procedures (Linington, 2001; Matamanda and Chirisa, 2018). As a result the constitutional system provide incentives for abuse of power which threatens citizen rights to private property.

The other challenge with regard to property rights is inequality in access to land is also evident along gender lines where women were traditionally denied access to property unless married (Goebel, 2005). This has negative effects on economic productivity of women and therefore human development. Though there are ongoing changes and promotion of gender equality in access to land and property, cultural practices underestimate the value of landownership among women members.

Another key area of RBD is sanitation and access to water. Though the government and government agencies are responsible for providing adequate water, there are challenges in the implementation of universal access to water and sanitation. The quality of water and sanitation in both rural and urban areas have been deteriorating (Government of Zimbabwe, 2015). Access to water and sanitation has been affected by the transformation of water pricing from social to economic pricing where water is priced at full cost recovery. This compromises access to water services by the minority. This reflects inconsistency between the constitution and water management.

The right to participation in political, economic and development is a central concept in fostering RBD. Besides empowering citizens public participation also improves transparency and foster good governance (Chikuhwa, 2004). In the case of Zimbabwe, section 67 of the 2013 Constitution obliges the state to take measures to ensure participation of citizens in development (Government of Zimbabwe, 2013). The civil society can provide resources to improve the capacity of the government to implement projects centered on human development (Hellum *et al.* 2013). The civil society can lobby the government to take an active role in addressing societal needs. However, the capacity of the public to lobby central government depends on awareness of citizenship rights and the institutional powers for participation as success of RBD rests on the knowledge of rights (Madebwe, 2015). Improving citizenship awareness is done through public education and disseminating of the constitution provisions in different languages (Government of Zimbabwe, 2013). However, limited resources are commissioned to increase constitution awareness in Zimbabwe hence constitutional and citizenship knowledge is often poor (Chigwata, 2016). This represents a gap in constitutional communication despite the increase in levels of literacy.

Still on public participation, despite devolution of powers in urban development, provisions for participation under the Regional Town and Country Planning Act Chapter 29: 12 have not been streamlined. As a result they continue to promote representative participation through ward councilors which is subject to manipulation by ward councilors. This shows another form of elite capture. Consequently public participation in urban development remain passive as citizens are marginalized (Zinyama, 2014). This deprives citizens of their right to participation for empowerment. Other than participation of individuals, the constitution also provides for participation of civil associations including religious groups, academics and NGOs in development and implementation of RBD policy in Zimbabwe. Complementary to the public, NGOS are an influential actor in promoting RBD implementation in Zimbabwe. Typical NGOs active in RBD in Zimbabwe include WASH, DANIDA, World Bank and Dialogue on Shelter. The role of NGOs vary from community education to material and funding support for construction projects such as construction of social utility infrastructure like school, clinics and water supply infrastructure. On a positive note, NGOs help complement government efforts in improving human development in terms of access to housing, education and empowerment. However, since they have to work in collaboration with the government their ideologies are often diluted to accommodate government interests to guarantee approval of projects. This poses institutional challenges in NGOs executing responsibilities towards RBD. Where NGOs fail to comply with interests of ruling parties, projects are often terminated for political interests (Moyo, 2016). On the other hand implementation of global approaches of RBD without proper adjustment to the context further compromise effectiveness of NGO projects in human development (Vivian and Maseko, 2018). These factors compromises effectiveness of NGOs as a player in delivery RBD in Zimbabwe.

Despite provisions for devolution to the grassroots, power remains centralised in central government ministries. This is also compounded by the absence of devolution structures since power elites within the ruling part are unwilling to devolve powers (ActionAid, 2014). Centralising power within the ruling party and president has widened inequalities in power and therefore access to resources between elites and minority groups (Dzinetsa, 2012). The excess powers over land and land policy by the Ministry of Local Government has prompted elite capture, abuse of power and corruption by government officials in urban land governance (Muchadenyika, 2015). A typical example includes the politicization of land access in urban areas and excessive land grabs by local government officials in the name of housing cooperatives in most urban areas (Mutondoro, 2018).

Environmental rights are one of the critical aspects of RBD introduced in the 2000 constitution, where access to a clean environment and the right to use natural resources for economic and social betterment were considered (Zimbabwe Government, 2000). This is particularly relevant given the reliance of human livelihoods on the natural environmental resources particularly in rural areas of

Zimbabwe. However, the exercise of the enjoyment of the right to the environment has been militated against by lack of requisite institutions to educate the public on this right. Furthermore, failure to bring litigation in case of the violation of this right has been reported (Madebwe, 2015). The other challenge of the practice has been the lack of proper economic instruments like financial support for the realization of some of the environmental rights like access to clean water. Furthermore lack of environmental knowledge and capacity among citizens affect their capacity in managing and exercising environmental rights clearly accounting citizens (Chirisa and Muzenda, 2014).

Though the constitution provides for the implementation of RBD through providing rights in public participation, housing, property rights and environmental rights, RBD in Zimbabwe is still grappling. Major challenges such as political capture, institutional challenges, lack of resources and conflict between the constitution and subsidiary laws constrain implementation of the rights principles for human development.

DISCUSSION AND SYNTHESIS

There is a link between the constitutional development between South Africa, Kenya and Zimbabwe. One of the similarities is that constitutional development in all the three countries has a colonial origin. In addition though environmental, economic and social contexts differ human rights provisions in these counties is informed by the same policy at regional level which is the African Charter on Human Rights. Despite the similarities, these countries are at different levels regarding RBD. While the level of public participation in economic, social and political affairs is more pronounced in South Africa, public participation in Zimbabwe remains poor.

Poor governance is one of the challenges facing RBD in Zimbabwe. The capacity of the public citizens, NGOs and the judiciary as some of the key actors are limited by contested power relations. This emanates from the excess executive powers of the president which are often used to constrain initiative by other stakeholders for political interest. This is contrary to the case of countries such as the United States and South Africa where powers of the president are ceremonial and hence no excess control on other stakeholders. This shows the dominance of elite capture in the development and implementation of the constitution in Zimbabwe (Madhuku, 2010). Excess control by the government is used to weaken the capacity of the civil society and NGOs. This is contrary to the case of South Africa where the courts are independent of the government and have powers to provide checks on government powers.

There are differences in levels of civic participation in development matters across countries. The level of civic participation in development matters in the context of Zimbabwe is lower and more passive. On the other hand, in the case of South Africa and Kenya citizens have taken an active role through social mobilization and litigation (Andreassen and Barasa, 2013). In the case of South, Africa citizens are better empowered based on the constitutional structure that limits the power of the president as compared to the case of Zimbabwe. This limits the zeal of civil society to mobilize and claim their rights where these are violated. Conflicts between constitutional law and subsidiary legislation in Zimbabwe has been are a key challenge in the implementation of RBD for example in the case of access to water (Sithole *et al.* 2015). In the case of South Africa where the courts are independent, subsidiary legislation has been aligned to the constitution to ensure ease implementation of rights-based approaches. However, this has not been the case in the context of Zimbabwe where the judiciary acts under the directive of the presidency. The level of citizen participation in constitutional matters in Zimbabwe is lower as compared to citizen participation in counties such as the United States and South Africa where citizens are empowered and take an active role in claiming and protecting their rights. This is despite the provisions for the right to participation under Zimbabwe's 2013 Constitution. While the courts and judiciary have played an active role in the interpretation of the human rights bill and communication in the case of South Africa, the role of the judiciary in Zimbabwe has remained limited since they are controlled by the state. In addition, the limited autonomy of the state has reduced the possibility for litigation when citizens are denied fundamental human rights. This has tended to constrain the effectiveness of RBD in Zimbabwe.

CONCLUSION, RECOMMENDATIONS, AND POLICY OPTIONS

This aim of the chapter was to assess the trends in rights-based development (RBD) and citizenship in Zimbabwe based on constitutional knowledge. The results reveal that despite theoretical provisions for public participation in the constitution, there is a knowledge gap of the constitutional provisions among citizens hence the practice gap in building human capacity through public participation. Elite capture through laws of expropriation and compulsory acquisition of land and property are a barrier on the exercise of citizen rights to property. Furthermore centralized power systems and limited constitutional knowledge negatively affects the capacity of citizens, the civil society and NGOs to meaningfully engage in promoting RBD in Zimbabwe. Adding to this is ambiguity of the role of the constitution to politicians and other stakeholders as the constitution has been used as an instrument for advancing interests of ruling party elites.

The constitution needs to be regularly reviewed since it is the mother law of the nation. This reduces conflicts between the other acts and the provisions of the constitution. RBD needs to be established in Zimbabwe and this can only be achieved through good governance and transparency by the government. The decisions should not also be made based on constitutional interests where those in power only make decisions which show how powerful they can be yet ignoring the general public. As such, there is a need for citizen engagement, participation, and consultation in the constitution-making process. Various stakeholders should also take part and those who represent the public should push hard such that the problems of the public are set in agenda setting. The language used should also be easy to understand and interpret such that the public knows its rights based on the provisions in the constitution. There is a need for constitution review to increase the strength of the civil society as a check on the powers of government. Moreover, it is critical to have checks and balances on the powers of the executive to prevent abuse of power where parts of the constitution are amended to ensure the advancement of partisan interests and knowledge. Devolution is one of the factors that can be taken to improve RBD development. Though the concept of devolution is common in the theory of development in Zimbabwe, little has been done in practice as one of the development activities remain centralized with little power devolved to local levels. Strengthening the knowledge and capacity of the civil society by making them accountable actors at law can be another policy option. Rather than assuming the full responsibility for development rest with the state, citizens should be made aware of the equally important responsibility they can play to meet their human rights obligations through social mobilization. Communication of the constitution is one of the important take-off point getting the citizens to understand their rights and obligations as responsible owners of the development of their own society is a pertinent issue that should be addressed given that citizens have taken a passive role and assume the responsibility for development as sorely vested in the government. Strengthening the roles and autonomy of the courts particularly with regards to their powers of interpretation of the constitution for a shared definition of the human rights and entitlements is one of the important factors in fostering RBD. In addition, the court's role in litigation has an important role as far as the implementation of RBD is concerned. This is shown in the case of South Africa where the courts have taken an active role in promoting RBD.

REFERENCES

ActionAid. (2014). *The Dynamics of Devolution in Zimbabwe*. ActionAid.

Ambani, J., & Mbondenyi, M. (2015). A New Era in Human Rights Promotion and Protection in Kenya? An Analysis of the Salient Feature of the 2010 Constitution's Bill of Rights. In Human Rights and Democratic Governance in Kenya: A post-2007 Appraisal. Pretoria: Pretoria University Law Press (PULP).

An-Nai'm, A. (2006). African Constitutionalism and the Role of Islam. University of Pennsylvania Press.

Anderson, T., & Huggins, L. (2003). *Property Rights: A Practical Guide to Freedom and Prosperity*. Hoover Institution Press.

Andreassen, B., & Barasa, T. (2013). Kenya: Civic Action from confrontation to collaboration? In *Human Rights, Power and Civic Action: Comparative Analyses for Struggles for Rights in Developing Societies* (pp. 55–87). Routledge. doi:10.4324/9780203525821

Andreassen, B., & Crawford, G. (2013). *Human Rights, Power and Civic Action: Comparative Analysis of Struggles for Rights in Developing Societies*. New York: Routledge. doi:10.4324/9780203525821

Andrew, J. (2007). *Universal Human Rights: Origins and Development*. LFB Scholarly Publishing.

Beeman, R., Botein, S., & Carter, E. (2012). *Beyond Confederation: Origins of the Constitution a American National Identify*. University of North Carolina Press.

Chambers, R. (1997). *Whose Reality Counts? Putting the First Last*. London: Intermediate Technology. doi:10.3362/9781780440453

Chambers, R. (2006). *Poverty Unpercieved: Traps, Biases and Agenda*. Sussex, UK: Institute of Development Studies.

Chambers, R. (2014). *Rural Development: Putting the Last First*. London: Routledge. doi:10.4324/9781315835815

Charizeni, E. (2009). Strategies for Spatial Development in Zimbabwe. Academic Press.

Chen, J. (1999). *Chinese Law: Towards an Understanding of Chinese Law, it's Nature and Development*. London: Kluwer Law International.

Chigwata, T. (2016). Three Years into the Implementation of the Zimbabwean Constitution of 2013: Progress, Challenges, Prospects and Lessons. In C. Fombad (Ed.), *The Implementation of Modern African Constitutions: Challenges and Prospects* (pp. 78–107). Pretoria: Pretoria University Law Press.

Chikuhwa, J. (2004). *A Crisis of Governance: Zimbabwe*. New York: Algora Publishing.

Chirisa, I., & Muzenda. (2014). Environmental Rights as a Substantive Area of the Zimbabwe Constitutional Debate: Implications for Policy and Action. *Southern Peace Review Journal*, *2*, 104–121.

Compton, J. (2014). *The Evangelical Origins of the Living Constitution.* Harvard University Press.

Cornwall, A., & Nyamu-Musembi, C. (2004). Putting the Rights based Approach to Development into Perspective. *Third World Quarterly*, *28*(2), 1415–1437. doi:10.1080/0143659042000308447

Desoto, H. (2000). *The Mystery of Capital: Why Capitalism Triumps in the West and Fail Everywhere Else*. London: Black Swan.

Dzinetsa, G. (2012). *Zimbabwe's Constitutional Reform Process: Challenges and Prospects.* Institute for Justice and Reconciliation.

Edling, M. (2003). *A Revolution in Favour of Government: Origins of the U.S Constitution and the Making of the American State*. New York: Oxford University Press. doi:10.1093/0195148703.001.0001

Fai, Q., Zhang, W., & Than, F. (2015). *The Road to the Rule of Law in Modern China*. New York: Springer.

Ghai, P. (2014). Constitutions and Constitutionalism: The Tale of the 2010 Constitution. In Kenya: The Struggle for a New Constitutional Order. Zedbooks.

Goebel, A. (2005). *Gender and Land Reform: The Zimbabwean Experience*. London: McGill- Queen's University Press.

Government of Zimbabwe. (2000). *Zimbabwe's Constitution as Ammended at 19 April 2000/ Government of Zimbabwe*. Harare: Legal Resources Foundation.

Government of Zimbabwe. (2013). *Constitution of Zimbabwe, Amendment (No.20) Act 2013*. Harare: Parliament of Zimbabwe.

Government of Zimbabwe. (2015). *Zimbabwe Millennium Development Goals 2000-2015: Final Progress Report*. Harare: Ministry of Macro- Economic Planning and Investment Promotion.

Gready, P., & Ensor, J. (2005). *Re- Inventing Development?: Translating Rights-Based Approaches from Theory into Practice*. London: Zedbooks.

Griffin, S. (1996). *American Constitutionalism: From Theory to Politics*. Princeton University Press.

Griffin, S., & Griffin, M. (1996). *American Constitutionalism: From Theory to Politics*. Princeton University Press.

Grinlinton, D., & Taylor, P. (2011). *Property Rights and Sustainability: The Evolution of Property Rights to meet Ecological Challenges*. Boston: Martinus Nijhoff Publishers. doi:10.1163/ej.9789004182646.i-415

Hatchard, J., Ndulo, M., & Slinn, P. (2004). Comparative Constitutionalism and Good Governance in the Commonwealth: An Eastern and Southern African Perspective. Cambridge, UK: Cambridge University Press.

Haws, R. (2009). *The South's Role in the Creation of Bill of Rights*. University Press of Mississippi.

Hellum, A., Derman, B., Sithole, E., & Rutsate, E. (2015). Governance, Gender Equilty and the Right to Water and Sanitation in Zimbabwe: Contested Norms and Institutions in an Unstable Economic and Political Terrain. In *Water is Life: Women's Human Rights in National and local Water Governance in Southern and Eastern Africa* (pp. 300–450). Harare: Weaver Press.

Hickey, S., & Mitlin, D. (2009). *Rights Based Approaches to Develop: Exploring the Potential and Pitfalls*. Lunarian Press.

Kamete, A. (2006). Revisting Urban Housing Crisis in Zimbabwe: Some Forgotten Dimensions. *Habitat International*, *30*(4), 981–995. doi:10.1016/j.habitatint.2005.08.002

Katz, S. (2012). The American Constitution: A Revolutionary Interpretation. In R. Beeman, S. Botein, & E. Carter (Eds.), *Beyond Confederation: Origins of the Constitution and American National Identity* (pp. 23–37). London: University of North Carolina Press.

Lang, A., & Wiener, A. (2017). *Handbook on Global Constitutionalism*. Cheltenham, UK: Edward Edgar Publishing. doi:10.4337/9781783477357

Linington, G. (2001). *Constitutional Law of Zimbabwe*. Harare: Legal Resources Foundations.

Linington, G. (2012). Reflections on the Significance of Constitutions and Constitutionalism for Zimbabwe. In *Zimbabwe: Mired in Transition* (pp. 63–98). Harare: IDAZIM.

Lumumba, P., Mbondenyi, M., & Odero, S. (2014). *The Constitution of Kenya: Contemporary Readings*. Law Africa Publishing.

Madebwe, T. (2015). A Rights- based Approach to Environmental Protection: The Zimbabwean Experience. *African Human Rights Law Journal, 15*(1), 110–128. doi:10.17159/1996-2096/2015/v15n1a5

Madhuku, L. (2010). *An Introduction to Zimbabwean Law*. Harare: Weaver Press.

Martin, G., & Benjamin, I. (2014). Elites, Interest Groups and Average Citizens. *American Political Science Association, 12*(3), 564–581.

Mbondenyi, K., & Ambani, O. (2012). *New Constitution al Law of Kenya: Principles, and Human Rights*. African Law Publishing.

Mbondenyi, M., & Osogo, A. (2014). *New Constitutional Law of Kenya: Principles, Government and Human Rights*. Law African Publishing.

McGinnis, J., & Rappaport, M. (2013). *Originalim and the Good Constitution*. Harvard University Press. doi:10.4159/harvard.9780674726260

Mostert, H. (2002). *The Constitution al Protection and Regulation of Property and Its Influence on the Reforms of Private Law and Landownership in South Africa and Germany: A Comparative Analysis*. New York: Springer.

Moyo, K. (2016). Justiciable Property Rights and Postcolonial Land Reform: A Case Study of Zimbabwe. In *Justiciability of Human Rights Law* (pp. 363–388). Springer. doi:10.1007/978-3-319-24016-9_15

Moyo, W. (2014). Urban Housing Policy and Its Implications on the Low- Cost Earners of Harare Municipality, Zimbabwe. *International Journal of Asian Social Science, 4*(3), 356–365.

Muchadenyika, D. (2015). Land for Housing: A Political Resource- Reflections from Zimbabwe's Urban Areas. *Journal of Southern African Studies*, 2–19.

Murunga, Okello, & Sjogren. (2014). *Kenya: The Struggle for a New Constitutional Order.* Zed Books.

Mutondoro, F. (2018). *Housing Cooperatives, Political Symbols and Corruption in Urban Land Governance: The Case of Zimbabwe*. Academic Press.

Ndlovu, N. (2015). *Protection of Socio- economic Rights in Zimbabwe: A Critical Assessment of the Domestic Framework under the 2013 Constitution of Zimbabwe.* Diploma Verlag.

Ndulo, M. (2010). Zimbabwe's Unfinished Struggle for a Legitimate Constitutional Order. In L. Miller & L. Aucoin (Eds.), *Framing the State in Times of Transition: Case Studies in Constitution Making* (pp. 176–203). Washington, DC: United States Institute of Peace Press.

Nelson, P., & Ellen, D. (2008). *New Rights Advocacy: Changing Strategie of Development and Human Rights NGOs.* Georgetown University Press.

OCED. (2013). *Integrating Hunan Rights into Development: Donor Approaches, Experiences and Challenges.* World Bank Publications.

Olowu, D. (2009). *An Intergrative Rights-based Approach to Human Development in Africa*. Pretoria: Pretoria University Law Press.

Paul, E., & Dickman, H. (1989). *Liberty, Property and the Foundation of the American Constitution*. New York: State University of New York Press.

Phama, W., & Madi, P. (2016). The Role of Civil Society Organization and Chapter 9 Institutions in Implementing South Africa's Constitution. In C. Fombad (Ed.), The Implementation of Modern African Constitutions: Challenges and Prospects. Pretoria: Pretoria University Law Press.

Qing, J. (2013). *A Confucian Constitutional Order: How China's Ancient Past can Shape its Political Future*. Princeton University Press.

Raftopoulos, B., & Mlambo, A. (2009). *Becoming Zimbabwe: A History from Pre-Colonial Period to 2008*. Harare: Weaver Press.

Rosenfeld, M. (1994). *Constitutionalism, Identity, Difference and Legitimacy: Theoretical Perspectives*. London: Duke University Press.

Rwodzi, A., & Mubonderi, B. (2015). The Dilemma of the Patriotic Front and the Influence of the Zimbabwe-Rhodesia Government on Final 1979 Lancaster House Constitution. *International Journal of Humanities and Social Studies*, *3*(9), 215–220.

Sciulli, D. (1999). *Theory of Societal Constitutionalism: Foundations of a Non-Marxist Critical Theory*. Cambridge, UK: Cambridge University Press.

Screener. (2007). *The Language of Liberal Constitutionalism.* Cambridge University Press.

Sibanda, A. (1991). *The Lancaster House Agreement and the Post- Independence State in Zimbabwe*. Harare: Zimbabwe Institute of Development Studies.

Sithole, E., Feltoe, G., Derman, B., & Hellum, A. (2013). Rights Claiming and Rights Making in Zimbabwe: A Study of three Human Rights NGOS. In B. Andreassen & G. Crawford (Eds.), *Human Rights, Power and Civic Action: Comparative Analysis of Struggles for Rights in Developing Societies* (pp. 22–54). Routledge.

Tlakuka, P. (2004). Human Rights and Development. In P. Zelela & P. McConnaughay (Eds.), *Human Rights: The Rule of Law and Development in Africa* (pp. 109–187). University of Pennsylvania Press.

Tlakula, P. (2004). Human Rights and Development. In *Human Rights, the Rule of Law and Development in Africa* (pp. 100–119). University of Pennsylvania Press.

Uvin, P. (2004). *Human Rights and Development.* Lynne Reiner Publishers.

Vivian, J., & Maseko, G. (2018). NGOs and Sustainable Development in Zimbabwe: No Magic Bullets. *Development and Change*, *25*(1), 167–193. doi:10.1111/j.1467-7660.1994.tb00513.x

Vollan, K. (2013). *The Constitutional History and the 2013 Referendum of Zimbabwe: A Norwegian Special Report*. Norwegian Centre for Human Rights.

Zimbabwe Government. (2000). *Zimbabwe Constitution as Ammended at 19 April 2000/ Government of Zimbabwe*. Harare: Legal Resources Foundation.

Zinyama, T. (2014). Partiicpatory Budegeting in Zimbabwe: Experiences and Reflections form Harare City Council. *British Journal of Physical and Human Geography*, *1*(1), 1–44.

KEY TERMS AND DEFINITIONS

Citizen: A natural person entitled to the human rights and freedoms under the constitution.

Citizen Participation: The active engagement of citizens in development where they are empowered to own and control the development process.

Citizenship: The act of being a citizen which is acquired by birth, descent, or registration.

Constitution: The supreme law from which all other laws are made.

Empowerment: Building the capacity of citizens to determine and manage their own development usually through skills development.

Knowledge: The skill or know how.

RBD: Development that focus on human empowerment by providing the basic human rights and freedom or addressing policy concerns in these areas.

Rights: Claims or entitlement to which every juristic person is entitled to by virtue of being a citizen.

Zimbabwe: A former colony of the British located in Southern Africa.

Chapter 7
Problems Relating to the Right to Information in Turkey

Omur Aydin
Istanbul University, Turkey

ABSTRACT

Traditionally, public administration has always preferred to work behind closed doors. However, the concept of participatory democracy, which developed especially after the 1950s, encouraged citizens to participate more in the decision-making mechanisms of the state. Turkey experiences many problems in exercising the right to information, which was enacted in 2003, arising from the administration's attitudes and behaviors and also from the legislation. Foremost among these are the fact that citizens have not been made sufficiently aware of this right and that the administration is reluctant to share information. An analysis of the data and statistics in Turkey shows a rising trend in the exercise of this right by citizens between 2004-2015. However, considering the size of Turkey's population, the rate can still be deemed low. Post-2015 figures show a radical decline in citizens' exercising of the right to information. This situation may be explained by the painful process that Turkey experienced from 2015 onwards and the state of emergency implementations that followed.

INTRODUCTION

Public institutions have always tried to make public decisions in secret. On the one hand, this tendency has aimed to protect public administration from external influences and pressure group interventions, while on the other it has been a result of the public sector's habit of looking down on citizens. In the 1960s, new developments,

DOI: 10.4018/978-1-5225-8350-9.ch007

new movements and new administrative principles emerged in the field of public administration and democracy. The new understanding of public administration argued that the public sector must become more transparent when taking its decisions, be more participatory, and be based upon the principle of accountability. In the 20th century, in particular, government regulations relating to the daily lives of their citizens increased in number, and administrative actions and acts began to influence their lives more. Judicial review of the actions and acts of public institutions and organisations is one of the most important requirements of the rule of law and democratic state administration. From the 1960s onwards, legislative regulations were made in order to increase public participation in administrative processes, especially in Western democracies. In this period, international organisations also encouraged governments in this direction through the decisions, agreements and recommendations they made. The rapid transformation that took place in the fields of globalisation and communication especially after the 1990s brought about the obligation to protect personal data, and made it necessary for citizens to influence the decision-making mechanisms of their government more. In order to ensure this and create transparent administrative models based on participation, many governments started passing laws in those years that secured the right to information. International organisations such as the UN, the EU, the European Council, the World Bank and the OECD took efforts that supported these initiatives. Today, the right to information has become an indispensable part of the catalogue of constitutions addressing fundamental rights and liberties. The first legal regulation that directly formed a basis for the right to information in Turkey was the Law No. 4982 on the Right to Information of 9 October 2003. It can undoubtedly be stated that the European Union accession and harmonisation process were influential on the introduction of this law. In order to indicate the implementation of Law No. 4982 on the Right to Information, an implementation regulation was also issued on 27 April 2004. Then in 2010, the right to information became constitutional and was included in the Political Rights and Duties section of the 1982 Constitution, which is still in force.

The current study will firstly discuss the nature of the right to information and its function in a democratic society, and then describe the process of its introduction into legal texts. The next part will deal with the principles and rules necessary for the right to information to be realised. The regulations relating to the exercise of the right to information in Turkey and the procedures prescribed by those regulations will then be discussed. Finally, problematic areas relating to the right to information in Turkey and suggested solutions will be addressed.

CONCEPT AND BACKGROUND

In its simplest sense, the right to information can be defined as the right to access the information that public institutions and organisations hold in connection with their duties. By means of this right, citizens can obtain information that they are interested in or are curious about, regardless of whether such information relates to them or to public administration (Loucaides, 1995, p.5).

Since the 20th century in particular, administrative authorities have influenced, regulated and led the daily lives of citizens more. This situation increases administrative authorities' intervention in the lives of citizens and influences their rights and freedoms directly or indirectly. Judicial review of the administrative actions and acts of administrative authorities, which are so involved in daily life, is one of the most important necessities for the rule of law and for qualification as a democratic state.

The classic conception of representative democracy proposes that citizens can influence the decision-making mechanisms of the state by only voting in elections that are carried out at certain intervals. However, this opportunity for participation is limited and very ineffective in our day. Currently, therefore, a conception of participation reduced just to elections at certain intervals is insufficient. The concept of a participatory democracy considers each citizen to be an active player who continuously influences the decision-making mechanisms of the state. Modern democracy theories offer many tools that encourage individuals to participate in state administration and intervene in its decision-making mechanisms. The rapid changes and transformations produced by our epoch necessitate this interaction.

These developments in the understanding of democracy have also influenced the understanding of administration. Today, public administration and its extensions of authority must be grounded on the principles of participation, transparency and accountability. These principles open public administration to the review of citizens, help create a democratic society order, and contribute to democratic legitimacy.

The fact that administrative bodies are invested with the privilege of public power against the individual leads to a situation of inequality in state-citizen relationships and, consequently, individuals occasionally become vulnerable in the face of state interventions and regulations. Under this unequal relationship, it is very important for a democratic administration to ensure that its administrative authorities with public power privilege are restricted by law and reviewed judicially. There are various tools which can increase the democratic legitimacy of an administration and ensure the rule of law. The separation of powers, the supremacy and binding force of the constitution, guaranteeing of fundamental rights and freedoms, judicial review of the acts of legislative, executive and administrative bodies, pluralism, freedom of expression and association, freedom of the press and publication, and the concept of an open society are just a few examples. When considered in this context, the right to information is one of the main instruments for realising democracy and the rule of law. The right to information brings the administration closer to its citizens and it also enhances the trust that citizens have in the state. An increase in the functions of the state not only requires improvement of the quality of public service, but also renders the protection of citizens against the state an indispensable obligation.

In addition to the monitoring of the public sector through classical methods, it is essential that it is also monitored by its subjects. By ensuring a state's subjects are informed about the activities of the administration and that they can easily access information and documents, the trust they invest in the administration can be increased, and monitoring of the administration can be made much more efficient through their participation in the administration (Organisation for Economic Co-operation and Development [OECD], 2005, p. 2). The 1950s saw an embracement of the principles of administrative transparency and accountability as fundamental principles of public administration across the world, with international organisations publishing many standards and guides for establishing these principles.

Traditionally, public administration tended to conduct its work behind closed doors. This was because administrative work and general public service matters were perceived as internal matters of bureaucracy. Traditional bureaucratic structures tended to limit interventions from the external environment and interest groups in the decision-making processes and thus protect the interests of the public. It was believed that, in this way, wearing down of the public power would be prevented and its authority would be protected (Sengul, 2005, p. 2016). Undoubtedly, a certain extent of confidentiality is indispensable for administrative decisions to be taken and implemented properly. If, however, administrative secrecy and isolation are accepted as a rule rather than exception, citizens will be distanced from the administration, and a wall will be built between rulers and subjects. This will in effect "otherise" a state's subjects, which, in turn, will lead to displeasure in society and a breakdown of the relations between the administration and the governed. Clandestinity is a political-administrational disease. An administration with such a tendency will actually prevent the formation of a conscious public community and, by distancing people from the administration, lead citizens to miscalculate, err, and become introverted. Consequently, citizens will be incapable of understanding and questioning what is carried out for what reason and how (Kocak, 2010, p. 117).

The right to information ensures that the administration responsible for providing information is committed more to the rule of law ideal, while providing individuals with the opportunity to participate in the administration, even if partially (Inal, 2004, p. 13). Historical developments indicate that clandestinity in administration has long been dominant, but that transparency and, accordingly, the right to information, have gained importance in our day (Akillioglu, 1990, p. 806).

THE NATURE AND FUNCTION OF THE RIGHT TO INFORMATION

Many factors can be taken into consideration when identifying the place of the right to information in the classification of fundamental rights and freedoms. Although the right to information is closely related to freedom of expression (Mason, 2000, p. 225), it is also an extension and promoter of the right to improve one's corporeal and spiritual existence, the right to request the protection of one's personal data, and protection of private life. The right to information is also closely related to the political right known as the right to access. It is well known that rights and freedoms are classified in many ways in the literature on human rights. While some of these classifications take the historical process as their basis, others regard the nature of the right.

Historical classification is related to the emergence of human rights. It states that the development of human rights and the gains in this field did not occur coincidentally. They are the products of a historical struggle. In this classification of human rights based on the historical process, human rights are separated into certain stages or generations. It is possible to categorise the rights that have emerged to date as the first generation, the second generation and the third generation rights (the three generations of human rights). Such a classification not only shows a parallelism with the historical development of human rights theory and of its practice, but also facilitates a better understanding of the social dynamics in the process of these rights forming (Uygun, 2000, p. 21). The generational distinction was first suggested by Czech human rights expert Karel Vasak in 1979 (Kaboglu, 2013, p. 41). Accordingly, the first generation includes civil and political rights, the second includes socio-economical and cultural rights, and the third covers solidarity rights. From a historical perspective, these rights are the products of the era when the bourgeoisie as a social class in Medieval Europe tried to carve out a niche for itself and to force the political establishment to accept the rights it acquired. More precisely, the first generation rights were shaped in the bourgeoisie's struggle against the main elements of the old order, namely the aristocracy, the monarchy and the church.

The first generation of rights were articulated by the philosophers of the 17th and the 18th centuries and put into practice to a great extent through the American and French Revolutions. Behind the classic (civil and political) rights is the bourgeoisie. During the Age of Enlightenment when the intellectual infrastructure formed by the theories of French and English philosophers such as Jean-Jacques Rousseau and John Locke took effect, the bourgeois revolution was supported. Through the constitutionalist movement that arose in the 19th century, the bourgeoisie legalised the rights it acquired and attempted to implement them (Kaboglu, 2011, p. 226).

The first generation rights are based on liberal thinking. Aiming to restrain the state, these rights provide individuals with a private sphere which may not be intruded by the state, society or third persons. Classic rights protect individuals from the state. The most important thing that individuals need to exercise classic rights is to be free. The state's part is, mostly, to avoid interfering in individuals' private lives and to assume a passive attitude (Uygun, 2000, pp. 21-22). However while classic rights were guaranteed by constitutions during the 18th and 19th century in Europe, a great majority of people were unable to benefit from these rights due to poverty. It was understood in the course of time that ensuring people's freedom is not enough on its own to allow them to utilise their human rights. The reaction of the working class, which emerged during the Industrial Revolution, against class inequality, and the social and economic rights obtained as a result of class conflict comprise the second generation rights. A great majority of the second generation rights assign the state the task of providing a service. Their realisation, therefore, necessitates the use of huge financial resources.

The third generation of rights, on the other hand, began to manifest itself in the last half-century. They include, without restriction, the right to peace, the right to live in a disarmed world, the right to live in a healthy and balanced environment, the right to develop in economic and social terms, the right to self-determination, and the right to benefit from the joint wealth of humanity (Kaboglu, 2013, pp. 37-41). These rights are known as the "rights of solidarity" as their realisation requires solidarity of humanity, exceeding the boundaries of the state (Erdogan, 2004, p.143). The problems inflicted by scientific and technological advancements take the lead among the reasons behind the birth of the rights of solidarity. A joint effort between individuals, institutions and the state is needed for third generation rights to be realised. These rights are considered among those which can only be exercised collectively and which are steadily growing in importance in our day. The third generation rights are still in the making.

As regards the first and second generation rights, the former reflect a conflict and struggle between the bourgeoisie and the aristocracy, and the latter between the working class and the bourgeoisie, whereas third generation rights refer to solidarity rather than struggle. Examples of third generation rights include the right to self-determination, right to peace, right to development, right to humanitarian assistance, and right to live in a healthy and balanced environment.

George Jellinek is the first name that comes to mind with regard to the classification of human rights according to their qualities. Jellinek classified rights as either "status negativus", "status positivus" or "status activus" (Nowak, 2003, p. 48). In this differentiation, the position and status of an individual relative to the state and the quality of the action they expect from the state become determinant.

If the action expected from the state for fulfilling a right is non-intervention, non-obstruction and non-restriction, then this refers to a right with a negative status (status negativus). In the case of negative rights, an individual does not expect the state to perform any action; they will benefit from those rights without any contribution from the state. Positive rights are those which entail a positive intervention by the state. Thus, an individual can benefit from these rights only through state intervention. For instance, economic and social rights, such as the right to health, the right to education, social relief, etc. are considered within this category of rights. What lies behind the positive rights is the goal of eliminating social inequalities.

Active rights include the right to elect and to be elected, the right to found political parties, the right to enter public service, etc. Hence why these rights are also called "participatory rights". They can compel the state to act both positively and actively. The right to information is set forth among the political rights and duties in Turkey's Constitution.

As they are rights that are mainly asserted against the state by their very nature, human rights are often violated by the state. Although this appears paradoxical, protection of human rights is also one of the main obligations of the state. In its strict sense, the protection of human rights by the state means that the state itself must not violate and not allow the persons and groups under its control to violate these rights. Today, however, the protection of human rights is generally understood in a wider sense, and it is believed that the protection of human rights requires the state to create an economic, social and political environment favourable for human rights or for supporting those rights. Although it is acknowledged that human rights violations can also be committed by people or communities, the state is mainly responsible for protecting human rights and freedoms (Yuzbasioglu, 2000, p. 397). It is currently acknowledged that non-intervention is not the state's only obligation in the face of rights and that it also assumes a positive obligation. The European Court of Human Rights jurisprudence also provides wide coverage to the concept of positive obligation, and charges state administrations with both negative and positive obligations in order to effectively uphold rights.

In light of this basic outline of the theory of human rights, the right to information is a part of freedom of speech and, also, being a product of the individual right to self-development and political participation rights, it is situated at the point where many rights intersect (McDonagh, 2013, p. 27). From this point of view, the right to information is a multidimensional right. It is almost a prerequisite for the functioning of a democratic system. People start to participate in a country's administration thanks to the right to information. In this sense, the relationship between the right to information and freedom of speech is beyond being just a theoretical relationship. In order for individuals and interest groups to be active in a democratic society, they must be able to access information. Accordingly, individuals and groups of individuals can set the agenda (Peled and Rabin, p. 361). It must be mentioned that, in this sense, the right to information is one of the fundamental human rights. It is essential to the democratisation of totalitarian or, to say the least, undemocratic regimes based on force and violence, and to reducing the culture of secrecy. This development is also closely related to the establishment of the concept of accountability in societies. The emergence of more information on subject matters that concern society and individuals will enable a more effective exercising of the rights necessitated by personal rights and social life (Yasamis, 2004, p. 12). The basic function of the right to information is to ensure that citizens can have information on the acts and actions of the political power, which has a public nature, and that they can change and transform public policies (Hasdemir, 2014, p.111).

As mentioned above, the state has both negative and positive obligations in effectively realising this right. According to the literature relating to the right to information, various academicians consider this right within the scope of solidarity rights, which are third generation rights, among active rights within the scope of political rights (Roberts, 2001, p. 262), or among the first generation rights as a part of the freedom of thought and expression within the scope of negative rights (Sedley, 2000, p. 239, Bovens, 2002, p. 317).

In its very first session in 1946, the UN General Assembly adopted Resolution 59(I), stating: "*Freedom of information is a fundamental human right and ... the touchstone of all the freedoms to which the United Nations is consecrated.*" The 1995 Report to the UN Commission on Human Rights reads as follows: Freedom will be bereft of all effectiveness if the people have no access to information. Access to information is basic to the democratic way of life. The tendency to withhold information from the people at large is therefore to be strongly checked (United Nations Development Programme [UNDP, 2004, p. 8]).

The right to information also provides an opportunity for the embracement of democracy, the rule of law, and transparent, participatory administration.

The right to information is important for many reasons. These are the contributions it makes towards (UNDP, 2004, p. 8):

- Creating a more open and democratic society
- Reducing poverty
- Challenging corruption and enhancing transparency

The process in which the right to information gained importance was also a product of the changes of mentality in the field of public administration. In the 20th century, beginning at the end of the 1970s, criticisms of the traditional understanding of public administration intensified. The bureaucratic, ineffective, inefficient and cumbersome style of administration that builds a wall between rulers and its subjects was rapidly abandoned, and a new, transparent and accountable understanding of public administration involving participation and activity based on law and human rights was targeted instead. The classical model of public administration positioned the state as a unilateral determinant in its relationship with the governed. A state's subjects want the state to be in their service and take their demands into consideration and they criticise the slowness of bureaucracy and the deficiencies and insufficiencies of its operation. Questioning of the classic administration model brought about transparency in the administration's decision-making processes (Wall, 1996, p. 501). Openness in administration means visibility for everyone by means of participation in the administrative operation, being given permission to walk freely around the locations of the administration and to access its information and documents (Akillioglu, 1991, p. 9). In democratic thought, the ruler derives its power from the public. Political rulers obtain the authority to rule society from society and, therefore, they are accountable to society (Birkinshaw, 2006, p. 194). Besides, in a democratic order, citizens want to know how administrative activities influence them and whether their interests are taken into consideration (Richordson, 1974, p. 45).

Negative and positive obligations were mentioned above in the discussion of the tasks of the state regarding rights. Just as the demand for information is a right for an individual, providing information is a task for the state. As also stated above, the right to information basically serves two purposes. The first is to facilitate the monitoring of the administration by the people by increasing its accountability and ensuring political participation indirectly; the second is to establish a balance in the unequal relationship between the state and the individual by protecting the fundamental rights and freedoms of the individual against the state. The state is required to provide the public with access to certain information even if this is not demanded by the individual.

With the influence of globalisation in particular, international organisations have propounded the concept of governance and pioneered the breaking of the traditional understanding of public administration. Institutions like the United Nations Development Programme (UNDP), the World Bank, and the Organisation for Economic Cooperation and Development (OECD) have ensured that the concept of governance has entered the literature and have attempted to design its principles. The UNDP, in its 1997 policy paper, defined governance as: "the exercise of economic, political and administrative authority to manage a country's affairs at all levels. It comprises the mechanisms, processes and institutions through which citizens and groups articulate their interests, exercise their legal rights, meet their obligations and mediate their differences."

In 1992, the World Bank, which uses this concept most frequently and widely, defined governance as the method through which power is exercised in the management of a country's political, economic and social resources for development. Good governance is an essential complement to sound economic policies. Efficient and accountable management by the public sector and a predictable and transparent policy framework are critical to the efficiency of markets and governments, and hence to economic development. The Bank came to realise that most of the crises in developing countries are of a governance nature. Hence, the contemporary adjustment package emphasises governance issues such as transparency, accountability and judicial reform. In this context, the Bank has introduced a new way of looking at governance; good governance.

Using the concept of governance widely, international institutions generally refer to an order predominated by participation, transparency, accountability, inspection, and administrative ethics, virtue and merit (UNDP, 1997, OECD, 2005). According to the World Bank, good governance entails sound public sector management (efficiency, effectiveness and economy), accountability, exchange and free flow of information (transparency), and a legal framework for development (justice, respect for human rights and liberties).

In consideration of such aspects as these, the right to information characteristically completes the right to good governance. From a theoretical point of view, good governance means right, fair, impartial, effective, efficient and ethical operation of public administrations (Yasamis, 2004, p. 3). Thus, governance, codetermination and administrative openness are closely interrelated concepts that have emerged in parallel to the aforementioned purposes (Roberts, 2001, p. 507). In both those administrative acts that directly influence the individual and also in matters concerning the public, the essential reason for including the right to information is to improve the relationship between the administration and individuals. With the right to information, an environment of trust will form between the administration and the governed, and the relationship between them will gain a democratic quality. If citizens do not have any information about or never participate in the acts and actions of the administration, they will eventually need to question their own legal security. One of the main ways of preventing this is by establishing a bridge between the citizen and the administration (Colak, 2005, pp. 32-33). In the event that the administration fulfils its duty of providing information, that is, regularly informs the public about public services before taking decisions, without waiting for a request from its citizens (Eken, 2005, p. 128), this will also contribute to the strengthening of that connection. The first function of the right to information is to ensure transparency, and its second function is to protect individuals against the state. In this context, it can be said that the right to information is a whole consisting of three rights: the right to request the protection of one's personal data, the right to access official data, and the right to be informed on matters involving public benefit (Soykan, 2007, p.73).

LEGALISATION OF THE RIGHT TO INFORMATION

By its nature, the right to information is closely related to the right of petition. The right of petition has a wider content than, and also includes, the right to information. This right enables citizens to submit their wishes, requests, and complaints about themselves or about the public sector to the parliament or to public authorities. In this sense, the right of petition is a precursor and supporter of the right to information. The right of petition was legalised before the right to information. It is one of the most fundamental civil and political rights of citizens. Although it is not exactly known when it originally emerged but the place of the right of petition in positive law is traced to Magna Carta of 1215. The Commission for Objections and Complains established by a resolution of the House of Commons in England in 1571 is one of the first implementations of the right of petition. As a constitutional right, however, the right of petition took place in the French Constitution of 1791 for the first time. With the spread of representative democracy and the steadily increasing importance of individuality, this right, initially accorded only to certain groups, was extended so as to include all individuals in the 19th and 20th centuries (Hiz and Yuksel, 2004, p.15).

The right to information gained legal quality for the first time in Sweden. The Freedom of the Press Act of 1766, which was passed by the Swedish Parliament in 1766, also regulated the right to information for the first time. Subsequently, the French Declaration of the Rights of the Man and of the Citizen of 1789 entitled citizens to access budget related information, a similar right was given in the Netherlands in 1795, and then a Colombian law on political and local association accorded the right to request information possessed by the government in 1888.

In the United States of America, the Freedom of Information Act passed in 1966 and the Sunshine Act of 1974-1976 were the first legal arrangements in this field. Similarly, the concept of access to information began to gain importance in the UK in the beginning of the 1990s and became the subject of a legal arrangement in 2000 (Koksal, 2004, pp. 7-8). In France, three laws have been enacted to ensure transparency in public administration. These include the Law on Information Technology, Data Files and Civil Liberties dated 06.01.1978, the General Legislation on Access to Administrative Documents dated 17.07.1978, and the Law on Motivation of Administrative Acts and Improving Relations between the Administration and the Public dated 11.07.1979 (Gursel, 1998, p. 283).

In Denmark and Norway, laws on the procedure for access to information were issued in 1970. Denmark reviewed and revised its law in 1985. In France, the Administrative Procedure Act took effect in 1978, and another law on the respect for the private lives of individuals was passed in the same year. In the Netherlands, the Law on Access to Information of 1978 was revised in 1991. In Canada, laws on access to information and respect for the private lives of individuals were passed in 1982. Australia's law on access to information was made in 1982. After the end of the Cold War in the beginning of the 1990s, the former Eastern Bloc countries successively introduced laws on access to information.

The introduction of the right to information into the legal texts of nations became possible with the global dissemination of the principle of administrative transparency or openness that occurred in the aftermath of World War II (Kilinc, 2009). The 1990s saw an increase in the value attributed to the right to information, and many countries made legal and constitutional regulations on the subject (McDonagh, 2013, p. 25). Some countries recognised this right with decrees having the force of law, while others incorporated it into their constitutions.

The right to information also found a place in international documents. It has been included in the works of such international institutions as the UN, the European Council, the OECD, and the EU, and member states are encouraged to effectively uphold this right.

The Universal Declaration of Human Rights Article 19, which was declared by the United Nations General Assembly on 10 December 1948, described the right to information in the following way:

Everyone has the right to freedom of opinion and expression; this right includes freedom to hold opinions without interference and to seek, receive and impart information and ideas through any media and regardless of frontiers.

Also in Article 19 of the International Covenant on Civil and Political Rights, passed again by the UN in 1966, the right to information was set forth as a fundamental right, and the limitations that can be imposed on it were stated. The article stipulates:

Everyone shall have the right to freedom of expression; this right shall include freedom to seek, receive and impart information and ideas of all kinds, regardless of frontiers, either orally, in writing or in print, in the form of art, or through any other media of his choice.

International human rights organisations put the following principles forth in their evaluations on the right to information regulated in Article 19 of the International Covenant on Civil and Political Rights (Singh, 2014, p. 89, Article 19, 1999):

Maximum disclosure: Freedom of information legislation should be guided by the principle of maximum disclosure.

Obligation to publish: Public bodies should be under an obligation to publish key information.

Promotion of open government: Public bodies must actively promote open government.

Limited scope of exceptions: Exceptions should be clearly and narrowly drawn and subject to strict "harm" and "public interest" tests.

Processes to facilitate access: Requests for information should be processed rapidly and fairly and an independent review of any refusals should be available.

Costs: Individuals should not be deterred from making requests for information by excessive costs.

Open meetings: Meetings of public bodies should be open to the public.

Disclosure takes precedence: Laws which are inconsistent with the principle of maximum disclosure should be amended or repealed.

Protection for whistleblowers: Individuals who release information on wrongdoing – whistleblowers – must be protected.

These principles, which were set forth as a product of a joint effort, constitute a guide for governments on an effective law on access to information and on effective utilisation of the right to information.

Article 10 of the European Convention on Human Rights also regulates and guarantees freedom of speech and the right to information. The convention also explained in which situations and for what reasons this right may be limited. Article 10 of the Convention contains the following provision:

Everyone has the right to freedom of expression. This right shall include freedom to hold opinions and to receive and impart information and ideas without interference by public authority and regardless of frontiers.

In its established case law, the European Court of Human Rights also attributed a special value to freedom of expression and the right to information for the realisation of a democratic society, and has emphasised in many decisions it has made to date that the state is under negative and positive obligations to fulfil this right.

The recommendation entitled "Recommendation No. R (81)19 of the Committee of Ministers to member states on the access to information held by public authorities" made by the Committee of Ministers of the Council of Europe in 1981 highlighted that access to information is a right: "Everyone within the jurisdiction of a member state shall have the right to obtain, on request, information held by the public authorities other than legislative bodies and judicial authorities."

The Committee of Ministers of the Council of Europe made the following statement in its recommendation entitled "Recommendation of the Committee of Ministers to Member States on Access to Official Documents" (Council of Europe [COE], 2002) dated 21 February 2002: "Considering the importance in a pluralistic, democratic society of transparency of public administration and of the ready availability of information on issues of public interest, considering that wide access to official documents, on a basis of equality and in accordance with clear rules:

- Allows the public to have an adequate view of, and to form a critical opinion on, the state of the society in which they live and on the authorities that govern them, whilst encouraging informed participation by the public in matters of common interest;
- Fosters the efficiency and effectiveness of administrations and helps maintain their integrity by avoiding the risk of corruption;
- Contributes to affirming the legitimacy of administrations as public services and to strengthening the public's confidence in public authorities.

Considering therefore that the utmost endeavour should be made by member states to ensure availability to the public of information contained in official documents, subject to the protection of other rights and legitimate interests;

Stressing that the principles set out hereafter constitute a minimum standard, and that they should be understood without prejudice to those domestic laws and regulations which already recognise a wider right of access to official documents;

Considering that, whereas this instrument concentrates on requests by individuals for access to official documents, public authorities should commit themselves to conducting an active communication policy, with the aim of making available to the public any information which is deemed useful in a transparent democratic society, recommends the governments of member states to be guided in their law and practice by the principles set out in this recommendation."

As also suggested in the recommendation by the Committee of Ministers of the Council of Europe, in a pluralist and democratic society, the importance of a transparent administration and of public accessibility of the information on matters that concern the public steadily increases. The individual right to access official documents must be guaranteed in law and constitution in order to practice the principle of equality under better conditions, diminish the culture of secrecy, and establish openness, transparency and accountability in state administration.

Similarly, the right to information is included in Articles 11 and 41 in the Charter of Fundamental Rights of the European Union. Article 11 of the Charter contains the following provision:

Everyone has the right to freedom of expression. This right shall include freedom to hold opinions and to receive and impart information and ideas without interference by public authority and regardless of frontiers.

In Article 41 of the Charter, the following statement was made under the heading of the Right to Good Administration:

Every person has the right to have his or her affairs handled impartially, fairly and within a reasonable time by the institutions and bodies of the Union. This right includes: the right of every person to be heard, before any individual measure which would affect him or her adversely is taken; the right of every person to have access to his or her file, while respecting the legitimate interests of confidentiality and of professional and business secrecy; the obligation of the administration to give reasons for its decisions.

Another important work on this matter is the Aarhus Convention on Access to Information, Public Participation in Decision-Making and Access to Justice in Environmental Matters. This convention was signed in 1998. Article 3 of the Convention which covers environmental topics requires the parties to make all the legal arrangements needed by individuals for accessing environmental information, participating in decision-making, and accessing justice.

As can be seen, international conventions have recognised the right to information as a prerequisite for a democratic and transparent administration and have regulated it mostly along with freedom of expression. International regulations have undoubtedly had a significant influence on the legalisation of the right to information across the world. The fact that such rights have been regulated in the international field has had a supporting and driving effect on individual countries as well.

IMPLEMENTATIONS OF THE RIGHT TO INFORMATION IN TURKEY

The first legal regulation that directly formed a basis for the right to information in Turkey was the Law No. 4982 on the Right to Information of 9 October 2003. Although the Turkish law no. 4982 is the first legal regulation on the right to information, the efforts to legalise this right began in the mid-1990s. In that period, corruption allegations were a significant item of agenda in the political arena. In order to overcome the emerging crisis of political legitimacy, the ruling party of the time emphasised the discourses of transparent government, accountable administration, and democratization, and initiated the efforts for legislation on the right to information. However, these efforts did not fruit in those years (Hasdemir, 2014, p.117). It can be said that the EU Accession and Harmonisation process was undoubtedly influential in the enactment of the Law on the Right to Information in 2003.

The right of petition, which is considered to be the precursor of the right to information, was enacted much earlier in Turkey. The first legal document covering this right in Turkey is the Constitution of 1876. It governed the right of petition in its Article 14. This right is addressed in Article 82 of the Constitution of 1924, and in article 62 in the 4th section entitled "Political Rights and Duties" of the Constitution of 1961. As the Constitution of 1961 involved a more integrative approach on fundamental rights and freedoms compared to previous constitutions, it included many rights supporting the right of petition. The Constitution of 1982 governed the right of petition in article 74 in the section entitled "Political Rights and Duties". With the constitutional amendment made on 7 May 2010, the Right to Information was included in the Constitution, and the title of Article 74 was changed to "Right of petition, right to information and appeal to the Ombudsperson". The right to information was constitutionalised in this way, and it became more highlighted. It is important that the Constitution governed the right to information together with the right of petition. The right of petition is defined as the right of individuals to make written applications to competent authorities and to the Grand National Assembly of Turkey on their requests and complaints about themselves or the public sector. Although the right of petition partially fulfils the freedom of information of individuals, it is not as effective as the right to information in regard to this matter (Aras and Altinok, 2009, p.108). The right to information functions in a narrower and more specific context than the right of petition. The right to information only contains the right to access the information and documents held by public institutions and organisations. In the context of the right of petition, however, submission of requests and complaints is also involved. Thus, the right to information considers "to know" as a right rather than a need. This situation that does not stipulate an "interest requirement" is called a transition from the "need to know" principle, to the "right to know" principle (Hasdemir, 2016, p.68), and extends the scope of the beneficiaries of this right. For instance, in the first years of the implementation of the Law on the Right to Information, the applications made by trade associations to public institutions had been rejected due to the lack of interest violation. In the face of such rulings, trade associations applied to administrative justice, and the latter deemed those rulings contrary to law, claiming that they conflict with the principle of democratic and transparent management aimed by the Law on the Right to Information, and also with the principles of equality, impartiality, and openness (Aras and Altinok, 2009, p.110). In Article 74 of the Constitution entitled, "Right of petition, right to information and appeal to the ombudsperson", this right was set forth as below:

Citizens and foreigners resident in Turkey, with the condition of observing the principle of reciprocity, have the right to apply in writing to the competent authorities and to the Grand National Assembly of Turkey with regard to the requests and complaints concerning themselves or the public. The result of the application concerning himself/herself shall be made known to the petitioner in writing without delay. Everyone has the right to obtain information and appeal to the ombudsperson.

The following part of this study will address the content and the implementation of the legislation that covers the right to information in Turkey, and the related problem areas.

It can be argued that there are three main texts which set out the framework of the right to information in Turkey. Article 74 of the 1982 Constitution includes a provision on the right to information. Provisions relating to the content, essential uses, and limits of this right are given in Law No. 4982 on the Right to Information (2003) and in the implementation regulation dated 27 April 2004 demonstrating its implementation.

Article 1 of the Law on the Right to Information states the aim of this law as following:

The object of this law is to regulate the procedure and the basis of the right to information according to the principles of equality, impartiality and openness that are the necessities of a democratic and transparent government.

Meanwhile, the scope of the law is explained thus: "This law is applied to the activities of the public institutions and agencies and the professional organisations which qualify as public institutions."

The law defines the information and documents that can be a subject of the right to information in the following way:

Every kind of data that is within the scope of this law and is included in the records of the institutions. Any written, printed or copied file, document, book, journal, brochure, etude, letter, software, instruction, sketch, plan, film, photograph, tape and video cassette, map of the institutions and the information, news and other data recorded and saved in electronic format that is within the scope of this law.

Accordingly, the information and documents that may be requested are described as below: The application for access to information should relate to the information or the document that the institutions and agencies which are 15 applied possess or should possess due to their tasks and activities. The institutions and agencies may turn down the applications for any information or document that require a separate or special work, research, examination or analysis. Where the requested information or the document is at an institution other than the one that is applied, the petition shall be sent to the relevant institution and the applicant shall be notified accordingly.

It can be seen in the above regulation that public institutions and organisations may refuse those applications for the kind of information or documents which can only be provided as a result of separate or special work, research, examination or analysis. Requests for access to information are certain to increase the work load of the administration. However, concepts such as "special work" or "analysis", as mentioned here, can cause some applications to be easily considered under this scope and rejected.

According to the law, applications for access to information must be made through a petition that includes the name, surname, residence or work address of the applicant and their signature; where the applicant is a company, its title and address, and the signature of the authorised person together with a certificate of authorisation, to the institution that possesses the information or the document. The application can be made also through electronic or other types of communication tools, provided that the identity and the signature of the applicant can be legally determined.

Pursuant to Article 10 of the Regulation on the Right to Information, applications in the electronic environment or with other means of communication are also possible. Applications made by real persons applying for access to information through electronic mail are made by completing the form given in the annex with name-surname, residence or business address and Turkish ID number, in order to confirm their identity, and emailing this to the information unit of the institution that possesses the information or document.

Applications made by legal entities applying for access to information through electronic mail are made by completing the form given in the annex with the title and registered address and the signature of the authorised person, together with a certificate of authorisation and Turkish ID number, and emailing this to the information unit of the institution that possesses the information or document.

Institutions and agencies are obliged to provide the requested information within 15 working days. However, where the requested information or document is to be obtained from another unit within the applied institution and agency, or it is necessary to receive the opinion of another institution, or if the scope of the application pertains to more than one institution, access shall be provided within 30 working days. In this case, the applicant shall be notified in writing of the extension and the reasons for it within 15 working days. The 15 working day time limit shall be suspended at the time when the applicant is notified of the cost for the access to the information or the document stated in Article 10. The applicant shall be considered to have withdrawn the application unless the cost is paid within the next 15 working days. Institutions and agencies notify applicants in writing, or inform them in electronic format of the result of their applications regarding access to information. If the application is rejected, the applicant shall be notified of the reasons and the appeal mechanism against the decision.

An applicant whose application for access to information is rejected may appeal to the Board before appealing for judicial review within 15 days, starting from the official notification. The Board shall come to a decision within 30 days. Institutions and agencies are obliged to provide every kind of information and document that is required by the Board within 15 days.

As can be seen, the Law has also formed an institution to which the applicants whose request for access to information is refused can file their objections. Working for this purpose, the Board of Review of Access to Information has been charged with evaluating the objections made by applicants.

The Board is composed of nine members. The Council of Ministers appoint two members from the four candidates nominated by the General Board of the Court of Appeals and the Council of State from their members; three members from scholars of criminal, constitutional and administrative law who bear the title of professor or associate professor; one member among two candidates who are qualified to be elected as Chief of Bar and are nominated by the Turkish Bar Association; two members who have been serving as general directors; and a ninth member from the judges in service of the Ministry of Justice as recommended by the Minister.

Article 29 of the Law on the Right to Information states that disciplinary action will be taken against public officials committing negligence, fault, or deliberate misconduct in the implementation of the law. When this provision is evaluated with the provision of Article 5 stating, "Public institutions are required to apply administrative and technical measures to provide every kind of information and document, with the exceptions set out in this law, to provide the information for applicants; and to review and decide on the applications for access information promptly, effectively and correctly", it becomes obvious that public administration has been charged with positive obligations to put this right into practice effectively.

It follows that violating behaviours will be deemed a service failure, and lead to action for damage against the relevant administration.

Article 29 of the Law on the Right to Information states that disciplinary action will be taken against public officials committing negligence, fault, or deliberate misconduct in the implementation of the law. When this provision is evaluated with the provision of Article 5 stating, "Public institutions are required to apply administrative and technical measures to provide every kind of information and document, with the exceptions set out in this law, to provide the information for applicants; and to review and decide on the applications for access information promptly, effectively and correctly", it becomes obvious that public administration has been charged with positive obligations to put this right into practice effectively. It follows that violating behaviours will be deemed a service failure, and lead to action for damage against the relevant administration.

When all these arrangements are taken into consideration, it can be concluded that these legal provisions are in compliance with international norms to a great extent (Yasamis, 2004b, p. 61). However, as for the limitations and exceptions in the implementation of the right to information, many problems arise. As a matter of fact, many EU progress reports and European Court of Human Rights and European Council recommendation reports on Turkey clearly indicate that the problems regarding human rights in Turkey are not rooted in the legislation but in the implementation.

There can also be situations in which the disclosure of the information and documents held by the administration is not desired for a variety of reasons. In such situations, a delicate balance should be established between the individual interest in obtaining administrative information and documents and the public interest in the administration's withholding of the same. That is to say, in certain situations, public interest may necessitate that certain limitations be imposed on the right to information, provided that the aforementioned balance is observed (Doner, 2010, pp. 105-106).

Articles 15-27 of the Law on the Right to Information are allocated to exceptions of the right to information. These exceptions that are set forth by the Law can be listed as follows:

- Transactions that are not subject to judicial review- Transactions that are not subject to judicial review, those that affect the working life and professional honour of persons, are within the scope of this law. The right to information does not eliminate the restriction regarding the judicial review of the transaction.
- Information and documents pertaining to state secrets- Information and documents which qualify as state secrets, whose disclosure would clearly

cause harm to the security of the state, foreign affairs, national defence or national security, fall outside the scope of the right to information provided herein.

- Information and documents pertaining to economical interests of the state- Information or documents whose disclosure causes harm to the economical interests of the state or will cause unfair competition or enrichment fall outside of the scope of this law.
- Information and documents pertaining to state intelligence - Information and documents regarding the duties and activities of civil and military intelligence units fall outside of the scope of this law. However information and documents that affect the professional honour and working life of persons are within the scope of the right to information.
- Information and documents pertaining to administrative investigation- Information or documents related to an administrative investigation being conducted by the administrative authorities and which will; a) clearly violate the right to privacy of the individuals, b) endanger the security or the life of the individuals or the officials that are carrying out the investigation, c) jeopardise the security of the investigation, d) disclose the source of the information which needs to be kept secret, or endanger the procurement of similar information in connection with the investigation, fall outside of the scope of this law.
- Information or documents pertaining to judicial investigation and prosecution- Information or documents whose disclosure or untimely disclosure will a) give rise to a criminal offence, b) endanger prevention and investigation of the crime or endanger the legal procedure for the detention and the prosecution of the criminals, c) obstruct the proper operation of judicial duty, d) violate the right to fair trial of a defendant in a pending case, fall outside of the scope of this law.
- Privacy of individuals- With the proviso that the consent of the concerned individual has been received, information and documents that will unjustly interfere with the health records, private and family life, honour and dignity, and the economic and professional interests of an individual, fall outside of the scope of the right to information.
- Privacy of communication - Information and documents that violate the privacy of communication fall outside of the scope of this law.
- Trade secrets article - Information and documents that qualify as commercial secrets in law and commercial and financial information that is obtained by institutions from natural or legal persons on the condition of being kept secret fall outside of the scope of this law.
- Intellectual property (works of art and science)

- Internal opinions, information notes and recommendations
- Requests for recommendation and opinions

As can be seen, many exceptions are considered regarding the right to information in Turkey. These exceptions essentially conform both to Article 10 of the European Convention on Human Rights, which regulates freedom of expression, and also to Article 19 of the United Nations Covenant on Civil and Political Rights.

The principles set forth in the "Recommendation of the Committee of Ministers to member states on access to official documents", which was passed by the Committee of Ministers of the Council of Europe on 21 February 2002, allow one to carry out more specific evaluations and comparisons with regards to the subject at hand. The recommendation also explains the situations in which access to documents may be limited. The basic limitations described in the recommendation are listed as follows:

- National security, defence and international relations
- Public safety
- The prevention, investigation and prosecution of criminal activities
- Privacy and other legitimate private interests
- Commercial and other economic interests, be they private or public
- The equality of parties concerning court proceedings; nature
- Inspection, control and supervision by public authorities
- The economic, monetary and exchange rate policies of the state
- The confidentiality of deliberations within or between public authorities during the internal preparation of a matter

It can thus be seen that the limitations contained in the Law on the Right to Information in Turkey appear in a similar form in the recommendation of the Committee. In addition to describing the reasons for such limitations, however, the Committee also mentioned some principles to be considered when imposing these limitations. Accordingly, member states may limit the right of access to official documents. Limitations should be set down precisely in law, be necessary in a democratic society, and be proportionate to the aim of protecting.

These principles of limitation are also set forth in Article 13 of the Turkish Constitution of 1982. However, the Turkish authorities' margin of appreciation for the interpretation and implementation of these principles has been questioned and found to be unacceptable. Thus, in many individual applications made against Turkey, the European Court of Human Rights has ruled against Turkey and identified many violations of rights.

The European Council defines a democratic society as being based on pluralism and open-mindedness. In this framework, it assigns a qualified value to freedom of expression. If the criteria of a democratic society mentioned here are not adopted by nation states, the European Court of Human Rights will rule violations of right.

In Turkey, a mechanism is provided for filing an objection with the Board of Review of Access to Information in the case an information request is rejected. In the initial form of the Law No. 4982, this Board has been established only to review those objections made by individuals in the case their information requests are rejected by public institutions that see the requested information within the scope of "State secret", or "likely to damage the economic interests of the country". In this sense, the Board had been structured as an office that evaluates the status of secrecy. In the course of time, however, the drawbacks brought by limiting the Board's scope of authority because of these two reasons were understood and, with an amendment made with the Law No. 5432, dated 17 November 2005, the Board became a higher authority in the capacity of reviewing objections made for any information request rejected partially or completely (Hasdemir, 2014, p.128).

Since the day of its establishment, the Board of Review of Access to Information has assumed a significant role for the development of the right to information in Turkey. With the principles and practices it has formed in the course of years, the Board has expanded the scope of the right to information, and assumed an important role, transforming the negative attitude of public institutions in the face of information requests, and filling legislation-related gaps. Administrative organisations mostly tend to reject to provide the information requested by considering them within the scope of the exceptions stipulated in the law. The Board of Review of Access to Information, however, has been taking efforts to overcome this attitude within the context of the objections it receives. A significant part of the applications made especially in the first years of the implementation of the Law on the Right to Information related to the personal rights and records of public officials. Public institutions had rejected such information requests coming from public officials by considering these requests within the scope of "Institutions' Internal Regulations", which is one of the exceptions explained in Article 25 of the law. The Board of Review of Access to Information has developed a practice about the applications of objection it receives. Accordingly, the information and documents held by public institutions about their own personnel must be kept confidential against third persons but if such information and documents have a quality that can influence the professional life and dignity of a given person, then they must be open to that person (The Board of Review of Access to Information, 2007/1017).

In another instance, a person who was dismissed from the Specialist Gendarmerie School, which operated under the Ministry of Internal Affairs, requested to obtain the information and documents which related to his dismissal, but this request was rejected within the scope of "The Information and Documents Pertaining the State Secrets" exception contained in Article 29 of the law. However, stating that the nature of the subject matter information and documents affected the professional life and dignity of the person, the Board of Review of Access to Information ruled the information request to be fulfilled (The Board of Review of Access to Information, 2004/104). Similar examples include a jury report that formed the basis for a person's appointment to a teaching staff, an associate professorship list, the questions and the answer key of an OSYM (Student Selection and Placement Centre) exam, and a dismissal resolution of the Turkish Supreme Military Council (The Board of Review of Access to Information, 2004/140, 2004/77, 2010/2122). With the decisions it made in many similar examples, the Board contributed to the improvement of the right to information.

With the contribution of the Board of Review of Access to Information, which works under the Presidency of the Grand National Assembly of Turkey, an annual statistical report is issued within the scope of the right to information in Turkey. These reports allow one to assess the exercise of the right to information in Turkey and the related problem areas. The Right to Information Assessment Board files the statistical reports that it draws up annually to the Presidency of the Grand National Assembly of Turkey (TBMM), and these reports are announced to the public through the TBMM (The Grand National Assembly of Turkey Reports, 2004-2017).

By analysing the reports published by the Presidency of the TBMM between 2004-2008, which reveal details about the requests for access to information made to public institutions and organisations, it is possible to make some observations. According to the reports, the number of applications for access to information made to public institutions and organisations in 2004 was low, which is normal considering that the law was only introduced in that year. In 2004, the number of applications requesting access to information was 385,557 and the number of applications accepted and given access to information or documents was 347,959, while the number of applications requesting access to information in 2008 rose to 1,099,133. In 2008, the number of applications accepted and given access to information or documents was 947,428. Thus, the number of applications steadily increased from 2004 to 2008. These figures show that more than 85% of the applications received an affirmative reply. It should be emphasised that the rate of increase in the number of applications was 62% from 2004, the first year of application, to 2005.

As for the statistics between 2009-2012, there was again an upward trend from 2009; the number of applications increased from 1,091,589 in 2009 to 2,092,463 in 2012. It is observed that the rate of applications given access to information or documents again was more than 80% between these years. According to the statistics, although the upward trend between the years has occasionally decreased, there has been a regular increase in the number of applications. Considering that Turkey's population exceeds 80 million people, the overall number of applications is not very high, but the number of citizens benefiting from the right to information steadily increased year on year.

The 2013 report shows that the total number of applications in 2013 increased by about 33% when compared with 2012. The escalating trend of applications made to public institutions and organisations within the scope of Law No. 4982 on the Right to Information also continued in 2014. In this context, the total number of applications in 2014 increased by about 18% compared to the previous year. Again in 2014, the rate at which public institutions and organisations accepted requests for access to information increased. Thus, it is observed that as many as 95% of the applications made in 2014 were responded to positively.

As it can be seen, the number of applications requesting access to information steadily increased until 2014. In 2015, however, a radical change occurred and the number of applications declined for the first time. A total of 1,190,325 applications for access to information were made in this year. Out of these applications, 1,019,466 were accepted. Thus, about 85.6% of all applications made in 2015 to public institutions and organisations were replied to positively. Accordingly, the total number of applications made in 2015 decreased by 36% compared with the previous year. In 2015, the rate at which public institutions and organisations fulfilled the requests for access to information was also lower than in 2014.

A total of 1,552,721 access to information requests were made in 2016. Of these, 1,308,105 were accepted. This means that about 84.2% of the total number of applications received a positive answer from public institutions and organisations. Compared to 2015, applications increased in 2016. The total number of applications made in 2016 increased by about 23% compared with the previous year. In 2016, a decrease was seen in the acceptance of requests for access to information by public institutions and organisations. However, as many as 84.2% of applications received a positive response in this year. (This rate was 87.9% in 2004, 86.5% in 2005, 86.4% in 2006, 79.9% in 2007, 86.2% in 2008, 86.8% in 2009, 81.2% in 2010, 87.5% in 2011, 92% in 2012, 90% in 2013, 95% in 2014 and 85.6% in 2015).

A total of 1,806,958 applications were made in 2017. Of these, 1,459,234 received a positive response. Thus, public institutions and organisations accepted about 81% of all applications in this year. There was a higher number of applications made in 2017 than in 2016. The total number of applications made in 2016 grew by about 16% compared to the previous year.

A radical decline can be observed in the number of applications for access to information made from 2015-2017 compared with those from 2008-2014. Numbering 3,298,465 in 2014, applications suddenly fell to 1,190,325 in 2015, which corresponds to a decrease of 36%. It is observed that the number of applications made in 2015, 2016 and 2017 never reached the figures seen before 2014. However, public institutions and organisations have always responded positively to over 80% of applications. It can be argued that various factors, such as the political sparring and the tense environment which arose in Turkey in 2014, the attempted coup in 2016, and the state of emergency which was subsequently declared and which still continues, and the adverse developments in Turkey's relationship with the EU, all contributed significantly to this downward trend and that citizens assumed a passive attitude in the spheres of the right to legal remedies, freedom of expression and participation in political life.

Those whose information requests are rejected by public institutions can file an objection with the Board of Review of Access to Information, and then resort to administrative justice. An examination of the report entitled "Remedies against Rejected Information Requests", which the Board of Review of Access to Information declared to the public through the Grand National Assembly of Turkey (The Grand National Assembly of Turkey [TBMM] Reports, 2013 and 2017), it is possible to obtain some significant data. For example, in 2005, only 1120 of the 54,235 information requests rejected by public institutions became the subject of an objection filed with the Board of Review of Access to Information, and 1059 of these were rejected by the Board. In 2008, out of the 81,466 information requests rejected by public institutions, 1305 became the subject of an objection filed with the Board. In 2011, only 1569 of the 87,500 information requests rejected by public institutions became the subject of such an objection. In 2005, only 2109 of the 84,115 information requests rejected by public institutions became the subject of an objection filed with the Board. In 2017, only 2020 of the 115,941 information requests rejected by public institutions became the subject of such an objection, and 1534 of these were rejected by the Board. According to these statistics, the annual average of the objections filed with the Board upon a rejection by public institutions is only 2 percent. This situation is an indication of the citizens' shyness about their constitutional right to legal remedies.

In 2013, to mark the 10th anniversary of the recognition of the right to information in Turkey, the TBMM's Department of Media, Publications and Public Relations organised a workshop which included analyses and assessments to identify the failing aspects of the system, establish communication between the receivers and providers of the access to information service, share good practice examples, and ensure integrity of implementation. In the "Workshop on the Right to Information in its 10th Year" (TBMM, 2013) efforts were made to identify the problem areas relating to the exercise of the right to information in Turkey. The assessments and suggested solutions to these problems can be said to essentially focus on three areas. Some of the problems derive from the legal regulations on the right to information, some from the attitude of the administration, and some from citizens' perceptions.

The main problem deriving from the legislation and from the attitudes of the administration is identified as the fact that no definition or listing of the administrative institutions from which information can be requested is made in the Law on the Right to Information. Therefore, citizens may hesitate as to whether the organisation they want to appeal to for access to information is a public organisation. In this context, it was proposed to make a clear definition of which institutions are public institutions and organisations and show, as an appendix to the law, an open list of all the institutions and organisations that fall within the scope of the law.

Another problem is derived from the fact that there are no definitions for the concepts of "information", "document", "state secret", "commercial secret", "degrees of classified information", "denunciation", "complaint" and "suggestion" in the Law on the Right to Information. This deficiency leads to requests for access to information being rejected by public administrations as they interpret them as exceptional conditions stipulated in the law. Thus applications become subject to the arbitrariness of administrative institutions. Similarly, expressions such as "classified information" or "confidential information" appear to be open to arbitrary interpretation and to being considered as exceptions. The provision of Article 7 of Law No. 4982 on the Right to Information, which stipulates that "Institutions may turn down applications for any information or document that requires separate or special work, research, examination or analysis", is one of the most common reasons for rejections in practice. The reason for rejection set forth in this provision is occasionally exploited and misused in order to avoid having to respond to applications. To solve these problems it is necessary that special working groups be created, the efficiency of the Right to Information Assessment Board be improved and, in the case of public interest, information be made open to the public by restricting the principle of secrecy.

The main problem deriving from the organisation of the administration is the insufficient number of coordination units responsible for responding to applications for access to information within the structure of the administrative organisation. Also the fact that no specialist civil servants are employed in this area prevents an effective and efficient operation of these units. The real addressees for requests for access to information are the main service units. However, these units lack a systematic organisation for enabling the exercise of the right to information, and they have no mandatory in-service training for improving the competencies of their employees.

Another problem rooted in the administration is that petitions will be sent to another institution or organisation if the requested information or document is not available. The problem derives from the fact that it is not always possible to know which public organisation or institution holds the requested information or documents.

From their own point of view, citizens have stated that the law does not function properly because their applications are not answered (a) at all, or (b) sufficiently or satisfactorily, or (c) accurately.

The main problem deriving from the citizens themselves is that they do not know exactly what falls within the scope of the right to information, and that they submit all of their demands and complaints to the administration through this channel. This means extra time and cost for the administration, leading to waste of time and labour. Additionally, examples of misuse of this right are also encountered.

Some of the problems relating to the right to information originate from the exercisers of this right. In hostile or harassment cases, some persons happen to make numerous or repeated requests for access to information so as to impede the operation of the administration and, consequently, sabotage the public interest. Especially in the case of local and small administrations who have a limited number of staff, this situation causes the employees to suspend their essential tasks and spend a significant part of their working time on such applications, which prevents those citizens who wish to exercise their right to information or petition in goodwill from receiving the necessary attention, and leads to public services being interrupted due to the waste of time and resources resulting from this harassment.

Holding citizens accountable in the face of such situations, administrative officials have reported that information requests are often made for certain information which can easily be found in official websites, that citizens exploit the right to information mechanism even for matters which should actually be the subject of complaint and denunciation mechanisms, that sometimes the right to information is misused, that institutions are under heavy pressure from the load of information requests, and that, therefore, they fail to properly fulfil all requests.

As it can be seen, when it comes to the failure to efficiently implement the right to information, there are problems deriving from both the administration and its citizens. The leading problem originating from the administration in the exercise of the right to information is that officials tend to categorise the information and documents requested from them as exceptions. The main reason for this situation is the fact that the decision about where "confidentiality" begins and ends is left to the discretion of the administration to a great extent. In the doctrine, although no definition acceptable to all has been made for it yet, a "state secret" refers to the state's information and documents that must be kept secret (Hafizogullari, 2012, pp. 173-174). In this sense, a state secret is defined as information documents which, if made public, would clearly threaten or damage state security, foreign affairs, national defence, and national security (Kaya, 2005, p. 49). The concept of state secret is covered extensively by Turkish Criminal Code No. 5237. The concept is very wide and open-ended. For a piece of information to be considered a "state secret", it must have a legal basis and be determined duly. Nevertheless, administrative institutions occasionally evade transparency under the pretext of the concept of state secret. In order to prevent this arbitrariness, the elements used to define a state secret must primarily be identified. Moreover, it would be right for an independent organ or even a court to inspect, when appropriate, whether some information that the state claims to be a "secret" is actually a secret. According to the US legislation on the right to information, for instance, the government is required to provide sufficient and detailed information about why a piece of information requested within the scope of the right to information is a secret. US courts are also authorised to examine such documents before sending them to the related party's attorney, and in the event that the government fails to provide a sufficient and detailed justification about why the subject matter information is classified as secret and which public interest would be damaged if it were disclosed, then the court is authorised to rule that the information be disclosed (Martin and Hoffman, 1999, p. 490).

Therefore, in Turkey, any legal legislation adversely affecting the exercise of the right to information must be reviewed, and regulations about state secrets and classified documents must be drawn up in a clear and comprehensible manner so as to be subject to concrete criteria and, to the extent possible, judicial review. Furthermore, citizens must be informed in this regard and their awareness must be raised about the right ways to exercise this right. Staff at public institutions and organisations must be given training about this subject, coordination units relating to the right to information must be established, legal exceptions of the right to information must be established on more concrete criteria, and development of more consistent judicial decisions in this matter by the Right to Information Assessment Board must be supported.

CONCLUSION

As explained in this study, the right to information is one of the building blocks of a democratic state. In order to ensure a participatory, transparent and accountable administration, this right might be efficiently exercised in that country. Since the 1960s, the world's democracies have covered significant ground to ensure an effective use of this right. The right to information has been guaranteed by legal texts, and international organisations and international human rights authorities have developed sufficient principles, judicial decisions and guidance to ensure the effective use of this right. The right to information occupies an important place at the intersection of many rights such as freedom of expression, the right to privacy, personal data protection, and the right to self-improvement. At the same time, this right ensures that public administration is closer to the public, and increases its democratic legitimacy. As also mentioned in the current study, state administrations are under both negative and positive obligations to fulfil fundamental rights and freedoms. It is not sufficient for this right to be solely regulated in legal texts, laws or constitutions. The state is also responsible for effectively and practically projecting this right into real life. With the additional driving force of the EU accession process, Turkey recognised its citizens' right to information with a law introduced in 2003. This right became constitutional with a constitutional amendment made in 2010. As also referred to in this study, the legal regulations made by Turkey appear to be in compliance with international norms to a great extent. This compliance, however, must not just be made in written regulation, but transferred effectively to real life. In Turkey, the deficiencies and criticisms regarding the concepts of human rights and the rule of law do not derive from legal regulation and the Constitution, but mostly from implementation. Many amendments have been made to the 1982 Constitution, and its fundamental rights and freedoms have been rendered substantially compatible with the norms of international human rights. It is observed, however, that this compatibility exists in text only and is not transferred to the real world. Turkey is still judged as one of the worst violators of human rights at the European Court of Human Rights, and the EU progression reports continuously emphasise its deficiencies in the field of practice.

The problematic areas relating to the right to information in Turkey essentially originate from three points. The lack of expert personnel working in this area in the administrative structure is the first of these. Secondly, citizens have not been made sufficiently aware about the exercise of this right. An analysis of the annual statistics of the Right to Information Assessment Board has revealed that the number of applications is very low in comparison to the size of Turkey's population. Thirdly, public institutions behave arbitrarily in their interpretation of the exceptions stipulated in the Law on the Right to Information, and they exploit a wide discretion regarding what counts as classified documents and state secrets. According to the statistics on the years 2004-2015, an upward trend, even if not sufficiently high, stands out in the applications for access to information. After 2015, however, a radical decline occurred in these applications. In this context, the total number of applications in 2015 fell by about 36% compared with the previous year. As for the 2017 statistics, although an upward trend is observed again, currently the number is significantly below that of pre-2014. It can be argued that the disturbances suffered in Turkey's political life, the attempted coup, and the state of emergency declared in its aftermath, have all played a significant part in this decline. As also discussed above, the most important task of a state when it comes to fundamental rights and freedoms is to guarantee them with legal regulations. But a state's responsibility to uphold fundamental rights and freedoms does not finish there. The state has both negative and positive obligations in this regard. Each year, through the Right to Information Assessment Board, the Grand National Assembly of Turkey shares statistics about the exercise of the right to information in Turkey and observes rising and falling trends. But it does not suffice to simply share these statistics with the public. Problems relating to the exercise of the right to information must be identified as well and solutions must be applied. As a matter of fact, Article 5 of the 1982 Constitution stipulates the following: "The fundamental aims and duties of the State are to ensure the welfare, peace, and happiness of the individual and society; to strive for the removal of political, economic, and social obstacles which restrict the fundamental rights and freedoms of the individual in a manner incompatible with the principles of justice and of the social state governed by rule of law; and to provide the conditions required for the development of the individual's material and spiritual existence." This duty is also a part of the state's positive obligations that require it to remove political, economic and social obstacles blocking the right to information.

REFERENCES

Akillioglu, T. (1990). *Yonetimde Aciklik-Gizlilik ve Bilgi Alma Hakki. In Ulusal Idare Hukuku Kongresi* (pp. 806–815). Ankara: Ikinci Kitap, Kamu Yonetimi.

Akillioglu, T. (1991). Yonetimde Aciklik-Gizlilik ve Bilgi Alma Hakki. *AUSBFD*, *46*(3), 1–12.

Alasdair, R. (2001). Questions about Policy Transparency. *Public Administration Review*, *61*(4), 507–508. doi:10.1111/0033-3352.00055

Alasdair, R. (2001). Structural Pluralism and the Right to Information. *University of Toronto Law Journal*, 243–271.

Aras, Z., & Altınok, E. B. (2009). Türkiye'de Bilgi Edinme Hakki ve Uygulama Sorunlari. *Ankara Barosu Dergisi*, *67*(1), 107–112.

Article 19. (1999). *The Public's Right to Know Principles on Freedom of Information Legislation London*. Retrieved from https://www.article19.org/data/files/pdfs/standards/righttoknow.pdf

Bayraktar, K. (2004). Bilgi Edinme Hakki ve Sir Kavrami. Kazanci Hukuk, Isletme ve Maliye Bilimler Dergisi, 3, 7-11.

Bovens, M. (2002). Information Rights: Citizenship in the Information Society. *Journal of Political Philosophy*, *10*(3), 317–341. doi:10.1111/1467-9760.00155

Colak, I. (2005). *Bilgi Edinme Hakki ve Bilgi Verme Yukumlulugu*. Retrieved from http://e-akademi.org/makaleler/nicolak-1.htm

Council of Europe Committee of Ministers. (1981). *Recommendation No. R (81) 19 of The Committee of Ministers To Member States on The Access to Information Held By Public Authorities*. Retrieved from https://rm.coe.int/CoERMPublicCommonSearchServices/DisplayDCTMContent?documentId=09000016804f7a6e

Council of Europe Committee of Ministers. (2002). *Recommendation Rec(2002)2 of the Committee of Ministers to Member States on Access to Official Documents, Adopted by the Committee of Ministers 784th meeting of the Ministers' Deputies*. Retrieved from https://rm.coe.int/16804c6fcc

Doner, A. (2010). *Seffaf Devlette Bilgi Edinme Hakki ve Sinirlari*. Istanbul, Turkey: XII Levha Yayinlari.

Eken, M. (2005). Gizlilik Geleneginden Seffaf Yonetime Dogru. *TODAIE*, *38*(1), 113–130.

Erdogan, M. (2004). *Anayasal Demokrasi*. Ankara, Turkey: Siyasal Kitabevi.

Gursel, O. (1998). Idari Rejim Olarak Ornek Aldigimiz Fransa'da, Idari Usul ve Bilgi Edinme Hakkina Iliskin Duzenlemeler. *Gazi Universitesi Hukuk Fakultesi Dergisi Prof. Dr. Ihsan Tarakcioglu'na Armagan*, 281-290.

Hafizogullari, Z. (2012). Ceza Hukuku Duzeninde Devlet Sirri. *Hacettepe Hukuk Fakultesi Dergisi*, *2*(2), 172–177.

Hasdemir, T. A. (2014). Türkiye'de Kamusal İletisim ve Bilgi Edinme:10 Yilin Ardindan Panoramik Bir İnceleme. *Amme Idaresi Dergisi*, *47*(3), 111–144.

Hasdemir, T.A. (2016). Right to Information and Communication between Government and Citizens: Identifying Continuities and Discontinuities in the Practices of Turkey at the10th Anniversary of the Law on Right to Information. *İletisim Kuram ve Arastirma Dergisi, 43*, 64-76.

Hiz, Y., & Yilmaz, Z. (2004). *Bilgi Edinme ve Dilekce Hakki Aciklamali Notlu Gerekceli*. Ankara, Turkey: Seckin Yayincilik.

Inal, T. (2004). Bilgi Edinme Hakki ve Özel Hayata, Haberlesmeye, Ticari Sirlara, Fikir ve Sanat Eserlerine Iliskin Sinirlamalar. *Kazanci Hukuk. Isletme ve Maliye Bilimleri Dergisi*, *3*, 12–29.

Kaboglu, I. (2011). *Anayasa Hukuku Dersleri*. Istanbul, Turkey: Legal Kitabevi.

Kaboglu, I. (2013). *Ozgurlukler Hukuku*. Ankara, Turkey: Imge Kitabevi.

Kaya, C. (2005). *Idare Hukukunda Bilgi Edinme Hakki*. Ankara, Turkey: Seckin Yayinlari.

Kilinc, U. (2009). Bilgi Edinme Hakki Kanunu ve Turkiye Uygulamasi. Kamu Mevzuati Dergisi, *1*(2).

Kocak, S. Y. (2010). Kamu Yonetiminde Aciklik Icin Bilgi Edinme Hakki. *Selcuk Universitesi Sosyal Bilimler Enstitusu Dergisi*, *23*, 15–125.

Loucaides, G. L. (1995). The Right to Information. *Essays on The Developing Law of Human Rights*, *39*, 3–31.

Martin, K., & Hoffman, P. (1999). Safeguarding Liberty: National Security, Freedom of Expression and Access to Information: United States of America. In Secrecy and Liberty (pp. 481-505). Martinus Nijhoff Publishers.

Mason, A. (2000). The Relationship Between Freedom of Expression and Freedom of Information. In Freedom of Expression and Freedom of Information (pp. 225-238). Oxford University Press.

McDonagh, M. (2013). The Right to Information in International Human Rights Law. Human Rights Law Review, 13(1), 25-55.

National Assembly of Turkey. (2013). *Bilgi Edinme Hakki Çalistayi Sonuc Raporlari*. Retrieved from https://www.tbmm.gov.tr/bilgiedinme/bilgi_edinme_calistay_raporu.pdf

National Assembly of Turkey (2013 Report). (n.d.). Retrieved from https://www.tbmm.gov.tr/bilgiedinme/2013_yili_degerlendirme_raporu.pdf

National Assembly of Turkey (2017 Report). (n.d.). Retrieved from https://www.tbmm.gov.tr/bilgiedinme/2017_yili_degerlendirme_raporu.pdf

National Assembly of Turkey (2004-2017 Reports). (n.d.). Retrieved from https://www.tbmm.gov.tr/bilgiedinme/degerlendirme_kurulu_raporlari.htm

Nowak, M. (2003). *Introduction to the International Human Rights Regime*. Leiden: Martinus Nijhoff Publishers.

Organisation for Economic Co-operation and Development (OECD). (2005). *Modernising Government.* 31st Session of the Public Governance Committee, Paris, France.

Patrick, B. (2006). Freedom of Information and Openness: Fundemental Human Rights? *Administrative Law Review*, *58*(1), 177–218.

Peled, R., & Rabin, Y. (2011). The Constitutional Right To Information. *Columbia Human Rights Law Review*, *42*(2), 358–401.

Richordson, E. (1974). Freedom of Information. *Loyola Law Review*, *20*(1), 45–64.

Sedley, S. (2000). Information As a Human Right. In Freedom of Expression and Freedom of Information. Oxford University Press.

Sengul, R. (2005). Bilgi Edinme Hakki Kanunu Turk Kamu Yonetimini Camdan Eve Donusturur mu? *A.U.S.B.F.D.*, *60*(3).

Singh, R. K. (2014). Right to Information: The Basic Need of Democracy. *Journal of Education & Social Policy*, *1*(2), 86–96.

Soykan, C. (2007). Avrupa Insan Haklari Mahkemesi Ictihatlarinda Bilgi Edinme Hakki/ The European Court of Human Rights Case Law on The Right to Information. *AUHFD*, *56*(2), 63–74.

The Board of Review of Access to Information Decisions (2004/104, 2007/1017, 2004/140, 2004/77, 2010/2122). (n.d.). Retrieved from http://www.bedk.gov.tr/

United Nations Development Programme. (1997). Governance for Sustainable Human Development. UNDP policy document.

United Nations Development Programme. (1997). *Reconceptualising Governance Discusson Pape*. New York: Management Development and Governance Division.

United Nations Development Programme. (2004). *Right to Information Practical Guidance Note*. Bureau for Development Policy Democratic Governance Group.

Uygun, O. (2000). *Insan Haklari Kurami. Insan Haklari*. Istanbul: Yapi Kredi Yayinlari.

Wall, S. P. (1996). Public Justification and the Transparency Argument. *The Philosophical Quarterly*, *46*(185), 501–507. doi:10.2307/2956360

World Bank. (1992). *Governance and Development*. The World Bank. Retrieved from http://unpan1.un.org/intradoc/groups/public/documents/un/unpan022332.pdf

Yasamis, F. D. (2004). *Anayasa Hukuku ve Insan Haklari Acisindan Bilgi Edinme Hakki*. Ankara: Turk Idare Dergisi.

Yildirim, R. (1998). *Idare Hukuku Acisindan Bilgi Edinme Hak ve Ozgurlugu. In Idari Usul Kanunu Hazirligi Uluslararasi Sempozyumu.* Ankara, Turkey: Babakanlik Basimevi.

Yuzbasioglu, N. (2000). *Insan Haklarinin Ulusal Duzeyde Korunmasi.* Istanbul, Turkey: Yapi Kredi Yayinlari.

Section 2

Citizenship Exercise in a Networked Society

In this section, the practical importance of the constitutional and fundamental rights knowledge is applied to some specific areas, such as news, taxes, corruption, human reproduction, and others.

Chapter 8
Exercise of Citizenship in Network Society:
Cyberactivism and the Fight Against Fake News in the Brazilian Context

Ana Carolina Trindade Soares Cohen
Centro Universitário Tiradentes, Brazil

ABSTRACT

The chapter is based on the understanding that the citizens' lack of awareness of the rights inherent to the very guarantee of human dignity, as well as of the whole historical process that gave rise to the guarantee of such rights, is one of the reflexes that the absence of a citizenship education and for citizenship provoke, even affecting the high rate of dissemination of false news in Brazil. There is a recurrent need to deal with this type of problem, especially aggravated by the presidential race of 2018, where there is an increase in the reproduction of news whose reliability of the source is not verified, although they are evidently false, exaggerated, and sensationalist. While analyzing this problem, the study seeks to examine the harm of this practice to the exercise of citizenship.

INTRODUCTION

The understanding of citizenship is quite complex, since it is a historical concept, which therefore varies in time and space, and which also depends on the legal regime of each country, as Jaime Pinsky well observes, according to whom such understanding does not only vary "by the rules that define who is or is not the

DOI: 10.4018/978-1-5225-8350-9.ch008

holder of citizenship (by territorial or blood law), but also by the distinct rights and duties that characterize the citizen in each of the contemporary national states." (PINSKAY, 2015, p. 9).

Therefore, it is not a question of a uniform evolution of citizenship in all countries, which does not prevent the conclusion that there is "a process of evolution that runs from the absence of rights to its expansion, throughout history." (PINSKAY, p. 10).

In this context, the present study intends to examine the understanding of citizenship in the Brazilian legal context, as well as its practice, especially in relation to the exercise of citizenship in the network society and the fight against *fake news*.

The mass dissemination of false news via the internet is a worldwide problem. Before the advent of the world-wide computer network, the ability to spread false news was limited, even if one had the possibility of printing, with the newspapers, roads, etc., news did not spread with the ease and speed that is verified nowadays.

The manipulation of news and videos (called *deep fakes*) can represent a danger to democracy and the exercise of citizenship, threatening even the credibility of everything that is published, since people no longer know what is real and what is false.

In Brazil, in particular, the problem of false news is increasing, since the country still has an incipient democracy and the State cannot guarantee the effectiveness of fundamental rights, as assigned by the Constitution, especially those pertinent to the full exercise of citizenship.

The Brazilian Federal Constitution provides, in its art. 205, that "education, the right of all and the duty of the State and the family, shall be promoted and encouraged with the collaboration of society, aiming at the full development of the person, his preparation for the exercise of citizenship and his qualification for work."

Such a device therefore links education to the formation of citizenship: "education that does not prepare the individual to be the holder of citizenship and effectively be able to exercise it, marginalizes the person" (KIM, 2013, p. 31), excluding him from the context and the formation of a just and egalitarian society, "not only because of the omission in the provision of the educational service (private or public), but also when education does not return to the formation of this citizenship, when it is rendered in an inefficient and incomplete way" (KIM, 2013, p. 31).

The relationship between education and citizenship is narrow and symbiotic. Without understanding the rights (civil, social and political) that are guaranteed to them, and the instruments necessary to exercise them and claim them, the individual does not exercise his citizenship. In this scenario, although the concepts of education and citizenship are not confused, without that the individual will not have instruments to exercise it.

The understanding of citizenship is not, therefore, restricted to the quality of the holder of political rights in the strict sense, but, above all, to the "quality of the one who holds fundamental rights linked to the dignity of the human person" (KIM, 2013, p. 32).

The ignorance of these rights, as well as the historical process that led to their conquest, and the consequent alienation that the absence of a citizen education provoke, have a high impact on the dissemination of false news in Brazil: without knowing their rights and obligations constitutionally foreseen, the society reverberates news without even verifying the reliability of its source, although these are evidently false, exaggerated and sensationalist.

In a survey conducted by the Brazilian Federal Senate, it was found that few people really know the Constitution. 811 people over 16 years of age were heard from all over the country from September 18 to 30, 2013, and it was worrying that 7.8% of the sample had no knowledge of the Constitution and another 35.1% declare to have a low knowledge of this. On the other hand, only 5.3% of those interviewed stated that they were familiar with the constitutional text (SENADO, 2015).

When it comes to formal schooling, the Brazilian situation is equally disastrous. Only in the middle of the twentieth century did the process of expansion of basic schooling in Brazil begin, and its growth, considering the public school network, only occurred in the late 70s and early 80s.

In an evaluation carried out by the Programme for International Student Assessment (PISA) in 2015[1], Brazil ranked 63rd in science, 59th in reading and 66th in mathematics. The review is coordinated by the Organization for Economic Co-operation and Development (OECD) and has been applied in 70 countries/economies (OECD, 2015).

However, the unreflective dissemination of false news in the current network society is not only a reflection of the lack of formal education, but, above all, of citizen education. The understanding of citizenship runs through the possibility of the people becoming the "main part of the process of their social development and promotion" (KIM, 2013, p.33).

In this scenario, "information is a resource of power, by linking development with a society's ability to generate and apply knowledge", because it contributes to the exercise of citizenship, as it enables the individual to understand the dimension of the changes that are changing the world outlook as well as "offers the means of individual and collective self-adjustment action" (ROCHA, 2000).

On the other hand, the same internet that is easy and fast means of propagating false news is also an instrument to clarify them and is valued as an important means of propagating knowledge.

The purpose of the present study is to analyze the problem of the dissemination of false news in the Brazilian context and the harm of this practice to the exercise of citizenship. At the time of this analysis, it will seek to demonstrate that this problem stems from the lack of effective guarantee of a citizen education, which, in turn, includes the citizens' knowledge of their constitutionally foreseen rights and duties.

In this step, it also seeks to examine how the Internet can serve as a tool for citizens to be aware of those rights and obligations.

CITIZENSHIP IN THE WESTERN SOCIETY: BRIEF TESTS

As already pointed out, citizenship is a historical concept whose understanding varies in time and space. Moreover, "even within each national state, the concept and practice of citizenship has been changing over the last two or three hundred years" (PINSKAY, 2015, p. 09), which is due to the "greater or lesser incorporation of immigrants to citizenship", "the degree of political participation of different groups (the vote of the woman, the illiterate)", "to the social protection offered by the states to those who need it", which is evident in the breadth of the guarantee of social rights (PINSKAY, 2015, pp. 09-10).

In the Greek city-states, the members of the political communities were considered citizens, who established their laws and elected their rulers. They were the minority: male individuals "who enjoyed rights and had participation within cities" (KIM, 2013, p.18). Women, children, foreigners and slaves were not included in this list.

In ancient Rome, citizenship referred to the political situation of individuals who held certain rights. As Richard Pae Kim points out, it was a discriminatory sense, since "it served to indicate that a certain individual belonged to a higher class within society" (KIM, 2013, p.18).

The concept of citizenship has already been used to refer to Christians who were linked to the nobility and clergy, which was revealed in the Middle Ages when the Church became a political institution.

The Enlightenment and the Protestant Reformation, in turn, imbued with the ideas of realism and rationality, contributed to a new understanding of the sense of citizen, "as a free subject, and not only as having participation in the society in which he lives" (KIM, 2013, p. 18).

Notwithstanding the extension of political rights from the eighteenth century to the right to vote not only to certain people, the understanding of citizenship was still limited to the idea of political participation through voting.

The rapidity of the social changes that communities face in recent centuries makes "what in one moment could be considered a dangerous subversion of order, in the following it is a commonplace" (PINSKAY, 2015, p. 10): in Western democracies women are guaranteed the right to vote; this right has already been conditioned to ownership of assets, to the holding of positions or functions, to belonging to a certain ethnicity.

With the enlargement of the integration process, there is an equally broader understanding of citizenship, not restricted to one country alone, but to a group of countries united by common goals, such as the European Union, the Mercosur and NAFTA, according to Richard Pae Kim (2013, p. 19).

The author emphasizes that the Charter of Fundamental Rights of the European Union has recognized the rights, freedoms, guarantees and principles set out in these documents, reaffirming the rights deriving from constitutional traditions and international obligations common to the Member States, the Treaty of the European Union and the Treaties of the European Convention for the Protection of Human Rights and Fundamental Freedoms, "seeking the minimum in terms of protection of the dignity of the human person in the signatory countries", in order to conform the rights of citizens of this community (2013, p. 20).

In this context, it is important to highlight that the rights of citizenship are not confused with human rights, as José Roberto Fernandes Castilho observes.

Although there is a common area between them, "the rights of citizenship relate to the subjective public rights enshrined by a specific legal system, concrete and specific." Human rights, on the other hand, "refer to the human person himself as the source value of all social values." The discussion on human rights - more broadly - "is therefore placed on another plane of theoretical analysis. On the plane of the global, from the universal, from a natural-law perspective, not from the positive and topical one" (CASTILLO, p. 1).

It should be noted, however, that there is as yet no uniform legal doctrine as to the understanding of citizenship and therefore, of citizen. In many countries the exclusion of certain people from the concept of active citizenship - referring to the right of suffrage - and its understanding in a broad sense, is still evident.

Such restrictions are mainly due to the very understanding of the concept of citizenship, which has been reaching since the beginning of the nineteenth century those who meet the requirements established by law to achieve this category, and the rights of citizenship themselves were indicated by law (DALLARI *apud* KIM, 2013, p. 19).

In Brazil, the Federal Constitution of 1988 assures Brazilian citizens the right to vote (article 14, *caput*), as well as the right to stand for office in the Legislative and Executive branches. However, it did not restrict itself to this, having greatly expanded the rights of citizenship: citizens have the right to submit bills through popular initiative (article 14, III); to participate in a plebiscite and referendum (articles 14, I and II) on bills or government acts; to propose lawsuits foreseen with the objective of guaranteeing fundamental rights, such as the Popular Action (Article 5, LXXIII), the *writ of mandamus* (article 5, LXIX) and the court injunction (article 5, LXXI), which aim to "prevent abuses by authorities against the rights of a citizen or of all citizenship" (DALLARI, p. 1).

The Brazilian Constitution also provides for the necessary participation of community representatives in consultative and decision-making bodies on the rights of children and adolescents, and in the area of education and health: "this participation confers the exercise of citizenship rights and is very important for the democratization of society" (DALLARI, p. 1).

Moreover, as Dallari points out, the rights of citizenship are at the same time duties, since "the associative nature of the human person, the natural solidarity characteristic of humanity, the weakness of individuals isolated when faced with the state or powerful social groups" they turn themselves into "factors that make it necessary for everyone to participate in social activities." In addition, it is impossible to live democratically without the members of society expressing their opinions and wishes: "all this makes it essential for citizens to exercise their rights of citizenship" (DALLARI, p. 02).

CITIZEN EDUCATION AND EDUCATION FOR CITIZENSHIP: THE PERCUSSIONS OF EDUCATION IN BRAZIL

The general crisis that has engulfed the modern world everywhere and in almost every sphere of life manifests itself differently in each country, involving areas and taking different forms." One of the most characteristic and suggestive aspects of this crisis in America is "the periodic crisis in education (ARENDT, 2009, p. 221)

Although Hannah Arendt is focusing on her analysis of the events of the twentieth century in the United States, some of her conclusions are very close to the current reality in Brazil, which makes it possible to use them, especially when she states that "it takes no great imagination to detect the dangers of an ever-increasing decline in elementary patterns throughout the school system [...]" (ARENDT, 2009, pp. 221-222).

According to the author, "here there is more than the enigmatic question of why Johnny does not know how to read. Moreover, there is always the temptation to believe that we are dealing with specific problems confined to historical and national boundaries", which would be important "only to those immediately affected "(ARENDT, 2009, p. 222).

However, this belief has been shown to be "invariably false in our time: one can admit as a general rule in this century that anything that is possible in one country may in the foreseeable future be equally possible in virtually any other country" (ARENDT, 2009, p. 222).

Based on the assumption that "education is among the most basic and necessary activities of human society" (ARENDT, 2009, p. 222), it is not difficult to conclude that a crisis in education at any time is a cause for concern.

Although there is a relative consensus regarding the severity of the Brazilian educational situation, there is disagreement about the causes of this situation, as well as the measures necessary to recover it.

Education stems from community life and reveals, as well as essential, the level and quality of this very life in common.

"The democratic educational discourses that emerged in Brazil in the political opening movement were especially crystallized during the 1990s, beginning at the end of the 1980s, with the 1988 Constitution," also comprising "international post Declaration of Jomtien in 1990 in the National Education Guidelines and Basis Laws in 1996 and in the National Curriculum Parameters in 1998 "(VENERA, 2009, p. 232).

As Raquel Alvarenga Sena Venera observes, such documents "regulated the senses of the discourses of freedom, autonomy, participation of all, critical posture" and guide "the construction of the citizen." The author emphasizes that these discourses "emerged as flags of education from the political opening in Brazil and became rights and duties" (VENERA, 2009, p. 232).

In addition to being relevant, the issue of the education crisis implies a deepening of the reflections about the role of the education system in a country that is deeply embedded in international globalization and which is subject to changes in paradigms of work, subordination and production (GADELHA, 2017, p. 166).

As early as the 1960s, the reasons for the mismatch between the degree of economic growth through the process of industrialization and urbanization and the exclusion of the poorest and without access to education in Brazil were identified.

As Regina Maria Gadelha points out, the crisis that is taking place in Brazilian education is not recent, as it is the result of a deliberate policy of dismantling, implemented since the agreements of the Brazilian Ministry of Education with the United States Agency for International Development (USAID), "whose ideology in favor of markets was gradually being implemented in the country from 1965 onwards." The author stresses that "the emphasis was placed on the subordination of universities to the immediate interests of entrepreneurs and on training focused on technological areas to the detriment of the humanities, along with proposals aimed at eliminating the gratuitousness of public universities in the country", so that the project "clearly advocated the planning of an educational system geared to market imperatives" (2017, p. 168).

Nevertheless, the combination of an education and culture project aligned with the construction of a national project of a developed nation has always been on the agenda of Brazilian intellectuals, who "taught us to think the meaning of 'citizenship'" (GADELHA, p. 168).

Illiteracy in Brazil still presents itself as one of the most serious national problems: in the 1960s the majority of the Brazilian population was illiterate, although it worked in industries and urban activities, mostly paying taxes "without even being able to exercise the most basic right to citizenship, which is the vote". In this context, there were movements, such as the "Popular Culture Movement of Recife" (1962), adult culture and literacy, which aimed not only to teach reading but to exercise citizenship (GADELHA, 2017, p. 168).

According to Gadelha, Paulo Freire, a Brazilian considered one of the most famous thinkers in the history of world pedagogy, deepens the ideas that "in order to transform education, it must also involve the expansion of man, in the sense of knowing his location in society" (GADELHA, 2017, p. 168).

Freire thought of education as a practice for freedom, advocating a "direct and truly linked literacy linked to the democratization of culture, which would be an introduction to this democratization", leaving aside "any hypothesis of purely mechanical literacy." In this way, he talked about the education of the Brazilian man "in a position of awareness, in the immersion he had made in the process of our reality", with a view to transforming naivety into criticality, while being literate. (FREIRE, 1982, pp. 103-104)

Freire therefore started from the assumption that the normal position of man "was not only to be in the world, but with him, to have permanent relations with this world." In addition, he emphasized that "in these relations with reality and in reality, man is locked in a specific relation - from subject to object - from which results the knowledge expressed by language" (FREIRE, 1982, p. 104).

The author stresses that this relationship is made by man, regardless of whether or not he is literate, so that "it is enough to be a man to realize it. Just be a man to be able to capture reality data. To be able to know, even though it is merely opinionated. Hence there is no absolute ignorance, no absolute wisdom." However, man does not grasp the data of reality purely, but "along with the problem, with the phenomenon, it also captures its causal links. Seizes causality. The resulting understanding of abstraction will be so much more critical as the apprehension of authentic causation is made" (FREIRE, 1982, pp. 104-105).

The author concludes: whereas for the critical conscience authentic causation itself is always subject to its analysis, so that what is authentic today may not be tomorrow, "for the naive conscience, what seems to be authentic causality is no longer, once which gives it a static character, something already made and established". "That is why it is proper to the critical conscience to integrate it with reality, while the naive is its superposition to reality [...]". In this sense, "for the fanatic conscience whose pathology from naive to irrational, is itself the accommodation, the adjustment, the adaptation" (FREIRE, 1982, p. 105).

However, "the military dictatorship interrupted this process of building citizenship in Brazil", because, "despite a consensus on the strict relationship between development and the level of education accepted by all Brazilian leaders, education has lost its instrument objective since 1965 of transformation". (GADELHA, 2017, p. 169).

The results of this process are sadly observed, given that the "educational vision implanted in Brazil would turn in the direction of more retrograde pragmatism by adopting a purely rhetorical discursivity in which enrollments are statistics of only numerical character" (GADELHA, 2017, p. 169).

INFORMATION SOCIETY AND SOCIALIZATION OF INFORMATION: THE PROBLEM OF "FAKE NEWS" IN THE BRAZILIAN CONTEXT

Already in 1987, in the first edition of the work "O Espaço do Cidadão", Milton Santos warned that "modern man is perhaps more helpless than his ancestors, because he lives in an information society, which, however, refuses him the right to know". In addition, it points out that "the stock of information, including those that concern each individual in particular, is manipulated by a few (*sic*) persons, who may make misuse of it" (2007, p. 155).

Quoting H. Laborit (1986, p. 16), Milton Santos emphasizes that "only the generalization of information 'can give the citizen the dimension of a man'", therefore, "to live in ignorance of what goes on around when a most of the decisions that concern us are taken in light of this missing information, it does not contribute to the formation of an integral citizenship (SANTOS, 2007, p. 156)

The statement of Santos is crystal-clear when he emphasizes that "education should provide all people with the appropriate means to be able to absorb and criticize information, refusing its biases" as well as "protesting against its fragmentation, requiring that the news of each day does not interrupt the sequence of events, so that the film of the world is within the reach of all men" (2007, p. 157).

The actuality referred to above is confirmed especially when we are faced with the disastrous effects of the dissemination of false news, notably in the social media environment, and with a view to determining the direction of voting, by the way, one of the most classic understandings of the concept of citizenship, as discussed elsewhere.

The term network society, originally coined by Norwegian Professor Stein Bråten in 1981, has received a typical attribution that refers to the "information society" or "knowledge society."

"In this sense, what is emphasized in the concept of an 'information society' is the substantial and ever-present transformation of the activities and processes that take place within those societies [...]". It is "a society whose economy and in general all values and sectors, including the agrarian, industrial and service sectors, is increasingly characterized by the production of information" (MOLINARO; SARLET, 2013, pp. 65-66).

In reality, as Carlos Alberto Molinaro and Ingo Wolfgang Sarlet point out, the concepts of network society and the information society complement each other and demand each other (MOLINARO; SARLET, 2013, p. 66).

With the development of information and communication technologies, especially the Internet and online social networks, "unprecedented frontiers for human socialization have opened up, becoming important tools in the multiplication of discourses and the signification of new knowledge and senses" (ESPINDOLA, 2015, p. 02).

On the other hand, borders have also been expanded for the dissemination of false news, which has to some extent been "explained" due to the need to obtain information in a shorter time, in a society that is constantly evolving and embedded in the rapid development of information technology. Such necessity may lead to the data obtained to be considered real, without confirmation of its reliability.

In 2018 Brazil repeats what had already happened in the 2014 presidential elections, but which in the current election was revealed with more vigor and intensity, and therefore with more drastic effects.

The dissemination of false news constitutes a threat to one's own democratic values. One of the candidates for the post of national executive has been challenged because of the existence of evidence that private companies finance the disclosure of false news through the Whatsapp app[2].

In addition to the aforementioned losses regarding the aspects of public life, the propagation of false news is also harmful when analyzed from the perspective of private life.

Social networks are full of false information about the intimate aspects of the lives of certain people, and often, as is happening in Brazil, such aspects are created or manipulated in the sense of damaging, in addition, the very public life of these individuals, as in the case of the mass dissemination of false news against Brazilian Parliamentarians (Pedroso de Campos, 2017).

The citizen's fundamental right to information is indissolubly linked to the existence of a democratic society: in order for the citizen to be able to inform himself, and consequently make decisions and participate in social life, he needs information from various social fields. It seems contradictory, but it is consistent with Alina V. Popescu's conclusion that "the need for information has become more and more acute as the surplus of information on the market has become increasingly obvious" (2018, p. 607).

In this social context, the manipulation of information and the creation of false news are increasingly appearing, undermining the right to information and undermining democracy.

In order to respond to problems such as these, one must take into account the problem of economic development in Brazil, of inequality and popular participation in this same development, with the critical insertion of Brazilian man in the process of democratization, since democracy in the Brazil is still in its infancy.

More than a mere formal education, it is necessary to enable man to discuss his own problematic and his insertion in this problematic, "which warned him of the dangers of his time, so that, conscious of them, he would gain the strength and courage to fight, rather than being led and dragged by the perdition of his own 'self', subject to the prescriptions of others". It is necessary, therefore, an education that places man in constant dialogue with the other, which predisposes him to constant revisions, "to the critical analysis of his 'findings'", listening, asking, investigating (FREIRE, 1982, p. 90).

CYBERACTIVISM AS AN INSTRUMENT OF COMBATING "FAKE NEWS" AND EXERCISE OF CITIZENSHIP: EDUCATION AS A STARTING POINT.

One cannot understand, as Paulo Freire rightly points out, that in a society in transition education leads man to "quietist" positions, rather than one that leads him to search for truth in common. The very essence of democracy, he emphasizes, involves a fundamental note that is intrinsic to it: change.

Democratic regimes "are flexible, restless, because of this, it must correspond to the man of these regimes, greater flexibility of conscience", so that "the lack of this permeability seems to come from the most serious mismatches of the current democratic regimes, of the correspondence between the sense of change, characteristic not only of democracy, but of technological civilization", as well as of "a certain mental rigidity of man that, massifying himself, ceases to assume a consciously critical attitude towards life" (FREIRE, 1982, p. 90).

Freire points out that, excluded from the orbit of decisions, increasingly attached to small minorities, man is commanded by the advertising media, "to such a point that he trusts or believes nothing, if he did not listen on the radio, television or otherwise. read in the papers" (FREIRE, 1982, pp. 90-91).

Today, on the other hand, reveals that the eagerness for information and for being the possessor of information - of any kind - that makes it appear dominant, causes man to believe and reproduce information without any criterion, "hence his identification with mythical forms of explanation of their world" (FREIRE, 1982, p. 91).

Man must, therefore, realize his social and political responsibility, experiencing this responsibility and being aware of his right to this responsibility.

In this way an education is needed that will lead him to a new posture in the face of the problems of his time and space, which will lead him to be intimate of them: to an education "of research instead of the mere, dangerous and tedious repetition of stretches and statements disconnected from their very conditions of life''. An education, and therefore an actuation of vitality, is needed, not of the one who insists on the transmission of "inert ideas", which "the mind merely receives without using, verifying, or transforming into new combinations" (FREIRE, 1982, p. 93).

The Brazilian challenge is therefore not only to overcome the alarming rates of illiteracy, but to overcome purely mechanical literacy, and the perception of the need to also overcome our democratic inexperience.

The challenge also concerns overcoming the emptiness, "of liking the hollow word", of the emphasis on discourses, because "this whole oratory manifestation, almost always without depth, reveals, above all, a mental attitude. It reveals the absence of permeability characteristic of critical consciousness. And criticality is precisely the fundamental note of the democratic mentality" (FREIRE, 1982, p.95).

The lack of this criticality in education, the naive way of dealing with problems and discussing subjects superficially is one of the great characteristics of Brazilian education, and is also, in our view, one of the causes of mass reproduction of false news today. The internet only facilitated this massive reproduction.

On the other hand, at the time when the Internet is a facilitator or even a propellant of this uncritical act in the mass, cyber-activism can also be seen as an instrument to combat the reproduction of false news and the promotion of the exercise of citizenship. "Mass self-communication provides the technological platform for constructing the autonomy of the social actor, be it individual or collective, in relation to the institutions of society" (CASTELLS, 2013, p.15)[3].

Although, as already pointed out, Brazilian education does not lend the citizen to more inquisitive positions – on the contrary, passivity, memorized knowledge, not requiring "elaboration or re-elaboration" (FREIRE, 1982, p. 96) –, many groups have been using the virtual environment to seek dialogue, research and criticism, so fundamental to democratic action.

It is no wonder that the internet today revolutionizes social relations, by expanding borders and breaking space-time barriers, giving birth to the feeling of belonging to a global community. The convergence of people by common interests, according to Carolina Bonoto Espindola, "has been one of the most important phenomena brought by the new technologies of information and communication" (2015, p. 06), enabling the subject to act actively, to listen and to be heard.

Starting from this understanding, it is even mentioned in *cyber-citizenship* that, according to Carolina Espindola, "is beyond the city's belonging and participation in the functioning of the political institution", insofar as it is "a profusion of potentially aggregating contexts, where all subjects are, theoretically, included". Carolina emphasizes that "in addition to access and consumption, cyber-citizenship refers to the possibility of playing a role of belonging in a deterritorialized and interactive environment, creating interpersonal relations in a political, cultural and social perspective" (2015, p. 08).

In this scenario, social networks present themselves as a means for issues to be debated, thought and analyzed, causing "social movements to bring to the agenda of the public sphere questions that until then were silenced in the traditional media sphere" (ESPINDOLA, 2015, p. 09).

In fact, the emergence of new spaces for deliberation and political dialogue allows access to "'political' 'information" that has never been observed in nineteenth-century newspapers, salons and cafes, nor in the media and television abundance of the twentieth century, as pointed out by Piérre Lévy. In this sense, we have never seen "such an opening of the conversation space, a similar availability of instruments at the service of the citizen in order to influence their representatives" (*apud* ESPINDOLA, 2015, p. 9).

The exercise of democracy and citizenship is closely related to the possibility of popular participation. "There is no democracy without democratic communication. In this sense, social media can be thought of as tools of free and instant collaboration where spaces for debate and collective construction are promoted". Indeed, "models of decentralized public collaboration can create innovative solutions to issues neglected by hegemonic media" (ESPINDOLA, 2015, p. 9)

The technological advance, therefore, and the greater breadth of access to information and communication, combined with the understanding of citizenship and consequent belonging and awareness of responsibility, create "the possibility of approaching perspectives that previously seemed to exclude, inviting debate and reflection on all civil society " (ESPINDOLA, 2015, p. 9).

CONCLUSION

The Brazilian Federal Constitution is rich in instruments that constitute legitimate expression of citizenship rights. While they allow for popular participation in the exercise of political power, these instruments are extremely relevant "to guarantee the social and legal effectiveness of constitutional norms" (CASTILHO, p. 03), notably those that guarantee the exercise of citizenship rights.

However, as José Roberto Fernandes Castilho points out, "it is true that the process of advancing the guarantees of the rights of citizenship is much more a question of power than a legal question" (CASTILHO, p. 03).

The current understanding of citizenship expresses "the advance of substantial democracy itself, that is, one that moves towards social and economic equality" (CASTILHO, p. 03).

To that end, its fundamental basis lies in the effective guarantee of political education, understood here as citizen education - inclusive, critical, participatory, ethical, collective- and for citizenship.

Thus, rather than a basic and elementary social right, education is the way and the necessary condition that will enable both the conquest and the exercise of the rights of citizenship itself, which, in turn, as Castilho points out, "widen every day in return for the needs of man and human dignity" (CASTILHO, p. 04).

In this sense, there is nothing more to contradict and compromise the exercise of citizenship rights and popular emancipation "than an education that does not throw the student to the experiences of debate and analysis of problems and that does not provide conditions for true participation" (FREIRE, 1982, p. 93), fueling our democratic experience.

The increasingly wide dissemination of false news compromises this same democratic space and is a reflection of a taste for the word hollow, empty. The holders of power take advantage of this lack of criticality for their own maintenance in power, using the purely formal education or even the complete absence of this, to instill in the minds of people untruths that, so reproduced, become true absolute.

It is necessary, therefore, an education that inserts the individual into his reality and into the reality of those around him, "in an analytic contact with the existent, to prove it, to live it and to live it fully, practically" (FREIRE, 1982, pp. 93-94).

Education in Brazil follows in the same way Paulo Freire once pointed out in the 1980s: it is verbose, hollow and resounding. It does not communicate, "it makes communications, different things" (FREIRE, 1982, pp. 93-94).

Citizen education and citizenship requires, above all, a constant attempt to change attitudes, and virtual space is one of the instruments to do so, since it makes it possible to move away from habits of passivity and to approximate habits of insertion, participation and interference: "Seeking to break with the unidirectional nature of information and with the homogenization of ideals, social networks appear as an important tool for minority social movements that seek spaces" to disseminate knowledge and stimulate debates (ESPINDOLA, 2015, p. 14).

In this scenario, the internet presents itself as a democratic environment for the construction of new models of thought, especially because it enables a way to "'dribble' the traditional media, which, for the most part, do not offer space for public opinion to manifest" (ESPINDOLA, 2015, p. 14). It plays a fundamental role in the exercise of citizenship.

While the internet presents itself as an instrument, education is a pillar for the construction of citizenship. Citizen education and citizenship must first of all allow equal access to the Law, that is, to the knowledge of the legal order and public liberties by all people, even instrumentalizing them in the search for their extension.

Citizenship is learned. The Brazilian Constitution itself establishes, in its art. 205, that education should aim at "the full development of the person, his preparation for the exercise of citizenship and his qualification for work". "It expands to the extent that it is affirmed as a social practice, in addition to legal texts" (CASTILHO, p. 04).

The process of building and learning citizenship is old and must be constant, without pretending to be exhausted. It is up to Brazilians to incorporate these habits.

REFERENCES

Arendt, H. (2009). *Entre o passado e o futuro*. São Paulo: Perspectiva.

Castells, M. (2013). *Redes de indignação e esperança: movimentos sociais na era da internet* (C. A. Medeiros, Trans.). Rio de Janeiro: Zahar.

Castilho, J. R. F. (n.d.). *Cidadania: esboço de evolução e sentido da Expressão*. Retrieved from http://www.pge.sp.gov.br/centrodeestudos/revistapge/revista2/artigo8.htm

Dallari, D. A. (2001). Estado de direito e cidadania. In *Direito constitucional: estudos em homenagem a Paulo Bonavides*. São Paulo: Malheiros.

Dallari, D. A. (n.d.). *Direitos e deveres da cidadania*. Retrieved from http://www.dhnet.org.br/direitos/sos/textos/deveres.htm

Espindola, C. B. (2015). Cidadania na sociedade em rede: o ciberativismo e o combate à LGBTFOBIA. In *Anais do 3º Congresso Internacional de Direito e contemporaneidade: mídias e direitos da sociedade em rede*. Rio Grande do Sul: Universidade Federal de Santa Maria.

Espindola, C. B. (2015). Cidadania na sociedade em rede: o ciberativismo e o combate à LGBTFOBIA. In *Anais do 3º Congresso Internacional de Direito e contemporaneidade: mídias e direitos da sociedade em rede*. Rio Grande do Sul: Universidade Federal de Santa Maria.

Freire, P. (1982). *Educação como prática da liberdade*. Rio de Janeiro: Paz e Terra.

Gadelha, R. M. A. F. (2017). *Educação no Brasil: Desafios e Crise Institucional. Revista Pesquisa & Debate*. São Paulo: PUCSP.

Kim, R. P. (2013). *O conteúdo jurídico de cidadania na Constituição Federal do Brasil. Cidadania – o novo conceito jurídico e a sua relação com os direitos fundamentais individuais e coletivos*. São Paulo: Atlas.

Kim, R. P. (2013). *O conteúdo jurídico de cidadania na Constituição Federal do Brasil. In Cidadania – o novo conceito jurídico e a sua relação com os direitos fundamentais individuais e coletivos*. São Paulo: Atlas.

Laborit, H. (1986). *La nouvelle Grille (1974)*. Paris: Robert Laffont.

Lévy, P. (1999). *Cibercultura*. São Paulo: Editora 34.

Molinaro, C. A., & Sarlet, I. W. (2013). *Sociedade em rede, internet e Estado de vigilância: algumas aproximações*. Rio Grande do Sul: AJURIS.

Pedroso de Campos, J. (2017). *Is Jean Wyllys going to direct a film that shows Jesus as homosexual?* Retrieved from https://veja.abril.com.br/blog/me-engana-que-eu-posto/jean-wyllys-vai-dirigir-filme-que-mostra-jesus-como-homossexual/

Pinskay, J., & Pinskay, C. B. (2015). *História da Cidadania*. São Paulo: Contexto.

Popescu, A. V. (2018). *The impairment of citizen's right to information by "fake news" publication. In Challenges of the Knowledge Society. Public Law*. Nicolae Titulescu University Publishing House.

Programme for international student assessment (PISA). (2015). *Result from PISA 2015*. Retrieved from https://www.oecd.org/pisa/PISA-2015-Brazil-PRT.pdf

Rocha, M. P. C. (2000). *A questão cidadania na sociedade da informação.* Retrieved from http://www.scielo.br/scielo.php?script=sci_arttext&pid=S0100-19652000000100004&lng=en&nrm=iso&tlng=pt

Santos, M. (2007). *O Espaço do Cidadão.* São Paulo: Editora da Universidade de São Paulo.

Santos, M. (2007). *O Espaço do Cidadão.* São Paulo: Editora da Universidade de São Paulo.

Senado. (2013). *Pesquisa DataSenado mostra que poucos conhecem realmente a Constituição.* Retrieved from http://www.12.senado.leg.br/noticias/materiais/2013/10/25/pesquisa-datasenado-mostra-que-poucos-conhecem-realmente-a-constituicao-do-pais

Venera, R. A. S. (2009). *Sentidos da educação cidadã no Brasil. Educar.* Curitiba: UFPR.

ENDNOTES

1 Data from the evaluation conducted in 2018 have not yet been released.

2 As reported in several national media: "Polícia Federal vai investigar uso de WhatsApp para fake news", available at https://oglobo.globo.com/brasil/policia-federal-vai-investigar-uso-de-whatsapp-para-fake-news-23172204; "Procuradoria Regional Eleitoral pede inquérito sobre fake news relacionadas a Bolsonaro e Haddad", available at <https://politica.estadao.com.br/noticias/eleicoes,pgr-pede-inquerito-sobre-mensagens-em-redes-sociais-relacionadas-a-bolsonaro-e-haddad,70002555170>. Considering that the object of the present study does not specifically refer to the analysis of how the spread of fake news had an impact on the outcome of the presidential elections in Brazil, it is recommended, as a deepening on this subject, the reading of the articles: "Eleições com fake news?: Uma semana dentro de 272 grupos políticos no WhatsApp mostra um Brasil dividido e movido a notícias falsas," by Juliana Gragnani, of BBC News Brazil in London, available at <https://www.bbc.com/Portuguese/ Brazil-45666742>; "O impacto das fake news nas eleições presidenciais", available at <http://cnseg.org.br/cnseg/servicos-apoio/noticias/o-impacto-das-fake-news-nas-eleicoes-presidenciales.html>; "Selective Exposure to Misinformation: Evidence from the Consumption of Fake News During the 2016 U.S. Presidential Campaign", available at <https://shorensteincenter.org/fake-news-2016-brendan-nyhan/>.

3 Castells emphasizes that "In our society, which I conceived as a networked society, power is multidimensional and is organized around networks programmed in each domain of human activity, according to the interests and values of qualified actors. The networks of power exercise it mainly by influencing the human mind (but not only) through multimedia mass communication networks. Thus, communication networks are decisive sources of power building" (p. 16).

Chapter 9
Dematerialization in Customs Taxation for Transparency in International Trade

Andreia Barbosa
Universidade do Minho, Portugal

ABSTRACT

Transparency is a quality that transcends many areas of law and is based on a fundamental principle that transcends the entire legal system and whose scope extends to all public and private actions to which legal relevance can be recognized. In the specific field of taxation in international trade, the importance of transparency has become proportional to the growing complexity of the terms in which cross-border trade in goods takes place. In deed, the more complex the exchanges are, the greater the level of control over them and the greater the degree of transparency required, both as regards the form of control and the specific terms in which transactions are performed. In any case, the requirements and effects of transparency are reflected in a digital context of dematerialization, but not, of course, of automation.

INTRODUCTION

Transactions of goods across borders - in particular those between economic operators of the Member States of the European Union and those of third countries or territories - are subject to a wide range of legal obligations, including tax obligations - which its raison d'être, and other extremely important purposes which we will have the opportunity to explore - the promotion of the effective functioning of the single market.

DOI: 10.4018/978-1-5225-8350-9.ch009

In the specific field of taxation in international trade, the importance of transparency has become proportionate to the growing complexity of the terms in which cross-border trade in goods takes place. That is to say, the more complex the exchanges are, the greater the level of control over them, and the greater the degree of transparency required, both as regards the form of control and the specific terms in which transactions are performed. In any case, the requirements and effects of transparency are reflected in a digital context of dematerialization, but not, of course, of automation. There is a growing internationalization of national economies, a dizzying advance of technologies and, in particular, of communications, bringing commerce to a new dimension in which the actions of citizens and companies are globalized.

In this sense, transparency in the taxation of international trade in goods takes on a complex of meanings: on the one hand, it constitutes a right to transparency that assists all economic operators and as a duty on them, through the digitization of their procedures, comply with the customs obligations to which they are attached. It also refers to a right of the Customs Authorities to make it easier to carry out their duties through procedural dematerialization and also as a duty to which they are attached and can not adopt a modus operandi other than that resulting from customs legislation and which is directed at facilitating legitimate international trade. In a very relevant but not a developmentally appropriate sense, the freedom of conformity of tax systems within the World Trade Organization should also be shaped by the principle of transparency, with the result that States should describe the type of fiscal measure adopted, its function and objectives, its cost or benefit in terms of tax revenue and its economic evaluation in terms of effectiveness in achieving the stated objectives.

Schematically, the consequential chain in this existing domain is as follows:

Dematerialization → Transparency → Fostering international trade

The Construction of the Legal-Tax Discipline of International Trade

The construction of the legal-tax discipline of international trade is based on an evolutionary process that has been consolidated over the years and has been impacted by the constant changes in the paradigms of the terms in which trade in goods develops. For this reason, this discipline is still under construction, due to the lack of stagnation in the field of international trade, which, although difficult to obtain the "stability" we consider as a necessary quality for the coherence of a tax system, presents the advantage of bringing legal reality closer to reality.

In the context of customs duties, from the eighteenth and nineteenth centuries, there were growing concerns in Europe about the multiplicity of taxes and the complexity of the systems then in force, as well as because "the most basic idea of the European Community is fiscal idea" (Terra & Wattel, 2012, p. 9). Consequently, a process of simplification has begun by eliminating or integrating some European customs systems, initially on a bilateral basis, but gradually extending to countries with geographical, commercial and economic affinities. In 1944 the conditions for the emergence of the Customs Convention within the Benelux Economic Union were met. In 1948 customs duties were abolished in the transactions of goods carried out between the Member States of the Union and a common customs tariff was introduced.

Moreover, alongside the introduction of a single currency in the European area, the creation of a Customs Union is one of the most important historical milestones in the process of European integration, in the sense that it emerged as a solution to political and economic concerns that were made to feel. "Projects for customs unions and other special tariff arrangements between states independent of each other politically are today widespread, and many persons look to them as at least a partial solution for the major eonomic and political problems in the international field" (Viner, 2014, p. 1). In the words of Schuman (1950), the Customs Union represents one of the most ambitious "concrete achievements", building a genuine solidarity between the Member States of the European Union, which has contributed to preventing the emergence of conflicts and to promoting better quality of life of the peoples of Europe, for the prosperity and security of the Union (Schuman, 1950). The Customs Union, which represents one of the first examples of successful integration in the European Union, has not been built at once and must be seen not as an event but as a has had an impact in the most diverse fields of States, with effects, in particular, at the legislative, judicial, political and administrative levels. With regard to the extent of the effects of a customs union, Leopold Kohr (1949, p. 9) said that "the economies inevitably become one of the waters of two lakes after dam separating them has been removed."

In addition, the Customs Union created brings together all the elements that the doctrine says are essential to customs unions: (i) the absence of customs duties in trade intra-union; (ii) the existence of a common customs tariff; (iii) the unit of the customs territory; (iv) uniformity of customs legislation; (v) the existence of common revenues.

Thus, in the European context, there is an umbilical relationship between the Customs Union and the free movement of goods between Member States, within the single market - that is, within an area without internal frontiers, where it is guaranteed the freedom of movement of the four factors of production of a market (goods, people, services and capital). The Customs Union is the guardian of the single market. Moreover, the Court of Justice of the European Union has repeatedly held that the first is that the second is necessarily guaranteed by the system as a whole and in accordance with the general nature of the prohibition of customs duties on the movement of goods between Member States, regardless of the purpose of its introduction or the destination that the revenue obtained would have. The rationale for the ban is essentially the obstacle to the free movement of goods in customs duties, in an idea that has been introduced and consolidated by globalization.

The phenomenon of globalization dictating a change in the «paradigms of life», of social, economic and political relations, has consequently influenced the world of law, promoting the change of «legal paradigms». In particular, the concept of globalization is essentially used to signify the growing and intense integration and interdependence of the various national economies, eliminating barriers to trade and the movement of capital and, in general, removing obstacles to the free movement of all factors production.

In view of the impact of globalization on trade, promoting them and making them even essential to the survival of States, restrictions on international trade began to emerge as potential enemies to this international trade should be developed in a safe and simple environment, eliminating unnecessary customs and administrative costs. Moreover, globalization and trade without frontiers stem from the idea that since its origin, goods have been found in the common heritage of mankind, intended for use by all men. There is, therefore, and thus has been recognized as something obvious, a natural right of every man to use the created goods, based on the principle of the universal destiny of goods (Alais, 2006, p. 271-272). It is in this sense customs duties are considered as "(...) flagrantly incompatible with free movement of goods and services" (Terra & Wattel, 2012, p. 9).

And with particular relevance to the present text is the idea that the legal discipline of international trade, in a context of globalization, should be guided by principles. More concretely, in the domain of the legal-tax system of international trade, the fundamental principles of taxation in international trade return to the essential values or the abstract rules that must define the main guidelines of the legal-tax regimes, systematizing them, structuring - inspiring them, benefiting from a generalized recognition by the subjects of the legal relationship established - States, international institutions, economic operators, citizens, among others.

It is considered necessary to overcome the unprincipled casuism, from a solid theoretical construction, away from practices outlined in the margin of the Law. Even if there are issues with a high technicist substrate that are further away from «humanitary» considerations, it is possible to find elements that are inherent in it and that allow us to withdraw from the legal-tax discipline of international merchandise trade the concern to protect dignity human. This is precisely because we are still in the field of law and, as in all its branches, it is a question of finding solutions that will serve and be used by men.

It will be sought, therefore, to identify the main crossings that pass through the system, which give rise to taxation in international trade and whose consideration may lead, on the one hand, to the obligation of the Authorities to adopt a principologically oriented action and, for that reason, especially shielded because it is fundamentally sustained and, on the other hand, that the taxation that would result from the application of the established rules can not occur when it means a preterite of some or some of the established principles, considering that they are part of the block of juridicity and that are endowed with binding.

Thus, it is through the identification of a set of basic principles to the tax system that the values or ideals of justice and coherence are constructed and achieved. It is a principiological basis that upholds justice and coherence, functioning each of these values as a presupposition of the other, in a relation of mutual prejudice.

The fact that, according to the majority view, «international trade should be developed in a safe and simple environment by eliminating unnecessary fiscal and administrative costs», it does not in itself allow a conclusion to be drawn that existing taxation, simply because it exists, renders the system unfair or inconsistente (Teixeira, 2018, p. 173). The fairness and consistency of taxation will be in accordance with the terms of the imposition of such taxation, and such terms should be based on a set of principles that are especially aligned with the specific field of international trade. Consecrated that remain and applied that are the principles, it is not necessary to fear for the taxation, knowing that of the same one stems the important virtuality of financing of the States.

It is true that customs duties have been accused of being a factor restricting international trade and have therefore been 'disposed of' in regional economic integration processes (for example, in the European Union and in Mercosul) and multilateral negotiations on the liberalization of world trade (GATT - General Agreement on Tariffs and Trade (1947) and World Trade Organization (1995). In this sense, and in the light of the post-World War II example of multilateral trade liberalization negotiations, the reduction and / or elimination of customs duties would be desirable for the promotion of world trade and globalization. Liberalization, achieved in this way, would lead to a general improvement in living standards, the achievement of full employment and an increase in real incomes.

Nonetheless, taxation is associated with extra-tax effects (other than revenue collection), aimed at protecting domestic markets, protecting public health and the environment, contributing to the transparency of these effects

The Tax and Customs Administrative Activity

The tax and customs administrative activity refers to all acts of the Customs Authorities (in the designation of European customs legislation) or the Tax and Customs Authority (in the designation of Portuguese legislation – *Autoridade Tributária e Aduaneira*) for the application of tax and customs rules to specific cases (in particular, the rules on VAT - Value-added tax - and customs duties in the field of international goods transactions). The aforementioned Authorities are true subjects of Law, to which is recognized the ownership of certain subjective legal situations, deserving of guardianship. Among these legal situations are subjective rights of a concrete and determined nature - such as the right to the perception of tax revenue in relation to that economic operator - and legal powers of an abstract nature - such as the power to take the necessary steps for the discovery of material truth in relation to any economic operator; the power to issue binding tariff information or information on origin. For each of these active subjective situations, the customs authorities will have a passive legal situation, to which a particular subject (e.g. the economic operator) is attached: for example, the duty to deliver the VAT); to control its operations and the flow of goods; and to enable customs inspections to be carried out.

In accordance with Article 5 (1) of the Union Customs Code, customs authorities shall refer to the customs administrations of the Member States responsible for the application of customs legislation, as well as to any other authority, which, under national law, are competent to apply certain customs legislation.

It is in Article 3 of the Union Customs Code that the mission of the Customs Authorities is established, stating that they are, first and foremost, responsible for supervising the international trade of the Union, thereby contributing to the implementation of the external dimension of the internal market, the common commercial policy and other common Union policies relating to trade and the security of the global supply chain. In particular, customs authorities shall institute measures aimed in particular at:

- To protect the financial interests of the Union and its Member States;
- Protect the Union against unfair and illegal trade, while encouraging legitimate economic activities;
- Ensure the protection and security of the Union and its residents, as well as the protection of the environment, where appropriate, in close cooperation with other entities;
- Maintaining an appropriate balance between customs controls and facilitation of legitimate trade.

Customs authorities therefore play an important leading role in the implementation of fiscal policies and techniques for the pursuit of heteronomically determined legislative interests and which subsume the idea of pursuing the public interest and promoting legitimate international trade (Lux, 2007, p. 1). In particular, the interest in revenue collection is not solely concerned, and the Customs Authorities do not function as mere tax collectors. Indeed, in their mission, customs authorities function as guarantors of the protection and safety of society, since, at the external frontier, it is their responsibility to ensure that the introduction of goods into the customs territory complies with the vast and dense legislation, in cooperation with competent authorities in matters of technical, environmental, cultural, public health, protection of fauna and flora, and control of dual use goods, torture, proliferation, among others. In addition, since transactions involving persons and entities from different jurisdictions are concerned and their goods are being transported across borders, tax and customs officials play an important role as vigilantes when entering the European Union. First of all, it is for them to control products imported from third countries which cross the common external frontier of the European Union in order to collect customs duties, VAT and excise duties and to protect the interests of the Union and its citizens in different ways. The transformation of the Customs Union into a single market has led to the elimination of internal economic frontiers between Member States and this development has reinforced the importance of external border controls, with a focus on these controls.

The achievement of the purposes underlying VAT and customs duties is thus directly dependent on efficient, organized and properly equipped customs authorities. The customs officials, who control the correct application of legal provisions, are true guardians of the Union's foreign policy, resulting from the aforementioned Article 3 of the Union Customs Code a complex of duties on them.

Thus, the Union Customs Code has emerged as the backbone of the Customs Union on the European Union and presents a set of solutions aimed at facilitating the terms of international trade, with a clear concern in the security field, as has been seen, to the customs authorities, an important role. In addition, it leaves it to the Member States to adopt, in particular, the measures necessary to give effect to the objectives set out in the Union Customs Code, in order to ensure that customs control - which appears as the «first defense» and «last control» of the which enters and leaves the customs territory - is implemented as efficiently and effectively as possible. Thus, theoretically, Member States may choose different approaches to fulfill the mission entrusted by the Union Customs Code to their Authorities. In the abstract, the scenarios could be as follows:

- A minimalist approach: in this case, the requirements resulting from the Union Customs Code are achieved through the smallest possible number of changes internally, without neglecting the necessary legislative changes brought by the Union Customs Code and adapting information technology systems. However, this type of approach may mean that a wide range of benefits arising from the Union Customs Code and the failure to follow up on the digitization measures in the customs field can not be achieved, to the detriment of agility and safety.
- An adapted approach: the philosophy of this approach is to correct problems related to international trade in goods and already felt through the implementation of the Union Customs Code itself. Instead of complying to the extent possible with the requirements of the Union Customs Code, the impending changes in the digital domain, organization, procedures and internal legislation are considered as an integral part of the Union Customs Code implementation. By using Union Customs Code as a way of responding to other requests and problems, in theory the conditions for designing a stronger and more cohesive Customs Authority are created and the benefits arising from Union Customs Code are enhanced. In this case, the risk is compounded by the complexity underlying this type of approach which may lead to non-compliance with the deadlines set in the Union Customs Code.

The activity carried out in this field is carried out in the course of various acts, which may be merely material acts - for example, the analysis of the accounts of an economic operator or the receipt of a document - as individual legal acts which establish legal effects in the sphere of an economic operator - for example, the settlement of customs duties or the rejection of a complaint.

The administrative activity triggered (i) is legally framed - due to compliance with, inter alia, the principles of constitutionality, legality, proportionality and mandatory reporting; (ii) enjoys a presumption of legality and (iii) may be jurisdictional.

The practice of all acts by the customs authorities presupposes a complex of steps, a gradual series of operations, from which results the procedural character of the tax and customs activity. Specifically, each act must have relative autonomy - having a specific purpose - it must be in connection with the other acts and there must be a causal relationship between each one of them, maintaining its sequential order.

It will be precisely within the scope of the authorities that the digitization will have a great impact, influenced the way the procedures are done and, consequently, the decisions themselves.

Dematerialisation at the Service of Transparency

Each tax solution causes problems in the trade and each solution in the trade brings tributary problems. Thus, although digitization can be attributed relevant advantages, the concrete terms of operation must be legally defined. Not only to ensure that the objective of transparency is met, but also to avoid breach of essential dimensions.

With special relevance, tansparency comes from requirement of good administration.

It is Article 41 of the Charter of Fundamental Rights of the European Union inserted in its Chapter V, entitled «Citizens Rights», which enshrines the «Right to good administration». According to the aforementioned provision, everyone has the right to have his affairs handled impartially, fairly and within a reasonable time by the institutions and bodies of the European Union. In particular, the right to good administration is broken down into a set of various rights, including, in particular, the right of any person to be heard before any individual measure is taken that would adversely affect his right of any person to have access to the files relating thereto, while respecting the legitimate interests of confidentiality and professional and commercial secrecy, and the obligation on the part of the Administration to give reasons for its decisions.

In this sense, it is possible to bring transparency requirements to all segments of the right to good administration, considering that they all presuppose the clarity of administrative action, combined with the need for efficiency and effectiveness, in favor of a growing sense of confidence in the activity developed.

Therefore, the idea that the principle of pursuing the public interest, which is evidently based on good administration and enshrined in Article 266 of the Portuguese Republic Constitution presupposes a transparent performance. Transparency, in addition to upholding rights and duties, then emerges as a sub-principle of the principle of pursuing the public interest. This is a particularly relevant reflex in the field of commercial transactions of goods, which are increasingly complex and require assertive actions and stability promoters.

The consequence of this conclusion is that actions that are not transparent (maxime, oblivious to the demands of dematerialization) will themselves be invalid, assuming that the principles are parameters of control of the administrative activity, which are part of the block of juridicity and, in particular, the fundamental structure of the legal-tax discipline, which must remain firm and solid, despite the variation, transitoriness and profusion of the applicable rules (Raimundo, 2015, p. 207).

From the perspective of economic operators and Customs Authorities, this conclusion is particularly relevant: for the former, because it represents a reinforcement of their guarantees and, for the latter, it serves as an incentive for the adoption of a principally oriented action and, for this reason, especially armored, for being fundamentally and constitutionally sustained.

In particular, there are several provisions of customs legislation from which the idea is that transparency is associated with digitization / dematerialization, but not with automation.

For example, from the point of view of the Customs Authorities, on the one hand, the dissemination of customs legislation, administrative decisions not having an individual character and the forms for applications that may be submitted in the form of a duty, which must be met digitally, in particular, through the Internet, through a free and open access platform. On the other hand, the customs control of goods and, to a large extent, the customs procedure as a whole, are now based on digital mechanisms and electronic data transmissions.

In deed, transparency is associated with digitization / dematerialization and it is in this sense that since 2003 the ideas of 'customs and paperless trade' have been disseminated by the European Commission. The objective is to promote, in a harmonious way by the States integrated into the Customs Union, a modern customs service, which communicates electronically with commerce, based on so-called «electronic customs». It is, therefore, a matter in which the law and the new technologies are in close connection. The last years have served to improve and implement the intended modernization, and the necessary legal instruments have been created and adapted so that it can say, with the greatest possible security, that the digitization in the customs taxation is done under the Law.

The Union Customs Code established the obligation of total computerization and dematerialization in the customs field, through electronic data processing techniques. In this way, the winds of technological change are felt, both for economic operators and for the customs authorities themselves, and both are required to adapt their procedures to the technological reality.

It is also in this sense that the MASP - Electronic Customs Multi-Annual Strategic Plan - is a tool for the management and planning of IT projects in the customs context and has been developed by the Commission in partnership with the Member States, Article 8 (2) of the e-Customs decision - is subject to constant revisions, as a result of the technological evolution achieved and the new requirements detected.

The rationale for digitization in the context of customs taxation may be based primarily on three grounds, which may be valid both from the perspective of economic operators and from the customs authorities.

The first of the reasons that can be attached to the digitization is simplification. This is the reason which seems to be the most obvious and which leads us back to the need to simplify and speed up the control and enforcement of obligations linked to the import and export of goods. The complexity and slowness normally associated with customs procedures and the need to implement new administrative practices based on risk analysis will have dictated, to a large extent, the need for de-duplication through the use of new technologies. The objective - which seems ambitious to us, considering that the complexity underlying international trade seems difficult to blur - is to improve the efficiency of the organization of customs controls and to allow an uninterrupted flow of information, customs formalities and a reduction in the administrative burden.

In particular, simplification can be reflected in several ways, including:

- The possibility for electronic data exchange between Customs throughout the Union to be possible where necessary and in the framework of any customs procedure or any other purpose related to the movement of goods at the Union's borders;
- The possibility for operators to be able to submit their declarations in electronic form and from their premises, regardless of the location of the goods within the Union;
- The possibility that the selection of goods for customs control in Customs be based on an automated risk analysis;
- The interconnection of customs electronic systems with systems in other areas of taxation.

The second reason, which turns out to be also a consequence of the first, is the need to ensure intense scrutiny of the terms in which international trade is implemented, which is well understood in view of the extra-fiscal purposes underlying the collection of duties customs, which go beyond the design of revenue collection and which extend to the whole set of extra-fiscal purposes that we have already had the opportunity to identify. Thus, the role of the Authorities in achieving these objectives is of the utmost importance, and for this reason the legislator gives them wide powers of control of the goods. By way of example, Customs Authorities may:

- Carry out customs controls of the goods they deem necessary. Customs controls may include checking the goods, taking samples, checking the accuracy and completeness of the information contained in a declaration or notification, and the existence, authenticity, accuracy and validity of the documents, the accounting of operators and other records, the inspection of means of transport, baggage and other goods carried by persons or persons and the carrying out of official inquiries and other similar acts;

- Verify the accuracy and completeness of the information contained in the customs declaration, the temporary deposit declaration, the entry and exit summary declarations, the re-export declaration or the re-export notification, and the existence, authenticity, accuracy and validity of any and may examine the declarant's accounts and other records relating to the operations in respect of the goods in question or the commercial operations relating to those goods; and
- Carry out subsequent checks on the information provided and on the documents, forms, authorizations or data relating to the transit operation, in order to verify that entries, information exchanged and stamps are authentic.

The fact that scrutiny is carried out electronically reduces the margin of error, the possibilities of information leakage and, as a consequence, enhances revenue collection through the collection of customs duties and meets the other purposes underlying taxation in commerce customs duties.

It is also important to point out the reasons why operators have to adapt their own internal procedures digitally in order to obtain the advantages conferred on them by the legislator. Digitization therefore contributes to tax planning, given the advantages that, within a framework of full legality, can mean. The opportunities to which we refer and which presuppose the digitization, could be, in particular, the following:

- The granting of an authorization retroactively to benefit from inward or outward processing, temporary importation or end-use arrangements or for the operation of storage facilities for the customs warehouse of goods. To that end, certain requirements must be fulfilled which presuppose a computer platform capable of storing and sharing a wide range of information, essentially relating to the treatment of goods.
- The granting of the status of authorized economic operator, which strengthens a relationship of greater confidence with the Authorities. Among the criteria for the granting of status, the applicant is required to demonstrate a high level of control of his operations and the flow of goods through a system of management of trade registers and transport records, allowing for appropriate customs controls.

However, the digitization that occurs through the voluntary action of economic operators in favor of a reduction of risks and, consequently, of the tax burden, must also be considered. In particular, we refer to the programs developed for the purpose of tracking the goods, to help in the correct classification of goods, in the definition of the flow of goods according to the trade agreements entered into, in the fulfillment of customs obligations, in particular of an incidental or formal nature and in identifying the Incoterms that may be used. There are also tools for graphically visualizing risk areas and opportunities for improvement - either from a group perspective or individually and that provide a benchmarking of the initial business income to help identify possible improvements in internal procedures. This is a digitization to which operators voluntarily subscribe - since, despite the fact that they are tasks that could be developed manually without using the technologies, they would be at least more time consuming - and that is usually developed within the scope of the consultancy on the basis of the idea that the revision based on the modernization of customs procedures contributes to the creation or development of a strategic vision of the business.

But voluntary digitization may be relevant to the Customs Authorities themselves in order to make their operation more efficient and effective. By way of example, the Internet of things can signify important opportunities by facilitating the tracking and monitoring of goods more safely and automatically through the application of Radio Frequency Identification or Near-Field Communication technologies in handling of the goods. Portable X-ray systems are another example of new technologies that can be implemented by the Authorities, allowing them to examine large quantities of goods more quickly. Moreover, the line of defense to be created must coincide with the borders, in order to make the controls more effective.

However, the digitization carried out in the customs area is not unrelated to particular challenges.

The first concerns the protection afforded to the data to which the Authorities have access. As we have seen, the software can reveal a considerable amount of information about the economic operators and the activity developed by them, which may even be confidential.

In this respect, Article 12 of the Union Customs Code stipulates that all information obtained by the customs authorities in the exercise of their powers, which are confidential or provided on a confidential basis, are covered by the obligation of professional secrecy. Such information shall not be disclosed by the competent authorities without the express authorization of the entity providing them. However, such information may be disclosed without authorization if the customs authorities are obliged or authorized to do so under the provisions in force, in particular as regards data protection or in legal proceedings. In addition, confidential information may be communicated to the authorities and other competent authorities of countries or territories outside the customs territory of the Union for the purpose of customs cooperation with those countries or territories under international agreements or Union legislation in the field of common commercial policy. However, any disclosure or disclosure of information shall ensure an adequate level of data protection in full compliance with the relevant provisions in force.

Related to the disclosure of data, there is a second challenge related to the possibility of software programs divulging data that put the respective operators in a situation of self-incrimination. In fact, since software can provide a more or less extensive set of information, data that incriminate economic operators are likely to be disseminated. This situation is capable of generating a discussion about the admissibility of these elements in the context of the criminal proceedings that may be instituted, considering that the Authorities only had access to them because the operators gave them up, as a result, for example, of a system failure which "unblocked" information that they did not intend to disclose or because the information was inserted there, the criminal nature of the information being unknown, or the fulfillment of the duties of cooperation. In this case, the information communicated in the framework of the cooperation shall be confidential, unless otherwise agreed. Moreover, Article 14 of the Union Customs Code provides that customs authorities and economic operators may exchange information which is not required by customs legislation with a view to mutual cooperation in the detection and prevention of risk. Such exchange, which may be effected under a written agreement, may include access by the Authorities to the operators' computer systems. In addition, Article 15 states that any person involved in the completion of customs formalities or in carrying out customs controls must provide the authorities with all the documents and information required, as well as the whole of the assistance necessary to carry out those formalities or controls. Even if, unless otherwise agreed by the parties, the information communicated in the context of the cooperation is confidential, the problem remains constant, given the possibility of a breach of confidentiality.

Without wishing to enter into the discussion about the possibility of using the evidence thus collected in the criminal proceedings that may be instituted, we will limit ourselves to say that this is a subject that, although it has already been discussed in other venues (in this case, essentially, of the evidence gathered in the tax inspection procedure), has not yet been raised in this particular area and should have been expressly safeguarded by the customs legislator.

Another challenge is the burden on economic operators of adapting their procedures to the new requirements. The creation and / or implementation of software programs entail significant investments due to the range of functionalities they will have to be able to achieve. At the cost associated with the acquisition of the computer system / program, the costs are increased by the respective maintenance and instruction of the employees who will have to learn how to work with them.

But it's not just the expense of digitization that gives rise to concern. They add to the burden on operators related to the most complete handling of the information. For example, operators control the data sources; protection of data against the risk of unauthorized access, loss, alteration and destruction; the registration of all the introductions, modifications and deletions of data with indication of their purpose, the precise moment in which they are made and of its author; the creation of mechanisms to detect and react to security flaws and technical problems in software and to keep their data for a certain period of time. We therefore consider that the burden of making simple what is by nature complex is largely the responsibility of economic operators.

In this sense, the requirements of proportionality are particularly important.

Such requirements have been taken into account by the legislature with regard to the activities of the customs authorities, but economic operators do not appear to have any prospect. Indeed, the digitization that economic operators have or can adhere to is justified in that, when implemented, it is not necessary to create a disproportionate administrative device in relation to the economic needs in question, and only a complete and effective will be able to avoid it. Thus, it is in the view of the Authorities that the requirements of proportionality are legislated. Although the legislator does not concretize what this device consists of, it is intuited that it will be redirected to the allocation of technical and human resources that allow to trace the transactional and tax reality of a particular entity.

On the other hand, it remained unclear what should be understood by economic needs. The relevance that this requirement assumes, in conjunction with the principles of security and legal certainty, calls for greater care of the legislator's resourcefulness and concreteness. But, of course, also for the Customs Authorities themselves, the correct delimitation of terms is fundamental so that the respective decisions are taken with a level of support as rigorous and complete as possible, in favor of an efficient and legally founded action, due to the principles of public interest and good administration.

Hoping to contribute to this densification, it seems clear that, from the subjective point of view, the economic needs must be verified in the sphere of the economic operator. More specifically, it will be in the sphere of the debtor or eventual debtor (who corresponds to the person liable for a customs debt) that the economic needs will have to be measured. From the objective point of view, and in summary form, they may, in our view, constitute economic needs, in the area of activities that focus on international trade, namely: compliance with large tax obligations, unaccompanied by the necessary increase in recipes; compliance with broad administrative and bureaucratic obligations, which entail increased investments so that procedures are adapted to the new requirements; failure to take advantage of opportunities granted by customs legislation; loss of market share due to the growth of competing operators; and consumer demand for goods.

Of course, these concerns are not as strong when the digitization is voluntary. However, taking into account that the use of new technologies in the customs context will mean an increase in economic activity, then voluntariness becomes an "almost obligatory" and the considerations that have hitherto been woven in this framework will also apply.

It must also be acknowledged that the legislative attempt to ensure compliance at least in part with the requirements of the principle of proportionality has been detected, on the grounds that a transitional period, valid until 31 December 2020, has been established for the development and operationalization of all IT systems required for the full implementation of the Union Customs Code.

Lastly, the possibilities of coordinating the digitization requirements laid down in the Union Customs Code with the customs situation experienced by third countries with which trade is established is also a challenge. This is all the more challenging the less technological development in third countries. In general terms, and according to MASP (in the revised version of 2017), the Customs Union computer systems will be built according to international standards, allowing interaction with third country systems.

However, the most important challenge is not the possibility of anticipating what kind of systems or software programs should be implemented in 5 to 10 years. The challenge, it seems to us, lies in the development of tools that have a level of versatility that is large enough to deal with the constant changes, although the basic idea does not undergo major changes - that of freedom in international trade.

However, compliance with the duty of transparency by digital means should not mean an automation of the administrative will, in the sense that the customs tax acts could be carried out without human intervention or with a reduced intervention. Officials and agents of the Customs Authorities should not be replaced by machinery which produces an independent will. If this were not the case, serious difficulties would arise from future accountability. In this sense, the objective of the current customs legislation, especially aimed at the respective digitization, was not to make the decision of the Authorities automated, but rather dematerialized, first of all because the automatic operating schemes alone can not produce an autonomous will, enlightened and thoughtful, as a human being is capable. In fact, automation alone is not capable of producing a legal act, and human intervention is always necessary. The objective of measures aimed at dematerialization in the customs field is therefore to improve the efficiency of the organization of customs controls, to allow an uninterrupted flow of information and to ensure the highest level of transparency for the Customs Authorities. Moreover, the automatic task of subsuming the facts to the norm must be the same: automatic, or syllogistic, in a task of uncritical subsumption, in which no valuation weights or choices in open spaces of graduation are required, be dispensed with.

In this respect, in the field of taxation in international trade, there is a growing dematerialisation of the administrative will, which can not, on pain of prejudicing the very purposes of taxation, become automatic in the name of the principle of good administration.

The growth of trade has led to the introduction of effective systems for the control of goods, since it is becoming increasingly impossible to intervene physically for this purpose, taking into account the time and effort required, as well as being a costly procedure for the parties involved. With progress, essentially at the technological level, control procedures have undergone a radical change and continue to evolve. The customs authorities therefore face the challenge of ensuring the normal flow of trade while maintaining, where necessary, effective control. To this end, modern working methods are applied in order to simplify controls and focus on areas where they are most needed or more effective. Thus, computerization, a posteriori controls, audits and the application of risk analysis are techniques that have been increasingly used, becoming more sophisticated.

Moreover, information technology is increasingly being used in relations between customs authorities and economic operators. As an exemple, customs declarations without paper support have contributed to reducing the length of the customs clearance process at borders. Computer systems have also been developed which allow National Authorities to exchange information with the European Commission's centralized databases. At the same time, the Commission played an important role in setting up new systems to complement existing national systems, thus allowing Member States' customs offices to exchange information between them at both national and European level.

The use of risk analysis methods allows the selection of consignments which, by their nature, value, origin or importer, may represent a certain risk. The use of these techniques allows customs to decide more objectively whether a particular consignment needs to be physically analyzed or not. It also helps to determine the level of controls to be applied, allowing customs to take some of these decisions before the goods concerned have reached the European Union's borders. However, the success resulting from the application of this type of technique depends on the rigor with which the data are introduced and the care with which they are collected.

Customs are increasingly inclined to carry out physical checks after the goods have been moved to the operators' premises. This greatly facilitates the movement of goods by reducing delays in ports and airports, while also contributing to a reduction in costs, since the goods will not have to be unpacked twice. The methods of verification after importation may be applied once the goods have arrived at their destination and have been released for free circulation. Currently, controls are increasingly based on operator accounting checks.

It is therefore clear that the new international trade frameworks have dictated the allocation to Customs of a new and more relevant role in promoting foreign trade and the competitiveness of enterprises, based on intensifying the fight against fraud and illicit trafficking, with a increasing use of risk analysis and risk management techniques, simplification and automation of customs procedures. It is true that the desire for simplification does not sometimes assess the reasons for the complexity involved. In addition, the sophistication of economic life, with an impact on the ways of transacting goods and services and on the ways of obtaining income, has as a corollary the need for the fiscal system to follow this sophistication, making it consequently and inevitably more complex - MARTINS, A. (2005), *A complexidade do sistema tributário: uma inevitabilidade económica?*, Lisboa, Portugal: Fisco. However, the simplification of procedures through digitization contributes to this.

Moreover, one of the purposes underlying the adoption of the Union Customs Code is to implement the concept of e-customs through computerization and dematerialization of the customs procedures of the Member States of the European Union. To this end, and following the decision of Decision No 70/2008 / EC of the European Parliament and of the Council, of 15 January 2008, on a paperless environment for customs and trade, Council Regulation (EC) No 2015/2447, of 24 November 1990, laying down certain transitional measures in cases where it has not yet been possible for the customs authorities and the undertakings themselves to provide themselves with the computer tools necessary for the full application of the Union Customs Code, being sure that from the end of 2020 all computer systems will have to be fully qualified. The objective is to improve the efficiency of the organization of customs controls and to allow an uninterrupted flow of information, in order to improve the efficiency of customs clearance procedures, to reduce administrative burden, to combat fraud, organized crime and terrorism, protect financial interests, intellectual property and cultural heritage, enhance the security of goods and international trade and improve protection of health and the environment.

It so happens that the use of the digital medium to carry out its mission should not make the administrative will automated, but merely dematerialized. Officials and agents of the customs authorities should not be replaced by machinery which produces an independent will. If this were not the case, serious difficulties would arise from future accountability. In this sense, the objective of the Union Customs Code, especially aimed at the digitization / modernization of customs, was not to make the decision of the Authorities automated, but rather dematerialized, first of all because the automatic operating schemes alone can not produce an autonomous will, enlightened and thoughtful, as a human being is capable. In fact, automation alone is not capable of producing a legal act, and human intervention is always necessary.

In addition, the automatic task of subsuming the facts to the norm must be the same: automatic, or syllogistic, in a task of uncritical subsumption, in which no valuation weights or choices in open spaces of graduation, and human intervention can not be dispensed with here (Rocha, 2018, p. 26).

In this respect, in the field of taxation in international trade, there is a growing dematerialisation of the administrative will, which can not, on pain of prejudicing the very purposes of taxation, become automatic, and name the principle of good administration.

From the perspective of economic operators, there are several reasons why they must adapt their own internal procedures digitally, in order to obtain the advantages conferred on them by the legislator. Digitization / dematerialization therefore contributes to an adequate tax planning, in view of the income that, within a framework of full legality, can mean. Such advantages - such as the granting of an authorization retroactively to benefit from a customs procedure and the granting of the status of authorized economic operator, which strengthens a relationship of greater confidence with the Authorities - are granted precisely because economic operators must now be supported on a digital basis and, therefore, provided with a higher level of transparency, thus allowing the Customs Authorities closer scrutiny.

In the light of all the foregoing, it is said that dematerialization is at the service of transparency in international trade, and that it falls on the Customs Authorities and on economic operators in the form of a duty - to act in accordance with the requirements of transparency -, and which at the same time corresponds to a right - to have transparent actions, for the sake of legal certainty and certainty, and for the facilitation of international trade itself. In these terms, it is the value of transparency that, together with others, should inform the performance of Customs Authorities and economic operators in the field of international trade.

CONCLUSION

The presence of technology defines the terms of tax in the international trade. But it is not just one technology. It is the convergence os all technologies: (i) transportation technologies; (ii) communication technologies and (iii) information technologies. All of those are converging to make a world and world trade that is ever more efficient. We finally achived the globalized society that is conected, and it is also multilateral.

The paradigm of international trade taxation is no longer the same as it was at the time when world peace was sought through the abolition of borders and the interdependent economy. Currently, taxation seeks to approximate the values, legal assets of each state, worldwide. And in this sense, the demands of transparency - at the various levels that have been identified - reflect this trend. Concerns about clarity of action are cross-cutting across most countries, and digitization at the service of taxation serves this purpose. The strength of international trade is recognized as requiring the creation of the necessary legal instruments.

Obviously, the exercise of citizenship - in the dimension one intends to adopt - implies, in the same way, transparent actions, both by the one who administers and the one who is administered.

REFERENCES

Félix Alais, H. (2006). *Los princípios del derecho aduanero, Teoría general y aplicación a la problemática de la infracción de declaración inexacta*. Buenos Aires: Facultad de Derecho de la Universidad Austral.

Kohr, L. (1949). *Customs Unions - A Tool for Peace*. Foundation for Foreign Affairs.

Lux. (2007). EU customs law and international law. *World Customs Journal*, 1.

Raimundo. (2015). Os princípios no novo CPA e o princípio da boa administração, em particular, in Comentários ao Novo Código do Procedimento Administrativo. Lisboa, Portugal: AAFDL.

Rocha. (2018). Lições de Procedimento e Processo Tributário. Coimbra, Portugal: Almedina.

Teixeira. (2018). Manual de Direito Fiscal. Coimbra, Portugal: Almedina.

Terra & Wattel. (2012). *European Tax Law*. Wolters Kluwer.

Viner, J. (2014). The Customs Union Issue, Edited and with an introduction by Paul Oslington. Oxford, UK: Oxford University Press.

Chapter 10
Corruption and Human Development Index:
A Global Picture of the Brazilian Panorama Between 2010 and 2018

Olívia Maria Cardoso Gomes
University of Minho, Portugal

Mara Karinne Lopes Veriato Barros
Federal University of Campina Grande, Brazil

ABSTRACT

Corruption is a human phenomenon that covers the whole world. It is a fact that public corruption gains more prominence than private corruption, because the state has the duty of accountability in a transparent way to taxpayers. As a result of this, the authors focus on the analysis of public corruption, which involves agents and public resources of the state. Therefore, this study has the main objective to verify if there is a relationship between IPC corruption (corruption perception index) and HDI (human development index), which posits the hypothesis that the greater the corruption, the lower the HDI indexes. In addition to the CPI and HDI variables, they also analyze the GDP of the countries in a secondary way. The global data analyzed indicate a high correlation between greater corruption and a lower index of human development, which may suggest problems of accountability.

DOI: 10.4018/978-1-5225-8350-9.ch010

INTRODUCTION

Corruption is a human phenomenon that covers the whole world and it is possible to observe it in every age, and an exciting topic that finds in Brazil a wide field of debate although there is evident difficulty to characterize it and to define it, it is possible realize that there is no sphere and hierarchy of power immune to this phenomenon.

It is a fact that public corruption gains more prominence than private corruption, first because the state has the duty to render accounts in a transparent way to the taxpayers, so as to exercise transparency in a form of accountability, according to public corruption is highlighted, which causes a greater social impact by diverting public resources, which in theory should be reverted to every society in the form of public policies. Due to this we focus in particular on the present work in the analysis of public corruption, that involving agents and public resources of the State.

According to Harada (2006, p.31), the state's financial activity is aimed at obtaining, managing and applying the financial resources necessaries for the attainment of the social well-being, if state activities deviate from that purpose through acts of corruption, such acts may interfere in the well-being and development of the whole society. In this sense, it is necessary to analyze the implications of the relationship between corruption and social development. However, the term development in this proposal is not only related to the economic aspect, but to human development.

Therefore, the present study aims to verify if there is a relationship between corruption and HDI (Human Development Index). We start from the hypothesis that the greater the corruption, the lower the HDI of the country. It is also intended to analyze the case of Brazil in the global scenario, adding the element Gross Domestic Product (GDP) to the HDI and other corruption data obtained from International Transparency (IT).

In this way, we will analyze the secondary data obtained through the Corruption Perception Index (CPI) of Transparência Internacional (TI), HDI data obtained through the United Nations Development Program (UNDP) and GDP data obtained through the Brazilian Institute Geography and statistics (IBGE).

In order to make the desired correlations, a bibliographic, empirical and explanatory research will be carried out. Subsequently, the quantitative secondary data (CPI, HDI and GDP for the years 2010 to 2018) will be collected and finally the correlation between the variables will be verified through the IBM Statistical Package for the Social Sciences (SPSS) program.

The issue is relevant due to the need to study the implications of corruption in state collection and the lack of work on these issues. In order to fill this gap, the concept of corruption highlighting public corruption and its effects on society.

ANALYZING THE CONCEPTS OF CORRUPTION, PUBLIC CORRUPTION, AND ACCOUNTABILITY

The term "corruption" has remote origin, comes from the Latin "*corruptio*" that means decomposition, putrefaction of the organic matter. According to the philosopher Aristotle corruption is "the change that goes from something to not being of that something". He analyzed the term by granting it negative character and suggested that corruption victimized the virtues of the human being in order to break it down, to decay it.

However conceptualizing the term is not something simple and there is almost a consensus among scholars in providing its difficulty. The problem occurs by the fact that the term from its origin to the present day has undergone changes and its understanding is influenced by time, space and culture, so that we do not intend to point out a complete and definitive concept in this work.

According to Bruno Wilhelm Speck investigations about the issue are divided into three generations. In the first generation there was a search for a single concept that dealt with the phenomenon, because it was believed that the different conceptions were a problem:

The first attempts that resulted in empirical surveys on corruption started from the assumption that the different models of conceptualization of the phenomenon represented a problem. The most common way out was to identify corruption from a definition close to that of the penal code. Nye's (1967) solution has become classic for this approach. According to this author, corruption represents a deviation from the formal duties associated with a public office, due to private benefits. Many authors have questioned this legalistic definition, since it would be suggesting a universalism that would not correspond to reality. (Speck, 2000, p.7)

Thus, the conceptual problem pointed out by many theorists of this generation consisted in the fact that there was a universalism, based on the penal definition, that did not correspond to the values and social behaviors, therefore the conceptual differentiations. In this sense, Speck (2000) points out Heidenheimer who suggested a new line of investigation, referring to social actors, and classified corruption as "black corruption", "gray corruption" and "white corruption".

The "white corruption" happens when the law condemns, but most people tolerate or recognize the conduct alleged as morally questionable; in "gray corruption" the actors evaluate behavior in a controversial way, there is no consensus among social actors whether the behavior is or is not corruption; and in "black corruption" the law and social norms are incontrovertible.

The first generation was a very important contribution to the debate by shifting the subject from the legal field to the social field, insofar as it is one of the most fit in the human reality.

In the second generation the contribution to the understanding of the theme occurred in a different way, especially in the 1980s through investment risk assessment companies that started to include the theme in the country analyzes with the objective of evaluating standards, institutions, culture and political practices to calculate the possibility of investment risk.

In order to measure corruption risk assessment companies take into account, for example, subjective perceptions of experts, interviews with companies and their executives, newspaper articles and began to create indexes to measure levels of corruption, as the creation of the Corruption Perceptions Index (IPCorr).

The IPCorr was created in order to provide a single indicator of corruption in different countries in a continuous and comparative way. The result was an Index that ranks from 0 to 10 each country analyzed. This index was of great importance, since it drew the attention of the world to the issue of corruption and its fight.

The third generation of research in turn, according to Speck (2000), search tools for intervention and reform of institutions, from that understanding the IPCorr suffer criticism because only measures the phenomenon and does not seek to change the reality of the countries with high rates of corruption. The discussion of the third generation revolves around verifying indices of seeking alternatives to guide institutional reform policies. Thus, it is necessary to understand the term Corruption. For Ramina (2002, p.25), although the phenomenon of corruption is currently of national and international interest, there is no consensus regarding a single definition and the subject treated in an area that oscillates between economics and political science.

Theoreticians who study the subject understand corruption as an act that injures operating standards of public administration. This way of understanding the phenomenon is intrinsically linked to public affairs; an act of corruption is committed by degrading public property for the benefit of the private sector. The United Nations, The World Bank and the IMF, which generally linked corruption to the abuse of public functions for private gain, followed this line of understanding.

Johnston and Kpundeh (2002, p.104) says that corruption is "*the abuse of functions or public funds or as the use of illegitimate means of influence by members of the public and private spheres.*" Such a view reduces the public waiting phenomenon, in that sense Elliott (2002) expands the concept by adding that corruption can occur in both private and public space.

There are those who believe that corruption also covers a much larger field, and corrupt those who do not meet certain moral standards and unbalance peace and social balance "*Others feel that corruption is something broader: this relates to acts* *that go against the public interest in a more general way (polluting a river could be an act of corruption according to this view)" (*Jordan, 2002, p.10).

Based on what was placed so far we can say that the concept of corruption involving public or private agents who commit unlawful in order to benefit, but in this light the public official to suffer threats or duress and because of that divert public funds, for example, is also being corrupted. In order to clarify this issue, we resort to Melo (2011), which outlines the concept of corruption based on constitutive elements:

Corruption in this work is understood as the action of an agent, public or private, who, in partnership with others, violate norms and captures resources for themselves or for their group or institution of which at least one is a part. There are three different elements in this concept: (a) agents; voluntary interaction and resources. Discussing these elements in detail aims to clarify the proposed concept. The purpose is to avoid the risk of confusing it with similar phenomena and avoid possible analytical errors. (Melo, 2011, p.58-59).

According to the author officers elements are actors (individuals or groups) public or private who are responsible for the manifestation of corruption, such agents are: The corrupt characterized by the privileged position it occupies in the organization and therefore enables the act of corruption, in general they are public agents; The corruptor is the agent that in partnership with the corrupt seek to capture resources of an organization (public or private), usually are private agents.

The voluntary interaction, as the name implies there must be the willingness of agents to capture resources, so that the individual who diverts public resources under threat will not be incurring corruption, but in another crime. The interaction can occur between the public and/or private space; the intersection of these two spaces aims to privatize public resources.

Resources are physically manipulable means such as amounts, values, products, goods and services. The interaction between corrupt, corrupt and refuse is given the triad name of corruption which according to Melo (2011) brings together the essential elements without which there can be no corruption phenomenon.

Under Brazilian legal perspective, means the criminal offenses defined by law in caputs Articles 333 and 317 of the Penal Code. Article 333 of the CP brings the concept of active corruption and article 317 defines passive corruption:

Art. 317 - Request or receive, for himself or for another, directly or indirectly, even if out of office or before assuming it, but because of it, improper advantage, or accept promise of such an advantage:

Art. 333 - To offer or promise an undue advantage to a public official, in order to determine him to practice, omit or delay an official act: Penalty - confinement, from two (2) to twelve (12) years, and fine.

Single Paragraph - The penalty shall be increased by one third if, due to the advantage or promise, the employee delays or omits an act of office, or practices it in violation of functional duty. (our emphasis).

By being typed as corruption illegal activity, that generally only comes to public via press scandals, lawsuits and criminal investigations is very difficult to assess their absolute levels of corruption crimes brought to the State through legal action cannot be taken as definitive indicators.

Taking into account what was put up here, the corruption could be understood as the tort where more than one agent, be it public or private, voluntary abuse their functions in order to influence members of the public and private spheres in order to capture undue resources for themselves or for third parties.

In the face of the intense debate that literature hangs around a concept it is clear that most of the scholars binds corruption to embezzlement of public funds, and this idea was reinforced by international institutions such as the World Bank and transparency International. The World Bank considers corruption as the abuse of public administration aimed at particular gains, the transparency International also adopted basically the same definition.

Currently, however, the transparency International has worked with the notion that corruption is the abuse of entrusted power for private gain, such a concept is applied to public and private sectors, making it clear that the index of corruption, that various of 0 to 100 where (0 It means a kind of highly corrupt and 100 indicates a country very clean) focuses on checking corruption in the public sector.

It is a fact that public corruption wins greater emphasis to private corruption, because most social impact and mobilize several international organizations that aim to combat it. Because of this we will be focusing in the present work the analysis of public corruption, that involving agents and or public resources, to analyze what their implications in relation to the State's financial activity and the implementation of public policies.

BRIEF CONSIDERATIONS ABOUT ACCOUNTABILITY

It difficult to define accountability. On a range of concepts the understanding seems more plausible, especially for getting fit in that traditionally conceived as corruption phenomenon in Brazil.

According to Gray (2001) the accountability is a process connected to an accountability, the duty that a given person or entity must provide a payback for a recipient. Such a concept used to work in a more adjusted public corruption which is what we want to emphasize; in the sense that the State must, by virtue of a fundraising by the taxpayer, should therefore give an account of these features to show that your fate has been the common good.

Complementing the idea of a certain connection between accountability, or rather between the lack of it with the corruption, Melo (2003) says that the ineffectiveness of accountability can generate public officials of fraud providing fertile ground for the development of corruption.

PUBLIC CORRUPTION AND ITS EFFECTS

The discussion about the effects of corruption is controversy; on the other hand, it is believed that corruption foments the efficiency and accelerate economic growth in the face of inefficient institutional mechanisms, since the State bureaucratic apparatus can generate costs, these costs minimized corruption which turns out unlock transactions and this would translate into greater economic growth.

On the other hand it is believed that corruption reduces efficiency, as it creates a series of mechanisms that make inefficient economic relations, increase the cost of transactions and reduce economic growth.

Corruption as "Second-Best"

Regarding the effects of public corruption for theoretical current it argues be corruption a vector of efficiency, an accelerator in front of lengthy institutional mechanisms; such power comes corruption as a kind of "Second-Best" term which can be translated as a second best choice; in this sense a certain level of corruption would be a better alternative to a slow and bureaucratic State, because it could provide economic growth and welfare improvement:

In this case, the corruption would act as an oil on the gears jammed the State bureaucracy, streamlining the processing of new investments that would result in greater economic growth. Following this same thought, and from the point of view of economic well-being, in a "second best" world with a priori existence of distorted incentives, adding more distortion, such as corruption, could increase the well-being. (Carraro, Fochezatto & Hillbrecht, 2006, p.04)

In this theoretical North, corruption remains a problem for the State, but ends up being as something positive in order to increase the efficiency of public inefficient gear and so provide social gains.

According to Leff (1964, p.396-397) corruption could increase the efficiency of the economic system because it would provide an alternative to bureaucratic system and competition would induce an increase of efficiency. The existence of corruption would imply that the privileges obtained by obtaining illegal benefits would be allocated to producers and to individuals who are more willing to pay them, these being the fittest and efficient.

For example, if in a country whose laws are very strict and bureaucratic apparatus prevents the speed of opening a company if that company offers a bribe to a public official to circumvent such obstacles, making harmful act against the State for the benefit of the particular, such form of corruption would serve as a better alternative to State inertia so that would benefit the company, employees and society. So understood the corruption would create a market that would provide trading alternative to legal impediments imposed by the State by minimizing costs and maximizing economic and social gains.

Corruption as Damage

The other line of thinking, prevalent among scholars, is that the corruption phenomenon is a great generator of prejudice to society because of your self cost, so vista corruption would minimize the ability of State action with regards to public policy, the Government spending, tax revenues, economic growth, investor distrust, among others.

In hand than claimed Leff (1964, p.396-397), Myrdal (1968, p.954) States that the bribery raises even more red tape, because the civil servant would create hindrance to receive more money.

According to Krueger (1990, p.18) public corruption undermines the legitimacy of the Government reducing your ability to comply with their contractual and legal obligations, discouraging private investment and weakening the economy. In this sense Rose-Ackerman firm that corruption is a symptom that something is wrong in the management of the State so that State institutions are being used to enrich corrupt staff:

Corruption is a symptom that something has gone wrong in the management of the state. Institutions designed to govern the interrelationships between the citizen and the state are used for personal enrichment and the provision of benefits to the corrupt. The prince mechanism, so often a source of economic efficiency and a contributor to growth, can, in the form of bribery undermine the legitimacy and effectiveness of government. (Rose-Ackerman, 1999, p.9)

Tanzi and Davoodi (1997, p.97-139) put that corruption is directly related to the large public works projects and the difficulty of monitoring of such works. According to the authors the political corruption induces an increase in the number, complexity, size of projects and conservation of public investments, so that claim that corruption has perverse effects on the quality of infrastructure. Such statements leads us to believe, due to corruption, public works financed by the collection of taxes, taxpayers can have their increased costs as a result of corruption.

As we can see, the phenomenon studied here relates closely with the public, with the administration of the resources of the state your destination and the common good of society which administers, so that if the State does not supervise the action of its public agents provision of services and implementation of their policies may result in acts of corruption by generating large costs to society.

In Brazil after the political opening in 1985 freaked to be greater interest in the discussion about the corruption in the country, that coupled with the greater emphasis given to the subject by various information vehicles that led the audience in State vulnerability concerning the effectiveness of its rules and the smoothness of your structure.

Several went to areas of knowledge that tried to explain the causes of corruption tupiniquim, and the hypotheses range from the way the Portuguese colonization, culture to excessive state intervention in the economy, here, however we seek to understand their inplicações on quality of life of society.

Silva, Garcia and Flag by applying a general equilibrium model for the period of 1998 in a survey developed by the Getúlio Vargas Foundation (FGV) in 2011, estimated to be R $6,000.00 per capita cost of corruption in Brazil this year, this means to say that the corruption would be responsible for a cost of approximately 68% of GDP (Carraro et al, 2006). In an attempt to measure the impact of corruption facing the gross domestic product (GDP) Carraro et al (2006), the impact of corruption On the economic growth of Brazil: also applying the general equilibrium model reached a the result of the volume of resources involved.

Based on caught up to the moment you can see that the corruption contributes to inefficiency of the Government leading to a crisis of governability that's ability to identify social needs and that governance is the ability that the State has to implement public policy and achieve collective goals, such as using money raised via taxes on important social needs identification and implementation of public works of quality that effectively meet collective needs.

METHODOLOGY

In order to verify the relationship between the corruption perception index (CPI) and Human development index (HDI) initially analyze secondary data obtained through corruption perception index (CPI), transparency International (TI), HDI data obtained through the United Nations Development Programme (UNDP) and GDP data obtained through Trading Economics; also in this article we character research, quantitative, empirical and bibliographic.

The CPI of the transparency International is one of the most used in the world and ranks the countries and territories based on how corrupt is your public sector, to the IPC of most years studied you adopted the calculation for the countries through d sources originating from the past 24 months of independent institutions specialized in governance and business environment analysis.

The CPI was calculated using a simple average of the standardized scores; the sources are standardized by subtracting the mean of the data, and dividing by the standard deviation (z score) and then resized on average of 45 and 20 standard deviation:

The formula for standardization is: $= \dfrac{x_i - media(x)}{\text{standard deviation}(x)} * sign * 20 + 45$

To reflect the changes that were made to the method used to resize the data sources, the scale on which the CPI is presented has also been updated, to 0-100 where (0 means a kind of highly corrupt and 100 indicates a country very clean). It is necessary to clarify that the CPI is not an index questioned by several scholars of the subject since the notes obtained by it methodology is based on perceptions, however due to the difficulties in measuring this phenomenon, the IPC is an index that Since 2005 has contributed to discussion of the theme and it comes search way of measuring corruption in the world, and therefore should be taken into account.

In your classic formulation, the HDI is composed by three indicators, which represent the opportunity of a long and healthy lives, access to knowledge and to have command over the resources to ensure a decent standard of living. Through the first two dimensions, it is intended to evaluate the achievement of well-being by adopting a lifestyle resulting from free choices and guided from the accumulated skills and knowledge. Already the command over resources indicates whether this process gave free of deprivation of basic needs, such as water, food and shelter (Chediek, Mulleady, Sharma, 2015).

The HDI is a unit that varies from 0 to 1. But for this hundred variables finish in that order of magnitude, it is necessary to establish minimum and maximum of each and make a series of calculations as shown in the following equation:

$$\text{Index} = \frac{actualvalue - \min imumvalue}{\max imumvalue}$$

Since 1999, this methodology is used. The main change with respect to previous calculations was the introduction of logarithmic base to reach the PPC, who ended up making the most reliable index in relation to its variation year to year. In addition to this change, the indexes cannot be compared simply by taking the previous year's report for this year, since other methodologies change every year and in each country (Project DHnet, 2018).

For the correlation between IPC and HDI 159 countries were analyzed, whose insertion criterion was to be present in all years surveyed. In order to facilitate the reading of the data, given the amount of countries were created groupings: with respect to the IPC corruption was classified as low, medium and high. The countries that have obtained score of 0 to 49.9 were grouped in high corruption, countries that have obtained score of 50 to 69.9 were grouped on average corruption and countries that have obtained score of 70 to 100 were were grouped into low corruption.

The HDI to your shift goes through a rating that establishes the ranking of countries. Thus, countries can be divided into: high human development-IDH above Average human development – 0.8 HDI of 0.5 to 0.799 Low human development-IDH to 0.499. The gross domestic product (GDP) is obtained by the sum of all goods and services of a country; Thus the classification proposed in this work, was performed as follows: Having the classification of countries Trading Economics site, divided into three levels (high, medium, and low GDP), high GDP is that assigned to the countries that are in the classification of place between the 1° to 53° rank, the average was assigned to countries between 54° to 106° and position between the classification of 107° to 159° were considered as having low level of GDP.

To carry out such a review was made a correlation between the variables through the Statistical Package for the Social Sciences (SPSS).

RESULTS AND DISCUSSIONS

The data collected were treated quantitatively through softwares Excel and Statistical Package for the Social Sciences (SPSS), which allowed elaborate statistics with a view to achieving the objectives of the research.

The table 1 presents descriptive statistics of the 159 countries data obtained from the corruption perception index (CPI) from transparency international, where the maximum value found for the IPC was 95 in the year 2017, coming very close to the maximum value of 100 assigned, in theory, to the country where there is no corruption. According to the evaluation methods of the Organization in the position of "less corrupt country in the world" in the period researched was the New Zealand (Cordeiro, 2018).

With respect to New Zealand and as to your state structure, Tower-if the trajectory of the New Zealand public administration the numerous administrative reforms implemented, until the consolidation of the current model: even with 29 ministries, there is a managerial public administration, lean, highly transparent structure, bureaucratic mechanisms optimized, focus on the efficiency of public services and, most important of all, impersonality, translated into a clear separation between Administration and politics.

Another important factor is the strict adherence to what we know as principle of economy, which aims at maximum exploitation of public resources; considering the public service as your final product and the taxpayer as the highest standard of client requirement (Marques, 2017).

Countries that already have obtained smaller CPI were the Afghanistan with note 8 in the years 2012 and 2013 and the Sudan with note in the years 2013 and 2014. According to the transparency international corruption examples vary and range from the distribution of public offices, distribution so excuse, justice for a price, daily tuition in Exchange for basic services, it, along with the opium trade – which is also connected to corruption -contributes to the negative trend in the country note on the IPC (Barkin, 2009).

To the human development index (HDI), table 2 presents the descriptive statistics of the 159 countries data obtained, the best value obtained for the HDI among the countries studied was 0.953 of Norway in the year 2017, very close to the maximum value, i.e. It is assumed that the better living conditions that population will have. Likewise, the countries with the worst living conditions of the population, will be with the index very close to 0.

The Norway (the country with the best HDI during the period researched) has a thriving economy based on the export of oil and natural gas; It has also been classified as happiest place on Earth, from the World Happiness Report 2017, a reflection of the good living conditions of the population, which has a high literacy rate and a high life expectancy (Polon, 2018).

Already the Country which obtained lower HDI during this period (2010 to 2017) was the Niger economically poorest nations in the world, possessing few arable land and few natural resources of commercial value. Among the various social problems are: malnutrition reaches 29% of the inhabitants; the infant mortality rate is 85 deaths

Table 1. Descriptive statistics of the data corruption Perception Index (CPI) to 159 countries in 2010 to 2017

Corruption Perceptions Index (CPI)	N	Minimum	Maximum	Mean
CPI – 2010	159	14	93	39,96
CPI – 2011	159	15	95	39,94
CPI – 2012	159	8	90	42,67
CPI – 2013	159	8	91	42,13
CPI – 2014	159	11	92	42,70
CPI – 2015	159	11	91	42,84
CPI – 2016	159	13	90	42,57
CPI – 2017	159	14	89	42,79
Valid N (listwise)	159			

Sources: International Transparency from 2010 to 2017, 2018

Table 2. Descriptive Statistics of Human Development Index (HDI) data for 159 countries in 2010 to 2017

Human Development Index (HDI)	N	Minimum	Maximum	Mean
HDI – 2010	159	0,318	0,942	0,67742
HDI – 2011	159	0,325	0,943	0,68286
HDI – 2012	159	0,336	0,942	0,68800
HDI – 2013	159	0,340	0,946	0,69257
HDI – 2014	159	0,345	0,946	0,69692
HDI – 2015	159	0,347	0,948	0,70074
HDI – 2016	159	0,351	0,951	0,70392
HDI – 2017	159	0,354	0,953	0,70654
Valid N (listwise)	159			

Sources: United Nations Development Programme, 2018

for every 1,000 live births; environmental sanitation services are insufficient; most of the population lives on less than 1.25 dollar a day and the illiteracy rate is 72%, according to data released in 2010 by the United Nations (UN) (Brazil School, 2018).

In table 3 it is shown that the 159 countries studied (74.8% of the total) had high corruption in the year 2011, and the year 2017 a low of 113 (71.1% of the total), having these countries 0 notes to 49.9 in IPC of transparency international, at the other end 21 countries s, 13.2% of the total presented low corruption in the years 2010 and 2012, and in 2017 also had a high to 24 countries, with 70 to 100 on the index of transparency international. The predominance of countries with high corruption demonstrates how this practice is widespread in the world.

Recently, Wang and You (2012) presented empirical evidence to which not all countries with high corruption suffer from a poor performance in growth. In the periods analysed, countries with low corruption levels have less propensity to increase these levels, on the contrary there is a tendency to decrease these levels of corruption.

The Brazil in the years studied obtained high levels of Corruption, arriving in 2017 to 37 points, three points compared to the previous study because of this the parents fell 17 positions in the world rankings of transparency international, occupying the same year 96th place, the worst the last five years.

The Brazil is still far from a satisfactory standard and the 2017 index only confirms this, and the combat of corruption be constant, it is necessary to improve the legal system through the judiciary, free and through the control of public agents, a strengthening of the institutions, a political reform, a cultural change that involves the improvement of structural conditions such as health, education and employment.

In table 4 we observed that there was between 2010 to 2017 1 increase in countries that joined the list of very high HDI. In 2017, 51 countries (32.1% of the total) had a very high HDI. For the same year at the other end of the scale, 36 countries (22.6% of the total) showed low levels of human development. In this case the Brazil is 23.9% of countries that had a high human development index in 2017, not very pleasant position, getting behind Latin American countries such as Venezuela and Cuba. The Brazil was stagnant for the third consecutive year in the human development index (HDI); from 2015 occupies the 79th placement among

Table 3. Ranking of the Corruption Perceptions Index (CPI) for 159 countries between 2010 and 2017

Corruption Perceptions Index (CPI)	Frequency	High Corruption	Frequency	Media Corruption	Frequency	Low Corruption
CPI – 2010	118	74,2	20	12,6	21	13,2
CPI – 2011	119	74,8	17	10,7	23	14,5
CPI – 2012	116	73	22	13,8	21	13,2
CPI – 2013	116	73	21	13,2	22	13,8
CPI – 2014	115	72,3	22	13,8	22	13,8
CPI – 2015	109	68,6	25	15,7	25	15,7
CPI – 2016	114	71,7	23	14,5	22	13,8
CPI – 2017	113	71,1	22	13,8	24	15,1

Sources: International Transparency from 2010 to 2017, 2018

the countries analyzed, ending a cycle of evolution seen between 2012 and 2014, when the country advance six places in the standings.

One of the indicators responsible for the maintenance of the tour of Brazil in ranking was. Life expectancy at birth of the Brazilian is 75.7 years, an indicator which year by year has been showing improvements. In 2015, for example, was 73.5. The area of knowledge, for your time, showed few changes.

The cross is a way of studying the relationship between the variables, at the crossroads between the IPC and the HDI ranking of 159 countries in years and 2010 to 2017. It was observed that the lower the highest human development index the index of perception of Corruption, of those countries (Figure 1). One can see that in the analysis period, from the year of 2010, had 47 countries, passing in 2017 the 35 countries with high IPC and low HDI.

This relative low HDI index and high CPI in 2017 22.01% of countries studied matches in the year 2017, Senegal, Ivory Coast and Niger, where this trend was observed in each year surveyed. Between the intersection of the high IPC with the very high HDI, we observe that in the period studied had a mild increase of 8 to 13 countries in this situation, having 8.18% of countries with this intersection in the year 2017, as examples are: Norway, USA, Canada, New Zealand Denmark, among others.

As the correlation is a measure of the degree of relationship between two variables, table 5 highlights this correlation between the Human Desenvimento index in proportion to the index of perception of Corruption. Second Dancey and Reidy (2006) where point a rank other than r = 0.10 to 0.30 (weak); r = 0.40 to 0.60 (moderated) and r = 0.70 until 1.00 (strong). Check in the table all the correlations

Table 4. Human Development Index (HDI) rankings for 159 countries between 2010 and 2017

Human Development Index (HDI)	Frequency	Very high	Frequency	High	Frequency	Médio	Frequency	Low
HDI – 2010	41	25,8	42	26,4	29	18,2	47	29,6
HDI – 2011	41	25,8	42	26,4	33	20,8	43	27
HDI – 2012	45	28,3	38	23,9	34	21,4	42	26,4
HDI – 2013	47	29,6	36	22,6	37	23,3	39	24,5
HDI – 2014	47	29,6	38	23,9	36	22,6	38	23,9
HDI – 2015	49	30,8	37	23,3	35	22	38	23,9
HDI – 2016	49	30,8	38	23,9	34	21,4	38	23,9
HDI – 2017	51	32,1	38	23,9	34	21,4	36	22,6

Sources: United Nations Development Programme, 2018

Figure 1. Crossing between the high Corruption Perceptions Index classification and the Human Development Index classification for 159 countries in the years 2010 to 2017

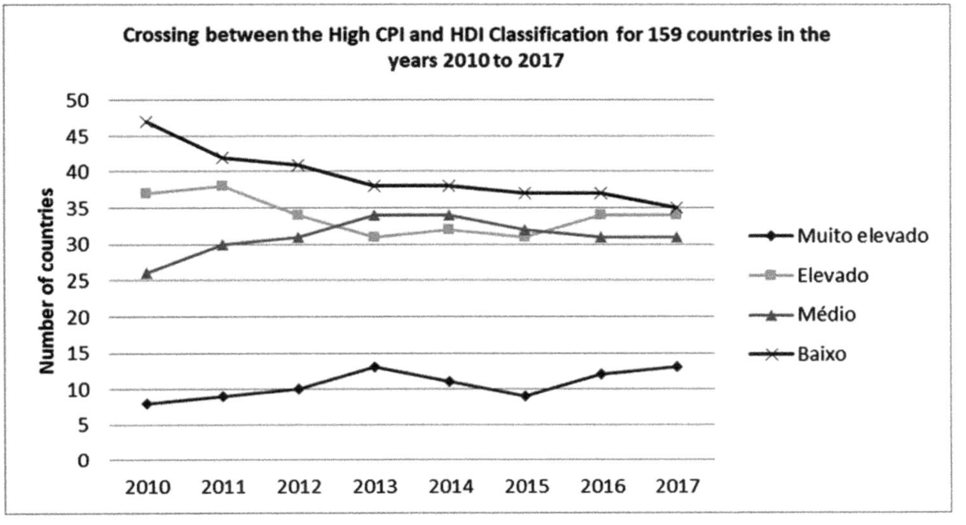

involving HDI and IPC the years surveyed are positive and also strong (between the 0.712 0.738). To give the answer of the correlation calculation in percentage values, apply the formula of the coefficient of determination: $\rho = r^2 x100$.

Knowing that the correlation coefficient (r) of the year 2017 was 0.738 have a coefficient of determination (r^2) of 0.5446. This means that the proportion of variance of a variable "explained" by the variance of the other in this case is 54.46%, i.e. has a correlation of more than 50% that can interfere in the result of the other. This interference of over 50% in all the years surveyed.

Studying the relationship between the variables by crossing, table 6 demonstrates the crossover between CPI and GDP ranking of 159 countries. It is noted in the table, 26 countries have high corruption and a high GDP, representing 16.35% of the countries studied that we can mention a few like Saudi Arabia, Greece and Romania, Lesotho and Kuwait.

Already in relation to the cross between HDI with GDP we have 34 countries with very high HDI and GDP, 21.38% of the countries studied. Of the 159 Countries surveyed that have low CPI, very high HDI and high GDP, by crossing are 12.58% among them we can mention New Zealand, Denmark and Finland.

Table 5. Correlations between the Human Development Index (HDI) and the Corruption Perceptions Index (CPI) for 159 countries in the years 2010 to 2017

		Corruption Perceptions Index (CPI)							
		2010	**2011**	**2012**	**2013**	**2014**	**2015**	**2016**	**2017**
HDI	2010	0,731**	-	-	-	-	-	-	-
	2011	-	0,719**	-	-	-	-	-	-
	2012	-	-	0,712**	-	-	-	-	-
	2013	-	-	-	0,719**	-	-	-	-
	2014	-	-	-	-	0,727**	-	-	-
	2015	-	-	-	-	-	0,733**	-	-
	2016	-	-	-	-	-	-	0,738**	-
	2017	-	-	-	-	-	-	-	0738**

**Correlation is significant at the 0.01 level (2 extremities).

Sources: United Nations Development Program (2018); Transparency International 2010 to 2017, 2018

Table 6. Crossing between the Classification of the Corruption Perceptions Index (CPI) and the Gross Domestic Product (GDP) for 159 countries in the year 2017

		GDP - 2017			**Total**
		Alta	**Média**	**Baixa**	
CPI – 2017	High Corruption	26	44	43	113
	Medium Corruption	08	05	09	22
	Low Corruption	20	04	00	24
Total		54	53	52	159
HDI – 2017	Very High	34	14	3	51
	High	10	17	11	38
	Medium	9	15	10	34
	Low	1	7	28	36
Total		54	53	52	159

Sources: United Nations Development Program, 2018; Transparency International from 2010 to 2017, 2018; Trading Economics, 2018

The correlations involving HDI and IPC with the GDP of 2017 are positive is also is also weak (0.232). The coefficient of determination (r^2) of just 0.054. This means that the proportion of variance of a variable "explained" by the variance of the other in this case is only 5.38%, i.e. There's a correlation, but too low to interfere with the result of another.

Among the 159 countries assessed in 2010 to 2017 by the NGO Transparency International, Brazil achieved scores between 37 to 43 on the perception of corruption in the world noted in Table 7. The classification of a nation indicates your position in relation to other countries and territories included in the index, on a scale of 0-100, where 0 means point that the country is regarded as highly corrupt, and 100 points, means that the country is considered to be very integrity.

The human development index in the period 2010 to 2017 in Brazil there was a small increase, leaving 0.727 in 2010 to 0.759 in 2017. In the short term, the HDI, therefore, does not reflect the sensitive improvements or deterioration in performance of the social indicators of the country.

Regarding the correlation between HDI and the CPI between the years 2010 to 2017 for Brazil (table 8) there was no statistical significance, this can occur in the program used (SPSS-IBM) due to the small amount of variables, that is, when you have a small the sample correlation can become meaningless to the program defaults.

FUTURE RESEARCH DIRECTIONS

The issue of corruption becomes even more relevant in today's networked societies because of greater access to information on the acts of corruption of public agents. The globalization of information generates in private individuals, users of public services, indignation and search for greater knowledge about the corrupt acts that benefit the private individuals and entail in the insufficiency of the public services.

Such insufficiency reflects on the human development of countries, precisely because the public resources that should invest in essential services such as education and health are diverted to other purposes. The effects of corruption and deficiency in accountability to the public restrict the exercise of citizenship rights when it withdraws from people the possibility of better acting in the political life of societies.

Table 7. Descriptive statistics of IPC, HDI and GDP data for Brazil in 2010 to 2017

	N	Minimum	Maximum	Mean
Corruption Perceptions Index (CPI)	8	37	43	39,75
Human Development Index (HDI)	8	0,727	0,759	0,746
Gross Domestic Product (GDP)	8	1793.99	2616.20	2233.85
Valid N (listwise)	8			

Sources: United Nations Development Program, 2018; Transparency International from 2010 to 2017, 2018; Trading Economics, 2018

Table 8. Correlations between the Human Development Index (HDI) and the Corruption Perceptions Index (CPI) for Brazil in the years 2010 to 2017

		IPC	IDH
IPC -	Pearson Correlation	1	,077
	Sig. (2-tailed)		,857
	N	8	8
IDH	Pearson Correlation	,077	1
	Sig. (2-tailed)	,857	
	N	8	8

** Correlation is significant at the 0.01 level (2 extremities).
Sources: United Nations Development Program (2018); Transparency International 2010 to 2017, 2018

Thus, the theme of the chapter is relevant and relates to the theme of the present book because the results found concerning the impact of corruption on the human development index are directly related to the knowledge of constitutional norms that declare fundamental rights and a series of obligations the promotion of social rights and quality public services.

CONCLUSION

In Brazil and in the world too if discusses about the lack of resources for public investment and corruption wins featured in this sense one that harms the finances of the State. The acts of public corruption ranging from tax evasion to the misuse of public resources, which leads to believe that the problems of particular social order is a reflection of corruption.

How do we know the main purpose of this work was to verify if there is relationship between corruption and HDI (Human development index), where it is postulated the hypothesis that the higher the corruption, lower the HDI of the country, also intends to analyze in the case of Brazil facing the global panorama, adding the element of gross domestic product (GDP) to the HDI and the data obtained from the transparency international corruption.

As seen in the data obtained the crossovers between HDI and IPC are positive and strong varying between 0.712 the 0.738, how it was possible to observe the results of the crossovers of the variavés referred to the years we have studied the possibility of more than 50% of a index interfere with each other.

The hypothesis that the higher the corruption, lower the human development index in the country, postulated in this study was corroborated by data arranged in Figure 1, where the intersection between the IPC and the HDI ranking of 159 countries in years and 2010 to 2017 presented that the lower the HDI higher the index of perception of Corruption. With respect to analysis of data only from Brazil the correlation between HDI and the CPI for the years studied were not significant.

From the world data analyzed that indicate high correlation between a greater corruption and a lower human development index, we can subjectively infer that accountability problems of public expenditure can account for such correlation, once the lack of transparency and an effective accountability on the part of the public can take both the public and private agent to commit acts of corruption.

REFERENCES

Barkin, N. (2009). *Afghanistan plummets in new ranking of corruption*. Retrieved from https: extra.globo.com/noticias/mundo/afeganistao-despenca-em-novo-ranking-da-corrupcao-199158.html

Brazil. (n.d.). *Criminal Code*. Retrieved from http://www.planalto.gov.br/ccivil_03/decreto-lei/del2848compilado.htm

Brazil school. (n.d.). *Niger*. Retrieved from <https: brasilescola.uol.com.br/geografia/niger.htm

Carraro, A., Fochezatto, A., & He, A. (2006). *The impact of corruption on the economic growth of Brazil: a general equilibrium model for the period 1994-1998*. Retrieved from http:www.anpec.org.br/encontro2006/artigos/a06a057.pdf

Chediek, J., Mulleady, A. I., Sharma, J., & Birth, R. (2015). Atlas of human development in the metropolitan regions of Brazil: Santos, Campinas, Maceió and the Paraíba Valley. Brasília, Brazil: UNDP, Ipea, FJP.

Cordeiro, T. (2018). *The secret of the most honest countries in the world*. Gazeta do Povo. Retrieved from http: www.gazetadopovo.com.br/ideias/o-segredo-dos-paises-mais-honestos-do-mundo-46ahc398rewn4doybhflmwh20

Dancey, C., & Reidy, J. (2006). Statistics without maths for Psychology: Using SPSS for Windows. Statistics without maths for Psychology: Using SPSS for Windows. Porto Alegre, Brazil: New Haven.

Elliott, K. A. (2002). *Corruption and the Global economy*. Brasília, Brazil: University of Brasília.

Gray, R. (2001). Thirty Years of Social Accounting, Reporting and Auditing: What (if anything) Have We Learnt? (v. 10, n.1). London, UK: Business Ethics, EuropeanReview.

Harada, K. (2006). *Financial law and tax law* (15th ed.). São Paulo, Brazil: Atlas.

Johnston, M., & Kpundeh, S. J. (2002). *Building A Clean Machine Anti-Corruption Coalitions and Sustainable Reform.* Retrieved from http://siteresources.worldbank.org/WBI/Resources/wbi37208.pdf

Jordão, R. P. (2002). *(Almost) perfect crime: corruption and money laundering in Brazil.* São Paulo, Brazil: Perseu Abramo Foundation.

Krueger, A. (1990). Government failures in development. *The Journal of Economic Perspectives, 4*(3), 9–23. doi:10.1257/jep.4.3.9

Leff, N. H. (1964). Economic Development Through Bureaucratic Corruption. In *Political Corruption: A Handbook.* New Brunswick, Canada: Transaction Plubishers. doi:10.1177/000276426400800303

Marques, E. (2017). *New Zealand and Brazil: lessons from the less corrupt country in the world.* Students for liberty – freer future. Retrieved from https: www.studentsforliberty.org/nova-zelandia-pais-menos-corrupto-mundo

Melo, C. A. V. (2003). *High Corruption in response to low levels of Accountability* (Unpublished Maters dissertation). Federal University of Pernambuco, Recife, Brazil.

Melo, C. A. V. (2011). Constituent elements and dynamic of corruption: a conceptual exercise (Ariús, v. 17, no. 2, Jul./dez). Brazil, Campina Grande: Federal University of Campina Grande.

Myrdal, G. (1968). *Asian Drama: An Inquiry into the Poverty of Nationsto (Vol. 2).* New York, United States of America: Pantheon.

Pinto, A. T., Windt, M. C. V. S., & Siqueira, E. A. S. (2000). National tax code. São Paulo, Brazil: Saraiva.

Polon, L. (2003). *HDI (Human development index) of the countries.* Retrieved from https: www.estudopratico.com.br/idh-indice-de-desenvolvimento-humano-dos-paises

Project DHnet. (2008). *How does the human development index HDI.* Retrieved from http: www.dhnet.org.br/dados/idh/idh/idh_como_funciona.pdf

Ramina, L. L. (2002). *International action against corruption.* Curitiba, Brazil: Juruá.

Rose-Ackerman, S. (1999). *Corruption and Government: Causes, Consequences, and Reform*. London, UK: Cambridge University Press. doi:10.1017/CBO9781139175098

Speck, B. W. (2000). *The costs of corruption*. Retrieved from https: bvc.cgu.gov.br/bitstream/123456789/2731/1/mensuracao_da_corrupcao_uma.pdf

Tanzi, V., & Davoodi, H. (1997). *Corruption, Public Investment, and Growth*. IMF Working Paper. Retrieved from http://www.imf.org/external/pubs/ft/wp/wp97139.pdf

The Brazilian Institute of tax planning (IBPT). (2012). *Brazilian tax burden 2012*. Retrieved from https: www.ibpt.org.br/img/uploads/.../cargatributaria2012ibpt.pdf

The Brazilian Institute of tax planning (IBPT). (2013). *Study on taxes/GDP x HDI*. Retrieved from https: www.ibpt.org.br/img/uploads/novelty/estudo/787/estudofinalsobrecargatributariapibxidhirbesmarco2013.pdf

Trading Economics. (n.d.). *GDP list of countries*. Retrieved from https: pt.tradingeconomics.com/country-list/gdp

Transparency International. (2010). *World Corruption Ranking. Corruption Perceptions Index 2010*. Retrieved from http://cpi.transparency.org/cpi2010/results/

Transparency International. (2011). *World Corruption Ranking. Corruption Perceptions Index 2011*. Retrieved from https://www.transparency.org/cpi2011/results

Transparency International. (2012). *World Corruption Ranking. Corruption Perceptions Index 2012*. Retrieved from http://cpi.transparency.org/cpi2012/results/

Transparency International. (2013). *World Corruption Ranking. Corruption Perceptions Index 2013*. Retrieved from https://www.transparency.org/cpi2013/results

Transparency International. (2014). *World Corruption Ranking. Corruption Perceptions Index 2014*. Retrieved from https://www.transparency.org/cpi2014/results

Transparency International. (2015). *World Corruption Ranking. Corruption Perceptions Index 2015*. Retrieved from https://www.transparency.org/cpi2015#results-table

Transparency International. (2016). *World Corruption Ranking. Corruption Perceptions Index 2016*. Retrieved from https://www.transparency.org/news/feature/corruption_perceptions_index_2016#table

Transparency International. (2017). *World Corruption Ranking. Corruption Perceptions Index 2017*. Retrieved from https://www.transparency.org/news/feature/corruption_perceptions_index_2017#table

United Nations Development Programme. (2018). *Human Development Reports 1990-2017*. Retrieved from http://hdr.undp.org/en/data

Wang, Y., & You, J. (2012). *Corruption and firm growth: Evidence from China*. Beijing, China: China Economic Review.

KEY TERMS AND DEFINITIONS

Accountability: Responsibility. To be accountable with transparency.

Corruption: Act or effect of bribing one or more persons on their own or another's behalf, by offering money.

Corruption Perception Index: Annual report corruption perceptions index (CPI) that orders the countries of the world according to the degree to which corruption is perceived to exist between civil servants and politicians.

Gross Domestic Product: Represents the sum (in monetary terms) of all final goods and services produced in a given region (whether countries, states, or cities) for a given period.

Human Development Index: Comparative measure used to rank countries by their degree of "human development" and to help classify countries as developed (high human development), developing (medium and high human development), and underdeveloped (low human development).

Public Agent: Anyone who exercises, even temporarily or without remuneration, by election, appointment, appointment, hiring, or any form of investiture or bond, mandate, position, job, or public function.

Public Resources: Set of assets that compose the public patrimony of a country.

Public Service: Is a service that is provided by the government to people who lives on its jurisdiction, either directly (through the public sector) or by financing the provision of services.

Chapter 11
Protection of the Communication and Digital Security of Mobile Phones as a Fundamental Right to Privacy:
A Study of the Jurisprudence of the Brazilian Superior Court of Justice

Nestor Eduardo Araruna Santiago
Universidade de Fortaleza, Brazil

Ana Monica Anselmo Amorim
Universidade de Fortaleza, Brazil

ABSTRACT

The central idea of this chapter is to discuss the notion of privacy arising from the use and exchange of messages through the use of mobile phones and whether police officers in charge of patrolling and public security may have access to the messages contained therein without proper judicial authorization. The authors focused on the position of the Brazilian Superior Court of Justice (STJ) on the subject, based on the decision rendered in the Appeal in Habeas Corpus (RHC) n. 51.531/RO. At this trial, protection was given to the new forms of communication and data contained in mobile phones under the constitutional terms of protection of privacy and non-unlawful obtaining of evidence, so that it will be necessary to issue a court order to get any informational elements found in messaging applications installed on a smartphone.

DOI: 10.4018/978-1-5225-8350-9.ch011

INTRODUCTION

The rights to privacy and intimacy (article 5, item X, of the Brazilian Federal Constitution of 1988 - CF) are protected as fundamental rights of individuals, so they can ensure the most intimate forum of the human being. The confidentiality of communications and data (article 5, item XII, CF) are aimed at preserving the fundamental rights referred to above, especially when there is state criminal prosecution activity targeted to obtain information contained in mobile phones or smartphones seized in situations of characterization of criminal offense.

In such cases, it is common for police officers to search text messages found on the device seized even without a court order, with the intention of verifying any information that may lead to the elucidation of crimes. It is important to say that the owners do not allow with the police practice, and in most cases they are "slightly threatened" to cooperate with law enforcement, providing the password to access the device.

It is discussed whether such behavior can be characterized as unlawful evidence, with the consequent breaking of the chain of custody. In order to do so, it is necessary to analyze the judgment of Appeal in Habeas Corpus (RHC) 51.531/RO from the Brazilian Superior Court of Justice (Superior Tribunal de Justiça, 2018), which considered *unlawful* to inspect the messages and data stored on the mobile phone of the person arrested without prior judicial authorization.

BACKGROUND

It should be emphasized that the present work is not intended to exhaust the topic of privacy and intimacy. The notions brought in are necessary to the aspiration of the research, considering that it is essential to conceptualize the right to privacy and intimacy and how it is related to the use of mobile phones. Or, being more specific, how technology is related to privacy and should be protected, taking for granted that this everyday relation brings some concerns, and the answers given by law and lawmakers not always are satisfactory.

Although the day-to-day use of smartphones rises, it seems important to accentuate it does not imply that the owners of this devices should give up the right to privacy. Protecting privacy should not be confused with hiding illicit behavior, once privacy and intimacy (as a narrower approach of privacy) are strictly linked to human dignity, which is protected by the Constitution (Vianna, 2004). The paradox is inevitable: the more we share our life experiences through the internet, the more we need to protect privacy, as it is a way to demonstrate freedom. Technological advances cannot condition the proper protection of freedom (Badaró, 2014; Schreiber, 2016). It is not wrong or exaggerated to say that this is one of humanity's greatest dilemmas today.

We can say that human dignity, treated as a fundamental principle of the federal constitution, can only be considered in its entirety if privacy is assured. The right to be with oneself, to have a right to an intangible sphere, far from the public eye (even to celebrities and public people) is revealed as one of the facets of personality. Of course, the understanding of privacy and intimacy extends also to all the belongings and objects of the human being, since these are often extensions of the personality.

It is well-known that in the chapter devoted to the description of fundamental individual rights in the CF there is the need to protect the confidentiality of correspondence, telegraphic communications, data and telephone communications. The same Constitution considered such inviolable secrets as a means of exercising the right to privacy among private individuals (article 5, item X), it also relativized this protection, allowing the "breach" of confidentiality of telephone communications by means of authorization issued by a judicial authority, in cases and in accordance with the procedure legally established only for purposes of criminal investigation or for criminal procedural instruction. Even if the seized telephone device does not have a password, judicial authorization for its analysis becomes indispensable (Lemos, Caldeira, Quintiere, 2016).

Thus, unlike the texts of the Brazilian Constitutions of 1946 and 1967, which had a categorical form on the inviolability of the secrecy of communications, oral or written, generating doubt about the validity of the Brazilian Telecommunications Code (Law n. 4177/1962, derogated by Law n. 9472/1997 and subsequent updates) regarding the possibility of violation of telecommunication by means of judicial authorization (Greco Filho, 2005), the current Constitutional rule relegated to the ordinary federal legislator the competence to discipline the subject.

The Brazilian Federal Supreme Court (STF – Supremo Tribunal Federal) was called to position itself regarding the reception of article 57 of the Brazilian Telecommunications Code according to CF. STF decided that, as long as there was no authorizing law, any evidence obtained through telephone interception, would be considered unlawful even if judicially granted.

While the Brazilian Federal Constitution of year 1988 protects the right to free expression of thought, regardless of the path chosen by the citizen, as a true exteriorization of the principle of the dignity of the human person (article 1, item III), on the other hand, defends the interest of the society not only for the search for factual and/or authoritative proof of the occurrence of an offense, but also - and especially - stipulates limits in the form of obtaining the same evidence, in the same line of protection of human dignity. What is interesting to note is that the CF, even though it was granted before the commercial emergence of the Internet and cutting-edge technological innovations in smartphone communication, has already provided for a general privacy protection clause for distance communications.

There is yet another point to consider, which somehow conflicts with the right to privacy. In Brazil, criminal organizations, as well as criminals in general, constantly use the message applications (apps) on cell phones to exchange information about illicit conduct planning. Among all apps, the most used in Brazil is *WhatsApp*, with about 120 million active users – one and a half billion worldwide. With an end-to-end encryption system, there is no way for a third-party to intercept the content of messages exchanged between two or more users. So, if someone wants to have access to the messages, a person must have the desired mobile phone to read or hear what was written or said.

Brazil has been in the news for some time due to their involvement in judicial decisions regarding the use of WhatsApp; forcing the company to deliver information to the Judiciaries that allegedly contained messages that pertained to criminal investigations. Of course, court decisions have failed to understand how information is sent in the application, because the encryption used not only prevents the company from having access to the content, but also prevents data from being stored on the server (Sydow, 2017).

So, it is possible for someone to say that the way information was obtained by the Judiciary was not modified by technology in the exchange of messages. Despite this, it is still common for police officers in charge of street surveillance to conduct personal searches in case of suspected crimes, immediately seizing the suspects' cell phones. They then ask the owner to enter the password so that they can read any messages exchanged via WhatsApp that can serve as evidence of criminal conduct.

THE LEADING CASE

The Brazilian Superior Court of Justice (Superior Tribunal de Justiça - STJ) ruling originated from Habeas Corpus judged by the Court of Justice of Rondônia (TJRO), a Northern Brazilian State, filed in favor of Leri Souza e Silva, accused of drug trafficking (Article 33 of Law n. 11343/ 2006). On March 18, 2014, Military Police of the State of Rondônia received information about unlawful conduct, possibly drug trafficking. As a result, they waited in a certain place until the arrest of the suspect and the seizure of his cell phone.

In the *writ* of habeas corpus, the thesis of nullity of the search promoted by the police authority in the mobile phone device seized during the caught-in-the-act arrest was supported, since the information contained in the apparatus has the same constitutional protection inherent to telephone secrecy. Finally, it was argued that access to data contained in the telephone could only be affected by judicial decision, and it was then an unlawful evidence, as prescribed by art. 157 of the Criminal Procedure Code (Código de Processo Penal – CPP).

The court said that the phone device was seized with the accused during his arrest, pointing out that the forensic examination performed in the device is based on article 6, items II, III and VII of the CPP, which determines to the police authority, as soon as it becomes aware of the criminal practice: a) to apprehend the objects related to the fact, after being released by the criminal forensic experts; b) collect all the evidence that serves to clarify the fact and its circumstances; and c) to determine, as the case may be, the examination of a body of evidence and any other forensic examination. It also stated that access to data contained in the device does not encounter the same impediment of telephone interception and that the police authority acted strictly for law enforcement.

TJRO denied the order of habeas corpus, citing precedent of the Brazilian Federal Supreme Court (Supremo Tribunal Federal, 2018), in which protection conferred by the CF would be inherent only to the communication of data and not to the data in themselves, although stored in computers or similar. Due to this decision, the defense appealed to STJ, supporting the same thesis already presented to the TJRO.

In April 2016, in the judgment of Appeal in Habeas Corpus (RHC) 51.531/RO (Superior Tribunal de Justiça, 2018), STJ considered *unlawful* to inspect messages and data stored on the mobile phone of the person arrested without prior judicial authorization, since it is a violation of the privacy and privacy of the person being investigated. After the seizure of the smartphone, the police authority should have filed a petition for the breach of confidentiality of the stored data. Lastly, the unlawfulness of the evidence produced were recognized, as well as those derived from it (Article 157 of the CPP), which should be taken from the case file.

ISSUES, CONTROVERSIES, AND PROBLEMS

The purpose of this chapter is to investigate the position of the Brazilian Superior Court of Justice on the subject, based on the decision rendered in the Appeal in Habeas Corpus n. 51.531/RO, of the rapporteur of the Justice Nefi Cordeiro (Superior Tribunal de Justiça, 2018). At this trial, protection was given to new forms of communication and data contained in mobile telephones under the constitutional terms of protection of privacy and non-unlawful obtaining of evidence, so it will always be necessary to issue a court order to get any informational elements found in messaging applications installed on one's smartphone.

In addition, other Justices of STJ also examined to determine whether there is a distinction in treatment arising from facts other than caught in the act arrest; for example, the issuance of a search warrant and seizure, or delivery of a mobile device by to the police.

Problems and research hypotheses are aimed at examining the inviolability of privacy and intimacy, the inviolability of data, and prohibiting the use of illegal evidence and its derivatives as fundamental rights, with an emphasis on protecting the confidentiality of data and telephone messages, and their subjection to judicial authorization for evidence in criminal proceedings, without mitigating the protection of fundamental rights as a result of a significant increase in crime.

THE JURISPRUDENCE OF STJ ON ACCESS TO SMARTPHONE DATA

In the global village, there is an era of communications dynamism, and smartphones are a palpable record of this. Modern mobile handsets have a multifunctionality that houses a significant portion of records relating to privacy and the privacy of its owner. They store not only messages or links, but also bank passwords, credit card data, photographs, appointment schedules, so constitutional protection must adapt and extend to new technologies. Not because they are new, but because they refer to a facet of the privacy and intimacy of their user.

This was a point made by Justice Rogério Schietti Cruz when speaking at the judgment of the Appeal in Habeas Corpus n. 51.531/RO (Superior Tribunal de Justiça, 2018), referring to the third-generation evidentiary law, which refers to "highly technological, invasive tests that allow the achievement of knowledge and results unattainable by senses and the traditional techniques adopted so far" (Knijnik, 2016).

It is important to emphasize the *distinguishing* made by Justice Schietti Cruz in the RHC 51.531/RO judgment regarding a 2004 positioning of Justice Gilmar Mendes in the judgment of Habeas Corpus (HC) 91.867/PA of the STF, which also deals with seizure of cell phone in the moment of arrest and access to data, but without access to the conversations contained in the device (Supremo Tribunal Federal, 2018). It is reminded that at the time, mobile phones were not connected to broadband Internet, which reveals the less intrusive character of the police check. It also points out that the messaging, photos and documents applications store the files in the phone memory, and it should be noted that most companies that offer such features do not save the files on their servers. What is deduced from the argument is that if the proof that were wanted to be stored on the servers that run the applications, it would be essential to submit a court decision determining the data routing so that the evidence would be considered lawful.

Regarding the seizure of mobile phones in situation of flagrant arrest and access to the content of messages and data contained therein, the STJ has solidified understanding on the subject. In a database search using the expression "WhatsApp prox10 conversation", 13 occurrences (judgments) were found, the oldest being judged in April 2016 – exactly the case that is being examined in this chapter - and the most recent in February 2018. And about the content of the judgments, there are distinctions of a qualitative nature as to the form of access to text messages.

In Habeas Corpus 372.762/MG, it should be noted that there were no arrests in the act of seizing the mobile phones, which were seized in compliance with the judicial order that authorized the search and seizure in the addresses linked to the patient and the other e-mails (Superior Tribunal de Justiça, 2018). Thus, new judicial authorization would be dispensable for analysis and use of stored data, since there was search and apprehension of the physical basis of the cellular telephone handsets.

Concerning the judgment by majority of votes of Appeal in Habeas Corpus 86.076/MT, it was decided by lawfulness in the investigation of mobile telephone equipment in the hypothesis in which the victim is dead, and that telephone was delivered to the police authority by his wife, interested in clarifying the facts that held him, since there was no more secrecy to protect the holder of that right (Superior Tribunal de Justiça, 2018). In this trial, Justice Sebastião Reis Júnior proposed a divergent vote, due to the fact that he understood that judicial authorization was essential for access to WhatsApp application data from the victim's telephone, even if the telephone been delivered by the wife of the victim to elucidate the crime committed against him, since it cannot be lost sight that the conversation maintained through this application is a form of written communication and immediate between the interlocutors, and, if accessed without judicial authorization, represents unauthorized interception of communications, making possible to break the chain of custody (Prado, 2014).

It can be said that the Brazilian Superior Court of Justice acted as a guarantor by requiring the issuance of a court order to access the data contained in the cellular device; distancing itself, however, from the activist form as it has been conducting the theme of telephone interceptions (Santiago, Costa, 2016), a matter that is related to the access to mobile data, and which, for consistency, deserves the same treatment, which shows that the STJ adopts a double behavior in relation to evidence obtained through telephone and data interception. In this sense, the STJ has been failing in its constitutional commitment to unify national jurisprudence.

FUTURE RESEARCH DIRECTIONS

In the year 2018 the Brazilian Data Protection Law was approved (Law n. 13708). The text guarantees greater control of citizens about their personal information, requiring explicit consent for data collection and use and requires the provision of options for the user to view, correct and delete such data.

Amongst many subjects, the law expressly excludes from the scope of protection the processing of personal data for public security purposes. The law also says that in this case, there will be special legislation, to be elaborated observing proportional measures and necessary to the service of the public interest, according to due process of law. It also prohibits companies from accessing this data.

In a society that is increasingly interconnected by digital means, and even access to the Internet is considered a fundamental right, it is important that only public power has access to data that can be used to the detriment of citizens. But even in these cases, it is important that there be legally established limits for state action.

Considering this, it is important that law researchers are concerned with establishing what the state boundaries would be, since the parameters established by law are too vague, and may give rise to relativizations based on the good faith of state agents.

CONCLUSION

Even in the case of *distinguishing* in relation to Appeal of Habeas Corpus 51.531/RO, there was consistency with the contents of protection of intimacy and privacy foreseen in the CF. Since there is a judicial warrant for search and seizure, there is no need to speak about issuing a new order to scan the contents of a smartphone. In the same way, the voluntary delivery of the device to the authorities eludes the unlawfulness in obtaining the proof, even if made by the wife of the deceased victim, in genuine exercise of renouncing the right of privacy. Although it is objected the necessity of a judicial warrant for access to the data of the telephone of the deceased for the validation of the informative elements contained in the evidentiary context, its delivery by the wife made the dispatch of the warrant unnecessary.

In any case, it is crucial to note that the position of the STJ in the decisions about non-invasion of smartphones at the moment of police approach is an important achievement aimed at the protection of intimacy and of privacy, despite a punitive discourse and violating fundamental rights and guarantees that has as its background the fight against crime.

ACKNOWLEDGMENT

We thank the University of Fortaleza (UNIFOR) for the financial and professional support regarding the development and presentation of this work.

REFERENCES

Badaró, G. (2014). *Processo penal*. Rio de Janeiro: Elsevier.

Brasil, Superior Tribunal de Justiça. (2018). *Habeas Corpus n. 372.762/MG*. 5ª. Retrieved from https://ww2.stj.jus.br/processo/revista/documento/mediado/?componente=ITA&sequencial=1631821&num_registro=201602540301&data=20171016&formato=PDF

Brasil, Superior Tribunal de Justiça. (2018). *Recurso Ordinário em Habeas Corpus n. 51.531/RO*. Retrieved from https://ww2.stj.jus.br/processo/revista/documento/mediado/?componente=ITA&sequencial=1497056&num_registro=201402323677&data=20160509&formato=PDF

Brasil, Supremo Tribunal Federal. (2018). *Habeas Corpus n. 91.867/PA*. 2ª. Retrieved from http://redir.stf.jus.br/paginadorpub/paginador.jsp?docTP=TP&docID=2792328

Brasil, Supremo Tribunal Federal. (2018). *Recurso Extraordinário n. 418.416/SC*. Retrieved from http://www.stf.jus.br/portal/jurisprudencia/listarJurisprudencia.asp?s1=%28418416%2ENUME%2E+OU+418416%2EACMS%2E%29&base=baseAcordaos&url=http://tinyurl.com/hews2gu

Knijnik, D. (2016). A trilogia Olmstead-Katz-Kyllo: o art. 5º da Constituição Federal do século XXI. *Revista da EMAGIS - Revista da Escola da Magistratura do TRF da 4ª Região*, *2*(4), 77-90.

Lemos, B., Caldeira, F., & Quintiere, V. (2016). Sobre as (i)legalidades no processo penal: breve reflexão a respeito do Whatsapp a partir da Lei n. 9.296/96 – um estudo de caso. In Interceptação Telefônica: os 20 anos da Lei n. 9.296/96 (pp. 45-62). Belo Horizonte: D'Plácido.

Prado, G. (2014). *Prova penal e sistema de controles epistêmicos: a quebra da cadeia de custódia das provas obtidas por métodos ocultos*. São Paulo: Marcial Pons.

Santiago, N. E. A., & Costa, D. K. A. (2016). Garantismo, encontro fortuito decorrente de interceptações telefônicas e a jurisprudência do Supremo Tribunal Federal e do Superior Tribunal de Justiça: rumo à ilicitude das provas. In Interceptação Telefônica: os 20 anos da Lei n. 9.296/96 (pp. 319-346). Belo Horizonte: D'Plácido.

Schreiber, S. (2016). Algumas reflexões sobre a medida cautelar de interceptação telefônica, 20 anos depois. In Interceptação Telefônica: os 20 anos da Lei n. 9.296/96 (pp. 445-463). Belo Horizonte: D'Plácido.

Sydow, S. T. (2017). Criptografia e ciência penal informática. *Revista dos Tribunais, 985*, 343-374.

Vianna, C. S. M. (2004). Da privacidade como direito fundamental da pessoa humana. *Revista de Direito Privado, 17*, 102–115.

ADDITIONAL READING

Dutra, L. (2007). *Busca e apreensão penal: da legalidade às ilegalidades cotidianas*. Florianópolis: Conceito Editorial.

Fayet, F. A., & Carvalho, A. V. (2018). *Whatsapp*, sigilo de dados e prova ilícita: Para dizer o óbvio. *Revista Brasileira de Ciências Criminais, 26*(140), 297–322.

Santiago, N. E. A. (Ed.). (2013). *Proibições probatórias no processo penal: análise do direito brasileiro, do direito estrangeiro e do direito internacional*. Brasília: Gazeta Jurídica.

Santoro, A., & Maduro, F. (Eds.). (2016). Interceptação Telefônica: os 20 anos da Lei n. 9.296/96. Belo Horizonte: D'Plácido.

Teixeira, T., Sabo, I., & Sabo, P. (2017). Whatsapp e a criptografia ponto-a-ponto: Tendência jurídica e o conflito privacidade vs. interesse público. *Revista da Faculdade de Direito da UFMG, 71*, 607–638.

Tucci, R. (2006). Ordem judicial de busca e apreensão e ilicitude da prova dela extrapolante. *Revista dos Tribunais*, 95 (848), 457-470.

KEY TERMS AND DEFINITIONS

Appeal of Habeas Corpus: It is a judicial measure that can only be used by the citizen because of an unfavorable decision rendered in the judgment of a writ of habeas corpus decided by the state courts or by the federal courts.

Brazilian Superior Court of Justice (STJ): According to Brazilian Federal Constitution, STJ is the constitutional court, empowered to resolve issues that directly concern constitutional violations.

Brazilian Supreme Court of Justice (STF): According to Brazilian Federal Constitution, the STJ is responsible for the uniformization of national jurisprudence, as well as ensuring the uniform application of federal legislation.

Caught in the Act Arrest (Flagrant): Arrest made by public agents when there is visual certainty of the infraction, or when the suspect has just practiced the alleged offense.

Habeas Corpus: It is a constitutional writ that seeks to protect the citizen against abuse of state power that curtails his freedom.

Chapter 12
Assisted Human Reproduction by Medical Techniques and the Respect of the Fundamental Rights and the Dignity of the Parts Involved

Roberto Wider
University of Minho, Portugal

ABSTRACT

Dealing with the subject of the fundamental rights of people involved in medically assisted reproduction, this chapter focuses on the issues surrounding the LGBTI+ population (lesbians, gays, bisexuals, transsexuals, intersexuals, and new genders that are being recognized). Within this group, the importance of biological children, even amongst those who cannot naturally reproduce, is also highlighted. Firstly, the author points out the laws that determine the child's protection, then compares them to real-life examples of actual situations of homophobia including physical and psychological abuse, understanding that children are also subject to the same abuse, not only due to sexual orientation discrimination and gender identity but also from having to grow up in a so-called unusual family structure. The author looks for an answer that will help strengthen the child's fundamental rights both before and after birth.

DOI: 10.4018/978-1-5225-8350-9.ch012

INTRODUCTION

Which fundamental human rights rule the breeding of IVF babies?

This is an issue which challenges our society as a whole, and not only law and healthcare professionals.

The importance of this subject is confirmed by articles in the international media, such as the one presented at the Brazilian newspaper, O GLOBO, published on the July 25th 2018. Its headline said: "Health and Reproduction - LIVES "in vitro"

Also, it is known through objective and official data released by the European Society of Human Reproduction and Embryology that since the birth of the first IVF baby on July 25th 1978, more than 8 million people were born from IVF fertilization (De Geyter, 2018).

Furthermore, the same data reports that 9% (nine percent) of Denmark's current population is the result of this technique! Therefore, we are dealing with a significant portion of our current society: lives produced "in vitro" (De Geyter, 2018).

However, these same techniques of assisted reproduction are also used by the LGBTI + population in order to generate biological children who may also suffer from the same homophobic reactions of the social environment to which they were brought.

What can be done in order to best protect the these children?

That will be analysed next.

DEVELOPMENT

One is not discussing here the extraordinary advance of this technique nor its effects, since it is undoubtedly crucial in the world we currently live in. Be that as far as family planning is concerned, as well as in the social and moral sphere.

However, it is also true that one can no longer judge these issues from an outdated family planning perspective, one which was the standard when these techniques were developed (over 40 years ago).

I have already pointed out in previous studies that we are experiencing new times in which accelerated social changes, unthinkable until now, are now happening. Even before societies and individuals are in a condition of accepting or determining what is socially accepted or not.

Scientific progress cannot be stopped. However it is fundamental that human dignity should be preserved as a greater value.

The nature of this issue deeply touches a myriad of human values, consequently showing a variety of approaches, from religious to sociopolitical, through psychic and emotional implications.

Therefore it raises both passionate emotions and interests, provoking heated debates, involving subjects such as eugenics and immortality, which are supported by antagonistic positions. All of these are issues that require an ethical approach and undoubtedly, appropriate legal rules (Wider).

In this challenging context, observe what one can learn from an extraordinary article published by the Portuguese magazine Visão, by its director Mafalda Anjos, on the 15th of June 2017. The title is remarkable:

Hey mom, go to the supermarket on the corner and buy me a pair of twins!

Taking into consideration the history of children's breeding, going through what happens nowadays, and dwelling on the future, the question arises:

How should this issue be addressed?

And what the prominent journalist refers to, is not a crazy hallucination. Since we know for sure that for many, going to the United States of America to "get" a child is a lifestyle.

And I would like to add that it is not even necessary to go to the United States anymore. You only need an internet connection and the right website.

Regarding the internet websites, one can of the news articles published on the Cryobank website states that a sperm bank in Los Angeles offers its customers an unusual service: they can choose a donor who is similar to a celebrity. Cryobank has a catalog of donors who resemble actors, athletes or celebrities, and deal with special requests (Cryobank, n.d.).

The purchased spermatozoids or egg cells are then brought to the purchasers and implanted in their own bodies (all of those who have a uterus, since it is not only the female bodies that can have this organ! There has been several cases of transexual couples in which the man became pregnant[1]) or implanted by surrogacy techniques.

What I propose in this article is the analysis of other current hypothesis, focussing on the principles of human dignity and responsible parenthood.

What are the most recent hypothesis?

It begins with the new family models currently recognized as well as the sex species declared by medicine.

On a previous article of mine, entitled "Family yes! Why not?", I have brought up this topic by indicating how many family models currently exist in our society (Wider, 2005).

I report objectively in that article, the types of families that are now recognized, which are ten (or more…)!

Three of them are the most known: marriage, stable union and single parenting (the latter could be between any parent and their descendants, or grandparents and their grandchildren and also relationships from other sources such as adoption, socio-affective paternity and homoaffective paternity - not necessarily biological).

Next there is the multi parenthood, also known as reconstituted family. They are composed by couples who were previously married (or with stable union) where the two or one of them have children of these previous unions.

The anaparental family (ana - without; parental - parents), considered by the coexistence between people who are either relatives or not and have a common family objective.

The eudemonist family, results from the coexistence between people through affective bonds and mutual solidarity.

Monoparenthood, it is the protection granted to a person who optionally lives alone (in Brazil this form of family grew 70% in the 90s, whereas in Portugal it already represents 8% of the population).

Transnational families result from relationships of people from different nationalities.

Parallel parenting is even when there is the obstruction of marriage by the man or the woman, a new family is constituted.

Homossexual families (already allowed by law in numerous countries - Portugal in 2010 - or by judicial recognition - Brazil 2013).

So far 10 family models are already known, but now one cannot deny the existence of the “polyamorous” model.

In Brazil there are already notary records of stable unions between a man and two women; between two women and one man and between three women[2]

One cannot discard other relevant aspects to this subject, which are the “Scientifically Recognized Sex Species (Louzada, 2016)”.

One was presented to the genders recognized by the medicine:

- **Gonadal Sex**: The gender based on the glands (ovary and testicles).
- **Morphological Sex**: The apparent sex.
- **Psychic (Psycho-Social) Sex**: The gender that the person feels as its own. Here we can talk about transsexualism, which occurs when despite the apparent sex, he or she feels as if part of another.
- **Legal or Civil Sex:** The one that appears on the individual’s birth certificate or identity card.

Due to the length of this aforementioned matter, however, this subject will not be the object of this article (it should be noted that the New York’s Commission on Human Rights has decided to formalize the multiplicity of gender identities and has come to recognize 31 types of genders![3])

What should be highlighted for this approach is the fact that there are always references in the declaration of these people (regardless being members of the new family models or of differentiated sexes) who wish to have biological children!

It is clear that Mafalda Anjos' declaration at the aforementioned articles has a very relevant humanitarian sense:

There is a solution for those who want children, but cannot or will not want to conceive them: it is called adoption.

But one also has the fundamental right to family planning.

In first place, this right has already constitutional recognition, as shown in the Brazilian Constitution, art. 226 § 7:

Based on the principles of the dignity of the human person and responsible parenthood, family planning is a free decision of the couple…

The Brazilian Civil Law repeats this rule in art. 1565 § 2, but the law number 9263 from 12/01/1996 assures these rights to every citizen and not just the couple. In the same context, the constitutional Portuguese legal order established at article 36 (Family, marriage and paternity) item I:

All citizens have the equal rights to constitute family and to get married

In this sense, the current legal scholars already work with the FAMILIES' Law and no longer in its singular form, as it has always been.

See, in this context, the work of Dimas Messias de Carvalho, Families' Law, Ed Saraiva, 4th ed. 2015, where it is now stated:

The species of families are broad and plural, and can be conceptualized using biological or socio-affective bonds; marriage or de facto union.; natural or substitute; unilinear or pluralistic, characterized by the affection and reciprocity of its members, in an ostensive and stable form.

Since this premise has been established, it is no longer possible to treat these parenting definitions as "unthinkable" as it happened to be a little more than ten years ago (Zambrano, 2006).

In this article it is already proposed the recognition of an alternative model, designated as "homoparental family" in which "the affective bond occurs between people of the same sex, including cases of transsexual and transsexual parenting". It is also observed that "such union do not have procreative capacity (in the biological sense) even though their components may have it individually."

Here we then return to the central theme of our work, namely the use of assisted reproduction techniques and the recognition of "equal legal dignity to heterosexuals, homosexuals, lesbians, bisexuals, transsexuals, transvestites, transgenders and intersexes", according to the preliminary draft of the charter of sexual diversity.

As aforementioned, the Brazilian law n9263/96 already ensures that family planning is a fundamental right recognized to all people. However there is no confrontation of the social reality consolidated within the LGBTI+ (an acronym adopted by the UN and Amnesty International to identify this part of society) share of the population.

As the lawyer and jurist, Carlos Roberto Siqueira Castro, rapporteur of the OAB[4] Federal Council[5], points out: "I claim that the proposal for Constitutional Amendment and the Draft of the Charter of Sexual Diversity, which are now under consideration, deal with issues of highest legal significance and importance for the implementation of fundamental rights in our country within the contemporary and postmodern context of the Democratic State of Law."

The Charter of Sexual and Gender Diversity is passing through the Brazilian National Senate as a draft bill since March 2018. One of the most influential leaders in this work of ensuring the rights of the LGBT population and criminalize homophobia is the lawyer and jurist, Doctor Maria Berenice Dias, who is the President of the OAB Sexual Diversity Commission and National Vice President of IBDFAM (Brazilian Family Law Institute). She has published a myriad of articles and lectures in this area, which can be consulted at www.ibdfam.org.br.

Among the fundamental proposals of this draft bill, one can highlight the recognition of equal legal dignity to the entire LGBT+ population, whether individually or in communion and in social relations, by "respecting the different ways of conducting their lives, according to their sexual orientation or gender identity."

The other fundamental rights include, among others, "the right to free sexual orientation and gender identity" and "the freedom to form a family and parental bonds".

Regarding the Right to the Family Life, "the right to paternity, adoption and the use of assisted reproduction practices" is foreseen (emphasis added by the author).

Also "the exercise of the rights deriving from family power cannot be limited or excluded due to sexual orientation or gender identity."

One come to the conclusion that homosexuals, lesbians, transsexuals, transvestites, transgender and intersex can generate biological children, including assisted reproductive practices.

It is thus a fundamental right recognized to them.

In this context, I propose now a questioning that I have not yet seen being analyzed under any circumstances:

And what about the children they have chosen/generated by the assisted reproduction technique? Do they have fundamental rights to be observed/preserved?

The Professor Maria Berenice, when explaining the need for the Charter of Sexual Diversity states that there is a great prejudice against the LGBT population, which is subject to persecution and violence and therefore cannot be left out of legal protection. She then adds:

The law is not enough to provide the rights. In order to ensure equal participation and opportunity in the economic, social, political and cultural life of the country, it is crucial to make the society aware of the equal dignity of heterosexuals, homosexuals, lesbians, bisexuals, transsexuals, transvestites, transgenders and intersex.

As far as I am concerned, she is absolutely right but the truth is that we are still working for a future condition in society through the creation of laws and awareness of all in order to end prejudice, persecution and violence.

Nevertheless, it is undoubted that the children generated within this context will still be victims of all these discomfort and therefore we shall return to our questioning:

"Which fundamental rights will these generated children be contemplated with, taking into account the principles and morals that rule the child's best interest?"

As a matter of fact, a child's best interest is already substantiated as a constitutional principle, as was established in our *Magna Carta*, in the article 227.

It is the duty of the family, the society and the State to grant with absolute priority, the right of life, health, food, leisure, professionalisation, culture, dignity, respect, freedom and family and community coexistence to all children, adolescents and young persons, as well as to safeguard them from all forms of neglect, discrimination, exploitation, violence, cruelty and oppression.

In the same sense, the Portuguese Constitution works towards the same idea (see article 69 line I).

It is of the utmost importance to bear in mind that, "according to its preamble, the Convention on the Rights of the Child - as contained in the Declaration on the Rights of the Child, from November the 20th 1959 - was created regarding the need to ensure the protection and special care for the children. It includes the appropriate legal protection, before and after the birth due to their disadvantaged condition as a result of their physical and mental immaturity (emphasis added by the author). It also takes into account that all over the world it exists children living in extremely adverse conditions and in need of special protection (Paes de Lira)"

Bear in mind then that such questioning does not mean a distinction between straight or homosexuals regarding the care and the treatment of the children since what matters in this field is the affection *per se.*

In relation to this question, by using the Socratic method, I allow myself not to make any statements about it. I would rather encourage, as a way of provoking reactions and motivating people (technical or not) to debate this subject, by pointing out ways and generating actions.

Notwithstanding, one must first of all understand the facts that are present in the lives of this segment that is so representative in our society. These facts are collected more than anything through the media and the social networks.

One can see, for example, the piece of news published by RFI (Radio France Internationale), a French public radio broadcasted abroad. On May 15th 2018, it was stated that "the number of homophobic acts" in France has risen for the second consecutive year and according to the organization SOS Homophobia, homophobic cases have continued to increase since reaching a record of 3,517 complaints in 2013 (year of the adoption of the law between same sex partners). In addition, the complaints received by SOS Homophobia detail various types of assaults, such as rejection, discrimination and threats of blackmail as well as physical assaults.

DW (Deutsche Welle), a public broadcaster in Germany, also announced on August 9th, 2017: "Germany sees an increase in cases of homophobic violence. Offenses against gays and lesbians increased 27% in 2016. Activists reported that hate crimes against homosexuals and transsexuals have become routine in the country."

In Portugal, Sapo.pt is an electronic publication considered as independent and strict. It announced on May 14th 2018 that "International Forum in Lisbon warns that LGBTI's rights in Europe have stalled." It also mentions that "according to ILGA-Europe, a non-governmental organization that gathers 490 organizations from over 45 European countries to defend human rights and equality for LGBTI people, fewer countries are adopting equality policies, including those that used to be traditional leaders."

Finally, it affirms that considering the classification of 49 European countries, the presence of populist and nationalist policies "can have a long-lasting impact on the lives of LGBTI people."

Still considering the events occurred in this area, the most striking ones are the news collected in several organs in Brazil. See, for example, those of Agência Brasil, from January the 18th 2018:

Survey indicates record deaths from homophobia in Brazil in 2017

Followed by: "in 2017, 445 lesbians, gays, bisexuals, transvestites and transsexuals (LGBTs) were killed in crimes motivated by homophobia. This number represents one victim every 19 hours."

This is reported by the NGO GGB (Gay Group of Bahia), who has been monitoring this for 38 years.The founder of this organ, the anthropologist Luiz Mott, pointed out at the NGO's website that:

These alarming numbers are just the tip of an iceberg of violence and blood. Since there are no official governmental statistics on hate crimes, such deaths are always underreported once the GGB database is based on news stories published in the media, the internet and personal declarations.

Hence the statement aforementioned by Professor Maria Berenice, that there is an enormous prejudice against the LGBT population, which has been the target of persecution and violence.

Returning now to the question that is the object of the analysis of this chapter: which measures can be taken to better protect the fundamental rights and human dignity of children generated by this population?

In relation to the children and the world of LGBTI+ population, two perspectives should be analyzed:

One concerns parenthood in relation to those who started or have been born with the characteristics of sexual and gender diversity.

At first, it is a difficult reality to absorb, because the expectation is related to the apparent sex or the sex attributed to them in the birth certificate.

Consequently, the failure to accept this reality causes serious suffering to these children, who are not accepted in their family environment. In addition to the aforementioned hostilities they are victims of, this failure can also lead to suicide, which also occurs in a dramatic proportion.

The GGB (Gay Group of Bahia) also reports, in 2017, the occurrence of 58 suicides in Brazil, of which 33 are gay, 15 are lesbians, 7 are transsexuals and 3 are bisexuals. This indicates that LGBTI+ population should be protected, not only by the force of law, but also by a cultural evolution of our current society.

But let us come back to the issues concerning the children brought to this world by the LGBTI + population through the use of medically assisted reproductive techniques.

Obviously, the question is not about to pondering whether the members of this social segment may or may not bear children. It is a right that they possess as human beings and that already is protected by legal rules, as pointed out above.

In her excellent article, Professor Heloísa Helena Barbosa, when dealing with the techniques of assisted reproduction to those who are not heterosexual, faces the question of the protection of the reproductive autonomy of transsexuals (Barbosa, 2012).

She also claims that "the fundamental right to reproduction, however, does not include the relation of rights considered "intangible" by the international legal order." Therefore, it can be removed in exceptional circumstances, where the law is threatened and requires a secure protection.

Subsequently, the author confirms the premise that justifies the question presented in this work:

"Although the right to reproduction constitutes one of the manifestations of the "principle and right to freedom," the effects of the act of generation necessarily interfere decisively in the sphere of interests of the child, who are also internationally recognized." In this sense, "that right can not be absolute, it will always be limited by the rights of unborn children, fundamentally for their right to dignity and the formation of their personality within a family.

The author mentions in her work two hypotheses that would justify an intervention of authorities in order to exclude the right to procreate: "if the sole and proven goal of the parent(s) would be to deliberately transmit serious illness to the offspring."

According to a piece of news published by BBC Brazil on the 12th of March 2008, "a deaf British couple has started a controversy by stating that they wanted to select a baby with the same characteristic (deaf) during the process of artificial fertilization"

In this case, what is the prevailing fundamental right: that of the parents in generating a child with the same handicap they have, or of the future generated child by having its integral health guaranteed?

It also mentions human cloning, which was prohibited in all its forms by a declaration from the United Nations General Assembly in 2005, because it is incompatible with human dignity and the protection of human life.

In addition to these unlawful hypotheses, it should be carefully considered the issue of generating a child only for the purpose of obtaining cells to cure illnesses of another child!

At the website Health IG, there is an analysis of those who are genetically selected to be born healthy and to be marrow and tissue donors for their siblings. Below there is an observation by physicians and geneticists that caution is needed so that these babies are not planned with the sole purpose to serve as "a cure" for the family (IG, 2013).

This issue was also the object of study at the International Seminar "Debating the Medically Assisted Procreation" from the University of Porto, on March 16th and 17th, 2017. The intervention of Professor Benedita Mac Crorie was relevant, with the analysis of item E - paragraph 2 of art. 67 of the Portuguese Constitution, together with Judgment 101\2009 of the Constitutional Court, when evaluating the unconstitutionality of Law no. 32\2006 (Mac Crorie, 2017)[6].

What was exposed in the case was the use of MAP (Medically Assisted Procreation) techniques for the treatment of another person's serious illness, usually a sibling. In that case, the hypothesis is: "being the new born generated precisely for the purpose of saving a third party, it is undeniable that it will be used as an instrument, for the pursuit of others' ends."

The decision of the Court did not follow the aforementioned hypothesis - with an argument also defended by the author. It was based on the argument that the "social aim of the action" was fulfilled, considering that the aim was the protection of the health of a third party in life risk.

With due respect, I do not follow this understanding, partly in accordance with the defeated vote of Maria Lucia Amaral. Besides, I also understand that the social aim of an action has a myriad of interpretations and consequences, which can largely surpass the best future interest for a child.

It is always necessary to foresee and to serve with absolute priority the best interest of the future child, as established in the aforementioned Article 227 of the Brazilian Constitution (1988).

It is clear from the judgment number 225/2018 of the Constitutional Court of Portugal, which dealt with the unconstitutionality of articles of the Law 32/2006 (Law of Medically Assisted Procreation). Specifically: Article 8 - gestation of substitution; Article 15 - Confidentiality and, Article 20 - Determination of parenting, a significant approach to the limits of this work, contained in page n.3, referring to decision n.87 / CNECV -2016.

In the following fragment, the Counselor Rita Lobo Xavier claims that:

I do not consider to be ethically acceptable to make the woman's beneficiaries of the WFP techniques over the rights of the unborn child, especially in the case of post-mortem insemination.

It should be noted that protective laws already exist. For the time being they are the same for children in the LGBTI + population and for other children. However it is certain that they are not enough to give those the effectiveness of protection and serve their best interest.

CONCLUSION

What matters is to actually give political and social visibility to the bioethical issues arising from this matter.

Conflict issues associated with heterologous reproduction such as that of filiation or those of the right to genetic identity and the donor's anonymity, often need socio political consensus mirrored in norms of law that are open to the difference and diversity of social practices.

The future is being built right now. Hence the need for investment in the training of agents (doctors, lawyers, judges, psychologists, social workers, nurses, educators, policemen, politicians and so forth) as well as organizational cultures capable of socially supporting the necessary changes against any form of discrimination, stigma and prejudice.

All things considered, after an interview with Professors Filomena Teixeira and Fernando Marques[7], we came up with the idea of an ethical-legal observatory of the implementation of the legislation on assisted reproduction, in order to monitor and regulate this implementation (Teixeira e Marques, 2017).

ACKNOWLEDGMENT

This chapter was translated by Ana Leticia de Figueredo Sampaio, University College Ghent, Belgium.

REFERENCES

Barbosa, H. H. (2012). *Professor at the State University of Rio de Janeiro - Protection of reproductive autonomy of transsexuals*. Florianópolis: Revista de Estudos Feministas.

Cryobank. (n.d.). *Donor Look-A-Likes*. Retrieved from https://cryobank.com/donor-search/look-a-likes/

De Geyter, C. (2018). *More than 8 million babies born from IVF since the world's first in 1978.* Retrieved from https://www.eshre.eu/ESHRE2018/Media/ESHRE-2018-Press-releases/De-Geyter.aspx

IG. (n.d.). *A geração dos bebês nascidos para curar.* Retrieved from: https://minhasaude/2013-05-02/a-geraçao-dos-bebes-nascidos-para-curar.html

Louzada, F. (2016), *intersexuality and Brazilian law* lecture at the Luso-Brazilian meeting of Right of Families in Lisbon.

Mott, L., & Michels, E. (2017). *Mortes violentas de LGBT no Brasil*. Grupo Gay da Bahia -Relatório 2017.

Teixeira, F., & Marques, F. (2017). Biologia e Gênero: outros olhares. Academic Press.

Wider, R. (n.d.). Assisted Reproduction - Aspects of Bioethics and Bioethics. Ed. Empresa do Diário do Minho Ltd. Braga.

Zambrano, E. (2006). Parentalidades "Impensáveis": Pais/Mães Homossexuais, Travestis e Transexuai. *Horizontes Antropológicos*, *12*(26), 123–147. doi:10.1590/S0104-71832006000200006

KEY TERMS AND DEFINITIONS

Assisted Reproduction: Medical technique for human reproduction.

Bioethics: Specific area of philosophical knowledge combined with biomedical sciences.

Biolaw: The integration of ethics, as a science of moral conduct, with the judicial rules that govern society.

Embryology: Study of the embryos before their implantation.

Homoparental Family: One in which the affective bond occurs between people of the same sex.

Homophobia: Rejection towards those who do not fit into the unique role of man or woman.

In Vitro "Lives": Human lives created outside the human body.

Replacement Pregnancy: Pregnancy with embryos in other wombs than their mother.

Sperm Banks: Centers for the collection of human semen.

ENDNOTES

1 See for example https//universa.uol.com.br/noticias/redaçao/2017/07/16/trans/gravido

2 Nevertheless, on the 26th of June 2018, the Brazilian National Council of Justice has determined that the notary offices should refrain from writing deeds from polyamorous unions.

3 Read more at: https://www.hypeness.com.br/2016/06/nova-york-agora-reconhece-31-diferentes-tipos-de-genero/

4 The Ordem dos Advogados do Brasil (OAB) is the Brazilian institution that regulates the lawyers' activities and represents them in general.

5 OAB's Federal Council is the department that disciplines all lawyers' activities.

6 Auxiliary professor of the University of Minho Law School.

7 Filomena Teixeira, Professora Coordinator of the School of Education - Polytechnic Institute of Coimbra. Effective member of the Center for Didactic Research and Technology in the Training of Teachers of the University of Aveiro.

Chapter 13
Bullying in the Work Environment and Human Dignity:
General Considerations About the Brazilian Reality

Iran Chaves Garcia Junior
Universidade do Minho – Braga, Portugal

Clovis Demarchi
Universidade do Vale do Itajaí, Brazil

ABSTRACT

This chapter deals with the dignity of the human person and moral harassment, bringing some specific considerations about Brazilian reality. The scientific objective is to demonstrate the concrete existence of an impact on the principle of human dignity when harassment occurs in the environmental work. It is a theme that is in the discussion guide mainly from the beginning of this century, although abuse and humiliation have always been practiced in labor relations, with the same current scope, which is a tool to achieve generally derogatory ends of the human condition and intensified by the action of globalization in the contemporary world. Besides impact directly on the person, moral harassment in the work environment results in consequences for society, for company (organization), and the state.

DOI: 10.4018/978-1-5225-8350-9.ch013

INTRODUCTION

This chapter has as its object the discussion about the dignity of the human person and bullying. The scientific objective is to demonstrate the concrete existence of an impact on the principle of the dignity of the human person when moral harassment occurs at work. Its specific objectives are: to present elements for a referential on the dignity of the human person; identify how, what is and how moral bullying develops; demonstrate how moral harassment at work violates the principle of the dignity of the human person.

Bullying is a phenomenon that occurs within working relationships, but must be identified, combated and punished whenever it is observed.

It is a topic recently discussed in the universe of work, although the abuse and humiliation have always been practiced in labor relations, with the same current scope, which is a tool to achieve generally derogatory ends of the human condition and intensified by the action of globalization in the contemporary world.

This issue brings to light all the humiliation and embarrassment suffered by many workers in their work environments. It also denotes, how cold and inhumane some people are becoming, intent on achieving "success" within their companies, bodies or institutions.

It is important to emphasize at the outset that bullying in the workplace presents serious consequences for both those who are persecuted and those around them, as well as causing harm and consequences to society as well as impacts on the company (organization) and the State.

The chapter is divided into five items, the first of which deals with general considerations about the dignity of the human person, the second about some historical and philosophical elements of the dignity of the human person, the third deals with aspects of conceptualizing moral harassment in the environment of work, the next item is about the possible dimensions of moral damage and finally addresses the consequences of bullying in the workplace for the individual, for society, for the company and the state.

To perform the work, the inductive method was used with bibliographical and documentary research.

CONSIDERATIONS ON THE DIGNITY OF THE HUMAN PERSON

At the beginning of this chapter, we see the idea of Paz (2009, p. 15.), which advises caution in addressing the principle of the dignity of the human person, since this principle has attracted more and more adherents. Thus, there is a prescription for this principle to be treated with rationality, since its indiscriminate application may represent a threat to democracy.

The author emphasizes that the legal discourse focused on the principle of human dignity has been a siren song that attracts and enchants legal discourse, sometimes to the detriment of critical reason. This clarification is important, considering that it is an objective of this work, in order to maintain a critical view of the issue of human dignity and harassment at work.

Defining a concept of dignity of the human person or even when this principle should be employed does not seem to be an easy task. It can be said that this is a biblical principle, going beyond the legal field. It appears in the Christian definition, when it is believed that man was created in the image and likeness of God, emphasizing his dignity and greatness.

Sarlet (2005, p. 16) emphasizes that there are difficulties in establishing a concept and this "certainly derives at least from the circumstance that one takes care of a concept of vague and imprecise contours, characterized by its ambiguity and porosity." Dignity is a concept that not only deals with aspects of human existence but refers to the right of every human person. Therefore, this conception portrays that the principle of dignity is intrinsic value to each person human being, being an integral quality of the human being, must be recognized, protected and respected.

Everyone is considered to be a holder of dignity regardless of status, social position, race, beliefs, sex, ability or any other personal or social attributes. Sarlet (2005, p.16) points to the realization that all, in principle, even the greatest of criminals "are equal in dignity, in the sense of being recognized as persons - even if they are not equally dignified in their relations with their fellow men, even with themselves. "

Because it is an intrinsic quality of the human person, this condition, in itself, considers the human person to be a dignity. Thus, it is inferred that dignity is prior to the formation of the State, exists a priori to the own right. Given its importance, it is recognized as the foundation of the legal order and, even if a certain normative system does not recognize it as such, its recognition must be recognized, since in all democratic constitutional systems, there is a determination that they should be recognized and fundamental rights.

For this reason, it is inadmissible to accept that people are treated as objects and not as subjects, considering that their rights surpass any individuality, making it a social imperative.

Thus, the term dignity carries with it a broader scope, the basis of which is respect for human rights. In other words, for the dignity of man to be respected, the a priori condition is the recognition of his condition as a human being that must be respected and considered by the State and members of its species. In this context, Bittar (2005, p. 302) emphasizes that "there is only dignity [...] when understood, understood and respected in its various dimensions, which necessarily imposes the expansion of ethical consciousness as a daily practice of respect for the human person ".

In order for the State to respect dignity, it is necessary to concretely secure individual rights alongside the social ones, both seen as reciprocally complementary, ensuring health, education, work and other rights that guarantee minimum conditions for a healthy and dignified life.

HISTORICAL-PHILOSOPHICAL SENSE OF THE PRINCIPLE OF THE DIGNITY OF THE HUMAN PERSON

The idea of human dignity refers to biblical times, permeating the development of Christian doctrine. In the medieval period, rising Christianity emphasizes that man was created in the image and likeness of God, in which "the human being is endowed with an intrinsic value of himself, and cannot be transformed into a mere object or instrument" as Sarlet points (2005, 29).

This conception highlights the notion of equality, regardless of its origin, ownership, color or race. In spite of the contradiction present in Christian doctrine, since it considered natural slavery and the superiority of the male figure in relation to woman, true equality, innate to the human being, was always present in the development of Christianity.

Justice, therefore, would be the guide of the conduct of any person and reference to the rulers, in which the sovereign should act to guarantee the common good and the dignity of all men.

The story also refers to the anthropological period of Greek philosophy, which highlighted ethical and political man as the center of philosophical discussion. Although he did not specifically address the issue of human dignity, the Greeks highlighted the figure of a man of universal and normative value. Greek reflection on man represented a break with mythical thinking. Mythology has built the image of man as subordinate to the mythical forces of the gods, responsible for directing their relations with other men and with nature, while Greek thinking, centered on reason, shows a man who aspires to knowledge, to justice. According to Sarlet (2005: 56), it is in this new conception of man that the understanding of dignity is developed.

From a philosophical perspective, the conception of the dignity of the human person is solidly based and prevails that every man, as an end in itself, has an intrinsic value, that is, dignity. The post-war Universal Declaration of Human Rights of 1948 contemplated "human dignity as a value to illuminate the universe of rights."

According to Piovesan (2005, pp. 41-53), "the primacy of the person, based on human dignity, is a response to the acute crisis suffered by legal positivism", since many atrocities were committed according to legality and this " legal order indifferent to ethical values, captured by the purely formal perspective "does not meet the opportunities of welcoming and protecting the human being.

In both the preamble and Article 1 of the UN Universal Declaration of Human Rights, "[...] recognition of dignity [...]is the foundation of freedom, justice and peace in the world; [and] all human beings are born free and equal in dignity and rights "

The thing, synonymous with material good, is priceless and replaceable. The human person puts himself above all price, has no equivalent and therefore becomes irreplaceable. Hence, it is concluded from Kantian thought that the human person is unique and has dignity. This conception enshrines the contemporary principle of the dignity of the human person, based on the assumption that man, by virtue of his human condition and independently of any other circumstance, has rights that must be recognized and respected by his peers and by the State.

Dignity is an individual attribute of the person. An "ideal or abstract being" (Sarlet, 2011, p. 120) has no dignity to be protected, since the lessons of human dignity and human dignity are not confused. The expression human dignity is linked to humanity, in its kind, and not to the human person, in his individuality. Humanity means human nature, and this is the reason for saying dignity of the human person, not human dignity, because in this case, the reference is to the human race and not to the individual who is part of this humanity.

Dignity is, in fact, the human person, from which he can not be withdrawn, except when he lacks his life, without prejudice to his rights protection. Of course, a "community (or social) dimension" is admissible, since "all are equal in dignity and as such coexist in a particular community or group" (Sarlet, 2011, 120).

In a literal term, the dignity of the human person is intrinsic to any human being, since "the life and birth of a person are the reasons for their dignity" (Siqueira Junior & Oliveira, 2009, p. The person, from his or her birth, carries with it his dignity, a concept corroborated by Nunes (2010, p. 49), when he affirms that dignity is "innate" to the person. Based on this inference, a criminal has human dignity, although his behavior is condemned by the legal system.

In the debate about dignity of the human person, some scholars adopt a posture of not considering it as an innate characteristic, maintaining that it must be built a priori, in the full human existence. In the unrestricted and full freedom of his existence, the human person conquers his dignity, making any type of discrimination inadmissible, since "all are equal before the law."

It is admitted that dignity is embodied in the human being, pointing out reason as a universal code of ethics, allowing man to organize his life within the ethical precepts, guided by a sense of respect for the laws. However, recognizing dignity only by the construction of man, in his existence, is not the best meaning for the principle.

The dignified life is what is expected during the existence, as intrinsic quality of the dignity that cannot be withdrawn from the man. As stated above, it is clear that the dignity of the person human being is prior to his or her own birth, configuring himself as essential to the human being from his conception.

However, it stands out that the human being is a social being and because of his sociability he cannot live isolated from his peers. Their experience in the social environment, their actions and their behavior make up their dignity and must be respected, but an important aspect must be observed: when there is a violation of the dignity of another, it is evident that the guardianship will be with the person victimized by the offense.

Thus, it will be necessary to incorporate into the concept of human dignity a social quality as a limit to the possibility of guarantee. That is, dignity is only an unlimited guarantee if it does not hurt another ", as Nunes (2010, p. 49) adds. It is not possible that the dignity of a person should be respected without, likewise, demanding the respect of another person, since the fundamental duty of a citizen is in observance of the principles, such as that of Roman law: honeste vivere (live honestly), alterum non laedere (do no harm to anyone) and suum cuique tribuere (give each one, what is due to him).

Man will always find the justification to resist arbitrariness and the pressures and repressions of rights that defy and cut the dignity of the human person, because, in disrespecting the human being, everything else will be disrespected. Thus, the dignity of the human person must be the end of law, and humanity, its greatest recipient. The Law assumes fundamental importance in the protection and promotion of human dignity, mainly for exercising the role of curbing possible violations.

Many countries, such as Brazil, have elevated the dignity of the human person as the basic foundation of the Democratic Rule of Law, in such a way that the legal system is based around the human being, considered a "convergent center of rights". In this way, all fundamental human rights must be guided by the source value of dignity. This is the case, for example, of work, which in the Democratic State of Law must be promoted by the fundamental and universal right to decent work, as clarified by Delgado (2006, p. 51).

The etymological root of the word dignity derives from the Latin dignitas, which corresponds to that which has value, which deserves esteem, honor and consideration. Regardless of the historical character of the extent and definition of what dignity of the human person is, given that at one time there was no mention of the rights of slaves, women or even workers exploited during the Industrial Revolution, it can be inferred from of the analysis of its etymological root, that it is born with the person.

Another important orientation is that human dignity as an intrinsic value is not the result of a constitutional text, since it precedes the law. Any fact or circumstance that contrasts with the human being damages his dignity. Nunes (2010, p. 51) mentions that "the human being is worthy because he is. It is innate. Inherent in its essence. "Therefore, the human being possesses, in being conceived, and even before receiving a name, the dignity conferred by life. That is, the life of man as an end in itself is reason that makes of dignity a fundamental value that can not be relativized.

Dignity is the innate characteristic of the human person, the "only being who understands an inner value, superior to any price, which does not allow equivalent substitution. Thus, dignity intrudes and is confused with the very nature of the human being ", as Silva (2009, p. 38) emphasizes.

In this way, it is inferred that dignity is born with life and not, necessarily, with the person. Dignity does not arise, as Rocha (2004, p. 87) shows, "as merit, but as an absolute value of the human being, an element that is intrinsic and intangible to him."

DEFINING BULLYING AT WORK AND ITS LEGAL CONTEXT

The idea of bullying emerged as an object of research at the end of the last century, when the Swedish psychologist Heinz Leymann conducted a survey with several groups of professionals and detected a phenomenon that he called "psychoterrorism." The psychologist coined the term mobbing (a derivative of mob, meaning horde or pack), by virtue of the similarity of the "psychoterror" with a rustic, coarse attack.

For the definition of bullying at work, it is necessary to take into account both cultural and organizational factors in each country. Many names are used and often mistakenly as synonymous with bullying. According to Prata (2006, p. 43), in Italy, the current expression is mobbing, especially by the influence of the German researcher Harald Ege, who conducted several studies there. In countries like USA, Australia and England the name used is bullying at work. Bully is the person who uses his strength or power to scare or injure the weakest people. Bullying is the use of force or power to coerce others out of fear.

Marie-France Hirigoyen emerged as one of the first to deal with these perverse relations, and thus distinguishes the terms:

The term mobbing is more about collective persecution or organizational violence, including deviance that can end physical violence. The term bullying is broader than the term mobbying. It goes from jokes and isolation to abusive conduct with sexual connotations or physical aggression. It refers more to individual offenses than to organizational violence. Bullying refers to subtler assaults, and therefore more difficult to characterize and prove, whatever its source. Even if they are close, physical violence and discrimination are primarily excluded, as violence is already taken into account in legislation. (Hirigoyen, 2009. p.85)

In this context, in order to characterize bullying at work, it is necessary to observe the frequency of conduct, types of acts that would be accepted as offensive and the duration of conduct. There are countries where humiliation and offenses in the workplace are not considered violence because they are commonplace in this environment.

According to Hirigoyen (2009, p. 17), it is possible to characterize bullying in a workplace as an abusive conduct that can be manifested by "words, gestures, acts, writings that will harm dignity, personality or the physical and mental integrity of the individual, "in this way, attitudes such as these can ruin the work environment as well, and especially, by jeopardizing employment.

Thus, according to Hirigoyen (2009), day-day stress, derived from the rudeness, nervousness, bad mood and subsequent repentance of the cause of the damage, would not typify bullying. In the same way, it is difficult to characterize harassment since it is difficult to interpret the sense in which the author is carrying out his action, which can be simply a joke of bad taste and in this way, would not be characterized as an organizational problem, but of personal behavior.

Harassment considerably affects interpersonal relationships within organizations, causing discomfort not only to the person who suffered the harassment but also to the people who are close to the problem, resulting, consequently, in a decrease in the work capacity of the team, since in relations The discomfort caused by the intentionality of disqualifying a member may reflect on the whole team.

It is observed that the scenario of globalization characterized by technological developments and flexibilizations and mobilities ended up generating an excessive competitiveness, these being some factors that caused profound changes in the organizations. These changes are intended to survive in the labor market. Human relations in these environments are also impacted, often becoming perverse. Some acts so often come to be considered normal.

Just as this reality of globalization produces an individualism that directly interferes in affective and social relations, and directly in the workplace. This new reality creates new types of friction and new realities to be regulated by law. This new context has consequences that directly interfere with the worker's life.

According to Dejours (2001, pp. 150-158), suffering is considered inherent to the work process and thus, can not be eliminated, since the subject is always subject to pressure and suffering at work, always needing an adjustment between subjectivity and the organization of work, prioritizing issues such as rhythm, journey, hierarchy, responsibility and control, in a collective vision. Thus, the more rigid the organization of work, the less significant content and the greater the chances of developing serious pathologies.

Still according to the author, suffering appears in the space of struggle between the desired well-being and mental illness or madness that presents symptoms such as depression, phobia, delusions among others.

As Hirigoyen (2002, p. 65) states, "it is a phenomenon that destroys the work environment, not only diminishing productivity, but also favoring absenteeism, due to the psychological damages it causes." The victim suffers all kinds of attacks by his tormentor, or executioners, from violent behavior or gestures to verbal aggression.

In reality, one thing is to take dedication and commitment in the work environment, another is to intimately reach the individual with offensive, humiliating or degrading words. Thus, bullying finds support in the power that fear establishes in the victim, as well as by humiliation and, on the other hand, by the connivance, silence and tolerance among the team members.

In this way, the concept of moral harassment was redefined, as the damages caused by its existence were observed, and the opportunity of punishment, now regulated in several labor laws. As Hirigoyen (2006, p. 17) points out, society has mobilized with a view to not only helping victims but taking concrete steps to compel companies and public authorities to implement effective preventive measures. "Bullying is surreptitious violence, unmentionable, but one that is nevertheless very destructive."

The harasser and the beleaguered are the main characters of the phenomenon of bullying in labor relations. As presented by Herigoyen (2006, p. 21), the harasser can be someone driven by the system as well as a person with a psychological predisposition. Most of the stalkers are people who present normality, but who can be elevated to this condition, due to the conjuncture of the work, or for other reasons that conjugate or not the existence of a psychological inclination.

Specifically in Brazil, given the context of globalization and the cultural heritage that remained before the slave regime, as well as the valorization that was given to the person and the worker, the incorporation of the idea of moral harassment in the work environment took time to be regulated, since certain acts considered today as harassment, until recently they were seen as "normal" behavior in the daily life of organizations, making it difficult for the victims to react, as well as their recognition by the Justice of the Work, since the term "moral damage" became part of the daily life of the Brazilian from this century.

It is important to point out that as moral damage affects the individual in particular, it can be understood that he is attained to a personality right, representing a true clause for the protection of human dignity and personality.

In this way, in protecting the rights of personality, the rights of the person as a worker are found in this context. In this reality, there is no way to distinguish the person from his work.

Considering the various forms of threat that people are facing, and understanding that in the work environment the person spends a large part of his life, especially in this context of globalization in which the workplace can be any place, it is possible, the violation of the rights of the personality, and as a form of bullying, happens in the work environment.

The Brazilian constitutional order is based on human dignity as well as on the protection of work and its valorization, so that when there is work without guarantee of respect for the individual rights of each worker, it is understood that there is a violation of the constitutional foundation of valorization work and the protection of the human dignity of the person who works.

In this way, it is understood that when work carried out without respect for the person and their dignity, thus failing to respect the fundamental rights of the worker, a direct violation of a constitutional foundation is taking place.

The Brazilian Constitution of 1988 sought the valorization of the human being, since, unlike the other constitutions that preceded it, it disposed the Fundamental Rights and Guarantees before the Organization of the State, thus prioritizing man in relation to the State.

Just as it strengthened the relationship of Constitutional Law with the Right of establishing in specific between Articles 7 and 11, a series of rights for workers. Specifically, in Article 7, it presented a minimum set of constitutionally guaranteed rights for both urban and rural workers. Even the single worker has guaranteed his rights, which provides for equality with the rights of workers with a permanent employment relationship. In Brazil, Labor Law, in addition to being directly related to the Constitution, relates to a large part of the Unconstitutional Laws, in the area of Civil Law, Business Law, Commercial Law, International Law, Criminal Law and others.

As the Brazilian Constitution is celebrating its 30th anniversary and the founding of Human Dignity and the valorization of work have come into force only in this constitution, it can be affirmed that the issue in Brazil is a new subject, firstly by the legislative question and the difficulty in characterizing and penalizing the action by its subjective characteristic and not always the damage is apparent and it becomes difficult to establish the causal relation. nexus, but on the other hand, the Higher Labor Court decided for the first time on the subject in 2001, from there to there are thousands of decisions across the country, with the most varied amounts of damages. There are bills in the National Congress that aim to create specific laws on workplace bullying.

The Brazilian labor court moral harassment opens the possibility for the worker to leave the job and to plead for the indirect termination of the contract. In general, bullying is covered by Article 483 of the Consolidation of Labor Laws (CLT), which establishes that the employee may consider terminating the contract and claim compensation when, among other reasons, services are to practice against him or someone in his family an act detrimental to honor and good reputation, contrary to good customs or unrelated to the contract, or even when treated by the employer or his hierarchical superiors with excessive rigor.

Specifically in Brazil, given the context of globalization and the cultural heritage that remained before the slave regime, as well as the valorization that was given to the person and the worker, the incorporation of the idea of moral harassment in the work environment took time to be regulated, since certain acts considered today as harassment, until recently they were seen as "normal" behavior in the daily life of organizations, making it difficult for the victims to react, as well as their recognition by the Justice of the Work, since the term "moral damage" became part of the daily life of the Brazilian from this century.

Therefore, it can be affirmed that the issue in Brazil is a new subject, firstly because of the legislative question and the difficulty in characterizing and penalizing the action by its subjective characteristic and not always the damage is apparent as well as it becomes difficult to establish the causal nexus, but on the other hand, the Higher Labor Court decided for the first time on the subject in 2001, from there to there are thousands of decisions throughout the country, with the most varied amounts of indemnities. There are bills in the National Congress aimed at creating specific law on moral harassment in the workplace.

The Brazilian labor court moral harassment opens the possibility for the worker to leave the job and to plead for the indirect termination of the contract. In general, bullying is covered by Article 483 of the Consolidation of Labor Laws (CLT), which establishes that the employee may consider terminating the contract and claim compensation when, among other reasons, services are to practice against him or someone in his family an act detrimental to honor and good reputation, contrary to good customs or unrelated to the contract, or even when treated by the employer or his hierarchical superiors with excessive rigor.

POSSIBLE DIMENSIONS OF MORAL HARASSMENT AT WORK

When the idea of dimension is presented, it is related to the form of concretization of the harassment, that is, by the relation between the author and the victim. It is important to emphasize that the victim is always harmed in action.

In this sense, harassment can occur in a top-down relationship, which is the most common dimension of harassment. The boss, hierarchically superior, over his subordinates.

A second possibility would be from the bottom up, but it is a rare situation that occurs when the subordinate or the subordinates use friendship or good relationship with a boss who is hierarchically superior to the immediate boss. In this case, the subordinates use a third (superior boss) to carry out harassment by means of hierarchically superior head.

There is the possibility of harassment between people of the same level. In this way, harassment is considered to be horizontal. It occurs when a person or group establishes harassment with partners. It is common to happen for the purpose of eliminating competitors. Or try to diminish someone who stands out.

Einarsen (2000, pp. 379-401), argues that bullying is a process, not a phenomenon, in which the victim faces aggressive behaviors that are frequent and violent each time. Remembering that bullying is a progressive process, the longer it takes, the hostile situation, the more frequent the insults, further aggravating the consequences. This causes, in the victims, the feeling that the treatment received was unfair.

At first the people involved do not want to be offended and play tricks and mistreatment. These attacks then multiply and the victim is then placed in an inferior situation and subjected to hostile and degrading maneuvers for longer periods. It is the repetition of vexations, of humiliations, without any effort to slow them down that makes bullying destructive.

As Hirigoyen (2006 p. 21) explains, psychological warfare in the workplace is compounded by two phenomena: abuse of power, which is quickly unmasked and not necessarily accepted by employees. The second is perverse manipulation, which happens insidiously but causes serious damage. The victim suffers various damages, reaching his self-esteem, which undoubtedly is an attack on his dignity.

The process by which the victim passes is not always easy to perceive, since in most cases it is a slow process, the perception becomes more apparent only when the victim's treatment is confronted with the received the other members of the work environment.

As Hirigoyen (2006, p.26) explains, over time, mutual phobias, between harasser and harassed, begin to emerge. The stalker begins to feel anger whenever he sees the victim and the same happens to feel complete discomfort and fear, when in the presence of the stalker. The aggressor always tends to trivialize his actions, always denying intentionality, but the intention to attack is latent.

For Freitas (2001 pp. 8-20) the whole process of harassment arises primarily from an abuse of power, later on narcissistic abuse occurs where the victim loses his self-esteem. For the author only the harassment is verified because there is a total disqualification of the victim who, due to lack of reaction forces, accepts in silence or is endorsed by the group. The victim, induced to error, finishes by chancelar what is said of her, loses concentration easily, which ends up promoting the flaws, theoretically predicted by the stalker.

CONSEQUENCES OF MORAL HARASSMENT FOR INDIVIDUALS AND SOCIETY

The following are some consequences of bullying in relation to the individual and society.

There is no doubt about the existence of harm to the individual as a victim of bullying. As Barreto explains (2005, p. 49), "what happens in harassment is the repetition of the act that intentionally violates the rights of the other, reaching its biological integrity and causing disorders to the psychic and physical health."

The pressure felt by the victim may even lead to his death, as the same author (2005, p. 36) has described in describing this situation, when punishments and controls culminate in exclusion from the workforce either through the temporary dispensation policy, stimulated dismissal or just cause, many are psychologically disorganized, lose their lives and commit suicide.

It is worth emphasizing the existence of several other diseases resulting from the somatization of the suffering coming from these situations of harassment. These are known psychosomatic diseases.

Dejours (1992, p 127) states that "somatization is a process by which conflict that can not find any way out mental disorder will unleash in the body endocrine-metabolic disorders, the starting point of an organic disease. "

Also in her studies Hirigoyen (2001, pp. 140-142) can observe that 52% of the victims presented several types of psychosomatic reactions. According to the author "after a certain time of evolution. psychosomatic disorders are almost always in the foreground. The body accuses aggression rather than the brain, which refuses to see what it can not understand. "

Hirigoyen (2001) can observe individuals presenting on weight of up to 20 kg, coming from harassment suffered. According to the author, people "suddenly gain weight (15 to 20 kg in a few months), digestive problems (gastralgias, colitis, stomach ulcers), endocrine problems (thyroid problems, problems with menstruation), increased hypertension, malaise, dizziness, skin ailments, etc. "After all the illnesses, whether physical or psychic, presented above, it is clear how devastating bullying is for the victim. Notwithstanding this, there are equally immeasurable damages to the victim's professional career.

The sense of incompetence that accompanies it is extremely painful. His absence from service and his removal for medical reasons takes him out of the professional routine. The victim is nervous, unable to communicate, either with the aggressor or with the other members of the team, and this picture resulting from the acts performed by the aggressor, ends up making it impossible to carry out their tasks and compromises their professional performance.

Certain that there is a decrease in quality and quantity of service performed, the victim ends up harming even more, not only himself but the whole group, further worsening his already worn image.

As noted by Heloani (2003, p. 59), "over time, harassment itself can generate pathologies in victims as it makes them believe that they are exactly what their perpetrators think or wish to be: inattentive, insecure, incompetent and fragile. " Continuing the author, "in some cases, the victim may go into a depressive process, impairing their performance at work and performing the prophecy induced by their tormentor."

This picture will inevitably lead to his withdrawal from the organization and, as Barreto (2000 p. 142) points out, "being unemployed or unemployed, even temporarily, is devastating to identity."

But, as Bradaschia (2007) explains, "it is also necessary to remember that the intention behind the harassment situation is for the victim to leave, to leave the company in this sense, constant attacks will undermine his professional confidence, affecting his chances of if put on the market ".

Thus, it is clear that all of these consequences for the victim may and probably will also compromise their future professional activities.

It is also worth mentioning the impacts also suffered by the victim's next of kin.

As Bradaschia (2007, p. 98) explains [...] the family suffers along with the worker [...] Family cohesion is impaired because the victim loses his interest in family projects and disengages himself from responsibilities and everyday family commitments'.

Hirigoyen (2002, p. 228), when discussing the reaction of victims of bullying, the author explains that "we do not have equal reactions to situations of moral harassment. Certain people, by their stories or personalities, are less able to protect themselves, suffer more, and have more difficulty defending themselves. "

As for the seriousness of the consequences left by bullying, Nasajon (2010, p. 4) explains that "the impact will be stronger if it starts from an allied group against a single person than if it comes from a single individual."

It is important to highlight that anyone can be a victim. However, the executioners and the people who witness these actions prefer to believe that only the most fragile or sick people are victims.

Although it often goes unnoticed, bullying also has consequences and damages for the whole society.

The removal of an individual from the labor market, whether temporary or permanent, acquired disease or dispensation, will clearly bring social reflexes.

As Freitas (2018, p. 6) states, "every time a capable professional is rendered incapable, every individual in that society pays the bill." Therefore, it is not only the individual or his family or the institution that will be suffering from consequences of the damage caused, but the whole society will be in solidarity in this process of bearing the consequences of the damage caused. For some the action or the consequence will be direct, for the great majority of society will be indirect.

As discussed earlier, bullying has serious consequences for both the harassed and those around him. Thus, it is of paramount importance that the victim be aware that there are punishments for such action. This awareness will tend to encourage victims to seek protection in the Judiciary.

Besides these considerations on the consequences for the individual and society, it is also necessary to point out that moral harassment impacts on the company (organization) and on the State.

With respect to the company (organization), bullying harms when the employee stops attending the work environment because of harassment issues. In legal language, we would say that absenteeism (absence) damages the normal course of the company. According to the level of specialization of the work performed and the quality of the employee, the greater the damage to the company.

Another damage that the company can see with harassment is the fall in productivity. This fall immediately occurs in the production of the harassed, just as it can be general when the environment becomes disturbed by psychological issues and that are external to the production process, this because the harassment impacts mainly on the moral aspect of the person or people involved.

A third harm to the company may be the need to change workplace to the harassed. This is because depending on the circumstance, the harassed employee cannot keep up with his job. Before the situation can be transferred or disconnected. In this context, according to specialization, the turnover generates costs much more costs than those anticipated by the employer.

In relation to the State, bullying in the workplace impacts on the worker's health care costs. The damages caused to the health of the worker that are the results of the moral harassment, by the Brazilian legislation, are considered as work sickness, and protected by the legislation, in specific can be cited article 20 of Law no. 8.219/1991. The legislation guarantees the worker, in this situation, the payment of social security benefit that is licensed from work for a period of more than fifteen days. This is an example of how bullying also impacts and damages the state

CONCLUSION

The dignified life is what is expected during the existence, as intrinsic quality of the dignity that cannot be withdrawn from the man. As stated above, it is clear that the dignity of the human person is prior to his or her own birth, configuring himself as essential to the human being.

However, it stands out that the human being is a social being and because of his sociability he cannot live isolated from his peers. Their experience in the social environment, their actions and their behavior make up their dignity and must be respected, but an important aspect must be observed: when there is a violation of the dignity of another, it is evident that the guardianship will be with the person victimized by the offense.

Respecting fundamental rights, having fulfilled them, means meeting the fundamental principle of the dignity of the human person.

Bullying has emerged as a subject of research in 1996 in Sweden at the hands of Heinz Leymann. This work psychologist conducted a survey with several groups of professionals and detected a phenomenon that he called "psychoterror".

For the definition of bullying at work, it is necessary to take into account both cultural and organizational factors in each country. Many names are used and often mistakenly as synonymous with bullying. It is the person who uses his strength or power to scare or injure the weakest people. What is very common in schools; Bullying is the use of force or power to coerce others out of fear.

In order to characterize bullying at work, it is necessary to observe the frequency of conduct, types of acts that would be accepted as offensive, and the duration of conduct. There are countries where humiliation and offenses in the workplace are not considered violence because they are commonplace in this environment.

Researchers, for the most part, acknowledge that bullying can occur in different directions, classifying this harassment into four types: bullying; downward harassment; bullying; mixed harassment.

Bullying develops within the organization's environment, destroying the tranquility of the victim and, to a certain extent, all who are there.

The working climate tends to deteriorate, since, as everyone is constantly witnessing or participating in these inhumane actions, a climate of tension is created involving both the victim and everyone present. Not only does it devastatingly affect the victim, but it compromises the proper development of the work tasks proposed by the institution.

A healthy work environment comes from a number of factors, ranging from interpersonal relationships to networking, motivation, and joint efforts.

There is no doubt about the existence of harm to the individual when subjected to bullying. The pressure felt by the victim can even lead to his death. There are a number of illnesses acquired by victims of bullying, among them: less energy and vitality; muscular tensions; sore muscles; unable to rest; palpitations; dizziness; psychosomatic problems and physical illnesses.

It is also worth mentioning the existence of several other diseases resulting from the somatization of suffering from these situations of harassment. These are known psychosomatic diseases.

It is important to highlight that anyone can be a victim. However, the executioners and the people who witness these actions prefer to believe that only the most fragile or sick people are victims.

Although it often goes unnoticed, bullying also has consequences and damages for the whole society.

The removal of an individual from the labor market, whether temporary or permanent, acquired disease or dispensation, will clearly bring social reflexes.

Therefore, it is not only the individual or his family or the institution that is suffering the consequences of the damage caused, but the whole society will be in solidarity in this process of bearing the consequences of the damage caused. For some the action or the consequence will be direct, for the great majority of society will be indirect.

Bullying has serious consequences for both the harassed and those who gravitate around them. Thus, it is of paramount importance that the victim be aware that there are punishments for such action. This awareness will tend to encourage victims to seek protection in the Judiciary.

The legal consequences of harassment include civil reparation for material and moral damages, which is supported by the Federal Constitution, the Civil Code and the Consolidation of Labor Laws, and whose competence for judgment lies with the Labor Court.

The victim of moral harassment is wounded in his dignity, going against one of the foundations of the Democratic State of Law on which many nations are based, as for example the Federative Republic of Brazil, provided for in Article 1, item III, of its Federal Constitution.

We know of the changes that have taken place within the factories and organizations in the last decades of the twentieth century: with the robotization of factories; restructuring of the means of production, and other needs to achieve goals, with a view to survival in an increasingly competitive market.

But individuals have changed too! If everything was accepted before, due to the directive power of employers, today is no longer so. This power, fortunately, has been reduced. The practices of humiliation, persecution and ill-treatment are less and less tolerated by both the victims and the people around them.

In order to prevent bullying in organizations, it is necessary, first, for management to recognize when it occurs, and once it has been detected that the persons responsible for its practice are properly investigated and punished. Also, that instruments be developed to curb them, in order to always maintain the best working conditions.

REFERENCES

Barreto, M. M. S. (2000). *Uma Jornada de Humilhações*. Disponível em http://www.assediomoral.org/spip.php?rubrique22

Barreto, M. M. S. (2005). *Assédio moral: a violência sutil. Análise epidemiológica e psicossocial no trabalho no Brasil*. Tese (doutorado em psicologia social) Pontifícia universidade católica, São Paulo. Disponível em: https://tede2.pucsp.br/handle/handle/17370

Bittar, C. E. B. (2005). *O Direito na Pós-Modernidade*. Rio de Janeiro: Universitária.

Bradaschia, C. A. (2007). *Assédio moral no trabalho: a sistematização dos estudos sobre um campo em construção*. São Paulo: Fundação Getúlio Vargas. Dissertação de Mestrado em Administração de Empresas. Disponível em: https://bibliotecadigital.fgv.br/dspace/bitstream/handle/10438/2231/50849.pdf

Dejours, C. (1992). *A loucura do trabalho: estudo de psicopatologia do trabalho* (5th ed.). São Paulo: Cortez Oboré.

Dejours, C. (2001). *A banalização da injustiça social* (4th ed.). Rio de Janeiro: FGV.

Delgado, G. N. (2006). *Direito Fundamental ao trabalho digno.* São Paulo: LTr.

Einarsen, S. (2000). Harassment and bullying at work: A review of the Scandinavian approach. *Aggression and Violent Behavior*, *5*(4), 379–401. doi:10.1016/S1359-1789(98)00043-3

Freitas, M. E. (2001). Assédio moral e assédio sexual: Faces do poder perverso nas organizações. *Revista de Administração de Empresas*, *41*(2), 8–19.

Freitas, M. E. (2007). Quem paga a conta do assédio moral no trabalho? *RAE-eletrônica, 6*(1). Disponível em: http://www.scielo.br/pdf/raeel/v6n1/a11v6n1.pdf

Heloani, R. (2003). Violência invisível. *GV executivo, 2*(3). Disponível em: https://rae.fgv.br/gv-executivo/vol2-num3-2003/violencia-invisivel

Hirigoyen, M. F. (2001). Le malaise dans le travail, harcèlement moral: démêler le vrai du faux. Paris: Syros.

Hirigoyen, M. F. (2002). *Mal estar no trabalho: redefinindo o assédio moral*. Rio de Janeiro: Bertrand Brasil.

Hirigoyen, M. F. (2006). *A violência perversa do cotidiano*. Rio de Janeiro: Bertrand Brasil.

Hirigoyen, M. F. (2009). *Assédio moral: a violência perversa do cotidiano* (11th ed.). Rio de Janeiro: Bertrand Brasil.

Nasajon, L. (2010). Assédio Moral no Trabalho. *Revista Ética e realidade atual*. Disponível em: http://era.org.br/wp-content/uploads/ARtigo_Leila_Assedio_Vers%C3%A3o-Final.pdf

Nunes, L. A. R. (2010). *O princípio constitucional da dignidade humana* (3rd ed.). São Paulo: Saraiva.

Paz, R. J. (2009). *O princípio da dignidade da pessoa humana: o caráter complexo da sua concretização em face da tensão entre democracia e constitucionalismo*. Dissertação de Mestrado, Unibrasil. Curitiba. Disponível em: https://www.unibrasil.com.br/wp-content/uploads/2018/02/mestrado_unibrasil_Rodnei.pdf

Piovesan, F. (2006). Direitos Humanos, o Princípio da Dignidade Humana e a Constituição Brasileira. Revista dos Tribunais.

Prata, M. R. (2006). *Anatomia do Assédio Moral no Trabalho uma Abordagem Transdisciplinar*. São Paulo: LTR.

Rocha, C. L. A. (2004). *O direito à vida digna*. Belo Horizonte: Fórum.

Sarlet, I. W. (2005). *Dimensões da Dignidade*. Porto Alegre: Livraria do Advogado.

Sarlet, I. W. (2011). *Dignidade da pessoa humana e diretos fundamentais*. Porto Alegre: Livraria do Advogado Editora.

Silva, J. A. (2009). *Curso de Direito Constitucional Positivo* (32nd ed.). São Paulo: Malheiros Editores.

Chapter 14
The Municipal Map in Portugal:
Such a Different Reality From France and Spain

Barbara Luize Iacovino Barreiros
Universidade do Minho, Portugal

ABSTRACT

The municipality is the basic territorial organization for almost all the Member States of the European Union and has approximately the same attributions in all these. Even so, the territorial structure of municipalities differs in each of the Member States, and it is possible to group them into two large groups: those that have implemented reforms with a consequent reduction in the number of these entities and those with a high number of municipalities. Although Spain is a neighbor of Portugal and Portugal gets some influences from France, in fact the territorial organization of municipalities corresponds to very different realities. Through this research you can see that Portugal did reform its municipalities while France and Spain failed to do so. However, they all recognize that there is a need to reform the territorial structure of municipalities.

INTRODUCTION

The territorial structure of municipalities differs in each of the Member States and can be grouped into two main groups: on the one hand Member States of European Union which have implemented reforms with a consequent reduction in the number of such entities, such as Portugal, Germany, Belgium and the Netherlands; and from other Member States with many municipalities, such as France and Spain.

DOI: 10.4018/978-1-5225-8350-9.ch014

Portugal pioneered this reform. Like this, in the nineteenth century, PASSOS MANUEL implemented a reform that reduced in Portugal more than 800 municipalities to about 351. The author considers that this reform served as a foundation for the current territorial organization of municipalities in Portugal because currently there are 308 municipalities in Portugal distributed between the mainland and the archipelagos of Madeira and the Azores. Most of them obtained the configuration and territorial structure approximated to the current one from this reform (Oliveira, 2013).

Thus, a hundred years after Portuguese reform, West Germany has reduced from about 24,500 to just over 8,000 counties, although, after reunification with East Germany, the number of counties has increased to over 16,000. Belgium, which for historical reasons, including its annexation to France by Napoleon Bonaparte which lasted until the Battle of Waterloo, had 2,586 municipalities, after the reform begun in the 1980s, merged the municipalities, reducing them to 589. The same happened in the Netherlands, which reduced the number of municipalities from 1,200 to 500. Also, Denmark, Norway and Sweden have significantly reduced the number of municipalities, currently counting some 300 municipalities. Also, Greece about 15 years ago has reduced from 6,000 municipalities to just over 1,000 (Jesus, 2018).

Differently, this was not the case in France and Spain. Attempts to reduce the number of municipalities have failed in these countries, but they have tried alternative solutions of cooperation and association.

However, the European Union has recently tried to reduce public spending and debt in the Member States, imposing either directly (in the case of Portugal and Greece in 2011) or indirectly the rationalization of the administrative apparatus. Besides that the theme of the reform and reduction of municipalities has been debated over time, for more than a century, in France and Spain, without success.

In this chapter it is essential to verify the reason why there are 308 municipalities in Portugal for a population of 10.561.614 habitants, while in Spain there are 8.000 municipalities for a population of 40.847.371 habitants, and in France there are 36.000 municipalities for 61.465.709 habitants.

The author intends to know the historical evolution of the municipal plan in Portugal with special emphasis on the reforms implemented by Passos Manuel and intends also to demonstrate why France and Spain have so many municipalities even if they recognize that it is necessary to change this reality.

The objective of this study is to demonstrate that without population and territory, municipalities are not able to perform the role assigned to them, so it is necessary to reform. To discuss such a complex issue, it is necessary to reflect before taking any restructuring measures. Portugal maybe an example to follow.

This subject is so complex that it is not possible to discuss all its aspects in this chapter. Thus, the author limited the study to the brief knowledge of the origins and reasons why France and Spain have so many municipalities while Portugal has a proportionately lower number. Also showed that France and Spain have resorted to cooperative figures to solve some of the problems suffered by small municipalities. The study of all other aspects and details will be study in another chapter.

It is important to clarify that the main study is about the territorial reform done in XIX century in Portugal. The author chose the examples of France and Spain not because only those countries have many municipalities (there are other countries who had also many municipalities). But, on the one hand, Spain is neighbor of Portugal however it has such a different reality. Proportionally Spain has more municipalities than Portugal and most of these are very small. On the other hand, France had a major influence on the Portuguese administrative organization. Thus, in 1832, Mouzinho da Silveira divided Portuguese territorial in provinces, counties and municipalities.

Before starts the main chapter is also important to explain that the organization of the State in France, Spain and Portugal are not the same. Although the Portuguese Constitution provides for three levels of local authorities, namely, regions, municipalities and parishes.[1] In fact, only the municipalities and the parishes were implemented. In France the territory is organized on three levels: Regions, Departments and Communes.[2] Also the State in Spain is organized territorially in municipalities, in provinces and in the Autonomous Communities that are constituted.[3]

It is important to note that France and Spain are organized on 3 levels. However, neither France nor Spain have a level below the municipality. That is, among these three countries, only Portugal has a level below the municipality: the parishes. It is important to make clear to the reader that parishes in Portugal do not correspond to the "Communes" in France neither to the municipalities in Spain. It is essential to elucidate to the reader that the parishes in Portugal do not correspond to the "Communes" in France or "Ayuntamientos" in Spain. In fact, it can be seen in Local Government Law of each one[4] that the duties of the parish in Portugal do not correspond to the duties of the "Communes" and "Ayuntamientos". So, the author insists: the parishes (lowest level in Portugal) does not match with the lowest level in Spain and France. Parishes in Portugal are not the same that communes in France or Ayuntamientos in Spain.

BACKGROUND

The reform towards reduction shows that many municipalities are not satisfactory from a functional point of view. It also suggests the need for a reform in the territorial structure of municipalities for the consolidation of local autonomy, since there can be no autonomy without population and territory. At the same time municipalities should not be too large. This subject is not easy to be approached and it is still unknown what criteria should be applied and the most correct strategy to be adopted in view of the ideal solution. As the author will demonstrate not only in Portugal but also in France and Spain discussed this issue of the ideal population size and territory size of a municipality. However, Portugal implemented a reform of the municipalities in 1836, allowing the reduction of more than 800 to about 351.

Luís Jordana De Pozas warned in the last century that "among contemporary local reforms, one of the most interesting ones is that carried out by Portugal" (1948).

Henry Roussillon defended that the study of this subject can be done under two concepts: a functional conception and organic conception. The functional conception starts from an assertion according the municipality is a result of the history and a natural social body. That's why its fundamental structure, more precisely its territorial dimension, can't be reformed. The authors who defend this thesis accepted that some municipalities are not able to assume certain functions, however, they understand that through the grouping of municipalities it is possible to manage in common the attributions that have been transmitted to them. For them, we are facing a functional crisis because today, municipalities have new technical and financial challenges but the problem to solved isn't structural. Like this, the municipalities must cooperate forming a group to able that what can't be done all alone. In its turn, the organic conception deals with the essence of the municipality. For the authors who defend this theory, the municipality isn't untouchable or eternal. The municipality characteristics changes with the evolution of the times and the history. In fact, there is no definition for the concept of municipality. When we compose the history, we verify that the characteristics of the municipalities change according to the times. Thus, for example, before the French revolution in 1789, France was the most populated country of the Europe and was divided into parishes. France had more than 60.000 parishes. In that time, the concept municipality was used only for the cities (De Pozas, 1948).

Royer Collard[5] defended the functional conception. for this author, the municipalities are a given, founded by history and as such intangible. the municipality preexist the law which can only see it and not create or modify it. Indeed, the municipality can be questioned only on very limited points. they are: the suppression of municipalities without inhabitants or too sparsely populated.

M. Carous, in a parliamentary discussion in France[6], about a Project of Law of the "Communautés Urbaines" said that: "*les communes sont des êtres vivantes faits de la chair et du sang de ceux qui les composents...*". Translating it means: the municipalities are a living being built of the blood of those who live there.

Mirabeau[7] defended that it must create a municipality "dans chaque ville, bourg ou communauté de campagne". Thus, France created more than 40.000 municipalities ("communes") like the lower-level administrative division. For years France will try to reduce the number of "communes" but without success and so it has come to rely on cooperation figures.

Otherwise, Pont Nemours, Condorcet, Syéyes and Thouret defended the organic conception.

Condorcet said that the population of a municipality must have 4.000 or 5.000 habitants minimum and 10.000 or 12.000 maximum. He also defended that the dimension of the territory must allow that in one day, a citizen that live fair from the center of the municipality can go and return from there, adding that three miles should be the maximum distance between each of these places (Condorcet, 1788).

Siéyes concept the territorial division in France basically municipal and Thouret has defended in 29th September 1789, in the National Assembly of France that each department will be divided in other divisions with 6 by 6 miles and this division determined the number of municipalities to be created (Sieyes, 1789). This thesis was presented to the Assembly against the thesis defended by MIRABEAU. Unfortunately, this thesis doesn't had success (Assemblee Nationale Constituante, 1791). At follow, France has had several unsuccessful attempts to reform the municipality. Recently France updates its territorial organization, reducing the number of regions, but it is not possible yet to achieve the reform of the municipality.

In Spain, Durán Garcia speaks about natural Law, saying that: "dogmática tradicionalista va sentando las bases de la institución sobre una concepción iusnaturalista (…) importada desde Francia, históricamente ha justificado la configuración natural del Municipio español (…)" (Garcia, 2016).

Martínez Marina[8] said: In Spain there are people who do not have any organization while others are organized by municipalities; some cities have the right to send a prosecutor to the courts and others do not; in general terms, each community has a different legal regime, a result of the individual Statutes inherited from royalty and medieval times.

Among the supporters of a municipal reform are names such as: FERNANDO ALBI (1966), PAREJO ALFONSO (2012), Jordana De Pozas, Soza Wagner, or Parada Vásquez (Bravo, 2014).

ALBI says that: There is, as we have said, total agreement among politicians, sociologists and economists, in which the majority of municipalities are anemic, they can't fulfill their most elemental purposes; they are not viable, in a word. What do they do? The answer is obvious; There is no other option: suppress them; since they are not an end in themselves, but simply, a means to carry out a set of activities for the benefit of the communities that reside in them, purposes that are of the first necessity, that are essential, and therefore, no reason can justify the deprivation of certain collectivities, making them worse off than others located within the same national territory. The suppression is imposed. These impotent collectivities must be eliminated by any of the two possible procedures: the fusion of several of them into a new broader one, or its annexation, pure and simple, to another better equipped.

Jordana De Pozas (1948) says: After many studies and controversies the idea seems to prevail that it is necessary to base the administrative organization on a strong and capable Municipality, but also that it would not be convenient to achieve it by eliminating the current and insufficient small Municipalities. Discarded by the negative experience of almost half a century the solution of "mancomunidades" or voluntary groupings, I understand that the best way to harmonize the embryonic subsistence of the current small Municipalities with the need to build the administrative building on strong and effective Municipalities would lead to these two Operations: reduce the small municipalities in question to a category that could receive the name of Council, and reserve the name of Municipality for the compound entity formed by the grouping of a plurality of Councils with each other or with a population of greater importance. It is not about the current minor local entities, an unfortunate name that should be abolished, but about authentic primary entities, like the Portuguese parishes ("freguesias") or the rural parish of England, with an elementary organization and a competence reduced to their real capacity and personal means. The desirable result of the operation would be that the 9,199 municipalities existing in 1960 would be reduced to less than half with a normal minimum number of about four thousand inhabitants (Puig, 1967).

Among those who, contrary, defended other alternatives to resolve the crisis of little municipality: Morell Ocaña (1984) and Rebollo Puig (1967) has observed that beyond the organic reduction and simplification of the legal system, it can also do diversity in terms of municipal competences and accept that small municipalities have less than medium and large municipalities.

Almeida Cerreda (2012) defends the cooperation between the municipalities is the better choice to resolve this issue.

However, both groups shared the diagnosis on the problem of small municipalities.

Otherwise, in Portugal, Sebastião Sarafana like Leon Poinsard defended that the municipality is a "circumscription administrative artificial composed of parishes (…) some ones are rural, others urban, arbitrarily grouped", "Most of those parishes do not have the smallest interest among them" and "some of them have its market, its hospital, or its train rail in another municipality".

António Candido De Oliveira (2010) defends that Municipalities without population and territory are not able to perform tasks that are required.

MAIN FOCUS OF THE CHAPTER

Issues, Controversies, Problems

The most relevant aspects of this crisis have to do with the role of municipalities, especially with their degree of autonomy. Municipalities without population and territory are not able to perform tasks that are required. Although, as the author pointed out above, almost all the European Countries have realized the need to reform and reduce the number of municipalities, in fact some of them failed to reduce. According to the conceptions explained above, the author will demonstrate that Portugal adopted an organic conception while France and Spain have adopted a functional conception. But all of them have debated politically on several occasions and recognize that without population and territory it is not possible to carry out the tasks conferred upon it. It is important to know the historical reason that gave rise to the number of municipalities currently existing in France, Spain and Portugal. It is also important indicate the levels of local authorities existing in each of these countries and the average size of each municipality in terms of population and territory.

The Functional Conception: France and Spain Have Failed to Reduce the Number of Municipalities and Opted for the Cooperation Between the Municipalities

The Issues in France

The origin of the number of the municipalities in France is the decision adopt in 1789. French's National Assembly decided to adopt the idea defended by Mirabeau. Like the author said above, he advocated that will be a municipality "*dans chaque ville, bourg, village ou communauté de campagne*". For him, the big municipality would mean that headquarters would be set up in the capital or in the more developed place. So, the poorer part of the territory, that means the rural parts, would be subjugated and victims of the richest. Maybe he was right in this respect. Portugal example demonstrated that the headquarters it is usually located in the more developed locality. This scenario might have been different if they adopted Thouret's opposing view.

More than 200 years passed, and France continues to have about 36.000 municipalities. But the tasks that municipalities may execute today is more complex than in the pass.

France has tried to reduce the number of municipalities several times. This pretension began shortly after the French revolution, which the doctrine bet in defining the municipality according to a territorial and populational standard that allowed big municipalities. It is necessary to conclude that small municipalities are not able to carry out their tasks.

Furthermore, the role of the municipality today is not the same than in French revolution's time. More than 200 years have passed and today municipalities are obliged to answer to new challenges. To solve these problems France chose to resort to association of municipalities ("Communauté de Communes", Syndicats Mistes", "District") but these figures give rise to other issues to solve.

In fact, France adopted a functional conception, so if the municipalities are a result of the history and a natural social body, its fundamental structure can't be reformed. It happens that France knows a small municipality can't perform its tasks properly because it has no budget and therefore personnel necessary for the purpose, thereby, decided to group the municipalities, each of them maintaining the status of local authority and not to create new local communities.

The legislator systematized these groups of municipalities ("Syndicat à vocation multiple", "district urbain", "communauté urbaine") in the category of public institutions ("établissements publics"). This is the first issue. Another one is the election of the council. The group of municipalities is not a local authority. Its institutions will have their elected council not by direct universal suffrage but indirect suffrage. This means that the members of the council would be designated by the municipal assemblies of each one of the municipalities grouped. It should be noted that the modality of designating these members is variable.[9]

Another issue is the municipality is not obliged to group together. Create a group of municipalities is just a faculty and not an obligation. The municipality can't be obliged to group with another one to perform the functions it can't do alone. It is true that the government encourages grouping by allocating funding but the decision to group must be taken by a qualified majority. So, to create a "Syndicat", "a District" or a "Communauté" it must be voted by two thirds of the municipalities involved or the half of the municipalities that represents two thirds of the population.

Therefor this entails another problem: in fact, the municipality isn't extinct, but a new level of administration emerges ("niveau Intercomunnale") and with this, other issues like appears. For example, in case of dissolution of the group and problems with the freedom of the municipality to group or not group with another municipality.

A change of paradigm occurred in 1971 with the law of July 16, 1971. This Law envisaged and encouraged the merger of municipalities. Moreover, it was entitled the law of fusion and grouping of municipalities and the groupings would be for a secondary plan. Nevertheless, it was also unable to cause the expected merger. But no success to merger municipalities.

Again in 2009, The French's National Assembly tried to reduce the number of the municipalities. Still they just achieved the Territorial's Reform Law n. 2010-1563, 16th decémber 2010, which provided for the possibility of merging municipalities. However, it is obvious that municipalities did not adhere to this faculty.

Currently, France tries some territory reforms. Since June 2014 the government discuss the problem of territorial organization. A first part has already been opened in January 2014 with the so-called law of modernization of territorial public action and affirmation of metropolises. The creation of a new status for the latter will begin a real clarification of the exercise of skills at the local level. On August 7, 2015, was promulgated on the law on the New Territorial Organization of the Republic (NOTRe) entrusts new powers to the regions and clearly redefines the competences attributed to each territorial collectivity. Maybe this is winds of change to an organic conception.

It should be noted that the local authorities in France are: the regions, the departments and the communes. Where the communes correspond to the lower level of local authorities and the regions the upper level.[10]And that the 36,685 French communes have different sizes: 955 communes have less than 50 inhabitants, 925 more than 10,000, and Paris, the most populated, more than two million. Most are small: half of the number of the communes have fewer than 400 inhabitants, one in four has less than 200 inhabitants. In total, 27,396 municipalities have fewer than 1,000 inhabitants (Institut National de la Statistique et des Etudes Economiques, n.d.).

However, in France it has 2,600 intercommunal structures (French public intercommunal cooperation establishments) and it is much larger than the intercommunal structures in other Countries of Europe: 21,000 inhabitants on average and 11,000 inhabitants for the smallest of them (the communities of communes), which is higher than the average size of municipalities in most European countries.

The Issues in Spain

Spain imported the French conception. The first Territorial Law in Spain was signed by José Bonaparte, in Sevilla, 17th April 1810. Just with the Cadiz Constitution the three elements of the municipality were established for the first time in Spain: population, territory and organization of the municipality. So today, Spain has many municipalities, especially in Galicia, and is aware that this is a problem to be solved. Like this, it has about 8.000 municipalities. It would serve 5,803 inhabitants. But, there are great differences between some provinces and others. The Provinces with municipalities with a small number of inhabitants are those of Soria (517 inhabitants per municipality), Teruel (609), Ávila (693) and Zamora (773). There is therefore a direct relationship between the population density of these provinces and the smaller municipalities. The largest municipalities are, apart from those of Ceuta and Melilla, which only have one; those of the provinces of Madrid (36,305 inhabitants), Murcia (32,766), Las Palmas (32,337) and Cádiz (28,229). The provinces with the highest number of municipalities are Burgos, with 371 municipalities; Salamanca, which has 362; Barcelona (311), Zaragoza (293), Guadalajara (288) and Navarra (282).

On the other hand, more than half of the Spanish town halls (4,873, according to 2012 data) have less than 1,000 inhabitants.

Anyway, some efforts were made to promote the merger of municipalities. The Law of 3rd February 1835 attributed to the "*diputaciones provincials*" the task of suppress municipalities. The standard was suppressing all municipality with less than 50 habitants. However, the Law previous an exception: even though the municipality had less than 50 inhabitants, could be maintained if other concrete circumstances advised it. More, the settlement of the number of inhabitants has become impractical in areas of high population density (Galiza it's an example). In fact, the only general and successful reform of the Spanish municipal map was made in accordance with the Municipal Law of 1845, which required the presence of a minimum of 30 neighbors (about 150 inhabitants) in the municipality as a necessary condition to conserve the town hall. In 1860, POSADA HERRERA presented a project establishing the abolition of the municipalities that did not gather 500 neighbors (about 2,500 inhabitants), although the continuity of the municipalities was also admitted. So, the standard of population isn't applied to those that were more than 12 km from the nearest town hall. Other projects appear in the same sense, but also no one obtained the success expected. However, although there have already been some examples of merger of municipalities, in fact, this process has been very slow, and it is a faculty not an obligation to the municipalities.

At the end of the fifties and beginning of the sixties, a favorable opinion was created for the revision of the municipal map, mainly with the aim of eliminating the smallest town councils. This state of opinion is part of a debate at European level on the need to optimize the structures of local government and echoes the first trials of reform of the municipal plant that were being produced in various countries of northern Europe. Thus, the natural law theory and the functional conception begins to be put aside and now the right of the State to indicate the elements of the municipality is undeniable to better fulfill its purposes.

The polemics about the reorganization of the local plant is always starting from the same assumptions: a high number of municipalities with small number of inhabitants implies the existence of duplicate administrative structures, which consume considerable resources, for its sustenance; resources that can be dedicated to other ends (Cerreda, 2012). But isn't easy merger municipalities. To solve the problem of small municipalities, without merger remain two alternatives: the diversification of competence and create a group of municipalities.

The diversification of competence would consist of examining and assessing, in terms of effectiveness and efficiency, the current attribution of tasks to the different territorial public entities, and, depending on the evaluation effected, proceed, eventually, to resign competencies. For example, smaller municipalities may lose some of their powers in favor of other local authorities (Provincias or Mancomunidades).

The promotion of administrative collaboration aims to unite the efforts of the municipalities involved to provide the services with the highest quality and efficiency.

Almeida Cerreda (2012) defends that the first option isn't the better option because requires a long period of study before being implemented. So, the second one, the cooperation between the administrative entities is the better choice.

The Spanish Law previous an open cast established by Article 4.5 of the LRJAP-PAC which provides: *"el contenido del deber de colaboración se desarrollará a través de los instrumentos y procedimientos que de manera común y voluntaria establezcan tales Administraciones"*. That means it consecrates a "numerus apertus" about cooperation mechanisms. Nevertheless, the main instruments of cooperation are: "Convenios intermunicipales", "encomienda de gestion intermunicipal", "Comunidades de municipios", "redes de cooperación territorial", "Mancomunidades", "Consorcios intermunicipales", "Sociedades intermunicipales", and "fundaciones intermunicipales".

It should be noted that the local authorities in Spain are: Comunidades Autonomas, Provincias and Municipios. Where the "municipios" correspond to the lower level of local authorities and the "comunidades Autonomas" the upper level.[11]

The Organic Conception: The Merger of Municipalities in Portugal Based on Passos Manuel Reform

Recalling, the organic conception deals with the essence of the municipality. The municipality isn't untouchable or eternal but its characteristics changes with the evolution of the times and the history. Portugal has adopted this conception. Like this, Passos Manuel did a reform of the municipalities and achieved to reduce more than 450 municipalities in Portugal. Before this reform Portugal had more than 800 municipalities. Today Portugal have 278 municipalities in the main Land.

The county division that exists today in Portugal is based on the reform of Passos Manuel, concretized thought the Decree 6th November 1836.which had the concern to combinate the ideal number of population and territory (Oliveira, 2013).

The liberal revolution in Portugal began in 1820, but it was only after the civil war of 1832-34 that the conditions for the consolidation of liberalism in Portugal were created. With this revolution a new cycle began in the administration of the country with the aim of making the management of the territory more effective.

Already in 1827 there was the concern with the rationalization of the Portuguese territory. The project no. 150 on the division of territory presented to the Chamber of Deputies on March 20, 1827 and it could be read: "it is necessary that the administrative divisions, each one of its kind, are not too large, on the other hand, the economy of the Treasury, the good proportion of the salaries, the capacity of the civil servants, and the facility in the performance of their duties compels us to give them a certain extension" (Caetano, 1972).

Thus, in this project, it was considered that the reorganization of the municipalities was all the more extensive and more complicated because it was necessary to gather more accurate information about the localities. Furthermore, like in France, the provision of Article 133 of the Constitutional Charter established that in all cities and towns now existing, and in the future for the creation, there would be Chambers.

But the proof is that the Chambers were elective, and only those who had at least one hundred thousand "réis" of net income could be City Councilmen. Consequently, small counties, with less than 200 "fogos", would not be able to form Electoral Chambers.

Mouzinho Da Silveira, with Decree No. 23 of May 16, 1832, divided the territory into 8 Provinces, 40 Counties and about 800 Counties. Although this Decree constituted the basis for the construction of the Modern State, the author did not detail it in this study, since Mouzinho did not reorganize the municipalities, maintaining, as mentioned above, the 800 municipalities of the old regime. In fact Mouzinho da Silveira adopted in part the ideas coming from France (Manique, 1989).

Subsequently, the Law of April 25, 1835 authorized the Government to proceed to the administrative division of the territory based on Districts, Counties and Parishes. The municipalities have therefore become the intermediate administrative entity located between the districts and the parishes. A Commission was set up to propose as a matter of urgency the administrative organization of the territory, which would be regulated by the following data: there should be on the continent 17 administrative districts that would be divided according to the map presented in 1827, that is, the 800 municipalities of the old regime.

It was only in 1836 that there was the courage to begin a reform of the county division.

Immediately afterwards, by Decree of May 17, the organ executive of the district was convoked extraordinarily. It was hoped that it would have an active role in the formation of the division project. In these terms, projects were sent with the map of the division of the municipalities of each district to each one, for them to adopt or suggest modifications. The criterion for maintaining a county was to have the number of citizens eligible for elective jobs to support the municipal burdens; combining this circumstance as much as possible with the distances and transits from one place to another and in relation to the capital of the county and the court, as well as the communications and habits of the residents. These bodies have not fulfilled their functions. Then the Queen, by the Ordinance of September 29, 1836, constituted a Commission composed by Franzini, Passos José (brother of Passos Manuel) and Joaquim Leal, to propose, without loss of time, a project for the administrative division of the territory.

After over a month, a report was drawn up by the Commission. This is one of the most important documents, since in a very simple and concise way it was indicated the difficulties that the members of the Commission were forced to overcome in order to propose a reform for the municipalities, the procedure adopted to prepare the proposal, and, above all, the reasons for the proposal that served as a basis for the reform of Passos Manuel elaborated through the Decree of November 6, 1836.

The Commission concluded that "Since the council is an integral part of the administrative division, it was soon recognized that the primitive organization still existing in these municipalities could not satisfy the purposes for which these municipal aggregations were instituted. Many of which were born under the old feudal influence". In fact, there were a lot of small counties, some of which had less than 20 "fogos" and even fewer, and that their moral and material resources were nil.

It was necessary to obtain the topography and statistics of the Kingdom, the sympathies, prejudices and interests of the local people, and to take into consideration the illustration of the inhabitants to hold the numerous elective offices.

The preparation of the proposed reorganization of the councils was based on five thousand maps and other descriptive documents of all the parishes of the Kingdom, elaborated and organized by the work of Franzini from 1822.

The Commission has taken into account the following: it took account of the electoral needs, in the sense that the municipalities should have sufficient population with passive electoral capacity capable of acceding to the elective positions provided for by the representative system; also took into account that very small municipalities do not have the capacity to use their revenues in works of public utility because the permanent expenses of the administration consume them in totality. It also considered the extension of the territory, communication difficulties and relative population. Thus, the Portuguese population to date was about 3,100,000 inhabitants unevenly distributed over the territory that had an extension of 3,150 leagues square. In summary, the criteria to be considered for the preparation of the proposal were essentially two: population and territory.

Passos Manuel decreed, through the Decree of November 6, 1836, that the continental territory of the Kingdom would be divided into 17 districts, composed of 351 municipalities. This reform, which is said to be provisional and dynamic, marked the beginning of the reorganization of the municipalities in Portugal (Figueiredo, 1950).

With this reform, more than 450 municipalities have been extinguished, but new municipalities have also been created.

The guideline introduced by this decree remained and throughout the nineteenth century the number of counties was still decreasing, approaching the current number, which is 278 counties in the continent. Changes were thus made in 1842, in 1853 and 1855, in 1878.

In 1867 by the reform of Martens Ferrão were extinguished still more municipalities and also parishes, passing the municipal map counting on a number much inferior to the half of the number of counties and parishes. However, this reform was the target of a popular revolt, the "Janeirinha", having had a very short life, not being at the origin of our municipal plant.

In 1898 around 50 municipalities were restored that included the districts of Aveiro, Beja, Braga, Bragança, Castelo Branco, Coimbra, Évora, Faro, Guarda, Leiria, Lisbon, Portalegre, Santarém, Viana do Castelo, Vila Real, Viseu, Funchal and Horta.

Nowadays there is the possibility of municipalities merging with others, but it is not verified in practice.[12]

It should be noted that the local authorities in Portugal are: "Região", "município" and "freguesia". But, Portugal has not yet the Regions. So, the "freguesias" correspond to the lower level of local authorities and the "municípios" the upper level of local authorities. To address the lack of regions, the Intermunicipal Communities were established. In any case, we will not discuss this aspect in this chapter.

In main Land no municipality has fewer than 1500 inhabitants. Just Corvo in The Azores Island has fewer than that. More than half of the municipalities in Portugal have more than 12000 inhabitants. Six municipalities have more than 200,000 inhabitants (World Population Review, 2018).

SOLUTIONS AND RECOMMENDATIONS

Merger or cooperation between the municipalities? The author recommends to States that have not yet done so, to prepare a study to reduce the number of municipalities. Municipalities without Population and Territory are not effective. The author defends a organic conception so it is desirable to merger because the municipality may change with history and with the real needs of citizens. It is useless to have a level of local administration that does not allow the development of localities and cannot promote the well-being of the citizens.

FUTURE RESEARCH DIRECTIONS

As the authors has demonstrated in this chapter, the problem of the territorial reform of the municipalities is also discussed in France and Spain. Although they have not yet been able to solve it. Because that, those Countries implemented alternative solutions of cooperation and association. In next chapters, the author pretends study in detail the advantages and issues of the merger or the cooperation between the municipalities in France and Spain. The objective is to demonstrate that cooperation does not definitively solve this problem of municipalities.

Also important is study the concept of municipality. This matter is essential before proceeding with any reform of municipalities. In fact, positive law does not give a definition of municipality and the classic definitions advanced by the doctrine are insufficient. Moreover, it is increasingly difficult to talk about strictly municipal matters.

CONCLUSION

It is not desirable municipalities with small numbers of inhabitants and little extension because without population and territory, municipalities cannot perform their tasks properly. That's why the Northern European Countries have undertaken reforms to reduce the number of municipalities some 60 years ago. Portugal was a pioneer in this reform, having reduced the number of munitions from 800 to around 351 in 1836. This means that small municipalities are not able to perform their tasks properly.

France and Spain have also understood that small municipalities are not able to carry out their tasks. And reduce the number of municipalities is also defended in France and Spain but failed to avenge. To overcome this problem, they have come to the aid of grouping them but maintaining the autonomy of each one of them. However, this solution is not satisfactory.

The key problem has to do with the role of municipalities. Another issue is to discover the ideal criterion about population and territory of a municipality and that can be so different in each State and even Region.

It should not be forgotten that each State has its administrative organization. Thus, Portugal, in fact, there are two levels of local authority: "freguesias" and "municípios" (parishes and municipalities) because regions established by the Portuguese constitution were never created; while France and Spain have three levels. France has "region", "děpartement" et "communes". Spain has "Comunidades Autonomas", "Provincias" and "municipios". It is essential, it is emphasized, that a definition of municipality and its role can be identified. It cannot be forgetting that in France the municipality has been the elementary unit since 1789. Below the municipality there is no local authority. Contrary to what happens in Portugal.

The author understands that it is very important to remember the words of Condorcet that that population of a municipality must have 4,000 or 5,000 habitants minimum and 10,000 or 12,000 maximum; and that the dimension of the territory must allow that in one day, a citizen that live fair from the center of the municipality can go and return from there, adding that three miles should be the maximum distance between each of these places. This criterion should be revised considering the current reality and the competences given to the municipal bodies and considering that nowadays there is more facility in communication and link between localities.

In any case, the reform of the municipalities in Portugal operated by Passos Manuel is an excellent example to follow. The author believes that the reform of the municipalities has been easier to implement since the most natural link between the citizens in Portugal is between them and the parishes. In any case, careful study is needed before a municipality reform to avoid what happened with Martens Ferrão that lasted about 15 days and ended with a popular revolt.

As the author shown in the text, France and Spain are based on a functional conception, so the municipality is a result of the history and a natural social body and that's why its fundamental structure, more precisely its territorial dimension, wasn't reformed yet.

The author doesn't agree with this thesis because defends that the local authorities, are simple tools of good administration and not a natural right. In addition, it is not possible to discuss the competences to be attributed to the bodies of local authorities, without first defining the role of the municipality.

The most important conclusion with this study is that the municipality exists to perform effectively the tasks assigned to them by the State and must carry them out for the good of the population. If they do not have the capacity to carry them out, then they must be extinct. Cooperation between municipalities may not be the best choice and may become poorly transparent.

REFERENCES

Albi, F. A. (1966). Las derivaciones inmediatas de la crisis del municipalismo. Revista de Estudios de Vida Local, 25.

Alfonso, P. (2012). *Apuntes para el debate sobre la planta y la articulación interna de la Administración local.* Retrieved from http://repositorio.gobiernolocal.es/xmlui/bitstream/handle/10873/1285/Apuntes_Parejo_10_22.pdf?sequence=1&isAllowed=y

Caetano, M. A. (1972). OS Antecedentes da Reforma Administrativa de 1832 (Mouzinho da Silveira). Revista da Faculdade de Direito da Universidade de Lisboa, 22, 7.

Catroga, F. (2014). *A Geografia dos Afectos Pátrios – As reformas politico-administrativas do Século XIX e XX.* Coimbra: Almedina.

Cerreda, A. A. (2012). La cooperación entre Municipios: una posible alternativa a la reordenación de la planta local en España. *Istituzioni del federalismo: rivista di studi giuridici e politici, 3*.

Cerreda, M. A. (2012). *La Cooperación entre Municípios en El Desarrollo de Funciones Administrativas y en la Gestion de Servicios Públicos*. Una Possible Alternativa a la Reordenación de la Planta en España.

Condorcet, M. A. (1788). *Essaie sur la Constitution et les Fonctions des Assemblées Provinciales* (Vol. 1). Paris: Bibliothèque Nationale de France.

Figueiredo, F. J. A. (1950). A reforma concelhia de 6 de Novembro de 1836. *O Direito, 82*.

Garcia, A. (2016). *La Fusión de Municípios como Estratégia*. Madrid: Editorial Dikinson Lda.

Institut National de la Statistique et des Etudes Economiques. (n.d.). *La Population Legale des Communes*. Retrieved from https://www.insee.fr/fr/statistiques/1280737

Jesus, B. (n.d.). *El eterno debate sobre la reforma del mapa municipal. El caso de Cataluña*. Retrieved from in https://dialnet.unirioja.es/ejemplar/162509

Manique, P. A. (1989). *Mouzinho da Silveira – Liberalismo e Administração Pública*. Lisboa: Ocaña.

Mirabeau. (1791). *Proccès Verbal des Séances de L'Assemblée Nationale de France ténues de l'année 1789 et suivantes*. Paris: Impression Nationale,

Morel, A. (1984). *La Administration Local*. Madrid: Tecnos.

Oliveira, A. C. A. (2010). Possibilidades de Reforma de las Actuales Estruturas Municipales y de su Régimen Jurídico. In *Problemas Actuais da Administração Municipal. Actas do 8º Colóquio Luso-Espanhol de Direito Administrativo*. Braga. NEDAL.

Oliveira, A. C. M. (2010). As condições necessárias para uma autonomia efectiva do município: a importância da população e do território. In *Actas do 8.º Colóquio Luso-Espanhol de Direito Administrativo - Problemas Actuais da Administração Municipal*. Braga: Universidade do Minho.

Oliveira, A. C. d. A. (2013). *Direito das Autarquias Locais*. Coimbra: Coimbra Editores.

Pozas, L. J. A. (1948). Las Tendencias Actuales del Régimen Local en Europa. *Revista de Estudios Políticos, 39-42.*

Puig, M. R. A. (1967). La Administración local en las Leyes Fundamentales españolas. Revista de Studios Politicos, 152.

Roussillon, H. A. (1972). *Les Structures Territoriales des Communes – Réformes et Perspectives d'avenir.* Paris: Librairie Générale de Droit et Jurisprudence.

Siéyes, A. (1789). *Quelques idées de Constitution Applicables à la Ville de Paris en Juillet 1789 par l'abbé Sieyès.* Paris: Bibliothèque Nationale de France.

World Population Review. (2018). *Portugal Population 2018.* Retrieved from http://worldpopulationreview.com/countries/portugal-population/

ENDNOTES

1 Article 236°, no. 1 Portuguese Constitution.

2 Article 72°, no. 1 French Constitution.

3 Article 137° Spanish Constitution.

4 Tasks of municipalities in Portugal – To read L. 75/2013, 12 September; in France: second part of Local Authorities Code; in Spain: L. 7/1985, 2 April.

5 Pierre Paul Royer-Collard was President of the French Chamber of Deputies, Lawyer, teacher, philosopher (21 June 1763 – 2 September 1845).

6 J.O, Sénat, déb. Parl., 8-11-1966, p. 1445.

7 A political and French parliamentary.

8 A noted Spanish jurist and historian.

9 Code des Collectivités Territoriales of France.

10 Article 72 of French Constitution.

11 Article 137 of the Spanish Constitution.

12 Article 1, no. 2, Law no. 22/2012 of 30 Mai 2012 (Approves the legal regime of the autarchic territorial administrative reorganization in Portugal).

Conclusion

At a time when the documents which form the basis for and the construction of the protection of human rights celebrate its anniversary (70 years of the Universal Declaration of Human Rights and 40 years of the European Convention on Human Rights, celebrated in 2018) It is pertinent to reflect on a central aspect of the texts: the citizenship exercise. This book starts from the premise that only effective communication and dissemination of the Fundamental Laws will contribute to the construction of enlightened citizens and, consequently, to the exercise of full and democratic sovereignty, especially in a networked society.

Throughout the book several chapters dealt with the subjects contained in the official documents, with two objectives: the first one was to understand where the people's sovereignty is foreseen and what dimension this prediction has in the Fundamental Laws; the second was to analyze the competencies of the different organs of sovereignty, whether in relation to their supervision, revision or application.

Much has been said about fundamental rights over the last few decades (Braga, 1977; Andrade, 2004; Amaral, 2010), on Constitutional power (Pinto, 1994), the material limits of revision (Lourinho, 2011, Castro, 2014) or even on the role of the Constitutional Court (Moreira, 2004). Several topics of the documents have been thought, their (re)creation and the accompaniment that the articles has as the society undergoes mutations. However, little has been discussed about the importance of communication, dissemination and, consequently, the people's knowledge of these documents and, fundamentally, of the Constitutions and what documents imply in terms of rights and duties. That is, on the exercise of sovereignty by the people beginning with the focal point in the same exercise of that same sovereignty: what do individuals know about the Constitutions and other documents protecting their Fundamental Rights?

This book reflected on the concept of people sovereignty manifest in the Fundamental Laws and on the mechanisms that people have at their disposal to acquire knowledge about them and, consequently, about Fundamental Rights and their exercise of sovereignty. Thus, it became urgent to address the topic of communication and dissemination, in a logic of guaranteeing access to documents to all citizens. In this connection, it was also pertinent to consider communication and dissemination as a role to be assigned to the official institutions from which such documents emanate, in order, inter alia, to ensure that the fundamental norms are complied with throughout its term.

If it is true that documents are publicly available, it may also be true that ignorance of technical language that allows an enlightened reading or even the size of documents are critical factors when it comes to decide to read, seek, or inquire about it. But if so, what role should official institutions have in the dissemination of the document, of the precepts stipulated therein, and in its adaptation to the current language? Does an education for fundamental rights make sense in an Education for Democratic Citizenship and Human Rights?

The 21st century presents new social demands, with citizens having to take an increasingly active position in the search for knowledge, and with more and more means at their disposal to do so. The demands go through the rapid change with which everything happens, but above all, because we live less and less isolated, each Nation is open to the World and cannot refuse to accept this fact, nor what comes from it.

Along with these changes and demands, the Constitutions need to adapt. Some have been doing so with successive revisions. But the adaptation may not be to the revision of the text, but also to the official institutions, since, as already mentioned, these are the ones that guarantee, among other occurrences, the application of the Fundamental Laws. Thus, the re-creation of official documents and institutions must be adapted to the new demands of the 21st century, education for citizenship and democracy as a backdrop, which is a guarantee of the freedom and responsibility of the people to exercise their sovereignty.

It is not considered to be an exclusive competence of the official internal institutions, but also of the international ones, as well as giving a proactive and accountable role to the people, especially in the exercise of their sovereignty, which, it is believed, requires the search for constant and interested information and knowledge. Communication and dissemination, along with the search for information, leads to more enlightened citizens, more capable of exercising sovereignty.

REFERENCES

Amaral, K. (2010). Os direitos fundamentais na Constituição Portuguesa de 1976: a eficácia dos direitos de liberdade e dos direitos sociais. *Direito, Estado e Sociedade*, *37*, 6-26. Retrieved from: http://www.jur.puc-rio.br/revistades/index.php/revistades/article/view/194/175

Andrade, J. (2004). *Os direitos fundamentais na Constituição Portuguesa de 1976*. Coimbra: Almedina.

Braga, A. (1977). Os direitos do homem e a Constituição. *Revista da Ordem dos Advogados, 2*, 437-450. Retrieved from: http://www.oa.pt/upl/%7B2307991a-ce4c-4d2b-b150-74265f914887%7D.pdf

Castro, V. (2014). Limites às Mutações Constitucionais: Revisão e Cláusula Pétrea. *RIDB – Revista do Instituto do Direito Brasileiro, 10*, 7657-7702. Retrieved from http://www.cidp.pt/publicacoes/revistas/ridb/2014/10/2014_10_07657_07702.pdf

Lourinho, S. (2011). Identidade constitucional, poder constituinte e os limites materiais de revisão ou cláusulas pétreas. *Conhecimento Interativo, 5*(1), 137-152. Retrieved from http://app.fiepr.org.br/revistacientifica/index.php/conhecimentointerativo/article/view/73/77

Moreira, V. (2004). O Tribunal Constitucional Português: a "Fiscalização Concreta" no Quadro de um Sistema Misto de Justiça Constitucional. *Direito Público, 1*(3), 62-88. Retrieved from https://www.portaldeperiodicos.idp.edu.br/direitopublico/article/view/1388/856

Pinto, L. (1994). *Os Limites do Poder Constituinte e a Legitimidade Material da Constituição*. Coimbra: Coimbra Editora.

Compilation of References

About the Court. (2018). *The Justices' Caseload.* Retrieved from: https://www.supremecourt.gov/about/justicecaseload.aspx

ActionAid. (2014). *The Dynamics of Devolution in Zimbabwe.* ActionAid.

Aggarwal, C. C. (2011). *An Introduction to Social Network Data Analytics.* Boston, MA: Springer. doi:10.1007/978-1-4419-8462-3

Ahranjani, M. (2017). The Prisonization of America's Public Schools. *Hofstra L. Rev., 45*(1097).

Akillioglu, T. (1990). *Yonetimde Aciklik-Gizlilik ve Bilgi Alma Hakki. In Ulusal Idare Hukuku Kongresi* (pp. 806–815). Ankara: Ikinci Kitap, Kamu Yonetimi.

Akillioglu, T. (1991). Yonetimde Aciklik-Gizlilik ve Bilgi Alma Hakki. *AUSBFD, 46*(3), 1–12.

Alasdair, R. (2001). Questions about Policy Transparency. *Public Administration Review, 61*(4), 507–508. doi:10.1111/0033-3352.00055

Alasdair, R. (2001). Structural Pluralism and the Right to Information. *University of Toronto Law Journal*, 243–271.

Albi, F. A. (1966). Las derivaciones inmediatas de la crisis del municipalismo. Revista de Estudios de Vida Local, 25.

Alexy. (2007). Teoria dos Direitos Fundamentais (2nd ed.). São Paulo: Malheiros.

Alfonso, P. (2012). *Apuntes para el debate sobre la planta y la articulación interna de la Administración local.* Retrieved from http://repositorio.gobiernolocal.es/xmlui/bitstream/handle/10873/1285/Apuntes_Parejo_10_22.pdf?sequence=1&isAllowed=y

Almeida, J. N. (2014). *Transparência e proporcionalidade no Financiamento dos Serviços de Interesse Económico Geral.* Porto: Vida Económica.

Alvarenga. (2011). *Aristides Junqueira. Reflexões sobre improbidade administrativa no direito brasileiro.* São Paulo: Editora Malheiros.

Álvaro, A. (2011). *Cidadania Digital: O Papel das TIC no Exercício da Cidadania dos Adultos* (Masters dissertation). Escola Superior de Educação de Coimbra, Coimbra, Portugal.

Alves, D. R. (2015, May). *Os direitos sociais na Constituição portuguesa. Conexão com o direito da União Europeia*. Paper presented at the meeting of Conferência Ibérica - "O Controlo Constitucional dos Direitos Sociais em ciclos de Crise Económica", Universidade Portucalense, Porto, Portugal.

Alves, D. R., & Moreira, F. C. (2018, July). *A Convenção Europeia dos Direitos do Homem e os seus laços com os direitos de segunda geração*. Paper presented at the meeting of IV Congresso Internacional Dimensões dos Direitos Humanos: "Direitos Humanos de 2ª Geração", na Universidade Portucalense, Porto, Portugal.

Alves, D. R. (2018). Os direitos sociais na constituição portuguesa: sua conexão com o direito da União Europeia. In *Temas Constitucionais – o direito constitucional no Brasil e na Península Ibérica* (pp. 11–33). São Luís, Brasil: SVT Editora.

Alves, D. R., & Silva, M. M. M. (2015). *O Estado Social e os Direitos Sociais - Um Novo Paradigma? In Cadernos de Dereito Actual, 3* (pp. 351–361). Santiago de Compostela: Espanha.

Amaral, K. (2010). Os direitos fundamentais na Constituição Portuguesa de 1976: a eficácia dos direitos de liberdade e dos direitos sociais. *Direito, Estado e Sociedade*, *37*, 6-26. Retrieved from: http://www.jur.puc-rio.br/revistades/index.php/revistades/article/view/194/175

Ambani, J., & Mbondenyi, M. (2015). A New Era in Human Rights Promotion and Protection in Kenya? An Analysis of the Salient Feature of the 2010 Constitution's Bill of Rights. In Human Rights and Democratic Governance in Kenya: A post-2007 Appraisal. Pretoria: Pretoria University Law Press (PULP).

Anastasia. (n.d.). *Exposição de Motivos do Projeto de Lei do Senado nº 349/2015*. Disponível em: https://legis.senado.leg.br/sdleg-getter/documento?dm=4407647&disposition=inline

Anderson, T., & Huggins, L. (2003). *Property Rights: A Practical Guide to Freedom and Prosperity*. Hoover Institution Press.

Andrade, J. (2004). *Os direitos fundamentais na Constituição Portuguesa de 1976*. Coimbra: Almedina.

Andreassen, B., & Barasa, T. (2013). Kenya: Civic Action from confrontation to collaboration? In *Human Rights, Power and Civic Action: Comparative Analyses for Struggles for Rights in Developing Societies* (pp. 55–87). Routledge. doi:10.4324/9780203525821

Andrew, J. (2007). *Universal Human Rights: Origins and Development*. LFB Scholarly Publishing.

An-Nai'm, A. (2006). African Constitutionalism and the Role of Islam. University of Pennsylvania Press.

Aras, Z., & Altınok, E. B. (2009). Türkiye'de Bilgi Edinme Hakki ve Uygulama Sorunlari. *Ankara Barosu Dergisi*, *67*(1), 107–112.

Arendt, H. (2009). *Entre o passado e o futuro*. São Paulo: Perspectiva.

Article 19. (1999). *The Public's Right to Know Principles on Freedom of Information Legislation London*. Retrieved from https://www.article19.org/data/files/pdfs/standards/righttoknow.pdf

Badaró, G. (2014). *Processo penal*. Rio de Janeiro: Elsevier.

Balaguer Callejón, F. (2005). *La configuración normativa de princípios e derechos constitucionales en la Constitución Europea*. RDCE.

Banerjee, A., Hanna, R., & Mullainathan, S. (2012). *Corruption*. Working Paper 12-08, Massachusetts Institute of Technology. Disponível em http://econwww.mit.edu/files/6607

Barbosa, H. H. (2012). *Professor at the State University of Rio de Janeiro - Protection of reproductive autonomy of transsexuals*. Florianópolis: Revista de Estudos Feministas.

Barker, R. G. (1968). *Ecological psychology*. Stanford, CA: Stanford University Press.

Barkin, N. (2009). *Afghanistan plummets in new ranking of corruption*. Retrieved from https: extra.globo.com/noticias/mundo/afeganistao-despenca-em-novo-ranking-da-corrupcao-199158.html

Barreto, M. M. S. (2000). *Uma Jornada de Humilhações*. Disponível em http://www.assediomoral.org/spip.php?rubrique22

Barreto, M. M. S. (2005). *Assédio moral: a violência sutil. Análise epidemiológica e psicossocial no trabalho no Brasil*. Tese (doutorado em psicologia social) Pontifícia universidade católica, São Paulo. Disponível em: https://tede2.pucsp.br/handle/handle/17370

Barros. (2008). *O Estado (in) transparente: limites do direito à informação socioambiental no Brasil (Doutoramento em Desenvolvimento Sustentável, Política e Gestão Ambiental)*. Brasília: Universidade de Brasília.

Barros. (2008). *O Estado (in)transparente: limites do direito à informação socioambiental no Brasil* (PhD thesis). University of Brasilia, Brasilia.

Bayraktar, K. (2004). Bilgi Edinme Hakki ve Sir Kavrami. Kazanci Hukuk, Isletme ve Maliye Bilimler Dergisi, 3, 7-11.

Beeman, R., Botein, S., & Carter, E. (2012). *Beyond Confederation: Origins of the Constitution a American National Identify*. University of North Carolina Press.

Bei, Z. A. (1996). A corrupção: Causas, consequências e soluções para o problema. *RAP*, *30*(3), 103–115.

Bell v. Itawamba County School Board, 799 F. 3d 379 (2015).

Bernheim, T. C., & Chauí, M. (2008). *Desafios da universidade na sociedade do conhecimento: cinco anos depois da conferência mundial sobre educação superior*. Brasília: UNESCO.

Bethel v. Fraser, 478 U.S. 675 (1986).

Bittar, C. E. B. (2005). *O Direito na Pós-Modernidade*. Rio de Janeiro: Universitária.

Board of Education of Pottawatomie County v. Earls, 536 U.S. 822 (2002).

Bonavides, P. (1988). Curso de Direito Constitucional (33ª ed.). São Paulo: Malheiros.

Bonavides. (2018). *Curso de Direito Constitucional* (33rd ed.). São Paulo: Malheiros.

Botelho, C. S. (2010). *A Tutela Directa dos Direitos Fundamentais*. Coimbra: Almedina.

Botelho, C. S. (2017). *Os direitos sociais em tempos de crise*. Coimbra: Almedina.

Bovens, M. (2002). Information Rights: Citizenship in the Information Society. *Journal of Political Philosophy*, *10*(3), 317–341. doi:10.1111/1467-9760.00155

Bradaschia, C. A. (2007). *Assédio moral no trabalho: a sistematização dos estudos sobre um campo em construção*. São Paulo: Fundação Getúlio Vargas. Dissertação de Mestrado em Administração de Empresas. Disponível em: https://bibliotecadigital.fgv.br/dspace/bitstream/handle/10438/2231/50849.pdf

Braga, A. (1977). Os direitos do homem e a Constituição. *Revista da Ordem dos Advogados*, *2*, 437-450. Retrieved from: http://www.oa.pt/upl/%7B2307991a-ce4c-4d2b-b150-74265f914887%7D.pdf

Brasil, Superior Tribunal de Justiça. (2018). *Habeas Corpus n. 372.762/MG*. 5ª. Retrieved from https://ww2.stj.jus.br/processo/revista/documento/mediado/?componente=ITA&sequencial=1631821&num_registro=201602540301&data=20171016&formato=PDF

Brasil, Superior Tribunal de Justiça. (2018). *Recurso Ordinário em Habeas Corpus n. 51.531/RO*. Retrieved from https://ww2.stj.jus.br/processo/revista/documento/mediado/?componente=ITA&sequencial=1497056&num_registro=201402323677&data=20160509&formato=PDF

Brasil, Supremo Tribunal Federal. (2018). *Habeas Corpus n. 91.867/PA*. 2ª. Retrieved from http://redir.stf.jus.br/paginadorpub/paginador.jsp?docTP=TP&docID=2792328

Brasil, Supremo Tribunal Federal. (2018). *Recurso Extraordinário n. 418.416/SC*. Retrieved from http://www.stf.jus.br/portal/jurisprudencia/listarJurisprudencia.asp?s1=%28418416%2ENUME%2E+OU+418416%2EACMS%2E%29&base=baseAcordaos&url=http://tinyurl.com/hews2gu

Brazil school. (n.d.). *Niger*. Retrieved from <https: brasilescola.uol.com.br/geografia/niger.htm

Brazil. (n.d.). *Criminal Code*. Retrieved from http://www.planalto.gov.br/ccivil_03/decreto-lei/del2848compilado.htm

Brazil. (n.d.). *The Comptroller General*. Available in https://relatorios.cgu.gov.br/Visualizador.aspx?id_relatorio=20

Caetano, M. A. (1972). OS Antecedentes da Reforma Administrativa de 1832 (Mouzinho da Silveira). Revista da Faculdade de Direito da Universidade de Lisboa, 22, 7.

Canotilho, J. J. G. (2003). Direito Constitucional e Teoria da Constituição (7.ª ed.). Coimbra: Almedina.

Canotilho, J. J. (2011). *Direito Constitucional e Teoria da Constituição* (7th ed.). Coimbra: Almedina.

Canotilho, J. J. G., & Moreira, V. (2007). *CRP Constituição da República Portuguesa Anotada (4.ª edição)*. Coimbra: Coimbra Editora.

Capelli, C. (2009). *Uma Abordagem para Transparência em Processos Organizacionais Utilizando Aspectos* (Unpublished doctoral dissertation). Pontifícia Universidade Católica do Rio de Janeiro.

Capelli, C., Engiel, P., Leite, J., Nunes, V., Tanaka, A., Santos, G., & Benjamim, K. (2014). *A Evolução do Modelo de Maturidade em Transparência Organizacional*. Rio de Janeiro: Universidade Federal do Estado do Rio de Janeiro. Disponível em https://www.researchgate.net/publication/303912288_A_Evolucao_do_Modelo_de_Maturidade_em_Transparencia_Organizacional/download

Cardoso, C. F. (1985). *A Cidade Estado Antiga*. São Paulo: Ática.

Carpenter v. United States 585 U.S. __ (2018).

Carraro, A., Fochezatto, A., & He, A. (2006). *The impact of corruption on the economic growth of Brazil: a general equilibrium model for the period 1994-1998*. Retrieved from http:www.anpec.org.br/encontro2006/artigos/a06a057.pdf

Carvalho, F. (2018). *Manual de Direito Administrativo* (32nd ed.). São Paulo: Editora Atlas.

Castells, M. (2003). A Era da Informação: Economia. In *O Poder da Identidade*. Lisboa: Fundação Calouste Gulbenkian.

Castells, M. (2013). *Redes de indignação e esperança: movimentos sociais na era da internet* (C. A. Medeiros, Trans.). Rio de Janeiro: Zahar.

Castells, M., & Cardoso, G. (2005). *A Sociedade em Rede: Do Conhecimento à Acção Política*. Imprensa Nacional – Casa da Moeda.

Castilho, J. R. F. (n.d.). *Cidadania: esboço de evolução e sentido da Expressão*. Retrieved from http://www.pge.sp.gov.br/centrodeestudos/revistapge/revista2/artigo8.htm

Castles, S. (2000). Underclass or Exclusion: Social Citizenship for Ethnic Minorities. In Citizenship, Community and Democracy. London: Macmillan Press. doi:10.1007/978-1-137-09068-3_2

Castro, V. (2014). Limites às Mutações Constitucionais: Revisão e Cláusula Pétrea. *RIDB – Revista do Instituto do Direito Brasileiro, 10*, 7657-7702. Retrieved from http://www.cidp.pt/publicacoes/revistas/ridb/2014/10/2014_10_07657_07702.pdf

Catroga, F. (2014). *A Geografia dos Afectos Pátrios – As reformas politico-administrativas do Século XIX e XX*. Coimbra: Almedina.

Cerreda, A. A. (2012). La cooperación entre Municipios: una posible alternativa a la reordenación de la planta local en España. *Istituzioni del federalismo: rivista di studi giuridici e politici, 3*.

Cerreda, M. A. (2012). *La Cooperación entre Municípios en El Desarrollo de Funciones Administrativas y en la Gestion de Servicios Públicos*. Una Possible Alternativa a la Reordenación de la Planta en España.

Chambers, R. (1997). *Whose Reality Counts? Putting the First Last*. London: Intermediate Technology. doi:10.3362/9781780440453

Chambers, R. (2006). *Poverty Unpercieved: Traps, Biases and Agenda*. Sussex, UK: Institute of Development Studies.

Chambers, R. (2014). *Rural Development: Putting the Last First*. London: Routledge. doi:10.4324/9781315835815

Charizeni, E. (2009). Strategies for Spatial Development in Zimbabwe. Academic Press.

Chavez, N., Grinberg, E., & McLaughlin, E. C. (2018, October 31). *Pittsburgh synagogue gunman said he wanted all Jews to die, criminal complaint says*. Retrieved from https://www.cnn.com/2018/10/28/us/pittsburgh-synagogue-shooting/index.html

Chediek, J., Mulleady, A. I., Sharma, J., & Birth, R. (2015). Atlas of human development in the metropolitan regions of Brazil: Santos, Campinas, Maceió and the Paraíba Valley. Brasília, Brazil: UNDP, Ipea, FJP.

Chemerinsky, E. (2017). *Constitutional Law*. Alphen aan den Rijn, The Netherlands: Wolters Kluwer Law & Business.

Chen, J. (1999). *Chinese Law: Towards an Understanding of Chinese Law, it's Nature and Development*. London: Kluwer Law International.

Chevalier, J. (1988). *Lê mithe de la transparence Administrative*. Paris: Centre Universitaire de Recherces Administratives et Politiques de Picardie, Informacion et Transparence Administrative, PUF.

Chigwata, T. (2016). Three Years into the Implementation of the Zimbabwean Constitution of 2013: Progress, Challenges, Prospects and Lessons. In C. Fombad (Ed.), *The Implementation of Modern African Constitutions: Challenges and Prospects* (pp. 78–107). Pretoria: Pretoria University Law Press.

Chikuhwa, J. (2004). *A Crisis of Governance: Zimbabwe*. New York: Algora Publishing.

Chirisa, I., & Muzenda. (2014). Environmental Rights as a Substantive Area of the Zimbabwe Constitutional Debate: Implications for Policy and Action. *Southern Peace Review Journal*, *2*, 104–121.

Colak, I. (2005). *Bilgi Edinme Hakki ve Bilgi Verme Yukumlulugu*. Retrieved from http://e-akademi.org/makaleler/nicolak-1.htm

Compton, J. (2014). *The Evangelical Origins of the Living Constitution*. Harvard University Press.

Condorcet, M. A. (1788). *Essaie sur la Constitution et les Fonctions des Assemblées Provinciales* (Vol. 1). Paris: Bibliothèque Nationale de France.

Constitution of Brazil. (1988). Retrieved from http://english.tse.jus.br/arquivos/federal-constitution

Cordeiro, T. (2018). *The secret of the most honest countries in the world.* Gazeta do Povo. Retrieved from http: www.gazetadopovo.com.br/ideias/o-segredo-dos-paises-mais-honestos-do-mundo-46ahc398rewn4doybhflmwh20

Cornwall, A., & Nyamu-Musembi, C. (2004). Putting the Rights based Approach to Development into Perspective. *Third World Quarterly, 28*(2), 1415–1437. doi:10.1080/0143659042000308447

Council of Europe Committee of Ministers. (1981). *Recommendation No. R (81) 19 of The Committee of Ministers To Member States on The Access to Information Held By Public Authorities.* Retrieved from https://rm.coe.int/CoERMPublicCommonSearchServices/DisplayDCTMContent?documentId=09000016804f7a6e

Council of Europe Committee of Ministers. (2002). *Recommendation Rec(2002)2 of the Committee of Ministers to Member States on Access to Official Documents, Adopted by the Committee of Ministers 784th meeting of the Ministers' Deputies.* Retrieved from https://rm.coe.int/16804c6fcc

Council of Europe. (2010). *Education for Democratic Citizenship and Human Rights Education (EDC/HRE).* Retrieved from https://www.coe.int/web/edc/charter-on-education-for-democratic-citizenship-and-human-rights-education

Coutinho, C., & Lisboa, E. (2011). Sociedade da Informação e da Aprendizagem: Desafios para a Educação no Séc. XXI. *Review of Education, 18*(1), 5–22.

Coutinho, C., & Lisbôa, E. (2011). Sociedade da Informação, do Conhecimento e da Aprendizagem: Desafios para Educação no Século XXI. *Review of Education, 18*(1), 5–22.

Cryobank. (n.d.). *Donor Look-A-Likes.* Retrieved from https://cryobank.com/donor-search/look-a-likes/

Cunha, J. (2018). Curso de Direito Constitucional (13ª ed.). Salvador: Editora Juspodivm.

Dallari, D. A. (n.d.). *Direitos e deveres da cidadania.* Retrieved from http://www.dhnet.org.br/direitos/sos/textos/deveres.htm

Dallari, D. A. (2001). Estado de direito e cidadania. In *Direito constitucional: estudos em homenagem a Paulo Bonavides.* São Paulo: Malheiros.

Dancey, C., & Reidy, J. (2006). Statistics without maths for Psychology: Using SPSS for Windows. Statistics without maths for Psychology: Using SPSS for Windows. Porto Alegre, Brazil: New Haven.

Davenport, T., & Prusak, L. (2000). *Working Knowledge: How Organizations Manage What They Know.* Boston: Harvard Business School Press.

de Andrade, V. (2001). Os Direitos Fundamentais na Constituição Portuguesa de 1976 (2.ª ed.). Coimbra: Almedina.

De Geyter, C. (2018). *More than 8 million babies born from IVF since the world's first in 1978.* Retrieved from https://www.eshre.eu/ESHRE2018/Media/ESHRE-2018-Press-releases/De-Geyter.aspx

Dejours, C. (1992). *A loucura do trabalho: estudo de psicopatologia do trabalho* (5th ed.). São Paulo: Cortez Oboré.

Dejours, C. (2001). *A banalização da injustiça social* (4th ed.). Rio de Janeiro: FGV.

Delgado, G. N. (2006). *Direito Fundamental ao trabalho digno.* São Paulo: LTr.

Desoto, H. (2000). *The Mystery of Capital: Why Capitalism Triumps in the West and Fail Everywhere Else.* London: Black Swan.

Di Pietro, . (2018). *Direito administrativo* (31st ed.). Rio de Janeiro: Editora Forense.

Diário da República Eletrónico. (n.d.). *Constituição da República Portuguesa: Princípios Fundamentais.* Retrieved from https://dre.pt/web/guest/legislacao-consolidada/-/lc/337/20181130l945/127959/diploma/indice

Dicionário da Língua Portuguesa. (2013). Porto: Porto Editora.

Doner, A. (2010). *Seffaf Devlette Bilgi Edinme Hakki ve Sinirlari.* Istanbul, Turkey: XII Levha Yayinlari.

Duarte, M. L. (2006). *União Europeia e Direitos Fundamentais - no espaço da internormatividade.* Lisboa: aafdl.

Duarte, M. L. (2011). *União Europeia - Estática e dinâmica da ordem jurídica eurocomunitária.* Coimbra: Almedina.

Dziekaniak, G., & Rover, A. (2011). Sociedade do conhecimento: características, demandas e requisitos. *DataGramaZero – Revista de Informação, 12*(5). Disponível em http://www.egov.ufsc.br/portal/conteudo/artigo-sociedade-do-conhecimento-caracter%C3%ADsticas-demandas-e-requisitos

Dzinetsa, G. (2012). *Zimbabwe's Constitutional Reform Process: Challenges and Prospects.* Institute for Justice and Reconciliation.

Edling, M. (2003). *A Revolution in Favour of Government: Origins of the U.S Constitution and the Making of the American State.* New York: Oxford University Press. doi:10.1093/0195148703.001.0001

Einarsen, S. (2000). Harassment and bullying at work: A review of the Scandinavian approach. *Aggression and Violent Behavior, 5*(4), 379–401. doi:10.1016/S1359-1789(98)00043-3

Eken, M. (2005). Gizlilik Geleneginden Seffaf Yonetime Dogru. *TODAIE, 38*(1), 113–130.

Elliott, K. A. (2002). *Corruption and the Global economy*. Brasília, Brazil: University of Brasília.

Emerson, T.I. (1977). Colonial Intentions and Current Realities of the First Amendment. *U. Pa. L. Rev., 125*(737).

Erdogan, M. (2004). *Anayasal Demokrasi*. Ankara, Turkey: Siyasal Kitabevi.

Espindola, C. B. (2015). Cidadania na sociedade em rede: o ciberativismo e o combate à LGBTFOBIA. In *Anais do 3º Congresso Internacional de Direito e contemporaneidade: mídias e direitos da sociedade em rede*. Rio Grande do Sul: Universidade Federal de Santa Maria.

Fagundes. (2010). O controle dos atos administrativos pelo Poder Judiciário (8ª ed.). Rio de Janeiro: Editora Forense.

Fai, Q., Zhang, W., & Than, F. (2015). *The Road to the Rule of Law in Modern China*. New York: Springer.

Félix Alais, H. (2006). *Los princípios del derecho aduanero, Teoría general y aplicación a la problemática de la infracción de declaración inexacta*. Buenos Aires: Facultad de Derecho de la Universidad Austral.

Ferranti, D., Jacinto, J., Ody, A. J., & Ramshaw, G. (2009). *How to improve Governance: A New Framework for Analysis and Action*. Washington, DC: Brookings Institution Press.

Ferreira, J., & Axt, M. (1999). Conhecimento, tecnologia e sociedade: Em busca de referências interpretativas da ação. *Interface, 3*(5), 95–109. doi:10.1590/S1414-32831999000200009

Ferry, K. A. (2018). Reviewing the Impact of the Supreme Court's interpretation of "Social Media" as Applied to Off-Campus Student Speech. *Loy. U. L.J.*, 49(*717*), 771.

Figueiredo, F. J. A. (1950). A reforma concelhia de 6 de Novembro de 1836. *O Direito, 82*.

Filho. (2018). Curso de direito administrativo (13ª ed.). São Paulo: Editora Revista dos Tribunais.

Forssbæck, J., & Oxelheim, L. (2014). The Multi-Faceted Concept of Transparency. *IFN Working Paper, nº 1013*. Estocolmo: Research Institute of Industrial Economics.

Fox, J. (2007). Government Transparency and Policymaking. *Public Choice, 131*(1-2), 23–44. doi:10.100711127-006-9103-3

Freire, P. (1982). *Educação como prática da liberdade*. Rio de Janeiro: Paz e Terra.

Freitas, M. E. (2007). Quem paga a conta do assédio moral no trabalho? *RAE-eletrônica, 6*(1). Disponível em: http://www.scielo.br/pdf/raeel/v6n1/a11v6n1.pdf

Freitas. (2018). *O artigo 22 da LINDB e os novos contornos do Direito Administrativo sancionador*. Disponível em: https://www.conjur.com.br/2018-jul-25/opiniao-artigo-22-lindb-direito-administrativo-sancionador

Freitas, M. E. (2001). Assédio moral e assédio sexual: Faces do poder perverso nas organizações. *Revista de Administração de Empresas, 41*(2), 8–19.

Gadelha, R. M. A. F. (2017). *Educação no Brasil: Desafios e Crise Institucional. Revista Pesquisa & Debate*. São Paulo: PUCSP.

Garcia, A. (2016). *La Fusión de Municípios como Estratégia*. Madrid: Editorial Dikinson Lda.

Ghai, P. (2014). Constitutions and Constitutionalism: The Tale of the 2010 Constitution. In Kenya: The Struggle for a New Constitutional Order. Zedbooks.

Glennerster, R., & Shin, Y. (2008). Does Transparency Pay? *IMF Staff Papers*, *55*(1), 183–209. doi:10.1057/palgrave.imfsp.9450028

Global Regulation. (2011). *Ex vi arts. 4 and 7, item IV of the Federal Law n. 12,527/2011*. Retrieved from https://www.global-regulation.com/translation/brazil/2895611/law-no.-12%252c527-of-november-18%252c-2011.html

Goebel, A. (2005). *Gender and Land Reform: The Zimbabwean Experience*. London: McGill-Queen's University Press.

Gomes, E. (2002). Gestão do conhecimento: definição conceitual, múltiplos usos e interpretações. In *Jornada de Prospecção Tecnológica e Gestão do Conhecimento: contextos de Sociedade da Informação, gestão do conhecimento e Prospecção tecnológica - uma tentativa de visão sistêmica, 1*. Brasília: Disponível. Retrieved from http://www.cgee.org.br/arquivos/pro0202.pdf

Gonçalves, L. (2013). *Direitos sociais: cidadania, política e justiça*. Rio de Janeiro: Sinergia.

Goss v. Lopez, 419 U.S. 565, 581 (1975).

Government of Zimbabwe. (2000). *Zimbabwe's Constitution as Ammended at 19 April 2000/ Government of Zimbabwe*. Harare: Legal Resources Foundation.

Government of Zimbabwe. (2013). *Constitution of Zimbabwe, Amendment (No.20) Act 2013*. Harare: Parliament of Zimbabwe.

Government of Zimbabwe. (2015). *Zimbabwe Millennium Development Goals 2000-2015: Final Progress Report*. Harare: Ministry of Macro- Economic Planning and Investment Promotion.

Gray, A. (2016, November). Freedom of speech: which country has the most? *World Economic Forum*. Retrieved from https://www.weforum.org/agenda/2016/11/freedom-of-speech-country-comparison/

Gray, R. (2001). Thirty Years of Social Accounting, Reporting and Auditing: What (if anything) Have We Learnt? (v. 10, n.1). London, UK: Business Ethics, EuropeanReview.

Gray, S. (2018, March). Thousands of Students Walked Out of School Today in Nationwide Protests. Here's Why. *Time Magazine*. Retrieved from http://time.com/5195960/national-school-walkout-march-14/

Gready, P., & Ensor, J. (2005). *Re-Inventing Development?: Translating Rights-Based Approaches from Theory into Practice*. London: Zedbooks.

Griffin, S. (1996). *American Constitutionalism: From Theory to Politics*. Princeton University Press.

Griffin, S., & Griffin, M. (1996). *American Constitutionalism: From Theory to Politics*. Princeton University Press.

Grinlinton, D., & Taylor, P. (2011). *Property Rights and Sustainability: The Evolution of Property Rights to meet Ecological Challenges*. Boston: Martinus Nijhoff Publishers. doi:10.1163/ej.9789004182646.i-415

Gursel, O. (1998). Idari Rejim Olarak Ornek Aldigimiz Fransa'da, Idari Usul ve Bilgi Edinme Hakkina Iliskin Duzenlemeler. *Gazi Universitesi Hukuk Fakultesi Dergisi Prof. Dr. Ihsan Tarakcioglu'na Armagan*, 281-290.

Häberle. (1997). *Hermenêutica Constitucional: a sociedade aberta dos intérpretes da Constituição – contribuição para interpretação pluralista e procedimental da Constituição. Tradução de Gilmar Ferreira Mendes*. Porto Alegre: Fabris.

Hafizogullari, Z. (2012). Ceza Hukuku Duzeninde Devlet Sirri. *Hacettepe Hukuk Fakultesi Dergisi*, *2*(2), 172–177.

Hancock, M., & Bradley, K. (2014). *UK Anticorruption Plan*. Disponível em www.gov.uk

Harada, K. (2006). *Financial law and tax law* (15th ed.). São Paulo, Brazil: Atlas.

Hargreaves, A. (2003). *O Ensino na Sociedade do Conhecimento: a educação na era da insegurança*. Porto: Porto Editora.

Hasdemir, T.A. (2016). Right to Information and Communication between Government and Citizens: Identifying Continuities and Discontinuities in the Practices of Turkey at the10th Anniversary of the Law on Right to Information. *İletisim Kuram ve Arastirma Dergisi, 43*, 64-76.

Hasdemir, T. A. (2014). Türkiye'de Kamusal İletisim ve Bilgi Edinme:10 Yilin Ardindan Panoramik Bir İnceleme. *Amme Idaresi Dergisi*, *47*(3), 111–144.

Hatchard, J., Ndulo, M., & Slinn, P. (2004). Comparative Constitutionalism and Good Governance in the Commonwealth: An Eastern and Southern African Perspective. Cambridge, UK: Cambridge University Press.

Haws, R. (2009). *The South's Role in the Creation of Bill of Rights*. University Press of Mississippi.

Hazelwood v. Kuhlmeier, 484 U.S. 260 (1988).

Hellum, A., Derman, B., Sithole, E., & Rutsate, E. (2015). Governance, Gender Equilty and the Right to Water and Sanitation in Zimbabwe: Contested Norms and Institutions in an Unstable Economic and Political Terrain. In *Water is Life: Women's Human Rights in National and local Water Governance in Southern and Eastern Africa* (pp. 300–450). Harare: Weaver Press.

Heloani, R. (2003). Violência invisível. *GV executivo, 2*(3). Disponível em: https://rae.fgv.br/gv-executivo/vol2-num3-2003/violencia-invisivel

Hickey, S., & Mitlin, D. (2009). *Rights Based Approaches to Develop: Exploring the Potential and Pitfalls*. Lunarian Press.

Hingels, A., Saltelli, A., Manca, A. R., Mascherini, M., & Hoskins, B. (2009). *Growing Cohesive Societies: The Characterization of Active Citizenship*. The 3rd OECD World Forum on "Statistics, Knowledge and Policy, Busan, Korea.

Hirigoyen, M. F. (2001). Le malaise dans le travail, harcèlement moral: démêler le vrai du faux. Paris: Syros.

Hirigoyen, M. F. (2002). *Mal estar no trabalho: redefinindo o assédio moral*. Rio de Janeiro: Bertrand Brasil.

Hirigoyen, M. F. (2006). *A violência perversa do cotidiano*. Rio de Janeiro: Bertrand Brasil.

Hirigoyen, M. F. (2009). *Assédio moral: a violência perversa do cotidiano* (11th ed.). Rio de Janeiro: Bertrand Brasil.

Hiz, Y., & Yilmaz, Z. (2004). *Bilgi Edinme ve Dilekce Hakki Aciklamali Notlu Gerekceli*. Ankara, Turkey: Seckin Yayincilik.

IG. (n.d.). *A geração dos bebês nascidos para curar*. Retrieved from: https://minhasaude/2013-05-02/a-geraçao-dos-bebes-nascidos-para-curar.html

Inal, T. (2004). Bilgi Edinme Hakki ve Özel Hayata, Haberlesmeye, Ticari Sirlara, Fikir ve Sanat Eserlerine Iliskin Sinirlamalar. *Kazanci Hukuk. Isletme ve Maliye Bilimleri Dergisi*, *3*, 12–29.

Iniciativa Nacional para a Sociedade da Informação. (1997). *Livro Verde para a Sociedade da Informação em Portugal*. Missão para a sociedade da Informação, Lisboa.

Institut National de la Statistique et des Etudes Economiques. (n.d.). *La Population Legale des Communes*. Retrieved from https://www.insee.fr/fr/statistiques/1280737

Jacoby Fernandes, J. U. (2018). *Lei nº 13.655/2018 e o resgate da segurança jurídica para os gestores públicos e órgãos de controle*. Disponível em: https://www.jmleventos.com.br/pagina.php?area=coluna-juridica&acao=download&dp_id=181

Jaeger, W. (2001). *Paideia: A formação do homem grego*. Rio de Janeiro: Martins Fontes.

Jellinek, Mendes, & Branco. (2018). Curso de Direito Constitucional (13th ed.). São Paulo: Saraiva.

Jesus, B. (n.d.). *El eterno debate sobre la reforma del mapa municipal. El caso de Cataluña*. Retrieved from in https://dialnet.unirioja.es/ejemplar/162509

Johnston, M., & Kpundeh, S. J. (2002). *Building A Clean Machine Anti-Corruption Coalitions and Sustainable Reform*. Retrieved from http://siteresources.worldbank.org/WBI/Resources/wbi37208.pdf

Jordão, R. P. (2002). *(Almost) perfect crime: corruption and money laundering in Brazil*. São Paulo, Brazil: Perseu Abramo Foundation.

Kaboglu, I. (2011). *Anayasa Hukuku Dersleri*. Istanbul, Turkey: Legal Kitabevi.

Kaboglu, I. (2013). *Ozgurlukler Hukuku*. Ankara, Turkey: Imge Kitabevi.

Kamete, A. (2006). Revisting Urban Housing Crisis in Zimbabwe: Some Forgotten Dimensions. *Habitat International*, *30*(4), 981–995. doi:10.1016/j.habitatint.2005.08.002

Katz, A. (2017, August). Unrest in Virginia: Clashes over a Show of White Nationalism in Charlottesville Turn Deadly. *Time Magazine*. Retrieved from http://time.com/charlottesville-white-nationalist-rally-clashes/

Katz, S. (2012). The American Constitution: A Revolutionary Interpretation. In R. Beeman, S. Botein, & E. Carter (Eds.), *Beyond Confederation: Origins of the Constitution and American National Identity* (pp. 23–37). London: University of North Carolina Press.

Kaya, C. (2005). *Idare Hukukunda Bilgi Edinme Hakki*. Ankara, Turkey: Seckin Yayinlari.

Ketzer, P. (2016). A irredutibilidade do conceito de confiança na epistemologia do testemunho. *Conjectura: Filosofia e Educação*, *21*(3), 496–513. doi:10.18226/21784612.v21.n3.03

Kilinc, U. (2009). Bilgi Edinme Hakki Kanunu ve Turkiye Uygulamasi. Kamu Mevzuati Dergisi, *1*(2).

Kim, R. P. (2013). *O conteúdo jurídico de cidadania na Constituição Federal do Brasil. Cidadania – o novo conceito jurídico e a sua relação com os direitos fundamentais individuais e coletivos*. São Paulo: Atlas.

Kim, R. P. (2013). *O conteúdo jurídico de cidadania na Constituição Federal do Brasil. In Cidadania – o novo conceito jurídico e a sua relação com os direitos fundamentais individuais e coletivos*. São Paulo: Atlas.

Klitgaard, R. (1994). *A corrupção sob controle*. Rio de Janeiro: Jorge Zaha.

Knijnik, D. (2016). A trilogia Olmstead-Katz-Kyllo: o art. 5° da Constituição Federal do século XXI. *Revista da EMAGIS - Revista da Escola da Magistratura do TRF da 4ª Região*, *2*(4), 77-90.

Kocak, S. Y. (2010). Kamu Yonetiminde Aciklik Icin Bilgi Edinme Hakki. *Selcuk Universitesi Sosyal Bilimler Enstitusu Dergisi*, *23*, 15–125.

Kohr, L. (1949). *Customs Unions - A Tool for Peace*. Foundation for Foreign Affairs.

Krueger, A. (1990). Government failures in development. *The Journal of Economic Perspectives*, *4*(3), 9–23. doi:10.1257/jep.4.3.9

Kuhn, T. S. (1970). *The Structure of Scientific Revolutions. Enlarged* (2nd ed.). Chicago: University of Chicago Press.

Laborit, H. (1986). *La nouvelle Grille (1974)*. Paris: Robert Laffont.

Lang, A., & Wiener, A. (2017). *Handbook on Global Constitutionalism*. Cheltenham, UK: Edward Edgar Publishing. doi:10.4337/9781783477357

Leff, N. H. (1964). Economic Development Through Bureaucratic Corruption. In *Political Corruption: A Handbook*. New Brunswick, Canada: Transaction Plubishers. doi:10.1177/000276426400800303

Lemos, B., Caldeira, F., & Quintiere, V. (2016). Sobre as (i)legalidades no processo penal: breve reflexão a respeito do Whatsapp a partir da Lei n. 9.296/96 – um estudo de caso. In Interceptação Telefônica: os 20 anos da Lei n. 9.296/96 (pp. 45-62). Belo Horizonte: D'Plácido.

Lenhart, A. (2015). *Teens, Social Media and Technology Overview*. Retrieved from http://www.pewinternet.org/2015/04/09/teens-social-media-technology-2015/

Levin, C. S. (2016). *Legal analysis: how far can schools go in limiting student speech online*. Retrieved from http://www.splc.org/article/2016/06/legal-analysis-student-speech

Lévy, P. (1999). *Cibercultura*. São Paulo: Editora 34.

Linington, G. (2001). *Constitutional Law of Zimbabwe*. Harare: Legal Resources Foundations.

Linington, G. (2012). Reflections on the Significance of Constitutions and Constitutionalism for Zimbabwe. In *Zimbabwe: Mired in Transition* (pp. 63–98). Harare: IDAZIM.

Liu, Y., & Ying, X. (2010). Review of Social Network Sites: Definition, Experience and Applications. In *Proceedings of The Conference on Web Based Business Management* (pp.749-752). Scientific Research.

Loucaides, G. L. (1995). The Right to Information. *Essays on The Developing Law of Human Rights*, *39*, 3–31.

Lourinho, S. (2011). Identidade constitucional, poder constituinte e os limites materiais de revisão ou cláusulas pétreas. *Conhecimento Interativo*, *5*(1), 137-152. Retrieved from http://app.fiepr.org.br/revistacientifica/index.php/conhecimentointerativo/article/view/73/77

Louzada, F. (2016), *intersexuality and Brazilian law* lecture at the Luso-Brazilian meeting of Right of Families in Lisbon.

Lumumba, P., Mbondenyi, M., & Odero, S. (2014). *The Constitution of Kenya: Contemporary Readings*. Law Africa Publishing.

Lux. (2007). EU customs law and international law. *World Customs Journal*, 1.

Madebwe, T. (2015). A Rights- based Approach to Environmental Protection: The Zimbabwean Experience. *African Human Rights Law Journal*, *15*(1), 110–128. doi:10.17159/1996-2096/2015/v15n1a5

Madhuku, L. (2010). *An Introduction to Zimbabwean Law*. Harare: Weaver Press.

Manique, P. A. (1989). *Mouzinho da Silveira – Liberalismo e Administração Pública*. Lisboa: Ocaña.

Mansell, R., & Tremblay, G. (2015). *Renovando a visão das Sociedades do Conhecimento*. São Paulo, CETIC.br.

Marques, E. (2017). *New Zealand and Brazil: lessons from the less corrupt country in the world*. Students for liberty – freer future. Retrieved from https: www.studentsforliberty.org/nova-zelandia-pais-menos-corrupto-mundo

Martin, K., & Hoffman, P. (1999). Safeguarding Liberty: National Security, Freedom of Expression and Access to Information: United States of America. In Secrecy and Liberty (pp. 481-505). Martinus Nijhoff Publishers.

Martínez. (2015). Derecho al acceso a la información public in el Uruguay. In *Access to Public Information* (p. 220). Belo Horizonte: Forum.

Martínez. (2015). Derecho al acceso a la información pública em el Uruguay. In *Acesso à Informação Pública*. Belo Horizonte: Fórum.

Martin, G., & Benjamin, I. (2014). Elites, Interest Groups and Average Citizens. *American Political Science Association, 12*(3), 564–581.

Martins, A. M. G. (2007). A Proteção dos Direitos Fundamentais em Portugal e a Constituição Europeia. *REE, 1*(2).

Martins, A. M. G. (2010). *A igualdade e a não discriminação dos nacionais de Estados terceiros legalmente residentes na União Europeia – da origem na integração económica ao fundamento na dignidade humana*. Coimbra: Almedina.

Martins, A. M. G. (2017). *Manual de Direito da União Europeia*. Coimbra: Almedina.

Martins, M., & Mogarro, M. (2010). A Educação para a Cidadania no Século XXI. *Revista Iberoamericana de Educación, 53*, 185–202.

Mason, A. (2000). The Relationship Between Freedom of Expression and Freedom of Information. In Freedom of Expression and Freedom of Information (pp. 225-238). Oxford University Press.

Masson, G., & Mainardes, J. (2011) A Ideologia da Sociedade do Conhecimento e suas Implicações para a Educação. *Currículo sem Fronteiras, 11*(2), 70-85. Retrieved from http://www.curriculosemfronteiras.org/vol11iss2articles/masson-mainardes.pdf

Mattos. (2010). *O limite de improbidade administrativa: comentários à Lei nº 8.429/92* (5th ed.). Rio de Janeiro: Editora Forense.

Mazzali, R., & Ercolin, C. A. (2018). *Governança corporativa*. Rio de Janeiro: Editora Fundação Getúlio Vargas.

Mbondenyi, K., & Ambani, O. (2012). *New Constitution al Law of Kenya: Principles, and Human Rights*. African Law Publishing.

Mbondenyi, M., & Osogo, A. (2014). *New Constitutional Law of Kenya: Principles, Government and Human Rights*. Law African Publishing.

McDonagh, M. (2013). The Right to Information in International Human Rights Law. Human Rights Law Review, 13(1), 25-55.

McGinnis, J., & Rappaport, M. (2013). *Originalim and the Good Constitution.* Harvard University Press. doi:10.4159/harvard.9780674726260

Medauar. (2003). *O direito administrativo em evolução.* São Paulo: Revista dos Tribunais.

Mello, C. A. B. (2013). *Curso de Direito Administrativo. 30ª edição.* Malheiros Editores.

Melo, C. A. V. (2003). *High Corruption in response to low levels of Accountability* (Unpublished Maters dissertation). Federal University of Pernambuco, Recife, Brazil.

Melo, C. A. V. (2011). Constituent elements and dynamic of corruption: a conceptual exercise (Ariús, v. 17, no. 2, Jul./dez). Brazil, Campina Grande: Federal University of Campina Grande.

Merloni, F. (2008). *La Transparenza Amministrativa.* Milano: Giuffrè.

Minersville School District v. Gobitis, 310 U.S. 586 (1940).

Ministério Público Federal. (2018). *Nota Técnica Conjunta nº 1/2018.* Disponível em: http://www.mpf.mp.br/atuacao-tematica/ccr5/notas-tecnicas/docs/Nota%20Tecnica%201_2018.pdf

Mirabeau. (1791). *Proccès Verbal des Séances de L'Assemblée Nationale de France ténues de l'année 1789 et suivantes.* Paris: Impression Nationale,

Miranda, J. & Medeiros, R. (2010). *Constituição da República Anotada* (2nd ed.). Coimbra: Coimbra Editora.

Miranda, J. (2014). *Manual de Direito Constitucional.* Coimbra: Coimbra Editora.

Misztal, B. (1996). *Trust in modern societies.* Cambridge, UK: Polity Press.

Mitchell, C. (2017). *Supreme Court Declines to Hear Free Speech Case.* Retrieved from http://www.splc.org/blog/splc/2017/04/keefe-certiorari-denied

Molinaro, C. A., & Sarlet, I. W. (2013). *Sociedade em rede, internet e Estado de vigilância: algumas aproximações.* Rio Grande do Sul: AJURIS.

Moreira, V. (2004). O Tribunal Constitucional Português: a "Fiscalização Concreta" no Quadro de um Sistema Misto de Justiça Constitucional. *Direito Público, 1*(3), 62-88. Retrieved from https://www.portaldeperiodicos.idp.edu.br/direitopublico/article/view/1388/856

Morel, A. (1984). *La Administration Local.* Madrid: Tecnos.

Morin, E. (1990). *Introduction à la pensée complexe.* Paris: ESF.

Morse v. Frederick, 551 U.S. 393 (2007).

Mossberger, K., Wu, Y., & Crawford, J. (2013). Connecting citizens and local governments? Social media and interactivity in major U.S. cities. *Government Information Quarterly, 30*(4), 351–358. doi:10.1016/j.giq.2013.05.016

Mostert, H. (2002). *The Constitution al Protection and Regulation of Property and Its Influence on the Reforms of Private Law and Landownership in South Africa and Germany: A Comparative Analysis*. New York: Springer.

Mott, L., & Michels, E. (2017). *Mortes violentas de LGBT no Brasil*. Grupo Gay da Bahia -Relatório 2017.

Motta. (2018). *Alterações na LINDB valem para todos, não só para o controle, 2018*. Disponível em: https://www.conjur.com.br/2018-jun-14/interesse-publico-alteracoes-lindb-valem-todos-nao-controle

Moyo, K. (2016). Justiciable Property Rights and Postcolonial Land Reform: A Case Study of Zimbabwe. In *Justiciability of Human Rights Law* (pp. 363–388). Springer. doi:10.1007/978-3-319-24016-9_15

Moyo, W. (2014). Urban Housing Policy and Its Implications on the Low- Cost Earners of Harare Municipality, Zimbabwe. *International Journal of Asian Social Science*, *4*(3), 356–365.

Muchadenyika, D. (2015). Land for Housing: A Political Resource- Reflections from Zimbabwe's Urban Areas. *Journal of Southern African Studies*, 2–19.

Mulin, J. (2016). *This Is How Facebook Has Changed Over the Past 12 Years*. Retrieved from https://www.eonline.com/uk/news/736977/this-is-how-facebook-has-changed-over-the-past-12-years

Murunga, Okello, & Sjogren. (2014). *Kenya: The Struggle for a New Constitutional Order*. Zed Books.

Mutondoro, F. (2018). *Housing Cooperatives, Political Symbols and Corruption in Urban Land Governance: The Case of Zimbabwe*. Academic Press.

Myrdal, G. (1968). *Asian Drama: An Inquiry into the Poverty of Nationsto (Vol. 2)*. New York, United States of America: Pantheon.

Nasajon, L. (2010). Assédio Moral no Trabalho. *Revista Ética e realidade atual*. Disponível em: http://era.org.br/wp-content/uploads/ARtigo_Leila_Assedio_Vers%C3%A3o-Final.pdf

National Assembly of Turkey (2004-2017 Reports). (n.d.). Retrieved from https://www.tbmm.gov.tr/bilgiedinme/degerlendirme_kurulu_raporlari.htm

National Assembly of Turkey (2013 Report). (n.d.). Retrieved from https://www.tbmm.gov.tr/bilgiedinme/2013_yili_degerlendirme_raporu.pdf

National Assembly of Turkey (2017 Report). (n.d.). Retrieved from https://www.tbmm.gov.tr/bilgiedinme/2017_yili_degerlendirme_raporu.pdf

National Assembly of Turkey. (2013). *Bilgi Edinme Hakki Çalistayi Sonuc Raporlari*. Retrieved from https://www.tbmm.gov.tr/bilgiedinme/bilgi_edinme_calistay_raporu.pdf

National Center for Education Statistics. (2018). *Fast Facts: Computer and Internet Use*. Retrieved from: https://nces.ed.gov/fastfacts/display.asp?id=46

Nations, D. (2017). *What Is Twitter, and Why Is it So Popular?* Retrieved from https://www.lifewire.com/what-is-twitter-3486519

Nations, D. (2018). *What Is LinkedIn and Why Should You Be on It?* Retrieved from https://www.lifewire.com/what-is-linkedin-3486382

Ndlovu, N. (2015). *Protection of Socio- economic Rights in Zimbabwe: A Critical Assessment of the Domestic Framework under the 2013 Constitution of Zimbabwe*. Diploma Verlag.

Ndulo, M. (2010). Zimbabwe's Unfinished Struggle for a Legitimate Constitutional Order. In L. Miller & L. Aucoin (Eds.), *Framing the State in Times of Transition: Case Studies in Constitution Making* (pp. 176–203). Washington, DC: United States Institute of Peace Press.

Nelson, P., & Ellen, D. (2008). *New Rights Advocacy: Changing Strategie of Development and Human Rights NGOs*. Georgetown University Press.

Neto & Freitas. (2018a). *A função normativa da administração pública e a Lei 13.655/2018.* Disponível em: https://www.conjur.com.br/2018-jun-14/opiniao-funcao-normativa-administracao-publica-lindb

Neto & Freitas. (2018b). *O artigo 22 da LINDB e os novos contornos do Direito Administrativo sancionador.* Disponível em: https://www.conjur.com.br/2018-jul-25/opiniao-artigo-22-lindb-direito-administrativo-sancionador

Neto, J., Valentim, M., & Júnior, O. (2013, May). *Information Society, The Knowledge or Communication? Issues of information's appropriation.* Paper presented at the V Seminário em Ciência da Informação, Londrina.

Neto. (2018). *Resposta aos comentários tecidos pela Consultoria Jurídica do TCU ao PL nº 7.448/2017.* Disponível em: https://www.conjur.com.br/dl/parecer-juristas-rebatem-criticas.pdf

Neto, L. (2016). A educação para a democracia: um propósito de solidariedade social e intergeracional. In *Educação e(m) Democracia*. Porto: Editorial UP.

New Jersey v. T.L.O. 469 U.S. 325 (1985).

Nhacuongue, J. A., & Ferneda, E. (2012). A construção do conhecimento na atualidade: um olhar sobre o impacto da tecnologia. *DataGramaZero – Revista de Informação, 13*(7). Disponível em https://repositorio.unesp.br/handle/11449/114787

Nowak, M. (2003). *Introduction to the International Human Rights Regime*. Leiden: Martinus Nijhoff Publishers.

Nunes, L. A. R. (2010). *O princípio constitucional da dignidade humana* (3rd ed.). São Paulo: Saraiva.

OCDE. (2014). *Perspectivas das políticas de Educação em Portugal*. Lisboa: OCDE – Organização para a Cooperação e o Desenvolvimento Económico.

OCED. (2013). *Integrating Hunan Rights into Development: Donor Approaches, Experiences and Challenges.* World Bank Publications.

Oliveira, A. C. A. (2010). Possibilidades de Reforma de las Actuales Estruturas Municipales y de su Régimen Jurídico. In *Problemas Actuais da Administração Municipal. Actas do 8º Colóquio Luso-Espanhol de Direito Administrativo.* Braga. NEDAL.

Oliveira, A. C. d. A. (2013). *Direito das Autarquias Locais.* Coimbra: Coimbra Editores.

Oliveira, A., & Bazi, R. (2008). Sociedade da Informação, transformação e inclusão social: A questão da produção de conteúdos. *Revista digital de Biblioteconomia e Ciência da Informação, 5*(2), 115-131.

Oliveira. (2012). Ativismo judicial, pragmatismo e capacidades institucionais: as novas tendências do controle judicial dos atos administrativos. *Revista Brasileira de Direito Público, 10*(39), 9-36.

Oliveira, A. C. M. (2010). As condições necessárias para uma autonomia efectiva do município: a importância da população e do território. In *Actas do 8.º Colóquio Luso-Espanhol de Direito Administrativo - Problemas Actuais da Administração Municipal.* Braga: Universidade do Minho.

Oliver, R. (2004). *What is Transparency?* New York: The McGraw-Hill Companies In.

Olowu, D. (2009). *An Intergrative Rights-based Approach to Human Development in Africa.* Pretoria: Pretoria University Law Press.

Oremus, W. (2014). *Facebook Was Born 10 Years Ago. Here's What It Looked Like.* Retrieved from http://www.slate.com/blogs/future_tense/2014/02/03/facebook_10th_anniversary_social_network_turns_10_looks_back_at_its_history.html?via=gdpr-consent

Organisation for Economic Co-operation and Development (OECD). (2005). *Modernising Government.* 31st Session of the Public Governance Committee, Paris, France.

Pacheco, F. (2017c). Cidadania Europeia: da livre circulação de pessoas ao gozo do essencial dos direitos conferidos pelo estatuto fundamental dos nacionais dos Estados-membros. In *Viagens Intemporais pelo Saber: Mapas, Redes e Histórias.* Porto: ISCAP, Centro de estudos interculturais – CEI.

Pacheco, F. (2011). *O Sistema de Protecção dos Direitos Fundamentais na União Europeia – Entre a Autonomia e o Compromisso. In Julgar* (pp. 11–28). Coimbra: Coimbra Editora.

Pacheco, F. (2016). *Tempo, vínculos e direitos: quando circular e permanecer não tende a ser o estatuto fundamental dos nacionais dos Estados-Membros, UNIO.* EU Law Journal.

Pacheco, F. (2017a). *Crise e viabilidade dos sistemas de segurança social: as facetas da cidadania europeia na jurisprudência recente do TJUE. Revista do Direito de Língua Portuguesa, REDILP Ano IV (9). Faculdade de Direito da Universidade Nova de Lisboa.* Quid Iuris.

Pacheco, F. (2017b). *Algumas reflexões sobre o conteúdo dos direitos sociais na União Europeia. In Os novos horizontes do constitucionalismo global.* Braga: APPCDM - Artes Gráficas de Braga.

Pacheco, F. (2017c). *Em nome da autonomia do Direito da União: algumas considerações sobre um parecer polémico. Debater a Europa, 16.* Aveiro: Imprensa da Universidade de Coimbra.

Pact of San José, Costa Rica. (n.d.). *Article 13 - Freedom of thought and expression.* Retrieved from https://www.oas.org/dil/access_to_information_American_Convention_on_Human_Rights.pdf

Parreira, A. (2017). Inovação, Novas Tecnologias e Complexidade. In Utopia, Anarquia e Sociedade. Coimbra: Almedina.

Parreira, A., & Silva, A. L. (2016). The use of numerical value of adverbs of quantity and frequency in the measurement of behavior patterns: transforming ordinal scales into interval scales. *Revista Ensaio – Avaliação e Políticas Públicas em Educação, 90.*

Parreira, A., Silva, A. L., & Moura, R. (2018). Transparência e Cidadania Organizacional: anticorrupção e sustentabilidade. In Emprego, Desenvolvimento e Coesão Social: Que Perspetivas para a Regulação Económica e Social? Lisboa: Associação Portuguesa de Profissionais em Sociologia Industrial, das Organizações e do Trabalho.

Patrick, B. (2006). Freedom of Information and Openness: Fundemental Human Rights? *Administrative Law Review, 58*(1), 177–218.

Paul, E., & Dickman, H. (1989). *Liberty, Property and the Foundation of the American Constitution.* New York: State University of New York Press.

Paz, R. J. (2009). *O princípio da dignidade da pessoa humana: o caráter complexo da sua concretização em face da tensão entre democracia e constitucionalismo.* Dissertação de Mestrado, Unibrasil. Curitiba. Disponível em: https://www.unibrasil.com.br/wp-content/uploads/2018/02/mestrado_unibrasil_Rodnei.pdf

Pedroso de Campos, J. (2017). *Is Jean Wyllys going to direct a film that shows Jesus as homosexual?* Retrieved from https://veja.abril.com.br/blog/me-engana-que-eu-posto/jean-wyllys-vai-dirigir-filme-que-mostra-jesus-como-homossexual/

Peled, R., & Rabin, Y. (2011). The Constitutional Right To Information. *Columbia Human Rights Law Review, 42*(2), 358–401.

Pellegrino, L., & Gerlaugh, R. (2004). Corruption's Effect on Growth and its Transmission Channels. *Kyklos, 57*(3), 429–457. doi:10.1111/j.0023-5962.2004.00261.x

Pereira. (Ed.). (2015). *Segurança jurídica e qualidade das decisões públicas: desafios de uma sociedade democrática, Brasília. 2015.* Disponível em: https://antonioaugustoanastasia.com.br/wp-content/uploads/2015/09/segurancajuridica.pdf

Phama, W., & Madi, P. (2016). The Role of Civil Society Organization and Chapter 9 Institutions in Implementing South Africa's Constitution. In C. Fombad (Ed.), The Implementation of Modern African Constitutions: Challenges and Prospects. Pretoria: Pretoria University Law Press.

Pinskay, J., & Pinskay, C. B. (2015). *História da Cidadania.* São Paulo: Contexto.

Pinto, A. T., Windt, M. C. V. S., & Siqueira, E. A. S. (2000). National tax code. São Paulo, Brazil: Saraiva.

Pinto, L. (1994). *Os Limites do Poder Constituinte e a Legitimidade Material da Constituição*. Coimbra: Coimbra Editora.

Piovesan, F. (2006). Direitos Humanos, o Princípio da Dignidade Humana e a Constituição Brasileira. Revista dos Tribunais.

Pítsica, G. (2012). Cidadania, transparência, proteção do erário e os Tribunais de Contas. *Revista Controle*, *10*(2), 98–110.

Polakiewicz, J. (1994). *Soziale Grundrechte und Staatszielbestimmungen in den Verfassungsordnungen Italiens, Portugals und Spaniens*. Zeitschrift für ausländisches öffentliches Recht und Völkerrecht.

Polcinski, G. (2017, February). *Good News for the First Amendment*. Retrieved from: https://knightfoundation.org/articles/good-news-for-the-future-of-the-first-amendment

Polon, L. (2003). *HDI (Human development index) of the countries*. Retrieved from https: www.estudopratico.com.br/idh-indice-de-desenvolvimento-humano-dos-paises

Popescu, A. V. (2018). *The impairment of citizen's right to information by "fake news" publication. In Challenges of the Knowledge Society. Public Law*. Nicolae Titulescu University Publishing House.

Pozas, L. J. A. (1948). Las Tendencias Actuales del Régimen Local en Europa. *Revista de Estudios Políticos, 39-42*.

Prado, G. (2014). *Prova penal e sistema de controles epistêmicos: a quebra da cadeia de custódia das provas obtidas por métodos ocultos*. São Paulo: Marcial Pons.

Prata, M. R. (2006). *Anatomia do Assédio Moral no Trabalho uma Abordagem Transdisciplinar*. São Paulo: LTR.

Proença, C. C. (2017). *Tutela Jurisdicional Efetiva no Direito da União Europeia*. Lisboa: Petrony.

Programme for international student assessment (PISA). (2015). *Result from PISA 2015*. Retrieved from https://www.oecd.org/pisa/PISA-2015-Brazil-PRT.pdf

Project DHnet. (2008). *How does the human development index HDI*. Retrieved from http: www.dhnet.org.br/dados/idh/idh/idh_como_funciona.pdf

Puig, M. R. A. (1967). La Administración local en las Leyes Fundamentales españolas. Revista de Studios Politicos, 152.

Qing, J. (2013). *A Confucian Constitutional Order: How China's Ancient Past can Shape its Political Future*. Princeton University Press.

Quadros, F. (1990). O princípio da exaustão dos meios internos na Convenção Europeia dos Direitos do Homem e a ordem jurídica portuguesa. *Revista da Ordem dos Advogados*, *50*(1), 124-126.

Queiroz, C. (2006). *Direitos Fundamentais – Teoria Geral*. Coimbra: Coimbra Editora.

Queiroz, C. (2006). *O Princípio da não reversibilidade dos Direitos Fundamentais – princípios dogmáticos e prática jurisprudencial*. Coimbra: Coimbra Editora.

Raftopoulos, B., & Mlambo, A. (2009). *Becoming Zimbabwe: A History from Pre-Colonial Period to 2008*. Harare: Weaver Press.

Raimundo. (2015). Os princípios no novo CPA e o princípio da boa administração, em particular, in Comentários ao Novo Código do Procedimento Administrativo. Lisboa, Portugal: AAFDL.

Ramina, L. L. (2002). *International action against corruption*. Curitiba, Brazil: Juruá.

Rato, H. (2010). Crise e Democracia: Resolução da Crise e Aprofundamento da Democracia. In Investigação e Prática em Economia. Parede: Principia.

Reoder, L. (2018). *What is Myspace?* Retrieved from: https://www.lifewire.com/what-is-myspace-2654923

Ribeiro, M. (1996). *O Princípio da Imparcialidade da Administração Pública*. Coimbra: Almedina.

Richordson, E. (1974). Freedom of Information. *Loyola Law Review*, *20*(1), 45–64.

Riley v. United States, 573 U.S. __ (2014).

Rocha, M. P. C. (2000). *A questão cidadania na sociedade da informação*. Retrieved from http://www.scielo.br/scielo.php?script=sci_arttext&pid=S0100-19652000000100004&lng=en&nrm=iso&tlng=pt

Rocha. (2018). Lições de Procedimento e Processo Tributário. Coimbra, Portugal: Almedina.

Rocha, C. L. A. (2004). *O direito à vida digna*. Belo Horizonte: Fórum.

Rock, M. T., & Bonnett, H. (2004). The Comparative Politics of Corruption: Accounting for the East Asian Paradox in Empirical Studies of Corruption, Growth and Investment. *World Development*, *32*(6), 999–1009. doi:10.1016/j.worlddev.2003.12.002

Rose-Ackerman, S. (1999). *Corruption and Government: Causes, Consequences, and Reform*. London, UK: Cambridge University Press. doi:10.1017/CBO9781139175098

Rosenfeld, M. (1994). *Constitutionalism, Identity, Difference and Legitimacy: Theoretical Perspectives*. London: Duke University Press.

Ross, C. J. (2016). Bitch, Go Directly to Jail: Student Speech and Entry Into the School-to-Prison Pipeline. *Temp. L. Rev.*, 88(*717*), 724.

Rotunda, R. D., & Nowak, J. E. (2017). *Treatise on Constitutional Law – Substance & Procedure*. Thomson West.

Rousseau, J.-J. (1999). *O Contrato Social*. Mem Martins: Publicações Europa-América.

Roussillon, H. A. (1972). *Les Structures Territoriales des Communes – Réformes et Perspectives d'avenir*. Paris: Librairie Générale de Droit et Jurisprudence.

Rubinstein, F. (2011). *Notas sobre a Transparência fiscal no direito financeiro*. São Paulo: Ed. RT.

Rwodzi, A., & Mubonderi, B. (2015). The Dilemma of the Patriotic Front and the Influence of the Zimbabwe-Rhodesia Government on Final 1979 Lancaster House Constitution. *International Journal of Humanities and Social Studies*, *3*(9), 215–220.

Saldanha, G. S. (2013). Transgramáticas: Filosofia da Ciência da Informação, linguagem e realidade simbólica. *Tendências da Pesquisa Brasileira em Ciência da Informação*, *6*, 1–30.

Sales. (2014). *O Direito de Acesso à Informação Pública Administrativa*. Rio de Janeiro: Lumen Juris.

Santiago, N. E. A., & Costa, D. K. A. (2016). Garantismo, encontro fortuito decorrente de interceptações telefônicas e a jurisprudência do Supremo Tribunal Federal e do Superior Tribunal de Justiça: rumo à ilicitude das provas. In Interceptação Telefônica: os 20 anos da Lei n. 9.296/96 (pp. 319-346). Belo Horizonte: D'Plácido.

Santos, M. (2007). *O Espaço do Cidadão*. São Paulo: Editora da Universidade de São Paulo.

Sarkar, S. (2012). The Role of Information and Communication Technology (ICT) in Higher Education for the 21st Century. *The Science Probe*, *1*(1), 30–40.

Sarlet, I. W. (2005). *Dimensões da Dignidade*. Porto Alegre: Livraria do Advogado.

Sarlet, I. W. (2011). *Dignidade da pessoa humana e diretos fundamentais*. Porto Alegre: Livraria do Advogado Editora.

Scholz, J. M. (2017). As apropriações dos direitos humanos no Brasil: O caso da Declaração Universal dos Direitos Humanos (1948) *Passagens. Revista Internacional de História Política e Cultura Jurídica*, *9*(2), 214–243. doi:10.15175/1984-2503-20179204

Schreiber, S. (2016). Algumas reflexões sobre a medida cautelar de interceptação telefônica, 20 anos depois. In Interceptação Telefônica: os 20 anos da Lei n. 9.296/96 (pp. 445-463). Belo Horizonte: D'Plácido.

Schutter, O. (2000). La contribution de la Charte des droits fondamentaux de l'Union européenne à la garantie des droits sociaux dans l'ordre juridique communautaire. *Revue Universelle des Droits de l'Homme*, *12*(1-2), 33–47.

Sciulli, D. (1999). *Theory of Societal Constitutionalism: Foundations of a Non-Marxist Critical Theory*. Cambridge, UK: Cambridge University Press.

Screener. (2007). *The Language of Liberal Constitutionalism*. Cambridge University Press.

Sedley, S. (2000). Information As a Human Right. In Freedom of Expression and Freedom of Information. Oxford University Press.

Senado. (2013). *Pesquisa DataSenado mostra que poucos conhecem realmente a Constituição.* Retrieved from http://www.12.senado.leg.br/noticias/materiais/2013/10/25/pesquisa-datasenado-mostra-que-poucos-conhecem-realmente-a-constituicao-do-pais

Sengul, R. (2005). Bilgi Edinme Hakki Kanunu Turk Kamu Yonetimini Camdan Eve Donusturur mu? *A.U.S.B.F.D.*, *60*(3).

Shaver, E.A. (2017). Denying Certiorari in Bell v. Itawamba County School Board: A Missed Opportunity to Clarify Students' First Amendment Rights in the Digital Age. *Brook. L. Rev., 82.*

Sibanda, A. (1991). *The Lancaster House Agreement and the Post- Independence State in Zimbabwe.* Harare: Zimbabwe Institute of Development Studies.

Siéyes, A. (1789). *Quelques idées de Constitution Applicables à la Ville de Paris en Juillet 1789 par l'abbé Sieyès.* Paris: Bibliothèque Nationale de France.

Sieyès, E.-J. (2002). *Qu'est-ce que le tiers état?* Paris: Éditions du Boucher.

Silva. (2012). Transparência e Controle social: Controle externo, controle social e cidadania. In *Revista do Tribunal de Contas do Estado de Minas Gerais, Ano 1, n. 1, Edição Especial.* Belo Horizonte: Tribunal de Contas do Estado de Minas Gerais.

Silva, J. A. (2009). *Curso de Direito Constitucional Positivo* (32nd ed.). São Paulo: Malheiros Editores.

Silva, S. T. (2010). *Direito Administrativo Europeu.* Coimbra: Editora Coimbra. doi:10.14195/978-989-26-0183-0

Singh, R. K. (2014). Right to Information: The Basic Need of Democracy. *Journal of Education & Social Policy*, *1*(2), 86–96.

Sithole, E., Feltoe, G., Derman, B., & Hellum, A. (2013). Rights Claiming and Rights Making in Zimbabwe: A Study of three Human Rights NGOS. In B. Andreassen & G. Crawford (Eds.), *Human Rights, Power and Civic Action: Comparative Analysis of Struggles for Rights in Developing Societies* (pp. 22–54). Routledge.

Snead, J. (2018). *Judge Kavanaugh and Technology Issues.* Retrieved from: https://www.heritage.org/courts/report/judge-kavanaugh-and-technology-issues

Soykan, C. (2007). Avrupa Insan Haklari Mahkemesi Ictihatlarinda Bilgi Edinme Hakki/ The European Court of Human Rights Case Law on The Right to Information. *AUHFD*, *56*(2), 63–74.

Speck, B. W. (2000). *The costs of corruption.* Retrieved from https: bvc.cgu.gov.br/bitstream/123456789/2731/1/mensuracao_da_corrupcao_uma.pdf

Sydow, S. T. (2017). Criptografia e ciência penal informática. *Revista dos Tribunais*, *985*, 343-374.

Tang, L., & Liu, H. (2010). *Community Detection and Mining in Social Media Synthesis*. Morgan & Claypool.

Tanzi, V., & Davoodi, H. (1997). *Corruption, Public Investment, and Growth*. IMF Working Paper. Retrieved from http://www.imf.org/external/pubs/ft/wp/wp97139.pdf

Teixeira, F., & Marques, F. (2017). Biologia e Gênero: outros olhares. Academic Press.

Teixeira. (2018). Manual de Direito Fiscal. Coimbra, Portugal: Almedina.

Terra & Wattel. (2012). *European Tax Law*. Wolters Kluwer.

The Board of Review of Access to Information Decisions (2004/104, 2007/1017, 2004/140, 2004/77, 2010/2122). (n.d.). Retrieved from http://www.bedk.gov.tr/

The Brazilian Institute of tax planning (IBPT). (2012). *Brazilian tax burden 2012*. Retrieved from https: www.ibpt.org.br/img/uploads/.../cargatributaria2012ibpt.pdf

The Brazilian Institute of tax planning (IBPT). (2013). *Study on taxes/GDP x HDI*. Retrieved from https: www.ibpt.org.br/img/uploads/novelty/estudo/787/estudofinalsobrecargatributariapibxidhirbesmarco2013.pdf

Tinker v. Des Moines Independent School District, 393 U.S. 503 (1969).

Tlakuka, P. (2004). Human Rights and Development. In P. Zelela & P. McConnaughay (Eds.), *Human Rights: The Rule of Law and Development in Africa* (pp. 109–187). University of Pennsylvania Press.

Tlakula, P. (2004). Human Rights and Development. In *Human Rights, the Rule of Law and Development in Africa* (pp. 100–119). University of Pennsylvania Press.

Trading Economics. (n.d.). *GDP list of countries*. Retrieved from https: pt.tradingeconomics.com/country-list/gdp

Transparency International. (2010). *World Corruption Ranking. Corruption Perceptions Index 2010*. Retrieved from http://cpi.transparency.org/cpi2010/results/

Transparency International. (2011). *World Corruption Ranking. Corruption Perceptions Index 2011*. Retrieved from https://www.transparency.org/cpi2011/results

Transparency International. (2012). *World Corruption Ranking. Corruption Perceptions Index 2012*. Retrieved from http://cpi.transparency.org/cpi2012/results/

Transparency International. (2013). *World Corruption Ranking. Corruption Perceptions Index 2013*. Retrieved from https://www.transparency.org/cpi2013/results

Transparency International. (2014). *World Corruption Ranking. Corruption Perceptions Index 2014*. Retrieved from https://www.transparency.org/cpi2014/results

Transparency International. (2015). *World Corruption Ranking. Corruption Perceptions Index 2015*. Retrieved from https://www.transparency.org/cpi2015#results-table

Transparency International. (2016). *World Corruption Ranking. Corruption Perceptions Index 2016*. Retrieved from https://www.transparency.org/news/feature/corruption_perceptions_index_2016#table

Transparency International. (2017). *World Corruption Ranking. Corruption Perceptions Index 2017*. Retrieved from https://www.transparency.org/news/feature/corruption_perceptions_index_2017#table

U.S. v. Jones, 565 U.S. 400 (2012).

UNESCO. (2018). *Information and communication technologies (ICT) Glossary*. Retrieved from http://uis.unesco.org/node/335129

United Nations Development Programme. (1997). Governance for Sustainable Human Development. UNDP policy document.

United Nations Development Programme. (1997). *Reconceptualising Governance Discusson Pape*. New York: Management Development and Governance Division.

United Nations Development Programme. (2004). *Right to Information Practical Guidance Note*. Bureau for Development Policy Democratic Governance Group.

United Nations Development Programme. (2018). *Human Development Reports 1990-2017*. Retrieved from http://hdr.undp.org/en/data

Uvin, P. (2004). *Human Rights and Development*. Lynne Reiner Publishers.

Uygun, O. (2000). *Insan Haklari Kurami. Insan Haklari*. Istanbul: Yapi Kredi Yayinlari.

Valle. (n.d.). *Direito fundamental à boa administração e governança*. Belo Horizonte: Fórum.

Vaz, M. A. (1998). *O enquadramento jurídico-constitucional dos «direitos económicos, sociais e culturais» in Juris et de Jure – nos 20 anos da Faculdade de Direito da UCP*. Porto: Universidade Católica Portuguesa.

Vaz, M. A., Carvalho, R., & Botelho, C. S. (1998). *Direito Constitucional*. Coimbra: Coimbra Editora.

Venera, R. A. S. (2009). *Sentidos da educação cidadã no Brasil. Educar*. Curitiba: UFPR.

Vernonia School District v. Acton, 515 U.S. 646 (1995).

Versteeg, M. (2017 August). What Europe Can Teach America About Free Speech. *The Atlantic*. Retrieved from: https://www.theatlantic.com/politics/archive/2017/08/what-europe-can-teach-america-about-free-speech/537186/

Vianna, C. S. M. (2004). Da privacidade como direito fundamental da pessoa humana. *Revista de Direito Privado*, *17*, 102–115.

Viner, J. (2014). The Customs Union Issue, Edited and with an introduction by Paul Oslington. Oxford, UK: Oxford University Press.

Vivian, J., & Maseko, G. (2018). NGOs and Sustainable Development in Zimbabwe: No Magic Bullets. *Development and Change*, *25*(1), 167–193. doi:10.1111/j.1467-7660.1994.tb00513.x

Vollan, K. (2013). *The Constitutional History and the 2013 Referendum of Zimbabwe: A Norwegian Special Report*. Norwegian Centre for Human Rights.

Wall, S. P. (1996). Public Justification and the Transparency Argument. *The Philosophical Quarterly*, *46*(185), 501–507. doi:10.2307/2956360

Wang, Y., & You, J. (2012). *Corruption and firm growth: Evidence from China*. Beijing, China: China Economic Review.

Watts v. United States, 394 U.S. 705 (1969).

West Virginia v. Barnette, 319 U.S. 624 (1943).

Wider, R. (n.d.). Assisted Reproduction - Aspects of Bioethics and Bioethics. Ed. Empresa do Diário do Minho Ltd. Braga.

Winkler, M.B. (2017). Executive Order "Protecting the Nation from Foreign Terrorist Entry into the United States": Violating First Amendment Rights or Altering Constitutional Provisions Granting Foreign Policy Powers to the President. *W. Mich. U. T.M. Cooley L. Rev., 34*(79).

World Bank. (1992). *Governance and Development*. The World Bank. Retrieved from http://unpan1.un.org/intradoc/groups/public/documents/un/unpan022332.pdf

World Population Review. (2018). *Portugal Population 2018*. Retrieved from http://worldpopulationreview.com/countries/portugal-population/

Yasamis, F. D. (2004). *Anayasa Hukuku ve Insan Haklari Acisindan Bilgi Edinme Hakki*. Ankara: Turk Idare Dergisi.

Yildirim, R. (1998). *Idare Hukuku Acisindan Bilgi Edinme Hak ve Ozgurlugu. In Idari Usul Kanunu Hazirligi Uluslararasi Sempozyumu*. Ankara, Turkey: Babakanlik Basimevi.

Yuzbasioglu, N. (2000). *Insan Haklarinin Ulusal Duzeyde Korunmasi*. Istanbul, Turkey: Yapi Kredi Yayinlari.

Zambrano, E. (2006). Parentalidades "Impensáveis": Pais/Mães Homossexuais, Travestis e Transexuai. *Horizontes Antropológicos*, *12*(26), 123–147. doi:10.1590/S0104-71832006000200006

Zimbabwe Government. (2000). *Zimbabwe Constitution as Ammended at 19 April 2000/ Government of Zimbabwe*. Harare: Legal Resources Foundation.

Zinyama, T. (2014). Partiicpatory Budegeting in Zimbabwe: Experiences and Reflections form Harare City Council. *British Journal of Physical and Human Geography*, *1*(1), 1–44.

About the Contributors

Ana Melro holds a Ph.D. in Information and Communication in Digital Platforms, from University of Aveiro and University of Porto (2013). A master degree in Sociology and a degree in Sociology (2004), from University of Minho. Ana Melro was post-doctoral fellow funded by FCT (2015-2017) at DigiMedia, University of Aveiro. Her research interests are: Ciberculture; New Media; Social Entrepreneurship and Innovation; Territorial Development; Smart Territories, Constitutional knowledge and citizenship exercise.

Lídia Oliveira has a degree in Philosophy from the University of Coimbra (1990), a Master's degree in Educational Technology from the University of Aveiro, in partnership with the University of Valenciennes (France) and Mons (Belgium) (1995), and a PhD in Sciences and Technologies of Communication from the University of Aveiro (2002). She has been a professor in the Department of Communication and Art (http://www.ua.pt) at the University of Aveiro since 1995 until the present. Her main scientific interest is in cyberculture studies and social network analysis. Her areas of interest are: Science and Technologies of Communication, ICT and Education, Multimedia, Social Network Analysis, Cyberculture Studies, Sociology of Communication, Information Systems, Digital Libraries, Time Studies, Science Communication, Communication in the Scientific Community (theoretical and empirical studies). She has published both nationally and internationally in peer review journals, book chapters and, conferences proceedings.

* * *

Maryam Ahranjani is an education law scholar whose main research interest is legal barriers to education access for vulnerable populations. She teaches or has taught in the areas of constitutional rights, education policy, criminal law, criminal procedure, and criminal sentencing. Fluent in Spanish and Persian, she has taught in several U.S. based law schools, as well as law schools in Guatemala City, Santiago de Chile, and Buenos Aires. Professor Ahranjani earned degrees from Northwestern University (BSEd, magna cum laude), American University Washington College of Law (JD), and University of Pennsylvania (LLM).

Dora Alves teaches European Union Law, History of Law, Constitutional Law, Constitutional Justice, Fundamental Rights and International Law at a private university – Universidade Portucalense Infante D. Henrique in Oporto, Portugal – since 1993. After taking the law degree in 1993, Dora Alves has worked as a lawyer registered at the Portuguese Lawyers Bar Association. She obtained a Master's degree in Law - European Integration at Law Department from the University of Coimbra (Portugal) in 1997 and have done her work under her PhD in Law at Vigo University (Spain). The thesis is about "The powers of investigation and sanction of the European Commission under the competition law" and took her PhD title in 2015. Dora Alves is academically interested in all subjects around Constitutional Law. Also lateral interest about respect of human rights and public versus private enforcement, always on competition field and always related to European Union Law.

Ana Amorim has a Master in Law and is a PhD student by the Post-Graduation Program in Constitutional Law, University of Fortaleza, Brazil (UNIFOR). Public Defender of the State of Ceará.

Nestor Eduardo Araruna Santiago is a Doctor of Law, with post-doctoral training at the University of Minho Law School. Professor of the Post-Graduation Program in Constitutional Law, University of Fortaleza, Brazil (UNIFOR). Criminal lawyer.

Omur Aydin is a member of Istanbul University, the Faculty of Political Sciences. He has a PhD in Constitutional Law and has been a lecturer at the department of Public Administration, Istanbul University since 1999. He stayed as an academic visitor at Essex University for his dissertation. His research interests focus on human rights, constitutional law, political life and intuitions. He is author of numerous peer-reviewed articles and book chapters in the above-mentioned areas. His current projects include freedom of speech and parliamentary immunity in Turkey.

Andreia Barbosa is a PhD Student, Professor at Universidade do Minho.

Barbara Barreiros is a PhD Public Law Student (University of Minho) Master in Local Authorities Law (University of Minho) Post-graduate in European Studies (University of Coimbra) Lawyer since 2007.

Mara Karinne Barros Graduated in Bachelor of Law from the State University of Paraíba (2008), Graduate Degree in History from the Federal University of Campina Grande (2002), Specialization in Public Policy and Management from the Federal University of Campina Grande (2014) and Specialization in Law Work and Work Process by the Faculdade Damásio de Jesus (2014) and Master in Natural Resources by the Federal University of Campina Grande (2018).

Kudzai Chatiza is a student of development planning and local governance working as a researcher and consultant at the Development Governance Institute (DEGI) Zimbabwe. Kudzai is the Institute's Director and Senior Consultant. He has over 24 years of work experience in development mainly in civil society and advisory services to governments and donors. He also teaches Development Planning & Development Management at the University of Zimbabwe's Planning School and Service Delivery Theory & Practice, Municipal Financing and Environmental Policy at the Midlands State University's School of Local Governance. Kudzai has research interests in spatial planning, pro-poor local governance and human settlements including work with/in slum settlements, water, sanitation and social protection. He has worked on different assignments in the SADC and East Africa Regions. He holds BSc and MSc in Rural and Urban Planning degrees (University of Zimbabwe 1992 & 1995) & PhD in Development Studies (Swansea University, 2008).

Innocent Chirisa: DPhil, MSc, BSc Hons. Rural & Urban Planning, (University of Zimbabwe), DipLMISR (IHS, Erasmus University), MZIRUP (Zimbabwe), Full Professor teaching Urban and Environmental Planning courses in the Department of Rural & Urban Planning, University of Zimbabwe. Currently is serving as the Deputy Dean of the Faculty of Social Studies, University of Zimbabwe. Also he is currently serving as the Acting Chairman of the Department of Rural & Urban Planning, University of Zimbabwe Prof Chirisa was recently appointed as a Research Fellow, Department of Urban and Regional Planning, University of Free State, Bloemfontein, South Africa for the period 2016 to 2020.

Ana Carolina Cohen is a PhD student in Legal Sciences, University of Minho (Portugal). Graduated in Law from Federal University of Alagoas (2006) - Brazil. Master in Public Law from the Federal University of Alagoas (2008). Adjunct Professor of the Law Course of Tiradentes University Center - UNIT, in the subjects General Theory of Civil Law, Family Law and Probate Law. She is a member of the Structuring Teaching Nucleus and of the UNIT Course Law School. She is a member of UNIT's Research Ethics Committee. She is a collaborating member of the Human Rights Group of the Justice and Governance Research Center - JUSGOV of the Law School of the University of Minho - Portugal.

Olivia Maria Gomes is a PhD student in Public Law from the University of Minho (Uminho). Master in Human Rights from the University of Minho (2011). Master degree recognized and revalidated by the Federal University of Paraíba (UFPB) (2013). Graduated in Law from the State University of Paraíba (UEPB) (2007). Lawyer, Professor and Adjunct Coordinator of Faculty's Law School Reinaldo Ramos FARR / CESREI, Campina Grande, PB. He is a collaborating member of the DH-CII (Center for Discipline Research) linked to the Science and Technology Foundation (FCT) and the Torture Map work group of the State Truth Commission of Paraíba state, Brazil.

Wendy W. Mandaza-Tsoriyo has lecturing experience in Zimbabwe in rural and urban planning as well as well as training experience in community capacity building and development in Zimbabwean marginalized communities. Wendy is currently studying for a PhD in Urban and Regional Planning. She holds an MSc in Rural and Urban Planning and a BSc in Rural and Urban Planning. Her research interests are in areas of urban design and management, spatial transformation of urban areas and participatory planning.

Emma Maphosa is urban and regional planner who graduated with a B. Sc Honors Degree in Rural and Urban Planning with the University of Zimbabwe in 2018. In 2017, Emma Maphosa got internship with Gutu Rural District Council in Masvingo, Zimbabwe. Her research interests are in property management, urbanisation, gender and women empowerment and transport planning.

Abraham R. Matamanda graduated from the University of Zimbabwe with a BSc degree in Rural and Urban Planning in 2013 and went on to obtain a Masters in Social Ecology in 2015. Currently he is a PhD student at the University of the Free State in the department of Urban and Regional Planning focusing on development of emerging Human settlements in The Global South, with special emphasis on Hopley, Harare, Zimbabwe. Abraham has presented his work at Conferences as well as published in international and national peer reviewed journals focusing on issues that include poverty and housing, housing and informality, water and sanitation. He is also concerned with the sustainability agenda as espoused in the Sustainable Development Goals; hence some of his work has been on environmental planning, where he tends to have a bias towards wetland ecosystems in urban areas. Basically, his researches focus on urban sustainability, environmental planning and management, rural development and the planning of cities and towns.

Marcilio Mello is a PhD in Legal Law at the University do Minho / Braga / PT. Master in Foundations of Constitutional Rights by the Federal University of Alagoas / Brazil. Prosecutor of the Public Prosecutor's Office of the State of Minas Gerais / Brazil.

Rui Moura is a Professor of Economics and Sociology; Integrated Researcher of Socioeconomic Sciences at the Center for Research and Social Studies (CPES) and the Center for Research in Politics, Economics and Society (CIPES) of the Universidade Lusófona de Humanidades e Tecnologias (ULHT); International Associate Consultant for MundiConsulting for Public Policy; member of the Editorial Board of the scientific journal Organizações & Trabalho of the Association of Professionals in Industrial Sociology, Organizations and Labor (APSIOT). Reviewer of the Education Policy Analysis Archives (A2 on Qialis Capes).

Fátima Pacheco teaches European Union Law, and International Law at Instituto Superior de Contabilidade e Administração do Porto (ISCAP - Politécnico do Porto), Portugal – since 1990. After taking the law degree in 1987 by University of Coimbra, she has worked as a lawyer registered at the Portuguese Lawyers Bar Association. She is a postgraduate in European Studies and International Justice. She obtained a Master's degree in Law in 1997 in International Relations and her PhD title in 2015, at Oporto's Catholic University. The thesis is about the Charter of Fundamental Rights of the European Union. She is an investigator of the Jusgov Research Center, in Minho Law School and the CEI, a research center in intercultural Studies of ISCAP.

Artur Parreira has a PhD, and is a Professor in Organizational Behavior; Scientific Methodology Coordinator at GESC- Grupo de Estudo de Sistemas Complexos.

Cátia Rosário holds a Master's degree in Business Management from the Lusófona University. Currently, she works in the field of management and financial consulting for various companies. Her research interests are innovation, human capital, ICT and determinants of countries' economic growth.

Ana Lorga da Silva is a Multivariate Data Analysis Researcher. Ana Silva is also Chairman of the board of Centro de Pesquisa e Estudos Sociais of ULHT and an Associate Professor.

Roberto Wider has a Master in Civil Law by the University of Coimbra, Portugal. Roberto Wider is also a PHD candidate for University of Minho, Braga, Portugal.

Index

E

F

G

H

I

K

L

M

N

O

P

R

S

T

U

W

Z